Studies in Critical Thinking, 2nd Ed

Studies in Critical Thinking, 2nd Ed

Edited by J. Anthony Blair

WINDSOR STUDIES IN ARGUMENTATION
WINDSOR, ON

Contents

Preface   xi

Part I. Introductory

Introduction   3

1. What critical thinking is   7
   Alec Fisher

Part II. On Teaching Critical Thinking

Introduction to Part II   29

2. Teaching critical thinking   31
   J. Anthony Blair and Michael Scriven

3. Validity   37
   Derek Allen

4. Teaching argument construction   51
   Justine Kingsbury

5. Encouraging critical thinking about students' own beliefs   57
   Tracy Bowell and Justine Kingsbury

6. Middle Ground: Settling a public controversy by means of a reasonable compromise   61
   Jan Albert van Laar

7. Using arguments to inquire   71
   Mark Battersby and Sharon Bailin

Part III. About Argument and Arguments

Introduction to Part III   85

8. Arguments and critical thinking   87
   J. Anthony Blair

9. The concept of an argument   101
   David Hitchcock

10. Using computer-aided argument mapping to teach reasoning   115
Martin Davies, Ashley Barnett, and Tim van Gelder

11. Argumentation schemes and their application in argument mining   153
Douglas Walton

12. Constructing effective arguments   181
Beth Innocenti

13. Judging arguments   191
J. Anthony Blair

14. An introduction to the study of fallaciousness   209
Christopher W. Tindale

Part IV. Other Elements of Critical Thinking

Introduction to Part IV   225

15. How a critical thinker uses the web   227
Sally Jackson

16. Definition   249
Robert H. Ennis

17. Generalizing   271
Dale Hample and Yiwen Dai

18. Appeals to authority: sources and experts   289
Mark Battersby

19. Logic and critical thinking   307
G.C. Goddu

20. Abduction and inference to the best explanation   329
John Woods

21. The unruly logic of evaluation   351
Michael Scriven

Index   373

Studies in Critical Thinking

Second Edition

Windsor Studies in Argumentation Vol. 8

Edited by J. Anthony Blair

WSIA Editors

Preface

Preface to the 1st edition

The distant origins of *Studies in Critical Thinking* lie in the recommendation of a committee of the *Association for Informal Logic and Critical Thinking* (AILACT) that an authoritative anthology on critical thinking should be prepared, with two ends in view. One was to be of service to new instructors of critical thinking courses. The other was to demonstrate to the scholarly community that critical thinking is a field that calls for serious and respectable academic attention.

More proximately, at the 2016 conference of the *Ontario Society for the Study of Argumentation* at the University of Windsor, Michael Scriven, who had been a member of that AILACT committee, convened a meeting to promote the idea of such a book and see what support there was for it. Somehow my long-time collaborator Ralph Johnson and I agreed to co-edit the book, with Scriven's guidance, if AILACT would give us a free hand. Having no other offers, AILACT agreed.

The idea of dividing the book into a section (Part II) with teaching material and one section (Parts III & IV) with material related to the theoretical underpinning of critical thinking came from Scriven, and Johnson and I happily adopted it.

About a year into work on the book, Johnson chose to withdraw from the project for personal reasons. So, while he played a role in the early planning, he cannot be held responsible for the final product.

Michael Scriven served as a consultant to the editors, and subsequently, to the editor. I cannot thank him enough for his encouragement, his always useful suggestions and for his general guidance and material support for the project.

I would like to thank the contributors, who met deadlines promptly, tolerated delays and editorial intrusion patiently, and produced either new work or suggested and adapted already-published work, both of extraordinary quality.

I am grateful to Leo Groarke and Christopher Tindale, the editors-in-chief of the Windsor Studies In Argumentation (WSIA) series for taking on the book's publication. Many thanks to Tamilyn Mulvaney, assistant to the Director of the Centre for Research in Reasoning, Argumentation and Rhetoric (CRRAR) at the University of Windsor, who provided invaluable assistance in the preparation of the manuscript, to Dave Johnston of Windsor's Leddy Library, who shepherded the manuscript through the PressBooks protocols, and to Ellen Duckman, for the cover.

I dedicate this book, with love, to my wife, June Blair, on whose support I constantly rely.

J. Anthony Blair
Centre for Research in Reasoning, Argumentation and Rhetoric
University of Windsor

Preface to the 2nd edition

The 1st edition of *Studies in Critical Thinking* was rushed to publication, with the consequence that it is sprinkled with rather more errors than should be tolerated. These have been corrected in this revised edition and the authors who wanted to have had the opportunity to further fine-tune their chapters.

I remain grateful to CRRAR's publishing arm, Windsor Studies in Argumentation, for arranging for the book's electronic distribution and for an inexpensive hardcover copy available from Amazon.

In addition to those listed in the Preface to the 1st edition, my thanks go to Waleed Mebane for his immaculate service as editorial assistant. Without his help, this 2nd edition would not have been possible. And many thanks to Ellen Duckman for the new cover.

My wholehearted thanks go to the anonymous donor whose generous grant to CRRAR financed the expenses entailed in the preparation of the book.

As ever, I thank my wife, June, with love, for her forbearance and support.

J. Anthony Blair
Centre for Research in Reasoning, Argumentation and Rhetoric
University of Windsor
June 2020

Original Publication of Essays

Chapter 4, © Justine Kingsbury, "Teaching Argument Construction" originally appeared in the Teaching Supplement of *Informal Logic*, 2002, Vol. 22, No. 1, pp. TS1-4.

Part of Chapter 9, by David Hitchcock, uses material from "The concept of an argument", pp. 518-529 in Hitchcock's book *On Reasoning and Argument: Essays in Informal Logic and on Critical Thinking* 2017, © Springer International Publishing AG 2017, used here with the kind permission of Springer.

Chapter 11, by Douglas Walton, originally appeared as "Argument Mining by Applying Argumentation Schemes" in *Studies in Logic* 2011, Vol. 4 (1): pp. 38-64, and is reproduced with permission of *Studies in Logic*, The Institute of Logic and Cognition, Sun Yat-Sen University, Guangzhou, China.

Chapter 14, © Christopher Tindale, "An Introduction to the Study of Fallaciousness" is a slightly modified version of Chapter 1 of his book, *Fallacies and Argument Appraisal*, 2007, published by Cambridge University Press, and reproduced with permission.

I

Introductory

Introduction

As we enter the third decade of the 21st century the need for critical thinking by voters, consumers, families, teachers, businesses, governments, and more is as urgent as ever. Formal instruction in critical thinking at the post-secondary level still usually occurs in a one-semester course offered to first-year students at colleges and universities, frequently but by no means always housed in philosophy departments or programs. The instructors tend to be junior faculty members whose own formal training in critical thinking, if any, tends to consist of the one-semester critical thinking course that *they* took as first-year undergraduates 5-10 years earlier, often supplemented by a couple of years' experience as teaching assistants for such a course while graduate students—time spent grading assignments and sometimes leading weekly tutorial sections. In many cases the critical thinking course a department offers has evolved from—and differs little from—the "introduction to logic" course, now supplemented with some informal logic. The result is that many instructors of critical thinking courses are thrown in at the deep end. Understandably, most reach for the textbooks on the market to stay afloat.

Textbook publishers have shown considerable interest in the profits available from the dedicated critical thinking course market, publishing scores of handbooks. Best sellers are revised frequently in minor ways to reduce resale. But textbook authors are rarely experts in every topic the publishers want covered to maximize sales, and even if they were, the sort of understanding that instructors should have in order to be at home teaching wide variety of topics pertinent to acquiring critical thinking skills and dispositions could not be included in an introductory textbook.

Granting exceptions, by and large critical thinking textbooks err on the side of the safety of tradition, and don't always reflect the latest research. With instructors themselves learning from the textbook any material unfamiliar to them that it contains, too often what the students receive is undigested and outdated.

Meanwhile "critical thinking" has become a buzzword, or buzz-term. It is found in virtually every college and university mission statement. Yet, simultaneously, its vagueness has been deplored and its intellectual respectability correspondingly denigrated. Although critical thinking is a capacity that is almost universally endorsed, its conceptualization and instruction have not been universally accepted as serious concerns.

The situation may be changing. An encouraging sign was the timely appearance in 2015 of the big *Palgrave Handbook of Critical Thinking in Higher Education*. It's a 630-page collection of 34 articles representing a wide range of theoretical viewpoints on a variety of issues related to the conception, the value and the pedagogy of critical thinking. Eight of the *Palgrave Handbook* contributors have authored chapters in this book.

S*tudies in Critical Thinking,* also contributes to the intellectual respectability of critical thinking, although in a quite different way. It has been prepared to serve the needs of the critical thinking course instructor (and the course teaching assistants) cast in the roles described above.

The book begins by confronting the question, What, precisely, *is* critical thinking? Alec Fisher shows in his introductory essay, Part I, that it has had a definite meaning that originated with Dewey and that has, with good reason, acquired accretions over the years. Although complex, the concept of critical thinking is quite clear. Fisher's essay provides some historical background for instructors and students, which also might be of interest to college deans as well as to the general reader.

Part II focuses on pedagogy. Anthony Blair and Michael Scriven are advocates of John Hattie's evidence-based approach to critical thinking instruction, and they offer as a taste some general outlines and some specific ideas designed to whet instructors' appetites and encourage them to look at the Hattie material when planning their courses. They also offer some critical reflections on the vexed state of institutional support for critical thinking instruction. The remaining chapters in Part II offer some inspiring examples of ways critical thinking instructors can design methods and tools that contribute to student learning.

Acquiring skills requires practice and acquiring complex skills such as those entailed in critical thinking requires practice in the elements of the skills. Derek Allen provides in Chapter 3 a graded exercise he has devised to teach one of those elements—assessing arguments in natural language for deductive validity.

Many who are adept at analyzing and assessing other people's arguments are inept at constructing arguments for themselves: the skills seem to be discrete. Justine Kingsbury has found the textbooks of little help in teaching how to construct arguments, especially with large classes. Chapter 4 contains an exercise she has devised for doing so.

Our compartmentalizing propensity tends to leave us with a blind spot when it comes to thinking critically about our own beliefs and attitudes. In Chapter 5, Dr. Kingsbury teams up with her colleague Tracy Bowell in developing a simple and ingenious assignment that encourages students to think critically about their own beliefs.

Critical thinking doesn't guarantee agreement. One of the more difficult thinking tasks is to resolve intractable disagreement by compromising. To do so, we need models to follow and practice in applying them. In Chapter 6, Jan

Albert van Laar provides one such model, along with an illustrative exercise with which to practice it.

We begin to think critically only after we already have an immense store of beliefs and other attitudes. Still, almost every day we are confronted with opportunities to add more, and some of these are about important matters that we want to get right. Mark Battersby and Sharon Bailin have a method for using arguments to test candidates for our endorsement, and in Chapter 7 they present an exercise to teach students how to employ it.

Readers are welcome to use any of the exercises in Part II as they are, or as modified to suit their particular pedagogical circumstances, or as inspirations for their own creative innovations. Their authors would welcome your feedback.

The chapters in Parts III and IV deal with the contents of critical thinking in two ways. Part III focuses on arguments. Because we express positive and negative critical reflections in arguments and we communicate them to others using arguments, argument is central to critical thinking. But the skills of critical thinking rely also on a substratum of theoretical understandings. The aim of Part IV has been to contain state of the art accounts, as formulated by leading scholars, of several of the most basic and widely applicable topics.

In Chapter 8 Anthony Blair contends there are two groups of meanings of 'argument', so that teaching argument analysis is a more complicated than it is often taken to be. Moreover, he argues, that there are many other things besides arguments that deserve the attention of critical thought.

Nonetheless, argument is central to critical thinking, and in Chapter 9, David Hitchchock submits the reason-giving concept of an argument to close critical analysis.

Critical thinking entails an ability to analyze the logical structures of such argument, breaking them down into their components and diagramming how they function to give reasons for beliefs and actions. In Chapter 10, Martin Davies, Ashley Barnett and Tim van Gelder, three of the pioneers of the method, demonstrate how to use available software to make computer-aided maps of arguments' structures.

Argument scheme research has become a central theme in argument theory. One of it's leading advocates, Douglas Walton, gives an account of argument schemes and their application, in Chapter 11.

Chapter 12 contains Beth Innocenti's account of the theory of constructing effective arguments. Her chapter provides the basis for exercises such as the one Kingsbury describes in Chapter 4.

In Chapter 13, Anthony Blair sets out what is involved in identifying, interpreting, displaying, evaluating and responding to argument—the elements of "judging" arguments.

The theoretical understanding of fallacies in arguments has enjoyed radical revision over the last half-century. In Chapter 14, Christopher Tindale gives an account of fallaciousness that reflects contemporary theory.

In Part IV we leave the central focus on argument behind and turn to other aspects of critical thinking.

Chapter 15 contains Sally Jackson's account of what critical thinking involves when applied to the web—and how the nature of the web calls for changes in how we should understand critical thinking.

Robert Ennis, one of the preeminent theorists of critical thinking of our time, in Chapter 16 applies his meticulous analysis to the kinds of definition and their nature.

Chapter 17 is Dale Hample and Yiwen Dai's primer in the concept at the heart of all scientific thinking, generalizing.

Since most of what each of us believes or knows comes not from our direct experience, but from the testimony of others, the critical thinker needs to know how to figure out whose "authority" to trust. In Mark Battersby's Chapter 18 addresses this vital question.

In differentiating critical thinking and logic, we do not mean to imply that logic has no place in critical thinking. A good way to incorporate logic is by introducing the logical concepts that are needed for critical thinking. G.C. Goddu does exactly that in Chapter 19.

There are plenty of handbooks and monographs on deduction and induction. On abduction?—not so much. In Chapter 20 John Woods explains what abduction is and reviews accounts of its connection to inference to the best explanation.

Those who teach that an evaluation is just an expression of a subjective preference need to read Chapter 21. In it, Michael Scriven not only explodes that myth, but also lays out the kinds of evaluation and their elements.

Studies in Critical Thinking makes no claim to be exhaustive. Nor can any of its chapters purport to be beyond dispute. What its contents do represent is some of the best and most up-to-date accounts of many of the concepts that play a role in critical thinking.

In the book's opening chapter, Alec Fisher spells out a conception of critical thinking that is shared by many scholars who have tried to understand this concept. It's the view of the nature of critical thinking that underlies the selection of the book's contents. So perhaps the best place to begin to read this book is at the beginning.

1

What Critical Thinking Is

Alec Fisher

Introduction

The modern "critical thinking" tradition has been developed by a number of leading thinkers, assisted by many others who have made contributions of their own. In this essay I will explain the ideas of these leading thinkers, showing how they have successively enriched the tradition whilst remaining true to its core ideas, with the result that we now have a rich and essentially coherent conception that can be used as a basis for designing lesson plans and for assessing critical thinking abilities. It is not uncommon for this core tradition to claim that Socrates was the originator of this approach to teaching and learning and this is worth remembering because it is clearly important to some of the contributors below and can help to maintain focus when questions arise.

1. John Dewey, "reflective" thinking (1909)

It is generally agreed that the modern critical thinking tradition derives from the work of the American philosopher, psychologist and educator, John Dewey (1859–1952). He called it "reflective thinking" and defined it as:

> Active, persistent, and careful consideration of a belief or supposed form of knowledge in the light of the grounds which support it and the further conclusions to which it tends. (Dewey, 1909, p. 9)

It is worth unpacking this definition because its elements have remained part of the core. Characteristically then, critical thinking involves "actively" subjecting the ideas we encounter to critical scrutiny, as distinct from just *passively accepting* them. For Dewey, and for everyone who has worked in this tradition subsequently, critical thinking is *essentially* an "active" process, one in which we think things through for ourselves, raise questions ourselves, find relevant information ourselves, etc., rather than learning in a largely passive way from someone else.

Again, characteristically the critical thinker takes time to weigh matters carefully—to "persist" and be "careful"—by contrast with the kind of unreflective thinking in which we all engage sometimes, for example when we "jump" to a conclusion or make a "snap" decision. Of course, we have to do this sometimes because we need to decide quickly or the issue is not important enough to warrant careful thought, but often we do it when we ought to stop and think—when we ought to "persist" a bit.

However, the most important thing about Dewey's definition is what he says about the "grounds which support" a belief and the "further conclusions to which it tends". The critical thinking tradition attaches huge importance to reasoning, to giving reasons and to evaluating reasoning as well as possible, and to valuing this focus. Characteristically, the critical thinker tries to reason skillfully in thinking about issues, by contrast with those who are unreasonable, unreflective, biased or dogmatic. There is more to be said about the components of Dewey's definition, but skillful reasoning is a key element.

2. Edward Glaser, building on Dewey's ideas (1941)

In the late 1930s Edward Glaser conducted a famous experiment in teaching critical thinking and, to his credit, he wanted to assess whether his methods had been successful, so he designed (along with co-author Goodwin Watson) what has become the world's single most widely used test of critical thinking, the *Watson-Glaser Critical Thinking Appraisal*. Glaser's remarkable experiment was a model for critical thinkers in that he tried to assess whether his teaching approach had succeeded.

Glaser defined critical thinking as:

> (1) an attitude of being disposed to consider in a thoughtful way the problems and subjects that come within the range of one's experience; (2) knowledge of the methods of logical enquiry and reasoning; and (3) some skill in applying those methods. Critical thinking calls for a persistent effort to examine any belief or supposed form of knowledge in the light of the evidence that supports it and the further conclusions to which it tends. (Glaser, 1941, p. 5)

This definition clearly owes a lot to Dewey's original definition. Glaser refers to "evidence" in place of "grounds" but otherwise the second sentence is much the same. The first sentence speaks about an "attitude" or disposition to be thoughtful about problems and recognizes that one can apply what he calls "the methods of logical enquiry and reasoning" with more or less "skill". The tradition has picked up on both these elements, recognizing that critical thinking is partly a matter of having certain thinking skills, but is also a matter of being disposed to use them (someone might be very skilled at, say, turning somersaults, but might not be disposed to do so).

Like many others who have worked in the critical thinking tradition, Glaser produces a list of the thinking skills that he sees as basic to or underlying critical thinking. In his case, these are the abilities:

(a) to recognize problems, (b) to find workable means for meeting those problems, (c) to gather and marshal pertinent information, (d) to recognize unstated assumptions and values, (e) to comprehend and use language with accuracy, clarity and discrimination, (f) to interpret data, (g) to appraise evidence and evaluate statements, (h) to recognize the existence of logical relationships between propositions, (i) to draw warranted conclusions and generalizations, (j) to put to test the generalizations and conclusions at which one arrives, (k) to reconstruct one's patterns of beliefs on the basis of wider experience; and (l) to render accurate judgments about specific things and qualities in everyday life. (Glaser, 1941, p. 6)

Much influenced by Dewey, Glaser also saw scientific thinking as a model of "reflective thinking", and this list is probably best understood as relating especially to scientific and similar thinking. It does, however, contain many elements that have been picked up by subsequent workers in the field. For more recent thinking see Facione (1990 and 2010) or Fisher and Scriven (1997, Chapter 3).

3. Robert Ennis and a widely used definition

Few people have contributed as much to the development of the critical thinking tradition as Robert Ennis. In 1962 he published a seminal paper "A Concept of Critical Thinking" and he has continued to contribute to the field ever since. His 1962 definition of critical thinking as "the correct assessing of statements" was too narrow and made no reference to critical thinking dispositions and habits of mind (see Siegel (1988) Ch.1 section 1), but he has developed many ideas in the field since then. The definition for which he is best known, and which has gained wide acceptance in the field, is:

Critical thinking is reasonable, reflective thinking that is focused on deciding what to believe or do. (See Norris and Ennis, 1989)

Again, the emphasis is on being "reasonable" and "reflective", which is in line with earlier definitions, but notice also that Ennis speaks of "deciding what to . . . do", which was not explicitly mentioned earlier. Since for Dewey the model of critical thinking was scientific thinking, he was largely concerned with what we believe, but on Ennis's conception deciding what to do is a proper part of critical thinking too; and one can do this with more or less skill, with more or less reflection, more or less reasonably, etc. Although some people have criticized this definition, its meaning is clear and it has been very widely used.

Like Glaser, Ennis has produced increasingly developed lists of critical thinking abilities and dispositions (Ennis, 1996) and we shall return to the latest of these shortly.

4. Richard Paul, "strong" critical thinking and "thinking about your thinking"

For some forty years, working within the evolving tradition outlined so far, Richard Paul developed his ideas about critical thinking, notably by introducing ideas about "fair-mindedness" and "strong" critical thinking into the tradition. "Fair-mindedness" and "strong" critical thinking require that thinkers take assumptions and perspectives that are quite different from their own *just as seriously as their own*. This is not easy to do, but Paul's ideas have been influential and have contributed significantly to the development of the tradition.

Paul famously distinguished between "weak" and "strong" critical thinking. Both of these are to be contrasted with "uncritical thinking", which is simply not reasoning things through very well. People who think uncritically are not clarifying issues as they should, assessing assumptions and implications, giving and critiquing reasons, applying intellectual standards, expecting people to give reasons for their actions and beliefs and valuing this, etc. Most people will be uncritical thinkers in some domains of their lives but Paul believed that most people are uncritical in many domains of their lives.

By contrast, those who engage in what Paul calls "weak" critical thinking might be good at reasoning things through, but such people will use this skill only to pursue issues from their own perspective, to pursue their own interests (narrowly conceived), to defend their own position, and to serve their own ends, without questioning these—without subjecting their own beliefs, assumptions and presuppositions to scrutiny. Most of us will be "weak" critical thinkers some of the time.

Someone who engages in "strong" critical thinking will also display skill at reasoning things through—will clarify issues where necessary, will assess assumptions and implications, give relevant reasons, apply intellectual standards, etc. But such a person (as contrasted with both the uncritical and the weakly critical thinkers) will *not* simply use this skill narrowly *to defend* their own position and interests, but will also employ it just as readily *to scrutinise* their own thoughts, beliefs and actions, their own judgements about their interests, their own goals, their own perspectives, even their own "world view". They will give equally serious weight to the different beliefs, goals, and assumptions, conflicting perspectives and opposing world views of others. In short, someone who engages in a good deal of strong critical thinking will live what Socrates called "the examined life", and this is Paul's ideal.[1]

Besides introducing the distinctive idea of "strong" critical thinking, Paul attached great importance to "thinking about one's thinking". Indeed Paul attaches such importance to it that some of his definitions (he has given several) look very different from the definitions given above because of the stress he puts on it. Here is an example:

> Critical thinking is that mode of thinking—about any subject, content or problem—in which the thinker improves the quality of his or her thinking by skillfully taking charge of the structures inherent in thinking and imposing intellectual standards upon them. (Paul, Fisher and Nosich, 1993, p. 4)

This definition is interesting because it draws attention to a feature of critical thinking on which teachers and researchers in the field seem to be largely agreed, that the only realistic way to develop one's critical thinking ability is through "thinking about one's thinking" (often called "metacognition"), and consciously aiming to improve it by reference to some model of good thinking in that domain.

Thus, for example, instead of (say) making a decision and then rationalizing it (as many of us often do) most scholars working in the critical thinking tradition agree that we should show students a good model of decision making: be clear what the problem is, think of alternative courses of action, work out the possible consequences of these and how likely they are, take objectives and values into account, come to a reasoned decision (see Swartz (1994) Chapter 2), then give them practice in using the model, self-consciously following it, then put them in real situations where they need to use it. The result should be that we can produce better thought-out, more reasonable decisions than most of us do in the absence of such practice.

5. Harvey Siegel: Being "appropriately moved by reasons" (1988)

During the 1980s more and more educators were becoming interested in critical thinking, in what it was and in how to teach it. Philosophers had long been prominent in developing the critical thinking movement and, in 1988, Harvey Siegel, a well-known philosopher of education, published an influential book called *Educating Reason*.

---

[1] For a review of Paul's fair-mindedness test that brings out some problems with the idea, see Fisher and Scriven (1997) pp. 137-144.

Although he was building on the tradition as it existed then, when Siegel introduced what he called his "reasons" conception of critical thinking, he was mainly interested in what it is to be a critical *thinker*. On his account "To be a critical thinker is to be appropriately moved by reasons." For him this means not only being *skilled* at reasoning things through, but also being *disposed* to do so, having certain *habits of mind*, and *valuing* basing beliefs and decisions on reasons, even when this runs counter to your own self-interest (cf. Paul on "strong" critical thinking). Siegel puts it like this:

> In order to be a critical thinker, a person must have [not only skills in reasoning, but also] certain attitudes, dispositions, habits of mind and character traits, which together may be labelled the "critical attitude" or "critical spirit". ... One who has a critical attitude has a certain *character* as well as certain skills: a character which is inclined to seek, and to base judgment and action upon, reasons; which rejects partiality and arbitrariness; which is committed to the objective evaluation of relevant evidence; and which values such aspects of critical thinking as intellectual honesty, justice to evidence, sympathetic and impartial consideration of interests, objectivity and impartiality. A critical attitude demands not simply an ability to seek reasons, but a commitment to do so; not simply an ability to judge impartially, but a willingness and desire to do so, even when impartial judgment runs counter to self-interest. ... For the possessor of the critical attitude, nothing is immune from criticism, not even one's most deeply-held convictions. (*Educating Reason*, p. 39.)

As Siegel says, the implication of this conception is that education aiming at developing critical thinking

> is a complex business which must seek to foster a host of attitudes, emotions, dispositions, habits and character traits as well as a wide variety of reasoning skills. (*Ibid.*, p. 41.)

For Siegel, being a critical thinker is closely related to being a rational person; his is a very Socratic conception, as is Paul's. However, it is worth noting that Siegel criticises Paul's conception of strong critical thinking on the ground that either it implies a self-defeating relativism (the question is, "which principles can be used to adjudicate between world views?") or it requires just the kind of "atomistic thinking" that Paul himself criticises as being central to the "weak" critical thinking tradition.

Either way, interesting and suggestive as it undoubtedly is, Siegel's conception of the critical think*er* goes further in some respects than the core tradition and may run into problems similar to those Paul's conception of "strong" critical thinking runs into, so we now leave it and move on to another conception.

6. Matthew Lipman: "Philosophy for Children" and *Thinking in Education* (1991)

Matthew Lipman was a professor of philosophy at Columbia University in New York. In the course of his teaching, he became convinced that even his philosophy students had not learned to think adequately before entering university and he became interested in working out how to teach students to think more skilfully. He quickly came to the view that schools needed to teach thinking skills long before students reach university, and he became famous for developing the Philosophy for Children Program, which included such treasures as *Harry Stottlemeier's Discovery*, a series of lessons for eight year old children, which aims to teach them how to think better.

In 1991 Lipman published *Thinking in Education*, in which he explained his ideas about teaching critical thinking. After some remarks connecting wisdom, judgment and critical thinking, he defined critical thinking as follows:

> I will argue that critical thinking is *thinking* that (1) *facilitates judgment because it* (2) *relies on criteria*, (3) *is self-correcting, and* (4) *is sensitive to context*. (*Ibid.*, Ch. 6., p. 116.)

and he explains the connection between judgment and criteria as follows,

> We are also aware of a relationship between criteria and judgments, for a criterion is often defined as "a rule or principle utilized in the making of judgments". It seems reasonable to conclude, therefore, that there is some sort of logical connection between critical thinking and criteria and judgment. The connection, of course, is to be found in the fact that critical thinking is skilful thinking, and skills themselves cannot be defined without criteria by means of which allegedly skilful performances can be evaluated. So critical thinking is thinking that both employs criteria and can be assessed by appeal to criteria. (*Ibid.*, p. 116)

The element in Lipman's definition that is least familiar is part (4) "*is sensitive to context*". He explains that this involves attending to,

1. *Exceptional or irregular circumstances.* For example, we normally examine statements for truth or falsity independent of the character of the speaker. But in a court trial, the character of a witness may become a relevant consideration.
2. *Special limitations, contingencies, or constraints* wherein normally acceptable reasoning might find itself prohibited. An example is the rejection of certain Euclidean theorems, such as that parallel lines never meet, in non-Euclidean geometries.

3. *Overall configurations*. A remark taken out of context may seem to be flagrantly in error, but in the light of the discourse taken as a whole it appears valid and proper, or vice versa. [Lengthy example given]
4. *The possibility that evidence is atypical*. An example is a case of over-generalizing about national voter preferences based on a tiny regional sample of ethnically and occupationally homogeneous individuals.
5. *The possibility that some meanings do not translate from one context or domain to another*. There are terms and expressions for which there are no precise equivalents in other languages and whose meanings are therefore wholly context-specific. (*Ibid.*, pp. 121f.)

Lipman's account of what critical thinking is has not caught on with the wider critical thinking community and is rarely referred to, but his books and materials for teaching philosophy/thinking to K-12 children have been very successful and contain many fascinating lesson plans which arise out of his basic conceptions.

7. Peter Facione: "Critical thinking: A statement of expert consensus for purposes of educational assessment and instruction" (1990)

Although Dewey, Glaser and the early Ennis had very little impact on educational practices in schools and colleges, things began to change in the 1970s. America had been embroiled in the Vietnam War for many years, and widespread student protest against the war included complaining that their college logic courses gave them no help in dealing with the arguments about the war. The philosopher, Howard Kahane, took these complaints seriously and in 1971 published his *Logic and Contemporary Rhetoric*, one of the first college-level critical thinking texts, which became enormously influential. Interest in teaching reasoning skills, thinking skills of one kind and another, even "critical thinking" skills, began to mushroom and by the 1980s many schools and colleges throughout North America were becoming explicitly committed to teaching critical thinking skills and dispositions.

However, there was no very clear view about what these were or how to teach and assess them and because philosophers had been heavily involved in characterising critical thinking, in designing college level programmes, and in trying to get it infused into the K-12 curriculum, the American Philosophical Association asked Peter Facione, himself a philosopher much involved in teaching and assessing critical thinking, to investigate the subject, in order to clarify what it was and how it should be taught and assessed.

To do this, Facione assembled a group of 46 educators who were agreed to be experts in critical thinking (including Ennis, Paul, Lipman and Johnson), and this group then used what is known as the Delphi Method to work towards a consensus view of what critical thinking is and what are its constituent skills and dispositions. The Delphi Method meant that participants shared their reasoned views with the rest, but did so anonymously under Facione's leadership (to avoid undue influence). He would circulate questions and views and would then pull together a summary of the responses before inviting further comments and responses; altogether he went through six rounds of consultation.

The report makes fascinating reading, partly because Facione did all he could to find consensus, but also because it is clear that there was still some disagreement among the participants.

Having said that, Facione did manage to articulate a consensus view about what critical thinking is (in terms both of its cognitive skills and its affective dispositions):

> We understand critical thinking to be purposeful, self-regulatory judgment which results in interpretation, analysis, evaluation, and inference, as well as explanation of the evidential, conceptual, methodological, criteriological, or contextual considerations upon which that judgment is based. ......
>
> While not synonymous with good thinking, CT is a pervasive and self-rectifying human phenomenon. The ideal critical thinker is habitually inquisitive, well-informed, trustful of reason, open-minded, flexible, fair-minded in evaluation, honest in facing personal biases, prudent in making judgments, willing to reconsider, clear about issues, orderly in complex matters, diligent in seeking relevant information, reasonable in the selection of criteria, focused in inquiry, and persistent in seeking results which are as precise as the subject and the circumstances of inquiry permit. Thus, educating good critical thinkers means working toward this ideal. It combines developing CT skills with nurturing those dispositions which consistently yield useful insights and which are the basis of a rational and democratic society. (Executive Summary p. 2)

As this "definition" says, the experts agreed that critical thinking has two elements: cognitive skills and affective dispositions, both of which need to be developed to produce critical thinkers.

The report says that the six skills of (1) interpretation, (2) analysis, (3) evaluation, (4) inference, (5) explanation and (6) self-regulation are "at the core of CT" and then details (over five pages) what these entail, whilst also emphasising that the appropriate "content knowledge" will always be required to arrive at rational judgements in any given domain.[2]

---

[2] The complete American Philosophical Association Delphi Research Report is available as ERIC Doc. No.: ED315 423 and the "Executive Summary" of its findings are easily available on the web.

8. Scriven: The evaluative definition of critical thinking

One last definition, due to Michael Scriven, is worth reviewing. Scriven has argued that critical thinking is "an academic competency akin to reading and writing" and is similarly fundamental to much of our lives. He defines it thus:

> Critical thinking is skilled and active interpretation and evaluation of observations and communications, information and argumentation. (Fisher and Scriven, 1997, p. 21.)

Like others, he defines critical thinking as a "skilled" activity, and he does so because critical thinking has to meet certain standards (of clarity, relevance, reasonableness, fairness, etc.) and one may be *more* or *less* skilled at this. He defines critical thinking as an "active" process (by contrast with the *passive* process of just accepting what one reads, hears or observes), and he does this partly because it involves *questioning* and partly because of the important role played by *metacognition*—thinking about your own thinking. He includes "interpretation" (of texts, speech, film, graphics, actions and even body language) because "like explanation, interpretation typically involves constructing and selecting the best of several alternatives [and it] is a crucial preliminary to drawing conclusions about complex claims". He includes "evaluation" because "this is the process of determining the merit, quality, worth, or value of something" and much critical thinking is concerned with evaluating the truth, probability or reliability of claims and the reasonableness of arguments, inferences, etc.

On Scriven's account, the objects of critical thinking are observations, communications, information and argumentation. He takes the term "information" to refer to factual claims (which may be false, lacking credibility, unreasonable, etc.) and the term "communications" to go beyond information to include questions (for example, "Do you favour affirmative action?"), commands, other linguistic utterances, signals, etc. (see Fisher and Scriven (1997). pp. 38, 39) and the term "argumentation" refers to material that presents reasons for some conclusion. Such argumentation may be explicit or implicit, hypothetical, dialectical or discursive (debates vs. intellectual exploration vs. proof) (*ibid.*, p. 44).

All that is fairly standard. However, the mention of "observations" is unusual. Scriven has long argued that "*observations*" may require critical thinking. For example, it may require considerable critical thinking to be sure what one has seen, heard, etc., either in weak light, or under the influence of strong emotions, or when apparently magical/paranormal things happen. Again, it may be quite hard to be sure what one has experienced, e.g., when you hear a bump in the night (*ibid.*, p. 57). Sherlock Holmes, a paradigmatic critical thinker, focused much of his thinking on the problem of how to interpret what he saw, or did not see (e.g., the dog that *didn't* bark in the night). Suppose one sees a TV news report, showing military film of a missile hitting its chosen target with great accuracy or suppose one views the brain scan of a stroke victim. Consider how much scope (and need) there is for critical thinking about what one has really seen—and not seen. Another good example is the way information is presented graphically; it looks as though the unemployment figures are suddenly much worse, but most of the vertical dimension of the graph has been cut off. And how do the figures normally move at this time of year—when many young people leave college and come on to the jobs market, etc.? There is plenty of room for and need for critical thinking in these cases too.

This is the last extension of the notion of critical thinking to which I here draw attention. I have run through this survey of definitions to give a sense of the development of the critical thinking tradition. It clearly has some core ideas, concerned with giving, evaluating and caring about *reasons*, but it has also developed from an idea based on a scientific model of thinking to one that includes *deciding what to do* and *critical observing* and *dispositions*. The critical thinking tradition has a core that has developed and changed to become the rich idea it is now.

9. The critical thinking skills, abilities or competencies

Many of those who have contributed to the development of the critical thinking tradition have produced lists of skills that are characteristic of the critical thinker. As I noted earlier, Edward Glaser, was the first to do this (1941 p. 6) but others who have produced such lists include Ennis (1962), (1987), (1991), (2011), Ennis and Norris (1989), Facione (1990), Paul (1992), Fisher and Scriven (1997), and others, so I shall now draw on the work which has been done by these pioneers, to produce a comprehensive list of critical thinking skills. Such a list is necessary to decide how to teach and how to assess critical thinking abilities (see Fisher and Scriven, pp. 85, 87).

I divide the skills into four basic groups.

9.1 Interpreting

These are basic skills (which may nonetheless be quite demanding) that one requires in order to be skillful in the higher-level activities mentioned below. Thus you may need to begin by being as clear as possible what the problem is, what is the question at issue, what is the author trying to convince the reader of, or what you observed. You will need to:

- understand and correctly articulate the meaning(s) of terms, expressions, sentences—perhaps also pictures/cartoons, graphs, signs, and other forms of presentation, etc.

- clarify and interpret expressions and ideas, by finding good or paradigm examples, drawing contrasts, specifying necessary and sufficient criteria, providing a paraphrase, providing analogies, etc.—to remove vagueness or ambiguity (*ibid.* p. 110).

Tests for active (or deep) understanding are typically requests to:

- identify what is implied by the material ("reading between the lines"); outline or summarize the material; translate it into other terms; extrapolate from it; to find the factual element in a highly emotional statement; to interpret correctly positions to which the interpreter is deeply opposed, etc. (*ibid.*, p. 98).

Much of this is very similar to what Facione lists under "interpretation". The least familiar reference in the first paragraph of this section is to *what one observed*. It is often hard to be sure how to interpret what we see, hear, etc., on TV, at the scene of a crime, when viewing conditions are abnormal, etc. What we observe will sometimes require interpretation rather than reflex labelling or simple recognition (e.g., reasoned identification of a rare species of flower, bird or rock formation) and this may require skilful reasoning (*ibid.*, p. 97).

9.2 Analyzing

Analysis in this context is essentially being clear about the reasoning involved in arguments of different kinds. These might aim to prove some claim, to support some explanation, to justify some decision, etc., and they might present evidence, use an analogy, proceed by comparing and contrasting alternatives, etc. (*ibid.*, pp. 111-112). In short the process of analysis is about identifying the elements in a reasoned case, its conclusion(s) (including main conclusions), the reasons presented in support of its conclusions, any assumptions or presuppositions implicit in the case but not expressed, including relevant background information (which may be factual claims, definitions, value judgments, recommendations, explanations, etc.) and the intended and actual inferential relationships among sentences and expressions, (etc.).

So, the question is whether, given some written or spoken material (say a newspaper editorial or a political speech or graphical presentation), it presents a reason or reasons in support of some opinion, point of view or conclusion(s). Of course, one also needs to identify any material that is extraneous to the argument, material that does not belong to the argument but that might divert (for example, a phrase intended to trigger a sympathetic emotional response that might induce an audience to agree with an opinion) (cf. Facione (1990), p. 7). Much of this section is similar to what Facione says about analysis (*ibid.*, pp. 7, 8)

Tests for this skill will typically ask the student to identify the conclusions and reasons presented for them, say what is assumed, identify similar patterns of reasoning, identify a flaw in reasoning, etc.

9.3 Evaluating

Several different kinds of evaluative activity are central to critical thinking. First, it is often necessary to make judgments about the relevance, acceptability, credibility or truth, of claims and assumptions that might be presented in words, graphs, pictures, etc. One might also need to judge the credibility of a witness, or other source.

A quite different activity is involved in evaluating inferences of different kinds. In general the question is whether the reasons genuinely support the conclusion and if so how strongly. Some reasoning is meant to be deductive/ conclusive, but much is not: it is meant to be persuasive in varying degrees from "beyond a reasonable doubt" to "reasonable in the circumstances". These different kinds of reasoning have to be evaluated by different standards. Some reasoning is analogical; some reasoning aims to give or justify explanations—sometimes causal explanations; some is intended to arrive at or justify decisions or recommendations. These all have to be evaluated in different ways. For example, with explanations the key question is often whether there are *other possible* explanations and whether these can be ruled out. With decisions or recommendations it is often crucial to look at alternatives and likely consequences. Some reasoning is based on hypothetical situations and this needs to be evaluated in distinctive ways. Some reasoning involves inferences to the merit (trustworthiness) of sources and procedures. These may identify individuals who might (or might not) be reliable authorities or they may be procedures (like using the polygraph or DNA) (*ibid.*, p. 99). There are many different kinds of reasoning, which need to be evaluated in different ways, often by different criteria.

Of course, some reasoning is mistaken, fallacious, or unconvincing in various ways, and one needs to be alive to formal, informal and other fallacies if one is to evaluate reasoning successfully. Furthermore, reasoning may support its intended conclusion, but there may be further/additional considerations that weigh for or against a given conclusion and that need to be taken into account in evaluating the argument/ conclusion as a whole (i.e., additional information might weaken or strengthen the argument).

The process of evaluating reasoning often requires creativity and imagination. One may need to be imaginative about (i) alternative strategies for solving a problem, or (ii) alternatives when faced with making a decision, or (iii) alternative hypotheses to explain something, or (iv) alternative interpretations of an observation, or (v) a variety of plans to achieve some goal, or (vi) a number of suppositions regarding a question or issue, etc. One may also need to extrapolate—to project the possible consequences of decisions, positions, policies, theories, or beliefs to assist in evaluating them.

Much of this is similar to what Facione says under the headings "evaluation", "inference" and "explanation", though it is more compressed.[3]

9.4 Thinking about one's own thinking: Self-regulation

Perhaps the most important skill/disposition/habit of mind of all for the critical thinker is that of applying critical thinking principles and practices to one's own ideas and communications, in writing or speaking, etc. This sort of self-regulation can be the hardest thing to do, which is partly why the typical critical thinking writing test can be very revealing (Fisher and Scriven, p. 39).

Whether producing responses to others or simply trying to think critically about something—perhaps with a view to presenting it in some form (written, spoken, pictorial, like pictures used for advertising or propaganda purposes, charts, etc. (cf. *ibid.*, p.100))—the crucial requirement is to apply the same standards that apply to the communications of others to one's own presentations (*ibid.*, p. 100). One needs to engage in the same active scrutiny of one's own work that is applied to others. So there is a need to be as clear as possible about the problem being addressed. Reasoning should be based on starting points that are as clear and reliable as possible. There is a need to be imaginative about what "other considerations" (including objections) might be relevant to the case—what might strengthen or weaken the presentation being constructed. The advocate needs to think about his or her claims and assumptions and justify them if possible or if the audience will demand it. It's necessary to take into account opposing points of view as sympathetically as one would wish one's own point of view to be treated. One needs to be as sure as possible of the soundness of one's inferences, made or implied, the suitability of one's presentation for the audience, the clarity of the presentation, its power and so on (*ibid.*, pp. 103, 104). To do all this is not easy and may well benefit from external help such as dialogue and discussion (*ibid.*, p. 100). For example, in arguing for a given position, one should try to anticipate (possible) reasonable criticisms/objections and others can help supply them.

This section is similar to what Facione says on "self regulation".

---

[3] For a vocabulary that can be helpful in connection with thinking about critical thinking, see Fisher and Scriven (1997) pp. 104-107.

10. Dispositions, habits of mind and values of a critical thinker

It is one thing to be skilled in some domain and another thing to display a tendency or disposition to use those skills. Though different in some respects, this is parallel to being courageous (funny, helpful or whatever) on a given occasion and being a courageous (funny, helpful or whatever) person. The critical thinker is someone who characteristically practices critical thinking. He or she does not simply display critical thinking skills in an examination but also characteristically deploys them in everyday situations or in the course of his or her work whenever good thinking matters.

Many of those who have worked in the critical thinking tradition have thought there was something very odd about having such thinking skills and not using them; indeed, if we look back at Glaser's definition, we see that he actually includes an "attitude of being disposed" to consider problems thoughtfully as part of his very definition of critical thinking.

For example, a skill in judging the credibility of evidence produces more reasonable beliefs than being rather more gullible—which is obviously better: one will be led astray less often and this is to one's advantage. So this skill is worth using whenever significant questions of credibility arise; it is valuable and it will pay to adopt the habit of using it, i.e., to be disposed to use it whenever it is appropriate.

There is no doubt that the critical thinking skills are generally valuable skills and having the habit of using them whenever it is appropriate will help in many ways, so the moral is that one should not just acquire the skills, but value them—and use them; in short become a critical *thinker*.

As Ennis has emphasized, there are some particular dispositions that are an important part of critical thinking—especially, being open-minded and trying to be well informed. The closed-minded person will lack the imagination so often essential to good critical thinking, and it is always important to try to be well-informed if one is to know what alternatives are realistic and worth considering, for example what alternative explanations need to be taken seriously when evaluating an explanation or what alternatives are realistic when faced with some decision.

It is widely agreed among the critical thinking community that it is not enough to teach the critical thinking skills mentioned above, but it is also very important to develop a range of dispositions or habits of mind if we are to develop critical think*ers*.

Facione, in his Delphi Report, lists what he calls the affective dispositions that the experts contributing to his report agreed were important for the critical thinker. Table 5 of the report (p. 13) spells these out:

Affective dispositions of critical thinking approaches to life and living in general:

- inquisitiveness with regard to a wide range of issues,
- concern to become and remain generally well-informed,
- alertness to opportunities to use CT,
- trust in the processes of reasoned inquiry,
- self-confidence in one's own ability to reason,
- open-mindedness regarding divergent world views,
- flexibility in considering alternatives and opinions,
- understanding of the opinions of other people,
- fair-mindedness in appraising reasoning,
- honesty in facing one's own biases, prejudices, stereotypes, egocentric or sociocentric tendencies,
- prudence in suspending, making or altering judgments,
- willingness to reconsider and revise views where honest reflection suggests that change is warranted.

Approaches to specific issues, questions or problems:

- clarity in stating the question or concern,
- orderliness in working with complexity,
- diligence in seeking relevant information,
- reasonableness in selecting and applying criteria,
- care in focusing attention on the concern at hand,
- persistence though difficulties are encountered,
- precision to the degree permitted by the subject and the circumstances.

It then discusses how these should be developed and the importance of teacher training for developing them.

11. "Critico-creative thinking": Critical thinking and being creative

Some people have preferred to use the term "critico-creative" thinking because the term "critical thinking" can sound "negative", as though one's only interest is in adversely criticizing other people's arguments and ideas. They want to emphasize the fact that to be good at evaluating arguments and ideas one often has to be imaginative and creative about other possibilities, alternative considerations, different options and so on. To be a good judge of issues it is not enough to see faults in what other people say; one needs to base that judgment on the best arguments one can devise (in the time available) and this often requires thinking of relevant considerations other than those presented, looking at issues from different points of view, imagining alternative scenarios and perhaps finding other relevant information; in short, one might need to be quite creative and imaginative.

The label "critico-creative" thinking is intended to stress these positive, imaginative aspects of critical thinking. Unfortunately the result is a rather unwieldy expression, and it has not caught on. So we continue to use the term "critical thinking" because it is now so widely used, whilst understanding it in this positive, imaginative sense. In this use it has the same sense in which one speaks, for example, of a theatre or film "critic"—as someone whose comments and judgments may be either positive or negative. In short, critical thinking is a kind of evaluative thinking that involves both criticism and creative thinking and that is particularly concerned with the quality of reasoning or argument which is presented in support of a belief or a course of action (see Fisher (2011) p. 14).

12. To conclude

The critical thinking tradition is a long one and is still developing. However, it is not too difficult to summarize the ideas contained in the tradition that we have just reviewed.

It is clear that critical thinking is contrasted with *unreflective* or *passive* thinking, the kind of thinking that occurs when someone jumps to a conclusion, or accepts some evidence, claim or decision at face value, without really thinking about it. It is a *skillful* activity, which may be done more or less well, and good critical thinking will meet various intellectual standards, like those of clarity, relevance, adequacy, coherence and so on. Critical thinking clearly requires the interpretation and evaluation of observations, communications and other sources of information. It also requires skill in thinking about assumptions, in asking pertinent questions, in drawing out implications—that is to say, in reasoning and arguing issues through. Furthermore, the critical thinker believes that there are many situations in which the best way to decide what to believe or do is to employ this kind of reasoned and reflective thinking and thus tends to use these methods whenever they are appropriate.

Does this attitude imply that there is just one correct way to think about any given problem? No. But it does imply that most of us could do it better than we do (that is, more skillfully/ reasonably/ rationally), if we asked the right questions. This tradition is all about improving our own thinking by considering how we think in various contexts now, seeing a better model and trying to move our own practice towards that better model. It does not imply that there is just one correct way of thinking that we should try to emulate, but that there are better ways of thinking than we often exhibit and that our poor thinking can be at least partially remedied by suitable practice.

Finally, it is worth pointing out that not all "good" thinking counts as critical thinking. For example, there is much routine thinking, speedy thinking, creative thinking, and more, which does not count as critical thinking. If one aims to interpret a claim or evaluate an argument one will often have to think of alternative interpretations or arguments. This is a creative activity (Fisher and Scriven pp. 66, 67) but quite different from literary or poetic creativity. Equally, plodding or straightforward reasoning (as when you solve a routine mathematical problem in a standard, well-learned way) is not critical thinking. Critical thinking only occurs when the reasoning, interpretation or evaluation is challenging and non-routine (*ibid.*, p. 72). Again, if you are working out an explanation this may well involve critical thinking, but if you are explaining something familiar to a third party it might not at all. Various other skills are excluded from being called critical thinking skills on our conception, for example being observant or watchful is different from critical observing, etc. (*ibid.*, pp. 94–96). The critical thinking tradition is rich and complex but understanding it and working within it pays tremendous dividends and is well worth the effort.

References

Dewey, J. (1998). *How We Think*. Dover Publications. (The beginnings of the modern tradition of critical thinking; first published by Heath and Co. 1909)

Ennis, R.H. (1962). "A Concept of Critical Thinking: A Proposed Basis for Research in the Teaching and Evaluation of Critical Thinking." *Harvard Educational Review*, 32, no. 1, 1962, 81-111.

Ennis, R.H. (1987). A Taxonomy of critical thinking dispositions and abilities. In J. Baron and R. Sternberg (Eds.), *Teaching thinking skills: Theory and practice*, 9-26. New York: W.H. Freeman.

Ennis, R.H. (1991). Critical thinking: A streamlined conception. *Teaching Philosophy*, 14 (1), 5-25.

Ennis, R.H. (1996). Critical thinking dispositions: Their nature and assessability. *Informal Logic*, 18 (2 & 3), 165-182.

Ennis, R.H. (2011). Critical thinking: Reflection and perspective—Part I. *Inquiry: Critical Thinking Across the Disciplines*, 26(1), 4-18.

Facione, P.A. (1990). The Delphi Report. Critical Thinking: A Statement of Expert Consensus for purposes of Educational Assessment and Instruction; Executive Summary. *California Academic Press*. The complete APA Delphi Report is available as ERIC Doc. No.: ED 315423.

Facione, P. (2010). Critical thinking: What it is and why it counts. California Academic Press. (Easy to find on the internet.)

Fisher, A. (2001, 2nd ed. 2011). *Critical Thinking: An Introduction*. Cambridge University Press.

Fisher, A. and Scriven, M. (1997). *Critical Thinking: Its Definition and Assess-ment*. Edgepress and Centre for Research in Critical Thinking, University of East Anglia. (Can be obtained from Edgepress.)

Fisher, A, Scriven, M and Ennis, R.H. (2012). A Survey of Critical Thinking/ Reasoning Tests that are Comparable to the Law Schools Admission Test. *Law Schools Admission Council.*

Glaser, E. (1941). *An Experiment in the Development of Critical Thinking*. Advanced School of Education at Teacher's College, Columbia.

Kahane, H. (1971). *Logic and Contemporary Rhetoric: The Use of Reason in Everyday Life*. Belmont, CA: Wadsworth Publishing Company.

Lipman, M. (1991). *Thinking in Education*. Cambridge University Press

Lipman, M. (1974). *Harry Stottlemeier's Discovery*. Institute for the Advance-ment of Philosophy for Children, NJ.

McPeck, J.E. (1981). *Critical Thinking and Education*. [Palgrave Macmillan] Martin Robertson. (The classic text which argues that critical thinking cannot be taught.)

Norris, S. and Ennis, R. (1989). *Evaluating Critical Thinking*. Pacific Grove, CA: Critical Thinking Press and Software. [Lawrence Erlbaum]

Paul, R. (1992). *Critical Thinking: What Every Person Needs to Survive in a Rapidly Changing World*. Foundation for Critical Thinking, Sonoma State Uni-versity, Rohnert Park, CA.

Paul, R., Fisher, A. and Nosich, G. (1993). *Workshop on Critical Thinking Strate-gies*. Foundation for Critical Thinking, Sonoma State University, Rohnert Park, CA.

Passmore, J. (1967). On teaching to be critical. In R.S. Peters (Ed.), *The Concept of Education*, pp. 192–211. Routledge and Kegan Paul. [Routledge 2009]

Scriven, M. (1976). *Reasoning*. New York: McGraw-Hill. (A classic text on how to improve reasoning skills.)

Siegel, Harvey (1988). *Educating Reason; Rationality, Critical Thinking and Education*. New York: Routledge.

Swartz, R.J. and Parks, S. (1993). *Infusing Critical and Creative Thinking into the Curriculum*. Pacific Grove, CA: Critical Thinking Press. (Very good account of how to teach transferable and critical thinking skills.)

Swartz, R. and Parks, S. (1994). *Infusing the Teaching of Critical and Creative Thinking into Elementary Instruction*. Critical Thinking Press and Software.

Swartz, R.J. and Perkins, D.N. (1989). *Teaching Thinking: Issues and Approaches*. Pacific Grove, CA: Midwest Publications. [Lawrence Erlbaum]

About the author:

Alec Fisher pioneered the development of critical thinking in the United Kingdom. He taught philosophy, logic and critical thinking in the University of East Anglia, Norwich, UK, where he was Director of the *Centre for Research in Critical Thinking.* He has conducted workshops on critical thinking in Britain, Europe. North America, South America, South Africa, Russia, and the Far East. He designed the *AS level examination in Critical Thinking* for OCR in the UK and was Chief Examiner for some years. His books include *The Logic of Real Arguments* (Cambridge University Press, 1988 and 2004), *Critical Thinking; Its Definition and Assessment* (Centre for Research in Critical Thinking and Edgepress 1997, co-authored with Michael Scriven) and *Critical Thinking: An Introduction* (Cambridge University Press, 2001 and 2011). He recently completed (with Michael Scriven and Robert Ennis) a report for the (US) Law School Admission Council, recommending changes to the Law School Admission Test.

II

On Teaching Critical Thinking

Introduction to Part II

Teaching critical thinking effectively requires considerable front-loading—designing the details of the course in advance—while at the same time having alternatives ready on hand to switch to in case a particular way of presenting a topic isn't working.

Those teaching the course for the first time will likely be looking for a textbook. Finding a textbook that is focused on critical thinking is easier said than done. Many textbooks marketed for critical thinking courses are devoted to argument analysis and assessment and elementary logic. The assumption of this book is that while skills in both of those contribute to critical thinking, they don't constitute it. Some textbooks marketed for critical thinking focus on problem-solving or on decision-making. These are activities whose effective performance can require critical thinking but they don't constitute critical thinking either. Instructors serious about teaching critical thinking are at best likely to find themselves in the position of needing to develop lesson plans and exercises that supplement the material in the textbook and wanting to skip chunks of the textbook, and indeed many feel the need to develop their own syllabus.

This part of the book begins, in Chapter 2, on teaching critical thinking, with, first, a brief account of John Hattie's "visible learning" pedagogy followed by a radical suggestion for teaching critical thinking. What is impressive about Hattie's recommendations is that they are based on a massive amount of evidence that Hattie accumulated and studied over many years of research. There follow five exercises of increasing complexity.

Derek Allen's exercise in Chapter 3, to use when teaching the logical concept of deductive validity, is straightforward and thorough. It can also serve as a model to copy in designing parallel exercises to use in teaching similar simple, discrete concepts.

In Chapter 4, Justine Kingsbury proposes a way to construct arguments, making them as good as the conclusion being argued for admits. She does it with a class of 200 students that meets for a mass lecture and also in small discussion groups. She introduces it after having spent some time in evaluating arguments, but it might also work, albeit differently, if it were taught before spending time in evaluating arguments.

In their exercise in Chapter 5, Kingsbury and her colleague Tracey Bowell describe an ingenious exercise designed to encourage students to apply to arguments for their own beliefs the standards they have learned to apply to others' arguments. This is an exercise in practicing what Richard Paul called "strong sense" critical thinking.

In Chapter 6, Jan Albert van Laar introduces an exercise in learning the value of compromising and methods of achieving a compromise in situations in which controversies cannot be settled otherwise. It's an ambitious learning device that can be packed into a 2-hour class or two 90-minute classes.

Chapter 7 contains Mark Battersby and Sharon Bailin's 4-lesson exercise in using arguments to inquire into the pros and cons of a controversial issue—thereby using arguments to help make up one's mind instead of to just to defend an opinion. Like van Laar's exercise, it would require at least a week's worth of class time.

2

Teaching Critical Thinking

J. Anthony Blair and Michael Scriven

2.1 An evidence-based approach *J. Anthony Blair*

The work of the Australian researcher of teaching and learning, John Hattie—*Visible Learning* (*VL* 2009) and *Visible Learning for Teachers* (*VLT* 2012)—inspires the general advice about teaching, and hence about teaching critical thinking, with which we begin the first part of this book.

Hattie's mantra is "Know thy impact". He argues that the evidence of about 1000 studies shows that a teacher should constantly be aware of what the students are learning (and what they are not learning) from the lessons. He contends that three "fundamental" principles should underpin teaching and learning at public schools (*VLT*, Preface).

1. Teachers should challenge students' intellectual and imaginative capacities. Thus ruled out are lowest common denominator materials, boring pedagogy, mindless busy work. There should be legitimate progression of learning throughout the course.

2. Students should be treated as developing human beings, with humanity, sensitivity and imaginative flair.

3. Teachers should strive to maximize students' potential for later learning and to be contributing members of a good society.

What makes Hattie's advice stand out is that it is powerfully evidence-based. He has analyzed close to 1000 studies of the effects on learning of different variables, He sums up his advice as follows:

> The simple principle underlying most of the syntheses discussed in this book is 'visible teaching and learning'. Visible teaching and learning occurs when learning is the explicit and transparent goal, when it is appropriately challenging, and when the teacher and the student both (in their various ways) seek to ascertain whether and to what degree the challenging goal is attained. Visible teaching

and learning occurs when there is deliberate practice aimed at attaining mastery of the goal, when there is feedback given and sought, and when there are active, passionate and engaging people (teacher, students, peers) participating in the act of learning. It is teachers seeing learning through the eyes of students, and students seeing teaching as the key to their ongoing learning. The remarkable feature of the evidence is that the greatest effects on student learning occur when teachers become learners of their own teaching, and when students become their own teachers. When students become their own teachers they exhibit the self-regulatory attributes that seem most desirable for learners (self-monitoring, self-evaluation, self-assessment, self-teaching). Thus, it is visible teaching and learning by teachers and by students that makes a difference. (*Visible Learning for Teachers, Maximizing Impact on Learning.* Pp. 17-18.)

One of the principal take-aways from Hattie's findings for teaching any subject—and so, also for teaching critical thinking—is that, of the factors over which teachers have control, the way the instructor approaches her and his teaching makes all the difference. Hattie distinguishes between experienced teachers and expert teachers. Expert teachers stand out in the following ways (pp. 28-33):

Expert teachers ...
- can identify the most important ways to present the subject they teach.
- are proficient at creating an optimal climate for learning.
- monitor learning and provide feedback.
- believe that all students can reach the success criteria. [Everyone qualified to take the course can, with effort, pass it.]
- influence surface and deep outcomes [A surface outcome might be exhibiting CT skills; a deep outcome might be internalizing the attitudes of a critical thinker.]

Advice to teachers:
- Discover what the students know and don't know about the subject as well as their attitudes and dispositions towards it. Begin there.
- Make learning intentions and criteria of success known at the outset of each lesson.
- As a teacher, aim for a balance between talking, listening and doing, and aim for a similar balance by students.
- Harness the positive power of peers to advance learning. Peers can help, tutor, provide feedback, provide friendship. Look for opportunities for cooperative learning and student tutoring.
- Encourage high, interesting, challenging, expectations.

Hattie divides *Visible Learning for Teachers* into three parts. The excerpts above come from Part 1—which describes where his ideas originate and the roles of teachers in the education process. Part 2 focuses on the lessons: preparation, starting the lesson, the flow of the lesson—(i) learning, and (ii) the place of feedback, and the end of the lesson. This part of the book is larded with ideas that have been tested and found effective. The third part emphasizes what Hattie calls "mind-frames"—the ways teachers and schools think about their roles. He lists eight that, he argues, have proven effective in producing success in reaching the goal of surface and deep student learning (pp. 181-189):

(1) Teachers/leaders believe that their fundamental task is to evaluate the effect of their teaching on students' learning and achievement.
(2) Teachers/leaders believe that their success and failure in student learning is about what they, as teachers or leader, did or did not do ... We are change agents!
(3) Teachers/leaders want to talk more about the learning than the teaching.
(4) Teachers/leaders see assessment as feedback about their impact.
(5) Teachers/leaders engage in dialogue not monologue.
(6) Teachers/leaders enjoy the challenge and never retreat to "doing their best".
(7) Teachers/leaders believe that it is their role to develop positive relationships in classrooms/staffrooms.
(8) Teachers/leaders inform all about the language of learning.

What is challenging about Hattie's analysis of the evidence is its implications for teaching critical thinking. We think we could do better with smaller classes. The evidence shows that class size is not a major variable. We think we could do better with better-motivated students—not the classrooms full of students for whom this is an option course (or worse, a required course outside their major) to which they aren't prepared to devote the time or invest the interest it requires. The evidence shows that committed teachers can turn such students into enthusiastic learners.

We cannot do justice to Hattie's recommendations and his defense of them. We strongly commend *Visible Learning for Teachers* (Routledge, 2012) to all critical thinking instructors.

2.2 A radical suggestion *Michael Scriven*

Thesis

The essential nature of critical thinking guarantees that, as taught in the usual ways, it will fail to show educationally significant (lasting) gains.

- "Taught in the usual ways" means taught in a single course (one quarter or one seminar long), using the typical approach (teacher-centric and single text focused).
- "The essential nature of critical thinking" is that it is the ability to distinguish, classify, identify and deal appropriately with general patterns of valid, good, weak and fallacious reasoning that recur across substantial ranges of subject matter within, and, especially, across disciplines.

Teaching this way fails in the usual situations for one or the other of two weaknesses. At the more general (macro) end it fails because it comes too close to trying to teach cognitive-linguistic IQ, which appears to be substantially genetic; and at the other (micro) end, where we laboriously endeavor to teach how to handle each of the 30 to 50 most important unsound or sound patterns of inference or representation, it fails because a single course is nowhere near long enough to cover and develop these sprawling skills.

In fact, the research results make clear that the whole undergraduate learning experience is not enough. So the claim that critical thinking can, and can only be taught comprehensively via subject matter instruction is also false. *A fortiori*—the college should not think that a three-course sequence of critical thinking is probably enough to yield big gains. Still, it's a significantly better approach than one course.

The other prong of the second horn that fatally skewers the hopes of success for anything like a conventional collegial critical thinking course (C4) is the relative weakness of the pedagogical approach used. As is clear from the brilliant analysis of nearly 1000 meta-studies by John Hattie (in the Visible Learning series of books), any approach is limited in its success by its approach to teaching as well as by the particular difficulty of its subject matter.

Reform

In order to get better results, some of the obvious components include:

(1) Allocate a sequence of three or if necessary more standard courses for coverage of critical thinking/argumentation/rhetoric.
(2) Allow no (or at least no new) teachers of critical thinking who have not developed an outline of texts, examples, and pedagogical guidelines for a 3-unit course that will be taught by using at least the peer-critiquing/

self-evaluating approach plus some other Hattie-backed technique(s) of their choice.

(3) A weak alternative to (2) is to allow only critical thinking courses that focus on a package of 3-6 one-term important patterns of good or bad inference/presentation skills, with a matching pre and post test on these only. In other words cut the goals heavily and the duration likewise. This approach has been occasionally adopted, e.g., for teaching argument mapping at the University of Melbourne, with significant positive results.

Several successful type (3) approaches might then be synthesized into a trial run 3-unit approach to something on the way to a successful full-scale course for teaching critical thinking.

Right now, we badly need new texts, texts that incorporate the "student as teacher" and other (Hattie) evidence-based approaches and good teachers for them, maybe a thousand as a first step.

About the authors:

J. Anthony Blair is a pioneer of the informal logic movement, co-authoring with Ralph H. Johnson the influential textbook *Logical Self-Defense*. With Robert C. Pinto and Katharine E. Parr, he wrote the critical thinking textbook, *Reasoning, A Practical Guide*. A founder and editor of the journal *Informal Logic*, he has published extensively in informal logic, critical thinking and argumentation. He is presently a Senior Fellow at the Centre for Research in Reasoning, Argumentation and Rhetoric (CRRAR) at the University of Windsor.

Michael Scriven was born in the United Kingdom, went to Australia from age 12 through a BA & MA at Melbourne in honors math. Returning to Oxford, he received a D.Phil in philosophy (thesis on explanation theory). He then held appointments (about four years each) at Minnesota, Swarthmore and Indiana; did summer teaching at Wesleyan and Harvard; did research in primatology in Austria; and two Institutions for Advance Study (on democracy and on the behavioral sciences). Next he spent 12 years at Berkeley, with eventually a split appointment between philosophy and education. He left UCB to start an institution for evaluation research at the University of San Francisco; ran an evaluation consulting business; was a Professor of Psychology at Claremont Graduate University; served was co-head of the School of Education at the University of Western Australia for twelve years; now back at Claremont as co-director of the Claremont Evaluation Center.

3

Validity

Derek Allen

A note for the instructor

I taught a two-semester reasoning course at the University of Toronto for many years. Enrolment was capped at 65. The course, open to students in all four undergraduate years, had no prerequisites. The first semester covered topics in informal logic, including argument recognition, argument analysis (by which I meant standardizing and diagramming arguments), and argument assessment. The second semester was devoted to ethical reasoning and legal reasoning.

I found that to develop enhanced reasoning skills students require repeated practice, so I assigned a number of exercises. Several of the exercises were mini-exercises worth 2% or 3% each. Others were longer exercises worth 7% each.

When introducing a new informal-logic topic, I used simple examples. More challenging examples followed in class, but for the most part I didn't rely solely on them for the purpose of preparing the students for the first-semester graded exercises. Instead, for each but one of these exercises I provided the students with a practice exercise that had been a graded exercise in a previous year. The students did the practice exercise outside class as part of their preparation for the corresponding graded exercise, and I posted answers and comments on the course website.

One of the graded exercises was a mini-exercise on assessing arguments for validity in natural/ordinary language. The term 'validity' was used in the course (and is used here) to mean *deductive* validity. Many instructors report that students often find validity a difficult concept to grasp, and this was my experience too. For this reason, I eventually decided to set *two* practice exercises for the mini-exercise on validity assessments, and to make the first of them a teaching exercise with step-by-step instructions for doing the assessments; the second practice exercise was a graded exercise from a previous year. An example of a step-by-step teaching exercise on validity assessments appears below; answers are given separately.

The exercise requires familiarity with the following topics (which I had covered earlier in the semester):

- Arguments in one or another of the senses in which they are understood in logic textbooks; validity (understood as deductive validity); the idea of an argument's being valid or invalid "as it stands" (that is, without the addition of any tacit premises); assessing an argument for validity in ordinary language (as distinct from assessing an argument for validity by using procedures of formal logic); entailment; entails; implies.
- Necessary and sufficient conditions; "if and only if"; indicative conditional statements; the antecedent and consequent of an indicative conditional statement; an indicative conditional statement implies that the truth of its antecedent is sufficient for the truth of its consequent and that the truth of its consequent is necessary for the truth of its antecedent; affirming/denying the antecedent/consequent of an indicative conditional statement; *modus ponens*; *modus tollens*.
- The possibility that a two-premise conditional argument that denies the antecedent or affirms the consequent and is therefore formally invalid may nevertheless be a valid argument in virtue of its content; this will be the case if the argument's non-conditional premise entails the argument's conclusion.
- The use of a modality (e.g., 'probably', 'necessarily') in an argument to indicate, at least roughly, the degree of support that the arguer thinks the premises provide for the conclusion.

The above list may include topics that you won't have covered in your course before you cover validity, or that you won't cover at all. In this event, you would need to edit the following practice exercise accordingly. Or, for whatever reason(s), you might decide not to use even an edited version of the exercise. In this event, the exercise would still serve as an example of a step-by-step teaching exercise, and you might decide to devise such an exercise yourself (on validity or another topic) for use in your course.

The arguments in the exercise below are ones that I made up; they don't come from "real-world" contexts such as the media or politics or court judgments or online discussions of social issues. This is deliberate. The exercise is for students who have just been introduced to validity, and the point of the exercise is to help them learn how to assess arguments for validity in natural/ordinary language. For such students, it's best, I believe, to start with arguments that have been devised specifically for this purpose and are free of the unclarities and complexities that often characterize arguments in "real-world" contexts. Once students have learned how to assess an assortment of such arguments for validity, they should be ready to try doing the same for selected "real-world" arguments.

Next, a comment about how the skill of assessing arguments for validity will have applications beyond the classroom. Whether an argument is a good one from a logical point of view depends (in part) on the nature of the connection between the argument's premises and its conclusion. If the conclusion must be true if the premises are true, then the connection between the premises and the conclusion is the strongest possible: if the premises are true, their truth guarantees that the conclusion is true. If we are considering whether to "buy" some argument we encounter, it's worth knowing whether the premises and conclusion are related in this way. If they are, then the argument is valid. Thus, students who become proficient at assessing an argument for validity, by determining whether the truth of its premises would guarantee the truth of its conclusion, acquire a useful logical skill—a skill they can apply to arguments they encounter in their daily lives beyond the classroom.

Finally, a transitional point. If the truth of an argument's premises would guarantee the truth of the conclusion, it would be logically impossible for the argument to have both true premises and a false conclusion, and so the argument would satisfy the condition for (deductive) validity stated at the beginning of the following exercise, namely: an argument is valid (that is, deductively valid) if and only if it is logically impossible that it has both true premises and a false conclusion.

A Practice Exercise on Validity

Review

An argument is **valid** (that is, *deductively* valid) if and only if it is **logically impossible** that it has both true premises and a false conclusion. A valid argument can't have the combination "true premises and false conclusion."

An argument is **invalid** if and only if it is **logically possible** that it has both true premises and a false conclusion.

Recall that in this course *assessing an argument for validity* means ARGU-ING *that the argument is valid or that it is invalid (NOT just asserting that it's valid or that it's invalid).*

Assess for validity each of the following arguments as it stands (that is, without adding any tacit premises):

(1) Figure 1 is square. Therefore, Figure 1 has exactly four sides.

Step 1: Identify the premise of the argument and the conclusion of the argument.

Step 2: Assume that the premise is true and ask yourself whether this assumption forces you to accept the conclusion as true.

Step 3: If you think that you must accept the conclusion as true if you assume that the premise is true, then you should conclude that the argument is **valid**. If you think that you are free to say that the conclusion is false even if you assume that the premise is true, then you should conclude that the argument is **invalid**.

Step 4: If you think that the argument is **valid**, how would you support (defend) this claim? If you think that the argument is **invalid**, how would you support (defend) this claim?

Step 5: Write out your validity assessment of the argument. Remember, this requires you to ARGUE that the argument is valid or that it's invalid; you can't just *assert* that it's valid or just *assert* that it's invalid.

For arguments (2)-(4), follow the same procedure as for argument (1).

(2) Figure 1 is square. Therefore, Figure 1 is small.

(3) Canada has more than nine provinces. Therefore, Canada has more than eight provinces.

(4) Canada has 20 provinces. Therefore, Canada has more than 10 provinces.

Arguments (1)-(4) above each have one stated premise. The next four arguments each have two stated premises.

(5) 1. Canada has 10 provinces.
     2. The U.S.A. has 50 states.
     Therefore,
     3. Canada has one-fifth as many provinces as the U.S.A. has states.

Step 1: Identify the premises of the argument and the conclusion of the argument.

Step 2: Assume that the premises are true and ask yourself whether this assumption forces you to accept the conclusion as true.

Step 3: If you think that you must accept the conclusion as true if you assume that the premises are true, then you should conclude that the argument is **valid**. If you think that you are free to say that the conclusion is false even if you assume that the premises are true, then you should say that the argument is **invalid**.

Step 4: If you think that the argument is **valid**, how would you support (defend) this claim? If you think that the argument is **invalid**, how would you support (defend) this claim?

Step 5: Write out your validity assessment of the argument. Remember, this requires you to ARGUE that the argument is valid or that it's invalid; you can't just *assert* that it's valid or just *assert* that it's invalid.

For arguments (6)-(8), follow the same procedure as for argument (5).

(6) 1. Canada has 13 provinces.
    2. The U.S.A. has 52 states.
    Therefore,
    3. The U.S.A. has four times as many states as Canada has provinces.

(7) 1. Canada has 20 provinces.
    2. The U.S.A. has 80 states.
    Therefore,
    3. Canada has one-quarter as many provinces as the U.S.A. has states.

(8) 1. The U.S.A. has 50 states.
    2. Canada has 10 provinces.
    Therefore,
    3. The U.S.A. has a larger land area than Canada has.

For arguments (9)-(11), follow the same procedure as for argument (1).

(9) 1. Jane plays several sports.
    Therefore,
    2. Jane likes sports.

(10) 1. Bryan's girlfriend has broken up with him.
    So it must be true that,
    2. Bryan is sad.

(11)   1.   Amy has been sneezing all day.
This means that,
    2.   Amy has a cold.

For argument (12), follow the procedure set out below it.

(12)   1.   If Jack was at the party, then Jill was at the party.
    2.   Jack was at the party.
Therefore,
    3.   Jill was at the party.

Step 1: Underline the antecedent and the consequent of premise 1.
Step 2: Decide which of the following sentences is true: (a) Premise 1 implies that the truth of its antecedent is **sufficient** for the truth of its consequent. (b) Premise 1 implies that the truth of its antecedent is **necessary** for the truth of its consequent.
Step 3: Premise 2 either affirms or denies the antecedent of premise 1, or it affirms or denies the consequent of premise 1. Which of these four things does it do?
Step 4: Given your Step 2 answer and your Step 3 answer, would you say that the conclusion of the argument must be true if the premises are true, or would you say that the conclusion of the argument could be false even if the premises are true?
Step 5: If you think the conclusion of the argument must be true if the premises are true, then you should conclude that the argument is **valid**. If this is your conclusion, how would you support (defend) it? If you think the conclusion of the argument could be false even if the premises are true, then you should conclude that the argument is **invalid**. If this is your conclusion, how would you support (defend) it?
Step 6: Write out your validity assessment of the argument. Remember, this requires you to ARGUE that the argument is valid or that it's invalid; you can't just *assert* that it's valid or just *assert* that it's invalid.

For argument (13), follow the same procedure as for argument (12).

(13)   1.   If Jack was at the party, then Jill was at the party.
    2.   Jack wasn't at the party.
Therefore,
    3.   Jill wasn't at the party.

For argument (14), follow the procedure set out below it.

(14) 1. If Jack was at the party, then Jill was at the party.
2. Jill was at the party.
Therefore,
3. Jack was at the party.

Step 1: Underline the antecedent and the consequent of premise 1.

Step 2: Decide which of the following sentences is true: (a) Premise 1 implies that the truth of its consequent is **sufficient** for the truth of its antecedent. (b) Premise 1 implies that the truth of its consequent is **necessary** for the truth of its antecedent.

Step 3: Premise 2 either affirms or denies the antecedent of premise 1, or it affirms or denies the consequent of premise 1. Which of these four things does it do?

Step 4: Given your Step 2 answer and your Step 3 answer, would you say that the conclusion of the argument must be true if the premises are true, or would you say that the conclusion of the argument could be false even if the premises are true?

Step 5: If you think the conclusion of the argument must be true if the premises are true, then you should conclude that the argument is **valid**. If this is your conclusion, how would you support (defend) it? If you think that the conclusion of the argument could be false even if the premises are true, then you should conclude that the argument is **invalid**. If this is your conclusion, how would you support (defend) it?

Step 6: Write out your validity assessment of the argument. Remember, this requires you to ARGUE that the argument is valid or that it's invalid; you can't just *assert* that it's valid or just *assert* that it's invalid.

For argument (15), follow the same procedure as for argument (14).

(15) 1. If Jack was at the party, then Jill was at the party.
2. Jill was not at the party.
Therefore,
3. Jack was not at the party.

Answers for the Practice Exercise on Validity

(1) 1. Figure 1 is square.
Therefore,
2. Figure 1 has exactly four sides.

Validity assessment: If the premise of this argument is true, the conclusion must also be true because by definition square figures have exactly four sides. Hence, the argument is valid as it stands.

(2) 1. Figure 1 is square.
    Therefore,
    2. Figure 1 is small.

Validity assessment: Even if the premise of this argument is true, the conclusion may be false because square figures need not be small. Hence, the argument is invalid as it stands.

(3) 1. Canada has more than nine provinces.
    Therefore,
    2. Canada has more than eight provinces.

Validity assessment: Nine is more than eight. Hence, if the premise of this argument is true (and it is true), then the conclusion must also be true. Thus, the argument is valid as it stands.

(4) 1. Canada has 20 provinces.
    Therefore,
    2. Canada has more than 10 provinces.

Validity assessment: Twenty is more than ten. Hence, if the premise of this argument were true, the conclusion would have to be true as well. Thus, the argument is valid as it stands.

(5) 1. Canada has 10 provinces.
    2. The U.S.A. has 50 states.
    Therefore,
    3. Canada has one-fifth as many provinces as the U.S.A. has states.

Validity assessment: Ten is one-fifth of fifty. Thus, if the premises of this argument are true (and they are true), then the conclusion must be true as well. Hence, the argument is valid as it stands.

(6) 1. Canada has 13 provinces.
    2. The U.S.A. has 52 states.
    Therefore,
    3. The U.S.A. has four times as many states as Canada has provinces.

Validity assessment: Fifty-two is four times thirteen. Hence, if the premises of this argument were true, the conclusion would have to be true as well. Thus, the argument is valid as it stands.

(7) 1. Canada has 20 provinces.
    2. The U.S.A. has 80 states.
    Therefore,
    3. Canada has one-quarter as many provinces as the U.S.A. has states.

Validity assessment: Twenty is one-quarter of eighty. Hence, if the premises of this argument were true, the conclusion would have to be true as well. Thus, the argument is valid as it stands.

(8) 1. The U.S.A. has 50 states.
    2. Canada has 10 provinces.
    Therefore,
    3. The U.S.A. has a larger land area than Canada has.

Validity assessment: Even if the premises of this argument are true (and they are true), the conclusion could be false, for the 50 states of the U.S.A. could be contained within a total land area equal to or smaller than the total land area within which Canada's 10 provinces are contained. Thus, the argument is invalid as it stands.

Comment: According to a World Statistics website,[1] Canada has a larger land area than the U.S.A. has; if so, then argument (8) has a false conclusion. But it has true premises. Thus, if its conclusion is false, then it has true premises and a false conclusion and is therefore invalid. Why? Because a valid argument cannot have true premises and a false conclusion; rather, an argument with true premises and a false conclusion is *in*valid.

(9) 1. Jane plays several sports.
    Therefore,
    2. Jane likes sports.

[1] www.mongabay.com/igapo/world_statistics_by_area.htm

Validity assessment: Even if it is true that Jane plays several sports, it may be false that she likes sports. It may be that she *hates* sports but plays several sports anyway because she is forced to do so by her parents. Thus, even if the argument's premise is true, the conclusion could be false, and so the argument is invalid as it stands.

(10) 1. Bryan's girlfriend has broken up with him.
       So it must be true that,
       2. Bryan is sad.

Validity assessment: Even if Bryan's girlfriend has broken up with him, he may not be sad. It could be that he wanted to break up with her and that she discovered this and decided to break up with him in order to deny him the satisfaction of being the one to initiate the break-up. His pride is hurt, but overall he's happy, not sad, because he wanted their relationship to end, and he's glad it has. Thus, even if the premise of the argument is true, the conclusion could be false, and so the argument is invalid as it stands.

Comment: Note that this assessment involves telling a story in which the premise of the argument is true, the conclusion is false, and there's no contradiction (no talk of married bachelors, for example). Note too that the argument's modality ("must") is irrelevant to the validity assessment. It tells us that the arguer thinks the argument's premise provides very strong support for the conclusion; but this is irrelevant to the question of whether in fact (no matter what the arguer thinks) the conclusion must be true if the premise is true.

(11) 1. Amy has been sneezing all day.
       This means that,
       2. Amy has a cold.

Validity assessment: Even if Amy has been sneezing all day, it could be false that she has a cold. It could be that she has a severe allergy (not a cold) and that this is why she has been sneezing all day. Thus, even if the premise is true, the conclusion could be false, and so the argument is invalid as it stands.

(12) 1. If Jack was at the party, then Jill was at the party.
       2. Jack was at the party.
       Therefore,
       3. Jill was at the party.

Validity assessment 1: This argument affirms the antecedent and is therefore valid by *modus ponens*.

Validity assessment 2: If the conditional premise of this argument is true, then if its antecedent ("Jack was at the party") is true this is sufficient for the truth of its consequent ("Jill was at the party"). If the argument's non-conditional premise ("Jack was at the party") is true, then the antecedent of the conditional premise is true. Hence, if both premises are true, the conclusion ("Jill was at the party") must also be true, and so the argument is valid.

Comment: In a graded assignment, it wouldn't be necessary to provide two validity assessments of the argument; one would be sufficient. The two assessments given here illustrate two different ways in which it can be argued that argument (12) is valid.

(13) 1. If Jack was at the party, then Jill was at the party.
2. Jack wasn't at the party.
Therefore,
3. Jill wasn't at the party.

Validity assessment: If the conditional premise of this argument is true, then if its antecedent ("Jack was at the party") is true this is sufficient for the truth of its consequent ("Jill was at the party"). If the argument's non-conditional premise ("Jack wasn't at the party") is true, then the antecedent of the conditional premise is false. But the consequent could be true even if the antecedent is false: Jill might have gone to the party because she heard that Jack wouldn't be there and she wanted to avoid him. Thus, even if the premises of the argument are true, the conclusion could be false, and so the argument is invalid.

(14) 1. If Jack was at the party, then Jill was at the party.
2. Jill was at the party.
Therefore,
3. Jack was at the party.

Validity assessment 1: This argument affirms the consequent and is therefore invalid unless its non-conditional premise (2) entails the conclusion (3). But (2) does not entail (3). The situation could be this: Jill was at the party, but Jack decided to stay home and do some validity assessments. This situation shows that (3) could be false even if (2) is true; hence, it shows that (2) does not entail (3). Given this fact and the fact that the argument affirms the consequent, the argument is invalid.

Validity assessment 2: If the conditional premise of this argument is true, then the truth of the consequent ("Jill was at the party") is *necessary* for the truth of the antecedent ("Jack was at the party"). But the truth of the consequent might not be *sufficient* for the truth of the antecedent, even if the conditional premise is true. It could be that:

>　(a) Jack was at the party if and only if Jill *and Vicky* were at the party; and that
>　(b) Jill was at the party, but
>　(c) Vicky was not at the party.

In this scenario, Jack was not at the party because a necessary condition of his being there (namely, Vicky's being there) wasn't satisfied. Thus, the conclusion of the argument ("Jack was at the party") could be false even if the premises are true, and so the argument is invalid.

Comment: As in the case of argument (12), it wouldn't be necessary in a graded assignment to provide two validity assessments of the argument; one would be sufficient.

>　(15)　1.　If Jack was at the party, then Jill was at the party.
>　　　　2.　Jill was not at the party.
>　　　　Therefore,
>　　　　3.　Jack was not at the party.

Validity assessment 1: This argument denies the consequent and so is valid by *modus tollens*.

Validity assessment 2: If the conditional premise of this argument is true, then the truth of the consequent ("Jill was at the party") is necessary for the truth of the antecedent ("Jack was at the party"). But if the non-conditional premise is true, then Jill wasn't at the party. Hence, if both premises are true, then a necessary condition for Jack's being at the party wasn't satisfied, in which case he wasn't at the party. Thus, if both premises are true, the conclusion must be true as well, and so the argument is valid.

Comment: As in the case of arguments (12) and (14), it wouldn't be necessary in a graded assignment to provide two validity assessments of the argument; one would be sufficient.

About the author:

Derek Allen is Professor Emeritus of Philosophy at the University of Toronto. For many years he taught an informal logic course called Modes of Reasoning for which he wrote extensive class materials. During his career he received several teaching awards including a Leadership in Faculty Teaching Award in recognition of an "outstanding contribution to teaching excellence in Ontario" and a 3M National Teaching Fellowship Award for "an exemplary contribution to teaching and learning" in a Canadian university. He has written a number of conference papers and commentaries in argumentation studies and has published journal and anthology articles in informal logic. He is a member of the editorial board of the journal *Informal Logic* and a past-president of the Association for Informal Logic and Critical Thinking (AILACT). He has been invited by Oxford University Press to write an encyclopedia article on critical thinking and will do so with three AILACT co-authors.

4

Teaching Argument Construction

Justine Kingsbury

Most critical thinking textbooks tell students nothing about how to construct good arguments of their own. Their focus is on the identification and evaluation of other people's arguments—as you would expect, since they are after all *critical* thinking textbooks.

Although teaching students how to evaluate arguments is the primary goal of critical thinking courses, such courses also provide the ideal context for the teaching of argument construction. Writing courses sometimes instruct students in how to write an argumentative essay, but they tend not to go into any detail about what differentiates a good argument from a bad one. By the middle of a critical thinking course, in contrast, students should have acquired some idea of what makes a good argument good, so they are well placed to be told how to construct one themselves. Although learning the difference between a good argument and a bad argument goes some way towards showing you how to construct good arguments of your own, it does not go all the way. Some explicit instruction is needed.

However, it is difficult to provide such instruction in a large lecture class. The best way to learn argument construction, once you have learned how to evaluate arguments, is to construct arguments and then have them evaluated either by your peers or by a tutor. How can you teach argument construction in a lecture? All that there is to say about it (given that the students already know how to evaluate arguments) can be conveyed in about five minutes.

Here is a method of teaching argument construction that I have developed to suit a teaching situation in which there are two one-hour lectures and one one-hour tutorial per week. The lecture class contains approximately two hundred students: each tutorial group contains between ten and twenty. One lecture and one tutorial are devoted entirely to argument construction. The lecture consists of a five-minute introductory spiel followed by an in-class exercise in which we construct an argument as a group. Then the students are given a homework assignment: a list of statements from which they are to choose one and construct the best argument they can for it. In the tutorial, their arguments will be presented to the class, and the class will make suggestions about how the argument could be improved.

The five-minute introduction

The introductory spiel begins by reminding the students of what constitutes a good argument, and then goes on to suggest the following method for constructing one:

(1) Consider your conclusion. If it is a conclusion that you believe, think about why you believe it, and write those reasons down. If the conclusion is not one which you believe, think "What reasons might someone have for believing that conclusion?" and write those reasons down.

(2) If you end up with several distinct sets of reasons, divide your reasons into related groups.

(3) Focus on one reason or group of related reasons. Consider whether or not there are any unstated premises that need to be added before those reasons will support your conclusion. If there are, add those premises.

(4) Consider whether or not your initial premises and unstated assumptions are plausible. Do they in turn need to be supported by additional premises to make them acceptable to your intended audience? Add as many such premises as you think are necessary. Now you have an argument.

(5) Evaluate your argument as if it were someone else's. Consider what objections to it might be raised by a reasonable and knowledgeable opponent. Are the premises plausible as they stand, or do they need further support? Do the premises provide enough support for the conclusion: if they were true, would they make the conclusion sufficiently likely? If not, adjust your argument accordingly. One way to test the amount of support the premises give the conclusion is to try to construct counterexamples: see if you can think of any situations in which the premises would all be true but the conclusion false. If you find any such counterexamples, then you should add premises, or adjust your premises, in such a way that the counterexamples are blocked, thus strengthening your argument.

The group exercise in constructing an argument

Having explained the method, I present the class with a claim for which we are going to construct arguments. It should be a claim that does not require any specialized knowledge to argue for, one that the students are likely to have thought about, and preferably one for which there are lots of different arguments. "God exists" works well. I invite the class to come up with reasons why a person might believe that God exists, and write all of their reasons up on the blackboard without comment. Here is a typical list.

- Most people believe that God exists.
- People have believed in God for a very long time.
- The Bible says so.
- How else could the world have come into existence?
- God talks to me inside my head.
- There are miraculous healings.
- People speak in tongues.
- I was brought up to believe that God exists.

If some of the reasons given seem to belong to the same argument, the students put them together, and then they choose a reason or set of reasons that we will turn into an argument. I ask them what premises need to be added before the reason(s) will provide strong support for the conclusion, whether these added premises are plausible, and whether the original reason or reasons is or are plausible. Often the premises require additional premises to support them. It is easiest to present this in the form of a diagram on the blackboard, the diagram method being one that the students have already learned while learning how to analyze and evaluate arguments.

On the following page is an example constructed in a recent critical thinking class (obviously, there are more premises that could be added).

The aim is to construct the best argument possible on the basis of the chosen premise or set of premises. Usually it will not be an absolutely watertight argument, and when it is as good as it seems to be getting, I sometimes ask the students to point out premises or links which are questionable.

Sometimes it turns out that nothing resembling a good argument can be constructed on the basis of the reason given. For example, there are no plausible premises which can be added which will make "I was brought up to believe that God exists" a good reason to believe that God exists: this is an explanation of why the person believes in God, rather than evidence supporting the claim that God exists. In such a case, or when we have successfully constructed an argument and still have more time, we go on to construct an argument based on one of the other reasons on the list.

The homework exercise

At the end of the lecture, the students are given a list of claims and asked to choose one of them and construct the best argument for it that they can. I tend to use somewhat controversial claims about issues that are currently in the news. Then the students bring their arguments along to the tutorial, and the class provides constructive feedback.

Tutors report that students have difficulty with the homework exercise, because by this stage they have been so schooled in how to detect fallacious arguments that they see the flaws in their own arguments before they even get as far as writing them down. This is all the more reason to persevere in teaching them this commonsense method of elaborating their actual reasons for belief into detailed and well-constructed arguments. It would be a pity if one of the effects of a critical thinking course were actually to *prevent* students from constructing good arguments of their own.[1]

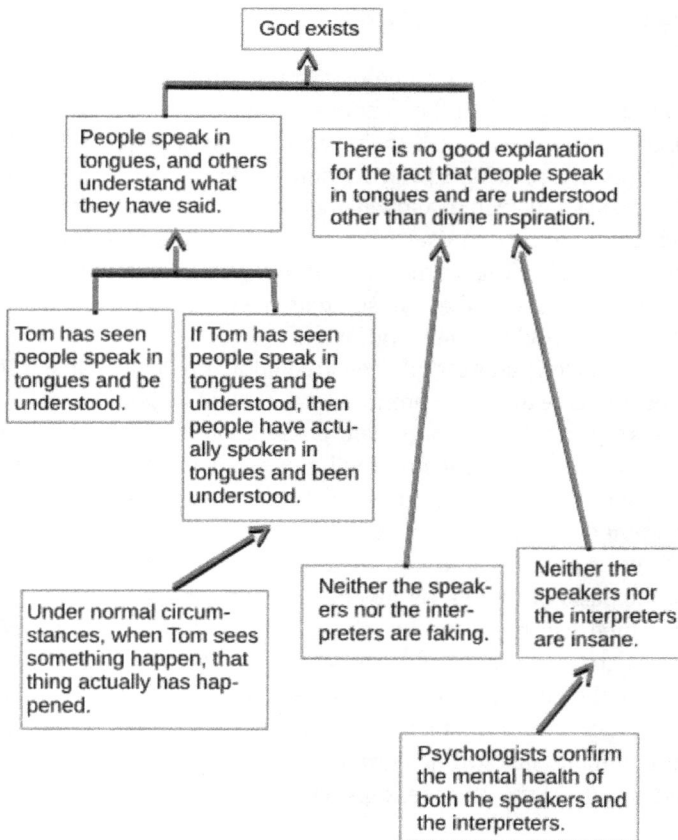

---

[1] Previously published in the Teaching Supplement to *Informal Logic*, 2002

About the author:

Justine Kingsbury is a Senior Lecturer in Philosophy, and currently Associate Dean (Postgraduate), in the Division of Arts, Law, Psychology and Social Sciences at the University of Waikato in Hamilton, New Zealand. She has taught critical thinking in a wide variety of formats and has published on virtue argumentation theory and on thinking critically about deeply held beliefs (with Tracy Bowell) and on the burden of proof (with Tim Dare), as well as on various topics in metaphilosophy and in philosophy of mind.

5

Encouraging Critical Thinking about Students' own Beliefs

Tracy Bowell and Justine Kingsbury

It is difficult to get students to think critically about their own beliefs about things that matter to them. This is a three-part exercise that addresses this problem.

Part I

The students are asked to pick some belief they care about and to give the best argument for it they can think of. We usually ask them to hand this in at the end of Week 2. Because this is very early in the course, we do not expect a very high standard of argument and we do not allocate many marks to this part of the assignment. Usually it is worth 5% of the final grade, and we grade it generously: anyone who has given an argument at all gets 3/5.

Part II

The students are asked to critically evaluate the Part I argument of one of their fellow-students and to provide constructive suggestions about how to improve it. Part II is due around the midpoint of the course or slightly later, and is worth 10% of the final mark for the course.

Part III

The students receive constructive feedback on their Part I argument from both the instructor and a fellow student (who has evaluated their argument in Part II). At the end of the course, hopefully having a better understanding than before of the difference between good and bad reasons for belief, the student improves their original argument in response to the feedback, presenting their improved argument both in standard form and as an argument tree and explaining why they have made the changes that they have (and, if they have rejected some of the suggestions given by their fellow-student or by the instructor, explaining why they have). Sometimes the feedback convinces them that their original conclusion was too strong, or even that it was completely misguided: in such cases, they are allowed to argue for whatever they now believe about the topic at issue. Part III is worth 15% of the final mark for the course.

Results

The final versions of the arguments are almost always greatly improved, and in those cases where students really have argued for something they feel strongly about, we hope (and we are explicit about this in class) that the process has provided a model for future examination of their own reasons for belief.

Practicalities and problems

1.   We anonymise the Part I arguments before distributing them to fellow-students. This seems particularly important since we have asked the students to argue for conclusions that they care about, and they may be sensitive about others in the class knowing what they have argued for. Genuine anonymity is not possible in a very small class: we have used this assignment only in classes of 50 or more students.

2.   An earlier version of this assignment did not include instructor feedback on the Part I arguments: the only feedback was from a fellow-student. This disadvantaged those students whose arguments were incompetently evaluated: the current version of the assignment ensures that all students get *some* useful feedback.

3.   There remains a problem for students whose Part I arguments are incompetently evaluated: if we give them the incompetent or unconstructive feedback from their fellow-student, they have the extra task of evaluating the feedback and seeing that it isn't useful. Since we, the instructors, have graded Part II and provided comments on it, one solution is to give the student receiving the peer feedback our comments on the peer feedback (with the grade removed). This is what we standardly do. There are however some cases in which the peer feedback is *completely* useless, and there are also cases in which the peer feedback is hostile. In those cases, we do not provide the student with the peer feedback, but we make sure that there is plenty of instructor feedback.

4. This assignment is labor-intensive from a grading point of view. It is important that the grading is done by an experienced instructor: for it to be gradable in a reasonable amount of time, the grader has to be able to quickly see what can be done to fix an argument, and this is a skill which can only be developed with long practice. The grading is time-consuming even for an experienced instructor, but we think the pay-off justifies the time spent—the three-part assignment helps students to see the usefulness of critical thinking and shows them how it can be applied to things that really matter to them.

About the authors:

Tracy Bowell works and publishes in the areas of Argumentation and Critical Thinking, especially virtue and argumentation, Philosophy of Education, Wittgenstein's Philosophy and Feminist Philosophy, and has taught critical thinking for the past 25 years. She is co-author (with Gary Kemp, Glasgow) of the textbook, *Critical Thinking: A Concise Guide*, 5th edition 2019. She currently holds the position of Pro-Vice Chancellor, Teaching and Learning at the University of Waikato, Aotearoa/New Zealand. Previously she was Senior Lecturer in Philosophy in the Philosophy Programme at Waikato.

Justine Kingsbury is a Senior Lecturer in Philosophy, and currently Associate Dean (Postgraduate), in the Division of Arts, Law, Psychology and Social Sciences at the University of Waikato in Hamilton, New Zealand. She has taught critical thinking in a wide variety of formats and has published on virtue argumentation theory and on thinking critically about deeply held beliefs (with Tracy Bowell) and on the burden of proof (with Tim Dare), as well as on various topics in metaphilosophy and in philosophy of mind.

6

Middle Ground: Settling a Public Controversy by Means of a Reasonable Compromise

Jan Albert van Laar

1. Introduction

Compromises have a questionable reputation, both in social and in personal life (Benjamin 1990; Margalit 2010). But not all disagreements allow of a substantial resolution, even if open-minded participants seriously attempt to convince one another. When the disagreement concerns action or policy, it can be useful to examine whether a well-reasoned compromise would be feasible. With the educational method Middle Ground, participants deliberate in an attempt to develop a reasonable compromise that settles a public controversy.

The method adds to the existing range of educational resources for students (high school and post-secondary education). Different from many critical thinking resources (e.g., Fisher 2011), reasoning assessment and critical dispositions are encouraged within the setting of a structured conversation. Different from debate or discussion-oriented education (e.g., Kuhn 2005; Hess 2009), Middle Ground targets specifically the cooperative exchange of reasons aimed at a reasonable compromise. In our view, young people should develop a point of view about the virtues and vices of compromises, and develop the skills and attitudes for construing, what they conceive of as, second-best yet socially optimal outcomes (Gutmann and Thompson 2012).

2. Scholarly background

Inspired by the deliberative shift in political philosophy (Elster 1995; Habermas 1996; Rawls 2005) various practical procedures for opinion formation and deliberative decision making have been developed, such as deliberative polls or town hall meetings (Fung 2003; Fishkin 2009). Middle Ground also incites deliberation, yet with a twist. It employs deliberative techniques to enable participants to negotiate a compromise agreement in a situation where they are unable to reach a genuine consensus, and to do so in a maximally transparent and non-manipulative way. In this way, it builds on a recent trend to study legitimate policy making in deliberative negotiation (see: Mansbridge et al. 2010; Steiner et al. 2004; Weinstock 2013; Wendt 2016). Middle Ground is tailor-made for issues that generate widely divergent opinions and feelings: gender quotas in business, corrective referenda, head scarves at university, the EU-Turkey refugee deal, but also the distribution of tasks in a group assignment, or the apportioning of a budget. Going through the procedure provides students with opportunities to discuss the quality of the result, to reflect on the process, and to draw general lessons about negotiation and compromise.

3. General design of the method

Before the three-step procedure starts, the moderator (e.g., teacher) sketches a (possibly fictive) scenario regarding a particular public controversy that pressures the participants to work towards a compromise. For example, they are supposed to be the members of a committee or board that must reach an agreement on a solution to the issue at hand. Ideally, the participants start from their authentic opinions, though sometimes it is needed or useful to ask some participants to assume the role of a specific stakeholder.

The first two parts of the procedure aim at encouraging diversity, whereas the third aims at an agreement (see Sunstein and Hastie 2015). Part 1 revolves around the expression of the participants' first policy preferences (i.e., those preferences not influenced by the need to accommodate dissenting others), and of the values, interests and perspectives that motivate them to have these preferences. In Part 2 the participants are pressed to temporarily deal with their differences of opinion as a practical problem of distributing or trading items or commitments to act—thereby "commodifying" as it were their opinions. Part 3 deals with the step-wise development of a compromise agreement, based on mutual concessions, and accommodating the variety of preferences and motives.

Participants reason and argue, yet not to convince others of the correctness of their firstly preferred solution, but (in Part 1:) to explain what motivates them and (in Part 3:) to find out what middle ground solution, if any, would be mutually advantageous (van Laar and Krabbe 2018a, 2018b, 2019. See: Holzinger 2004; Amgoud and Prade 2006; Fisher, Ury, and Patton 2011). In this way, they try to arrive at an outcome that each participant prefers to the status quo (i.e., a situation where no compromise is accepted) and that does not allow of an improvement that a sufficient number of others would be willing to endorse (Raiffa, Richardson and Metcalfe 2002). By means of a simple book-keeping device, participants keep track of their collective reasoning.

4. Learning objectives and applications

Middle Ground can be used for several learning objectives that are central in civic education and critical thinking: (a) gaining insight into (historical or topical) public controversies and political processes; (b) developing a point of view about the virtues and vices of compromises; (c) obtaining knowledge about the conditions for fruitful negotiation; (d) developing skills for cooperative argumentation, conversation, listening, and collective problem solving; (e) increasing moral and ideological sensitivity, empathy, spirit of compromise, integrity; (f) reducing polarization as well as group thinking.

The Middle Ground method has been applied at five faculties of the University of Groningen, The Netherlands (in courses on: academic skills, business ethics, philosophy of argument, leadership skills, and industrial engineering), and has been tested in social science courses at Dutch high schools. Also, a digital version has been developed, and access can be requested from the author.

5. The design of the method in detail

The details of the Middle Ground procedure will be introduced by means of an example, namely the controversy about what form of direct democracy to adopt on the national level in the Netherlands. It is assumed that about 20 students participate.

Prior to the Middle Ground procedure, the moderator provides the participants with (what is plausibly) a fictive scenario that puts some pressure on the participants to settle for a compromise. For example, the participants are asked to imagine that they are commissioned to provide the Dutch government with advice about the form of direct democracy to implement, and if they fail to provide detailed advice that receives the support of at least all committee members minus one, the country faces uproar and individual careers will get damaged.

At this preliminary stage, the moderator also helps the participants to form (three to five) parties of like-minded individuals. In order to arrive at parties of sufficient size the moderator can request some individuals to assume the role of a specific stakeholder with a specific opinion. In the example, Party Red is a strong supporter of parliamentary, representative democracy, and opposes referenda and all other forms of direct democracy. Party Green is a strong supporter of unfiltered, direct forms of democracy, and it opts for a constitutional change such that major policy decisions are required to get support from a referendum. Party Blue is sympathetic to introducing some forms of democratic innovation so as to give voice to the concerns of citizens, and it is especially attracted to the idea of connecting major policy decisions to a deliberating body of citizens who are selected by lot. Party Purple would be willing to allow for a restricted role for referenda, though it is hesitant when it comes to changing the existing rules of democracy.

In order to prompt thinking about their first preferences (in Step 1) as well as about the ways to commodify their differences of opinion (in Step 2), the moderator may provide the participants with some options: Who initiates a referendum? For what types of issue? Who is allowed to participate? What kind of turn-out threshold should there be, if any? For what kind of policy decisions? Advisory or binding? What role for public debate? What kind of majority is required?

Finally, the moderator explains that his/her role remains limited to explaining the purpose of each of the steps, and to keeping track of the time. What follows is a statement of the procedure that can be distributed to the participants.

Part 1: Policy Positions (30 minutes)

(a) Within your party, decide who—in Part 3—will act as the group's principal negotiator. (1 minute)

(b) Within your party, elaborate on your group's policy position (14 minutes)

1. Discuss your first policy preference.
2. Discuss your motivation: What are the values, feelings, interests and principles that lead you to prefer this policy?
3. Express your first policy preference and motivation by means of keywords, and record them on a position poster with the following format.

Party name:
Our first policy preference: [*use keywords*]

Our motivating values / feelings / principles / interests:
1. [*use keywords*]
2.
etc., ...

(c) Each party attaches its poster on a wall, and in a plenary session the groups inform one another about their positions, in 60 seconds, and answer questions. Only questions for clarification (such as "what do you mean by this phrase?" or "Why do you think this is valuable?") are allowed at this stage, and no criticism. (15 minutes)

Part 2: First Compromise Proposals (25 minutes)

(a) Discuss within your party how you might revise your firstly preferred policy by making some concessions that accommodate cherished values, feelings, interests or principles of other groups. Also discuss what concessions you would like other groups to make. (5 minutes)

(b) Within your party, express your first compromise proposal as well as the reasons why other groups might find this proposal (somewhat) attractive, and record them by means of keywords on a compromise poster with the following format. (5 minutes)

Party name:

Our first compromise proposal: [*use keywords*]
    Why other groups might want to adopt this proposal:
    1. [*use keywords*]
    2.
    etc., ...

(c) Each group attaches its compromise poster below its earlier position poster, and in a plenary session the groups inform one another about their compromise proposals, each time in 60 seconds, and answer questions. No restrictions apply as to the kinds of question. (15 minutes)

Part 3: Seeking Compromise (40 minutes)

(a) Within the separate parties: Each party discusses what compromise proposals to table, and how to respond to expected proposals from others, after having studied the rules of the plenary negotiation game (below). (10 minutes)

(b) Plenary negotiation game: In an inner circle, the principal negotiators try to arrive at an agreement, now and then consulting the other participants, located at an outer circle, in accordance with the following rules. (30 minutes)

Rule 1. By lot is it determined which principal negotiator starts, after which they take turns clockwise.

Rule 2. (a) At his/her turn, a principal negotiator tables, in 60 seconds, a compromise proposal, after which (b) there is limited time available for questions for clarification and critical questions. (c) On the whiteboard, the moderator numbers each such compromise proposal and characterizes it by means of keywords. Finally, (d) the moderator asks the other principal negotiators whether they are willing to endorse this proposal. If complete unanimity is not achieved among the principal negotiators, the next principal negotiator takes his/her turn; If complete unanimity is realized, Rule 4 applies.

Rule 3. Each principal negotiator can request once for a two-minute time-out when every negotiator can consult his/her party or align bilaterally with other parties.

Rule 4. As soon as the principal negotiators strike an agreement with complete unanimity, the moderator stops the negotiation and invites all other participants to cast their individual votes ("Yes, I am willing to endorse this compromise" or "No, I am not willing to endorse this compromise"), if needed preceded by round of questions for clarification. If the required supermajority has been achieved in the group at large (unanimity minus one) the participants succeeded in agreeing on a compromise; If not the procedure ends without an agreed upon compromise.

Rule 5. If there is still no unanimity among the principal negotiators when each of them has tabled two compromise proposals, the moderator invites all participants to cast their individual votes on each of the compromise proposals listed on the whiteboard, starting with compromise proposal #1, followed by #2, and so forth, until a proposal gets the required supermajority (unanimity minus one). There is no limit to the number of "yes" or "no" votes that a participant can submit. As soon as the required supermajority has been achieved for a proposal, the procedure ends with an agreed upon compromise; If no such supermajority is achieved for any proposal, the procedure ends without the participants agreeing on a compromise.

6. Students' evaluation

When the students have finished the middle ground procedure, the moderator (teacher) and students can evaluate the quality of the process, the quality of the outcome, and draw some general lessons.

(a) Process

1. Did we succeed in articulating our motivating considerations adequately? Did we neglect facts, values, perspectives, principles?
2. To what extent did our motivating considerations influence the outcome? Has one group's position been (dis)favored, and if so, how is that to be explained? To what extent do we think we grasped the essence of the other groups' positions?
3. To what extent was the outcome enabled by some kind of pressure? Or by some kind of manipulation? To what extent did we succeed in cooperating, when trying to advocate or push our positions?
4. Did we miss an opportunity to arrive at a more optimal solution?

5. To what extent did we feel we had to sacrifice the integrity of our position so as to enable the compromise?

6. What would we like to change in the procedure, or in a future execution of it?

(b) Outcome

1. Are we pleased with the outcome? Is it sufficiently coherent? Is it fair vis-à-vis the diverse perspectives in the group? How would we evaluate this outcome in the real world?

2. Did we change our individual positions as a result of the exchanges?

References

Amgoud, Leila and Prade, Henri (2006). Formal handling of threats and rewards in a negotiation dialogue. In: *Argumentation in Multi-Agent Systems: Second International Workshop*, ArgMAS 2005, Utrecht, The Netherlands, July 26, 2005: Revised Selected and Invited Papers, ed. by Simon Parsons, Nicolas Maudet, Pavlos Moraitis, and Iyad Rahwan, pp. 88-103. Berlin: Springer.

Benjamin, Martin (1990). *Splitting the Difference: Compromise and Integrity in Ethics and Politics*. Lawrence KS: University of Kansas.

Elster, Jon (1995). Strategic uses of argument. In Kenneth J. Arrow, Robert H. Mnookin, Lee Ross, Amos Tversky and Robert B. Wilson (Eds.). *Barriers to Conflict Resolution*. (pp. 236-57). New York: Norton.

Fisher, Alec (2011). *Critical Thinking: An Introduction*. Cambridge University Press: Cambridge.

Fisher, Roger, Ury, William and Patton, Bruce (2011). *Getting to Yes: Negotiating an Agreement without Giving In*, 3rd ed. London: Random House.

Fishkin, James S. (2009). *When the People Speak: Deliberative Democracy and Public Consultation*. New York: Oxford University Press.

Fung, Archon 2003. Recipes for public spheres: Eight institutional design choices and their consequences. *Journal of Political Philosophy* pp. 338-367.

Gutmann, Amy and Thompson, Dennis (2012). *The Spirit of Compromise: Why Governing Demands It and Campaigning Undermines It*. Princeton: Princeton University Press.

Habermas, Jürgen (1996). *Between Facts and Norms*. Cambridge: Polity Press.

Hess, Diana E. (2009) *Controversy in the Classroom: The Democratic Power of Discussion*. New York: Routledge.

Holzinger, Katharina (2004). Bargaining through arguing: An empirical analysis based on speech act theory. *Political Communication* 21, 195-222.

Kuhn, Dianna (2005). *Education for Thinking.* Cambridge Mass.: Harvard University Press.

Laar, Jan Albert van and Krabbe, Erik C.W. (2018a). Splitting a difference of opinion: The shift to negotiation. *Argumentation,* 32, 329-350. doi: 10.1007/s10503-017-9445-7

Laar, Jan Albert van and Krabbe, Erik C.W. (2018b). The role of argument in negotiation. *Argumentation* 32(4), 549-567. doi: 10.1007/s10503-018-9458-x

Laar, Jan Albert van and Erik C.W. Krabbe (2019). Criticism and justification of negotiated compromises: The 2015 Paris Agreement in Dutch Parliament. *Journal of Argumentation in Context* 8(1), 91-111. doi: org/10.1075/jaic.18009.laa

Mansbridge, Jane, Bohman, James, Chambers, Simone, Estlund, David, Follesdal, Andreas, Fung, Archon, Lafont, Christina, Manin, Bernard and Martì, José Luis (2010). The role of self-interest and the role of power in deliberative democracy. *The Journal of Political Philosophy,* 18, pp. 64–100.

Margalit, Avishai (2010). *On Compromise and Rotten Compromises.* Princeton NJ: Princeton University Press.

Raiffa, Howard, Richardson, John and Metcalfe, David (2002). *Negotiation Analysis: The Science and Art of Collaborative Decision Making.* Cambridge MA: The Belknap Press of Harvard University Press.

Rawls, John (2005). *Political Liberalism* (Expanded edition). New York: Columbia University Press.

Steiner, Jürg, Bächtiger, André, Spörndli, Markus and Steenbergen, Marco R. (2004). *Deliberative Politics in Action. Analysing Parliamentary Discourse.* Cambridge: Cambridge University Press.

Sunstein, Cass and Hastie, Reid (2015). *Wiser: Getting Beyond Groupthink to Make Groups Smarter.* Boston, Massachusetts: Harvard Business Review Press.

Wendt, Fabian (2016). *Compromise, Peace and Public Justification: Political Morality Beyond Justice.* Switzerland: Palgrave Macmillan.

Weinstock, Daniel (2013). On the possibility of principled moral compromise. *Critical Review of International Social and Political Philosophy* 16(4), 537-556.

About the author:

Jan Albert van Laar is researcher and lecturer at the Faculty of Philosophy of the University of Groningen (The Netherlands). After having defended his dissertation "The dialectic of ambiguity" he worked as a postdoc researcher on argumentative confrontations from a pragma-dialectical stance at the Department of speech communication, argumentation theory and rhetoric at the University of Amsterdam. With Erik C. W. Krabbe he published a series of articles on argumentative criticism and on the role of argument in negotiation. He developed the educational software package "Middle Ground" for training in and reflection on compromise formation. Presently, he publishes and teaches about: argumentation, compromise, dialogue types, deliberation, fallacies, philosophy of argument and public controversy

7

Using Arguments to Inquire

Mark Battersby and Sharon Bailin

1. Introduction[1]

An important function of argumentation is to inquire into issues that are controversial or the subject of debate in order to come to reasoned and reasonable judgments about them. The analysis and critique of individual arguments is one aspect of this process, helping to weed out bad arguments: arguments that provide little or no support for a particular position. It does not, however, on its own, get us to the goal of deciding what it *is* reasonable to believe or do. What is required is a comparative evaluation of the arguments on various sides of the issue.

Let us take, for example, the issue of whether physician-assisted dying should be legal. One could reject the argument that such a law would inevitably lead to the termination of the physically disabled as committing the slippery slope fallacy. But this would not, on its own, tell us whether or not such a law should be supported. Making this judgment requires comparatively evaluating the arguments both for and against physician-assisted dying.

Goal of the unit

To learn to use argumentation to make reasoned judgments about real, complex issues.

---

[1] This chapter is based on the approach to critical thinking detailed in *Reason in the Balance: An Inquiry Approach to Critical Thinking*. (S. Bailin & M. Battersby, Hackett 2016). The text shows how an inquiry approach can be used as the basis for an entire critical thinking course. For an examination copy, go to: https://www.hackettpublishing.com/reason-in-the-balance-second-edition-3991

Learning Objectives

Students will learn to:
- clearly identify the issue
- understand the various positions, the evidence and arguments on various sides of the issue, any objections and responses to the objections, and relevant alternative arguments and views
- understand the history and context of the debate
- evaluate the individual arguments
- comparatively evaluate and weigh the various pro and con arguments and come to a reasoned judgment

Method

We suggest using the following questions to guide the inquiry process:
- What is the issue?
- What kinds of claims or judgments are at issue?
- What are the relevant reasons and arguments on various sides of the issue?
- What is the context of the issue?
- How strong is each of the arguments?
- Weighing and balancing the evaluated arguments, what judgment should we come to?

Lesson Suggestions

We will demonstrate the methodology using a dialogue about a controversial issue (assisted dying) as the basis for the inquiry. Instead of dialogues, class inquiries could be based on a current issue of interest to students, a media piece, op. ed, blog post, online debate, etc.

2. Assisted Dying

Nancy: (looking at a Tweet on her cell phone) Right on! It's about time.

Ravi: What are you so excited about?

Nancy: They've just passed a law that physician-assisted suicide will be legal—actually they're calling it medical aid in dying. It's long overdue.

Ravi: Do you mean to say that you agree with the decision?

Nancy: Well of course. People have a basic right to control their own lives. And that's got to include the right to decide when to end it.

Ravi: Now wait just a minute. We don't condone killing in our society, and that's what we're really talking about.

Nancy: "Killing"—come on Ravi, that's rather loaded. Suicide is not a crime and helping someone to do what they have every right to do is hardly killing.

Ravi: But what about folks who are mentally incompetent or depressed? Are they really in a position to make those kinds of life and death decisions?

Nancy: There can be legal restrictions to deal with those potential problems.

Ravi: But you're forgetting something pretty basic, Nancy—the sanctity of human life is one of our most fundamental values.

Nancy: But there's also the issue of the quality of life. There's no justification for forcing dying people to endure intolerable suffering and for not allowing them to die with dignity.

Ravi: But there are ways to reduce suffering, like drugs, palliative and hospice care.

Nancy: That may be so, but it doesn't really address the issue of people's right to die if they so choose.

Ravi: Except that allowing assisted death will undermine support for hospice and palliative care.

Nancy: What reason is there for thinking that that will happen? I'm not aware that that's been the experience in places like the Netherlands which have legalized assisted death. And besides, allowing physician-assisted death would probably result in cost savings because we currently devote so much of our resources to end-of-life care.

Ravi: But making this type of life-and-death decision on the basis of money is clearly immoral.

Nancy: But the money could be used for other forms of health care where you could actually save lives.

Ravi: But what I'm most worried about is that this move will lead to all kinds of outcomes that we wouldn't want—like people being "helped to die" without their consent or being pressured to die by family members. This could be a problem especially for the elderly, who may feel pressed to choose to die in order to not be a burden on their family.

Nancy: We'd have to make sure that there are safeguards in place to prevent this.

Ravi: It could also encourage the idea that the disabled are dispensable and should be terminated. I know that several of my friends with disabilities are worried about exactly that.

Nancy: I don't really see how that would be an outcome of this type of law.

Ravi: And there's also the concern that, if mental suffering is included in the law, this could lead to lots of people with depression taking their own lives.

Nancy: I would think that clear procedures and restrictions could help to deal with those concerns.

Ravi: You're a lot more confident than I am that that we could control it in practice once it's allowed. And anyway, it's still involves taking a life and so I just can't support it.

LESSON 1[2]

Discussion of the nature of inquiry
Discuss how using arguments to inquire differs from using arguments to persuade. Emphasize the point that inquiry is not a matter of defending or attacking a particular position but involves, rather, an attempt to find the best view. It requires that participants show respect for the contributions of other participants, charitably interpret others' contributions, and direct criticisms at the arguments and not at the person who offers them.

What is the issue?[3]
Discuss the criteria for a well-formed and appropriate issue for inquiry.

- *Focused*—clear and precise; not overly broad
- *Question vs. topic*—e.g., *not* "Marijuana legalization" but *rather* "Should marijuana use be decriminalized in this state?"
- *Controversial*—a currently live question, e.g., *not* "Does the earth revolve around the sun?"; an issue with at least two plausible sides, e.g., *not* "Is killing innocent children wrong?"
- *Neutrally framed*—framed in a way that does not bias the inquiry in a certain direction, e.g., *not* "Should CEOs be paid excessive salaries?" but *rather* "Are the salaries paid to CEOs in large corporations justifiable?"

Have the students try to formulate the main issue raised in the "Assisted Dying" dialogue, using the criteria as a basis for the formulation and critique of suggested issue formulations. This activity, as well as most of the activities which follow, can be done most effectively in small groups that report back to the class. Alternatively, they can be done as a whole class discussion if numbers permit. Examples of *problematic* issue statements: "Assisted dying." "Is suicide wrong?" "Should doctors be allowed to kill their patients?

What kinds of claims or judgments are at issue

- *Factual*—focus on describing or explaining some aspect of the way the world is
- *Evaluative*—express an evaluation or assessment of an object, action, or phenomenon
  - *instrumental*—deal with the best means to an end
  - *ethical*—deal with questions of right and wrong, good and bad, etc.

---

[2] Several lessons might be done in one class period and some lessons may be extended over several.

[3] See *Reason in the Balance,* Chapter 7.

- Discuss the difference between factual claims or judgments and evaluative claims or judgments. It is also useful to distinguish among types of evaluative judgments, in particular, instrumental judgments and ethical judgments. Making these distinctions will be important when it comes to evaluating the various arguments because of the differences in the way the different types of judgments are evaluated.
- Have the students identify the type of judgment that is called for by the issue raised in the "Assisted Dying" dialogue, as they have formulated it. E.g., the issue "Should physician assisted dying be legal in this state?" calls for an evaluative judgment.
- Have the students also identify some of the sub-questions that would be involved in inquiring into the main issue and determine what kinds of judgments they would involve.
- E.g., "Is it right to force dying people to endure intolerable suffering?" (ethical judgment)
- E.g., "Have assisted dying laws in other jurisdictions undermined support for palliative care?" (factual judgment).

LESSON 2

What are the relevant reasons and arguments on various sides of the issue?[4]

- Have the students, working in groups, use an argument table to lay out the various arguments on both sides of the issue as represented in the dialogue, as well the objections to the arguments and responses to the objections. (Alternatively, have each student fill out an argument table as homework, then have them work in groups to compare and evaluate their tables.) We have supplied an example of a completed table, below.
- Then have the students add any arguments, objections, and responses that they can think of that are not included in the dialogue.
- Do an argument table as a class using the students' suggestions from their tables and using the following criteria:
  - that it includes all important arguments, objections and responses
  - that it represents the arguments, objections and responses in a balanced and fair way

---

[4] See *Reason in the Balance*, Chapter 8.

Sample Argument Table: Should physician-assisted dying be legal?

Argument Name	Argument Summary	Objections	Responses
MAIN PRO ARGUMENTS			
Right to die	Basic right to control one's life which includes right to decide when to end life		
Right to end suffering	Intolerable to insist that people suffer to their death	Other alternatives to reducing suffering, e.g., drugs, palliative care, hospice	
Quality of life	It is not just being alive that matters, but also quality of life		
Right to die with dignity	Individuals have right to die with dignity		
Health care costs	Could result in cost saving because of expense of end-of-life care	Making life-and-death decisions on basis of cost is immoral	Money could be used for other forms of health care to save lives
MAIN CON ARGUMENTS			
Murder	Amounts to murder, which is not condoned or legal in our society	Loaded language; It's aiding suicide, which is legal	
Sanctity of human life	Violates sanctity of human life, which is a fundamental value	Also issue of quality of life; dying with dignity	
Misuse by mentally incompetent	Depressed or mentally incompetent not able to make such decisions	Need to be legal safeguard to prevent this	
Slippery slope	Likely to lead to involuntary or pressured death	Need to be legal restrictions to prevent this	Might not be able to control it in practice.

Pressure on elderly	Elderly could feel pressure to end life	Need safeguard to prevent this	Might not be able to control it in practice.
Palliative care	Hospice and palliative care undermined	No reason to think this will be result	What is experience where it is legal?
Encourage termination of disabled	Encourage termination of disabled	No reason to think this will be outcome	What is experience where it is legal?
Depression	If includes mental suffering, could lead to depressed taking their life	Would need to be legal restrictions to prevent this	

What is the context of the issue?

- State of practice (current situation)
- Intellectual, Social, Political, and Historical Contexts

Controversial issues generally exist against a historical background, and in the context of social relations and social, political and intellectual views. With respect to the debate over assisted dying, the current state of legislation is important in terms of framing the debate (is it about establishing a new law or changing the current law?) and establishing the burden of proof (which generally lies with the view that goes against commonly accepted views or practices). It is also helpful for students to understand some of the worldviews which may underlie the positions, e.g., the notion of the sanctity of life may stem from religious beliefs; the claim that people have a right to decide when to end their lives is underpinned by the philosophical notion of autonomy.

- Have students research the aspects of context which are relevant to making a judgment on the issue of assisted dying, using the following questions as guides.
  - What is the current law with respect to assisted dying in your jurisdiction?
  - Is the issue currently being debated? What arguments are being offered by the various sides? Are there particular groups that are championing each of the sides?
  - Have there been particular cases either in the media or the courts which have fueled the debate?

- ∘ What worldviews (e.g., social, religious, political) inform the debate?
- ∘ What's happened in jurisdictions where assisted dying has been legalized?

One way to organize this task is to have students work in groups to create a joint wiki with their findings (this can be done outside class time).

LESSON 3

How strong is each of the arguments?[5]

- Have students evaluate the individual arguments in the table using the following questions as a guide:
  - ∘ Are there any fallacies or other obvious weaknesses?
  - ∘ To what degree are the factual claims well supported and credible?
  - ∘ To what extent do the evaluative arguments meet the relevant criteria?
  - ∘ Are the objections well-founded? To what extent do they count against the particular argument?
  - ∘ Are there additional arguments that have not been listed? If so, evaluate them as well.

Students will likely have covered the identification of fallacies in their course. Evaluating the factual claims will require outside research by the students (this can be a good homework assignment).

- Before they do the evaluation, discuss how to find reliable sources (refereed journals, look for expert consensus) and, especially, how to determine the credibility of websites, internet and social media sources.[6]
- Before they do the evaluation, discuss the criteria for evaluating evaluative claims:
  - ∘ ethical judgments: (1) the moral quality of the act (e.g., murder is wrong); (2) the duties and responsibilities of the actor (e.g., teachers have a duty of fairness to their students); and (3) the consequences of the act (e.g., will it benefit or harm people?)
  - ∘ instrumental judgments: how well the action achieves the desired goal. Point out that evaluative judgments often involve both ethical and instrumental judgments, i.e., to decide whether to do something, we need to ask not only whether the action will achieve a certain goal but also whether the action is morally acceptable.
  - ∘ Have the students add an "evaluation" column to their argument tables with a brief summary of their evaluation of each argument

[5] See *Reason in the Balance*, Chapter 9.

[6] See *Reason in the Balance*, Chapter 6.

LESSON 4

Weighing and balancing the evaluated arguments. What judgment should we come to?

At this point, students comparatively evaluate the various arguments to determine their weight in the overall case.

- Discuss the factors that contribute to the weight of an argument:
  - its credibility
  - how well it has withstood any objections
  - its degree of certainty or likelihood (e.g., the argument that the elderly might be pressured to take their own lives would be a strong moral objection to assisted dying if evidence from other jurisdictions showed it to be a likely consequence but would be much weaker if shown to be unlikely)

- Discuss the idea that arriving at an overall judgment will often involve weighing and balancing different, and sometime conflicting considerations, e.g., the preservation of human life versus individual autonomy; the benefits of alleviating suffering versus the risks of abuse, etc. Discuss some of considerations that go into such weighing and balancing:
  - the consideration of both means and ends
  - the consideration of both costs and benefits
  - the importance of considering a variety of criteria
  - the priority of moral considerations over other types of considerations.

- Discuss moves that can be helpful in arriving at a reasoned judgment:
  - establishing the burden of proof
  - identifying whether differences in how arguments are framed are contributing to disagreement
  - recognizing the valid points in each view and trying to take them into account

- Have the students come to a judgment on the issue of assisted dying (as they have formulated it), using the following questions as guides:
  - How much weight should we give to each of the pro and con arguments in light of their individual evaluation?
  - How can we weigh and balance the various considerations to come to a judgment?
  - Can we reach a judgment that incorporates the strengths and avoids the weaknesses of different views?

Point out that the overall judgment need not be a matter of deciding in favor of one side or the other of the debate as framed but may well be a modification, qualification, or combination of the positions (e.g., that physician-assisted dying should be legal but only with certain qualifications, restrictions, and procedures in place to safeguard against some of the concerns raised in the con arguments).

- One possible procedure is to have the students work in groups to do the comparative evaluation and discuss the overall judgment. Then have each student, as an assignment, explain the judgment they would come to and justify it with reference to how they have evaluated and weighed the arguments.

- An excellent strategy for promoting the careful consideration of both sides of a controversial issue is structured controversy. After the students have done their evaluation of the individual arguments, divide them into two groups and assign each group one of the sides to defend. Then switch roles and have each group defend the other side. At this point, one can have the whole group try to reach a collective reasoned judgment.

3. Pedagogy

This approach is best realized through an active and interactive pedagogy. Although there is an important place for instructor interaction with students through a lecture format, providing explanations, concepts, etc., and leading discussions, much of the value of the approach comes through having the students engaged in the learning activities. Students can work on tasks in groups, both during class and online, and either report back to the class or hand in the work as an assignment. In addition, some of the tasks can be done individually as homework, with students meeting in groups during the following class to offer each other critiques and suggestions as a basis for revision.

This series of lessons can be done as a complete unit, but it can also be extended by having students work on inquiries, either individually or in groups (or some combination), on issues of interest to them, using the structure of inquiry described here.

About the authors:

Sharon Bailin, Professor Emeritus at Simon Fraser University and a past president of the Association for Informal Logic and Critical Thinking, has authored an extensive corpus of internationally recognized work on critical thinking and on creativity, including the award-winning book, *Achieving Extraordinary Ends: An Essay on Creativity*. The conception of critical thinking which Bailin co-developed has formed the foundation of a major curriculum project for K- 12 schools; she has also designed and directed Masters programs on critical thinking for educators. Bailin is the author, along with Mark Battersby, of *Reason in the Balance: An Inquiry Approach to Critical Thinking* (2nd Ed. Hackett, 2016). Their new book, *Inquiry: A New Paradigm for Critical Thinking*, which describes their innovative approach to conceptualizing and teaching critical thinking, has been published by *Windsor Studies in Argumentation*. She and Battersby collaborated on CRITHINKEDU, a major European project to infuse critical thinking into higher education.

Mark Battersby is Professor Emeritus at Capilano University, where he taught for over 40 years. He has also taught critical thinking at the University of British Columbia, Simon Fraser University and Stanford University, and has presented numerous workshops. He was founder of the British Columbia Association for Critical Thinking Research and Instruction and led a Ministry curriculum reform initiative based on learning outcomes. He has written numerous articles on critical thinking, and is the author of *Is That a Fact?* (Broadview, 2nd ed., 2016), and, along with Sharon Bailin, *Reason in the Balance: An Inquiry Approach to Critical Thinking* (2nd ed. Hackett, 2016). Translations of both of books have been published in China. *Inquiry: A New Paradigm for Critical Thinking*, a selection of his and Bailin's papers on their innovative approach to critical thinking, has been published by Windsor Studies in Argumentation. He and Bailin collaborated on CRITHINKEDU, a major European project to infuse critical thinking into higher education.

III

About Argument and Arguments

Introduction to Part III

Since argument is so central to critical thinking, Part II, comprising seven chapters, has been set aside to focus on contemporary theories of, approaches to, and construction of argument.

In Chapter 8, Anthony Blair sets out two different referents of 'argument' and discusses the connection between the study of arguments and the study of critical thinking. In Chapter 9, David Hitchcock develops a careful analysis of the concept of an argument as, in the case of a simple argument, a set of reasons for or against a claim. Chapter 10, by pioneers and experts in the development of argument mapping software, Martin Davies, Ashley Barnett and Tim van Gelder, offers instructions for using some of the current computer assisted argument mapping (a.k.a. tree-diagramming) programs for the purpose of interpreting and displaying arguments. Chapter 11 is an introduction to argument schemes, which are widely referenced in the contemporary argumentation literature, by their most renowned theoretician, Douglas Walton. Chapter 12 outlines the theoretical framework that lies behind constructing arguments by rhetoric and communications scholar, Beth Innocenti. In Chapter 13 Blair lays out the different steps involved in judging arguments—identifying, interpreting, displaying, evaluating and responding to them—and sets out a variety of ways arguments may be assessed. Christopher Tindale's Chapter 14 expands on one method of evaluating arguments, namely assessing them for fallacies, at the same time providing an account of how fallacies have come to be understood in today's argumentation literature.

8

Arguments and Critical Thinking

J. Anthony Blair

Introduction

This chapter discusses two different conceptions of argument, and then discusses the role of arguments in critical thinking. It is followed by a chapter in which David Hitchcock carefully analyses one common concept of an argument.

1. Two meanings of 'argument'

The word 'argument' is used in a great many ways. Any thorough understanding of arguments requires understanding 'argument' in each of its senses or uses. These may be divided into two large groupings: arguments *made or used*, and arguments *had* or *engaged in*. This distinction has been described in two influential papers by Daniel J. O'Keefe (1977, 1982), who labelled them 'argument₁" and 'argument₂'. I begin with the latter.

> *1.1 An 'argument' as something two parties have with each other,*
> *something they get into, the kind of 'argument' one has in mind*
> *in describing two people as "arguing all the time"*

For many people outside academia or the practice of law, an argument is a *quarrel*. It is usually a verbal quarrel, but it doesn't have to use words. If dishes are flying or people are glaring at each other in angry silence, it can still be an argument. What makes a quarrel an argument is that it involves a communication between two or more parties (however dysfunctional the communication may be) in which the parties disagree and in which that disagreement and reasons, actual or alleged, motivating it are expressed—usually in words or other communicative gestures.

Quarrels are emotional. The participants experience and express emotions, although that feature is not exclusive to arguments that are quarrels. People can and do argue emotionally, and (or) when inspired by strong emotions, when they are not quarrelling. Heated arguments are not necessarily quarrels; but quarrels tend to be heated.

What makes quarrels emotional in some cases is that at least one party experiences the disagreement as representing some sort of personal attack, and so experiences his or her ego or sense of self-worth as being threatened. Fear is a reaction to a perceived threat, and anger is a way of coping with fear and also with embarrassment and shame. In other cases, the argument about the ostensible disagreement is a reminder of or a pretext for airing another, deeper grievance. Jealousy and resentment fuel quarrels. Traces of ego-involvement often surface even in what are supposed to be more civilized argumentative exchanges, such as scholarly disputes. Quarrels tend not to be efficient ways of resolving the disagreements that gives rise to them because the subject of a disagreement changes as the emotional attacks escalate or because the quarrel was often not really about that ostensible disagreement in the first place.

In teaching that 'argument' has different senses, it is misleading to leave the impression (as many textbooks do) that quarrels are the only species of argument of this genus. In fact they are just one instance of a large class of arguments in this sense of extended, expressed, disagreements between or among two or more parties.

A *dispute* is an argument in this sense that need not be a quarrel. It is a disagreement between usually two parties about the legality, or morality, or the propriety or correctness or advisability on some other basis, of a particular claim, act or policy. It can be engaged in a civil way by the disputants or their proxies (e.g., their spokespersons or their lawyers). Sometimes the disputing parties can settle their difference. In disputes over policies or entitlements, sometimes a third party such as a mediator, arbitrator or judge has to be called in to impose a settlement. Disputes over claims (e.g., "I was here first." *vs.* "No, *I* was."; "You can find that idea in Marx." *vs.* "No, it comes from Hegel.") can sometimes be settled by evidence; others involve conflicting value judgements (see Chapter 21).

A *debate* is another argument of this general kind. Debates are more or less formalized or regimented verbal exchanges between parties who might disagree, but in any case who take up opposing sides on an issue. Procedural rules that govern turn-taking, time available for each turn, and topics that may be addressed are agreed to when political opponents debate one another. In parliamentary or congressional debates in political decision-making bodies, or in formal intercollegiate competitive debates, strict and precise rules of order govern who may speak, who must be addressed, sometimes time limits for interventions. Usually the "opponent" directly addressed in the debate is not the party that each speaker is trying to influence, so although the expressed goal is to "win" the debate, winning does not entail getting the opponent to concede. Instead, it calls for convincing an on-looking party or audience—the judge of the debate or the jury in a courtroom or the television audience or the press or the electorate as a whole—of the superior merits of one's case for the opinion being argued for in the debate.

To be distinguished from a debate and a dispute by such factors as scale is a *controversy.* Think of such issues as the abortion controversy, the climate change controversy, the same-sex marriage controversy, the LGBT rights controversy, the animal rights controversy. The participants are many—often millions. The issues are complex and there are many disputes about details involved, including sometimes even formal debates between representatives of different sides. Typically there is a range of positions, and there might be several different sides each with positions that vary one from another. A controversy typically occurs over an extended period of time, often years and sometime decades long. But an entire controversy can be called an argument, as in, "the argument over climate change." Controversies tend to be unregulated, unlike debates but like quarrels, although they need not be particularly angry even when they are emotional. Like quarrels, and unlike debates, the conditions under which controversies occur, including any constraints on them, are shaped by the participants.

Somewhere among quarrels, debates and controversies lie the theoretical arguments that theorists in academic disciplines engage in, in academic journals and scholarly monographs. In such arguments theorists take positions, sometimes siding with others and sometimes standing alone, and they argue back and forth about which theoretical position is the correct one. In a related type of argument, just two people argue back and forth about what is the correct position on some issue (including meta-level arguments about what is the correct way to frame the issue in the first place).

The stakes don't have to be theories and the participants don't have to be academics. Friends argue about which team will win the championship, where the best fishing spot is located, or what titles to select for the book club. Family members argue about how to spend their income, what school to send the children to, or whether a child is old enough to go on a date without a chaperone. Co-workers argue about the best way to do a job, whether to change service providers, whether to introduce a new product line, and so on. These arguments are usually amicable, whether or not they settle the question in dispute.

All of these kinds of "argument" in this sense of the term—quarrels, friendly disputes, arguments at work, professional arguments about theoretical positions, formal or informal debates, and various kinds of controversy—share several features.

(1) They involve communications between or among two or more people. Something initiates the communication, and either something ends it or there are ways for participants to join and to exit the conversation. They entail turn-taking (less or more regimented), each side addressing the other side and in turn construing and assessing what the other has to say in reply and formulating and communicating a response to the replies of the other side. And, obviously, they involve the expression, usually verbal, of theses and of reasons for them or against alternatives and criticisms.

(2) They have a *telos* or aim, although there seems to be no single end in mind for all of them or even for each of them. In a quarrel the goal might be to have one's point of view prevail, to get one's way, but it might instead (or in addition) be to humiliate the other person or to save one's own self-respect. Some quarrels—think of the ongoing bickering between some long-married spouses—seem to be a way for two people to communicate, merely to acknowledge one another. In a debate, each side seeks to "win," which can mean different things in different contexts (*cf.* a collegiate debate vs. a debate between candidates in an election vs. a parliamentary debate). Some arguments seemed designed to convince the other to give up his or her position or accept the interlocutor's position, or to get the other to act in some way or to adopt some policy. Some have the more modest goal of getting a new issue recognized for future deliberation and debate. Still others are clearly aimed not at changing anyone's mind but at reinforcing or entrenching a point of view already held (as is usually the case with religious sermons or with political speeches to the party faithful). Some are intended to establish or to demonstrate the truth or reasonableness of some position or recommendation and (perhaps) also to get others to "see" that the truth has been established. Some seem designed to *maintain* disagreement, as when representatives of competing political parties argue with one another.

(3) All these various kinds of argument are more or less extended, both in the sense that they occur over time, sometimes long stretches of time, and also in the sense that they typically involved many steps: extensive and complex support for a point of view and critique of its alternatives.

(4) In nearly every case, the participants give reasons for the claims they make and they expect the other participants in the argument to give reasons for *their* claims. This is even a feature of quarrels, at least at the outset, although such arguments can deteriorate into name-calling and worse. (Notice that even the "yes you did; no I didn't;…; did; didn't" sequence of the Monty Python "Having an argument" skit breaks down and a reason is sought.)

There are extensive literatures on each of these species of arguing. The kinds of argument listed so far are all versions of the communicative events of *arguing* or *having* an argument (see Daniel J. O'Keefe, 1977, 1982). Some might think that this is not the sense of 'argument' that is pertinent to critical thinking instruction, but such arguments are the habitat of the kinds of argument that critical thinkers need to be able to identify, analyze and evaluate. The second sense of 'argument' might be roughly characterized as follows:

> *1.2 An argument as something a person makes (or constructs, invents, borrows) consisting of purported reasons alleged to suggest, or support or prove a point and that is used for some purpose such as to persuade someone of some claim, to justify someone in maintaining the position claimed, or to test a claim.*

When people *have* arguments—when they engage in one or another of the activities of arguing described above—one of the things they routinely do is present or allege or offer reasons in support of the claims that they advance, defend, challenge, dispute, question, or consider. That is, in *having* "arguments," we typically *make and use* "arguments." The latter obviously have to be arguments in different sense from the former. They are often called "reason-claim" complexes. If arguments that someone has *had* constitute a type of communication or communicative activity or event, arguments that someone has *made or used* are actual or potential contributions to such activities. Reason-claim complexes are typically made and used when engaged in an argument in the first sense, trying to convince someone of your point of view during a disagreement or dispute with them. Here is a list of some of the many definitions found in textbooks of 'argument' in this second sense.

- "... here [the word 'argument'] ... is used in the ... logical sense of *giving reasons* for or against some claim." *Understanding Arguments*, Robert Fogelin and Walter Sinnott-Armstrong, 6th ed., p. 1.
- "Thus an argument is a discourse that contains at least two statements, one of which is asserted to be a reason for the other." Monroe Beardsley, *Practical Logic*, p. 9.
- "An argument is a set of claims a person puts forward in an attempt to show that some further claim is rationally acceptable." Trudy Govier. *A Practical Study of Arguments*, 5th ed., p. 3.
- An argument is "a set of clams some of which are presented as reasons for accepting some further claim." Alec Fisher, *Critical Thinking, An Introduction*, p. 235.

- Argument: "A conclusion about an issue that is supported by reasons." Sherry Diestler, *Becoming a Critical Thinker*, 4th ed., p. 403.
- " Argument: An attempt to support a conclusion by giving reasons for it." Robert Ennis, *Critical Thinking*, p. 396.
- "Argument – A form of thinking in which certain statements (reasons) are offered in support of another statement (conclusion)." John Chaffee, *Thinking Critically*, p. 415
- "When we use the word argument in this book we mean a message which attempts to establish a statement as true or worthy of belief on the basis of other statements." James B. Freeman, *Thinking Logically*, p. 20
- "Argument. A sequence of propositions intended to establish the truth of one of the propositions." Richard Feldman, *Reason and Argument*, p. 447.
- "Arguments consist of conclusions and reasons for them, called 'premises'." Wayne Grennan, *Argument Evaluation*, p. 5.
- Argument: "A set of claims, one of which, the conclusion is supported by [i.e., is supposed to provide a reason for] one or more of the other claims. *Reason in the Balance,* Sharon Bailin & Mark Battersby, p. 41.

These are not all compatible, and most of them define 'argument' using other terms—'reasons', 'claims', 'propositions', 'statements', 'premises' and 'conclusions'—that are in no less need of definition than it is. In Chapter 9, David Hitchcock offers a careful analysis of this concept of an argument.

Some define argument in this second sense as a kind of communication; others conceive it as a kind of set of propositions that can serve communicative functions, but others as well (such as inquiry). Either way, the communicative character, or function, of arguments has been the subject of much of the research in the past several decades. Most recently what some have called "multi-modal" argument has attracted attention, focusing on the various ways arguments can be communicated, especially visually or in a mix of verbal and visual modes of communication. Some have contended that smells and sounds can play roles in argument communication as well. This area of research interest would seem to have relevance for the analysis of arguments on the web.

1.3 Argumentation

'Argumentation' is another slippery term. It is used in several different senses.

Sometimes it is used to mean the communicative activity in which arguments are exchanged: "During their argumentation they took turns advancing their own arguments and criticizing one another's arguments." Sometimes 'argumentation' denotes the body of arguments used in an argumentative exchange: "The evening's argumentation was of high quality." And occasionally you will find it used to refer to the reasons or premises supporting a conclusion, as in: "The argumentation provided weak support for the thesis." 'Argumentation theory' is the term often used to denote theory about the nature of arguments and their uses, including their uses in communications involving exchanges of arguments.

2 The relation between critical thinking and argument

2.1 Arguments are both tools of critical thinking and objects of critical thinking

In one what must be one of the earliest handbooks on critical thinking, John Dewey wrote:

> In ... [one] sense, thought denotes belief resting upon some basis, that is, real or supposed knowledge going beyond what is directly present. ... Some beliefs are accepted when their grounds have not themselves been considered .... such thoughts may mean a supposition accepted without reference to its real grounds.
> ...
> Such thoughts grow up unconsciously and without reference to the attainment of correct belief. *They are picked up—we know not how. From obscure sources and by unnoticed channels they insinuate themselves into acceptance and become unconsciously a part of our mental furniture.* Tradition, instruction, imitation—all of which depend upon authority in some form, or appeal to our advantage, or fall in with strong passions—are responsible for them. Such thoughts are prejudices, that is, prejudgments, not judgments proper that rest upon a survey of evidence. (John Dewey, *How We Think*, pp. 4-5, emphasis added.)

People—all of us—routinely adopt beliefs and attitudes that are prejudices in Dewey's sense of being prejudgments, "not judgments proper that rest upon a survey of evidence." One goal of critical thinking education is to provide our students with the means to be able, when it really matters, to "properly survey" the grounds for beliefs and attitudes.

Arguments supply one such means. The grounds for beliefs and attitudes are often expressed, or expressible, as arguments for them. And the "proper survey" of these arguments is to test them by subjecting them to the critical scrutiny of counter-arguments.

Arguments also come into play when the issue is not what to believe about a contentious issue, but in order just to understand the competing positions. Not only are we not entitled to reject a claim to our belief if we cannot counter the arguments that support it; some would say we have no right to say we have a thorough understanding of a claim if we cannot formulate the arguments that support it to the satisfaction of its proponents.

Furthermore, arguments can be used to investigate a candidate for belief by those trying "to make up their own minds" about it. The investigator tries to find and express the most compelling arguments for and against the candidate. Which arguments count as "most compelling" are the ones that survive vigorous attempts, using arguments, to refute or undermine them. These survivors are then compared against one another, the pros weighed against the cons. More arguments come into play in assessing the attributed weights.

In these ways, a facility with arguments serves a critical thinker well. Such a facility includes skill in recognizing, interpreting and evaluating arguments, as well as in formulating them. That includes skill in laying out complex arguments, in recognizing argument strengths and weaknesses, and in making a case for one's critique. It includes the ability to distinguish the more relevant evidence from the less, and to discriminate between minor, fixable flaws and major, serious problems, in arguments. Thus the critical thinker is at once adept at using arguments in various ways and at the same time sensitive in judging arguments' merits with discrimination, applying the appropriate criteria.

Moreover, arguments in the sense of "reason-claim" complexes surround us in our daily lives. Our "familiars", as Gilbert (2014) has dubbed them—our family members, the friends we see regularly, shopkeepers and others whose services we patronize daily, our co-workers—engage us constantly in argumentative discussions in which they invoke arguments to try to get us to do things, to agree, to judge, to believe. The public sphere—the worlds of politics, commerce, entertainment, leisure activities, social media (see Jackson's chapter)—is another domain in which arguments can be found, although (arguably) mere assertion predominates there. In the various roles we occupy as we go through life—child, parent, spouse or partner, student, worker, patient, subordinate or supervisor, citizen (voter, jurist, community member), observer or participant, etc.—we are invited with arguments to agree or disagree, approve or disapprove, seek or avoid. We see others arguing with one another and are invited to judge the merits of the cases they make. Some of these arguments are cogent and their conclusions merit our assent, but others are not, and we should not be influenced by them. Yet others are suggestive and deserve further thought.

We can simply ignore many of these arguments, but others confront us and force us to decide whether or not to accept them. Often it is unclear whether someone has argued or done something else: just vented, perhaps, or explained rather than argued, or merely expressed an opinion without arguing for it, or was confused. So we initially might have to decide whether there is an argument that we need to deal with. When it is an argument, often in order to make up our minds about it we need first to get clear about exactly what the argument consists of. So even before we evaluate this argument we have to identify and analyze it. (These operations are discussed in Chapter 12.)

In the end we have to decide for ourselves whether the argument makes its case or falls short. Does the conclusion really follow from the premises? Is there enough evidence to justify the conclusion? Is it the right kind of evidence? Are there well-known objections or arguments against the conclusion that haven't been acknowledged and need to be answered satisfactorily? Can they be answered? And are the premises themselves believable or otherwise acceptable? Are there other arguments, as good or better, that support the claim?

Critical thinking can (and should!) come into all of these decisions we need to make in the identification, the analysis and the assessment of arguments.

2.2 Critical thinking about things other than arguments

Many critical thinking textbooks focus exclusively on the analysis and evaluation of arguments. While the centrality of arguments to the art of critical thinking is unquestionable, a strong case can be made that critical thinking has other objectives in addition to appreciating arguments. In their analysis of the concept of critical thinking, Fisher and Scriven suggest the following definition:

> Critical thinking is skilled and active interpretation and evaluation of *observations* and *communications, information* and argumentation. (1997, p. 21, emphasis added)

We agree with the gist of this claim, but notice what Fisher and Scriven propose as the objects to which critical thinking applies. Not just argumentation, but as well observations, communications and information. About observations, they note that:

> What one sees (hears, etc.) are usually things and happenings, and one often has to interpret what one sees, sometimes calling on critical thinking skills to do so, most obviously in cases where the context involves weak lighting, strong emotions, possible drug effects, or putatively magical or parapsychological phenomena. Only after the application of critical thinking—and sometimes not even then—does one know what one "really saw". ... When the filter of critical thinking has been applied to the observations, and only then, one can start reasoning towards further conclusions using these observations as premises. (*Ibid.*, p. 37)

An example is the recent large number of convictions in the U.S.A. that originally relied on eyewitness testimony but that have been overturned on the basis of DNA evidence.[1]

The DNA evidence proved that the accused was not the culprit, so the moral certainty of the eyewitness had to have been mistaken. The observation of the eyewitness was flawed. He or she did not think critically about whether the conditions needed to make a reliable observation were present (e.g., were strong emotions like fear involved? was the lighting good? has he or she ordinarily a good memory for faces? was there time to observe carefully? were there distractions present?). Neither, probably, did the lawyers on either side, or else they immorally suppressed what should have been their doubts. As a consequence of poor critical thinking about observations, innocent people languished in jail for years and guilty parties went free.

Communications are another object for critical thought. When in reply to Harry's question, "How are you doing?" Morgan says, in a clipped and dull voice and a strained expression on her face, "I'm fine", Harry needs to be aware that "How are you doing?" often functions as equivalent to a simple greeting, like "Hi" and so the response "Fine" could similarly be functioning as a polite return of the greeting, like "Hi back to you", and not as an accurate report of the speaker's condition. Harry needs to notice and interpret other aspects of Morgan's communication—her lethargic tone of voice and her anxious facial expression—and to recognize the incompatibility between those signals and the interpretation of her response as an accurate depiction of Morgan's state of well-being. He needs to employ critical interpretive skills to realize that Morgan has communicated that she is not fine at all, but for some reason isn't offering to talk about it.

If President Trump did in fact say to his then F.B.I. director James Comey, about the F.B.I. investigation of former National Security Advisor Michael Flynn "I hope you can let this go", was it legitimate for Comey to interpret the President's comment as a directive? And was Comey's response, which was simply to ignore President Trump's alleged comment, an appropriate response? What was going on? It takes critical thinking to try to sort out these issues. Taking the President's alleged comment literally, it just expresses his attitude towards the FBI investigation of Flynn. But communications from the President in a tête-à-tête in the White House with the Director of the FBI are not occasions for just sharing attitudes. This was not an occasion on which

---

[1] According to the Innocence Project, "Eyewitness misidentification is the greatest contributing factor to wrongful convictions proven by DNA testing, playing a role in more than 70% of convictions [in the U.S.A.] overturned through DNA testing nationwide." (https://www.innocenceproject.org/causes/eyewitness-misidentification/, viewed August 2017).

they could step out of their political roles and chat person-to-person. The President can legitimately be presumed to be communicating his wishes as to what his FBI Director should do, and such expressions of wishes are, in this context, to be normally understood as directives. On the other hand, for the President to direct that an ongoing investigation by the FBI be stopped, or that it come up with a pre-determined finding, is illegal: it's obstruction of justice. So Comey seemed faced with at least two possible interpretations of what he took the President to be saying: either an out-of-place expression of his attitude towards the outcome of the Flynn investigation or an illegal directive. Which was the President's intention? However, there are other possibilities.

Was President Trump a political tyro whose lack of political experience might have left him ignorant of the fact that the FBI Director has to keep investigations free of political interference? Or might Trump have thought that the Presidency conveys the authority to influence the outcome of criminal investigations? Or might President Trump have been testing Mr. Comey to see if he could be manipulated? And Mr. Comey could have responded differently. He could have said, "I wish we could let this go too, Mr. President, but there are questions about General Flynn's conduct that have to be investigated, and as you know, we cannot interfere with an ongoing FBI investigation". Such a response would have forced the President to take back what he allegedly said, withdrawing any suggestion that his comment was a directive, or else to make it plain that he was indeed directing Comey to obstruct justice. In the event, apparently Mr. Comey did not take this way out, which would at once have displayed loyalty to the President (by protecting him from explicitly obstructing justice) and also have affirmed the independence of the FBI from interference from the White House. Perhaps he thought that the President clearly had directed him to obstruct justice, and judged that giving him an opportunity explicitly to withdraw that directive amounted to overlooking that illegal act, which would be a violation of his responsibilities as Director of the FBI. If so, however, simply not responding to the President's comment, the path Comey apparently chose, also amounted to turning a blind eye to what he judged to be President Trump's illegal directive.

As these two examples illustrate, the interpretation of communications, and the appropriate response to them can require critical thinking: recognizing different functions of communication, and being sensitive to the implications of different contexts of communication; being sensitive to the roles communicators occupy and to the rights, obligations, and limits attached to such roles.

As Fisher and Scriven acknowledge, "defining *information* is itself a difficult task." They make a useful start by distinguishing information from raw data ("the numbers or bare descriptions obtained from measurements or observations", *op.* cit., p. 41). No critical thinking is required for the latter;

just the pains necessary to record raw data accurately, In many cases, though, the interpretation of raw data, the meaning or significance that they are said to have, can require critical thinking.

One might go beyond Fisher and Scriven's list of other things besides arguments to which critical thinking can be applied. A thoughtful appreciation of novels or movies, plays or poetry, paintings or sculptures requires skilled interpretation, imagining alternatives, thoughtful selection of appropriate criteria of evaluation and then the selection and application of appropriate standards, and more. A good interior designer must consider the effects and interactions of space and light and color and fabrics and furniture design, and coordinate these with clients' lifestyles, habits and preferences. Advanced practical skills in various sciences come into play. A coach of a sports team must think about each individual team member's skills and deficiencies, personality and life situation; about plays and strategies; opponents' skill sets; approaches to games; and much more. Conventional approaches need to be reviewed as to their applicability to the current situation. Alternative possibilities need to be creatively imagined and critically assessed. And all of this is time-sensitive, sometimes calling for split-second decisions. The thinking involved in carrying out the tasks of composing a review of some work of literature or art or of coaching a sports team can be routine and conventional, or it can be imaginative, invoking different perspectives and challenging standard criteria.

The list could go on. The present point is that, while argument is central to critical thinking, critical thinking about and using arguments is not all there is to critical thinking.[2]

References

Bailin, Sharon and Battersby, Mark (2010). *Reason in the Balance, An Inquiry Approach to Critical Thinking,* 1st ed. Toronto: McGraw-Hill Ryerson.

Beardsley, Monroe C. (1950). *Practical Logic.* Englewood Cliffs, NJ: Prentice-Hall.

Chaffee, John (1985). *Thinking Critically.* Boston: Houghton Mifflin.

Dewey, John (1910, 1991). *How We Think.* Lexington, MAD.C. Heath; Buffalo, NY: Prometheus Books.

Diestler, Sherry (2005). *Becoming a Critical Thinker,* 4th ed. Upper Saddle River, NJ: Pearson Education.

---

[2] I owe the general organization and many of the specific ideas of this chapter to a series of lectures by Jean Goodwin at the Summer Institute on Argumentation sponsored by the Centre for Research in Reasoning, Argumentation and Rhetoric at the University of Windsor.

Ennis, Robert H. (1996). *Critical Thinking.* Upper Saddle River, NJ: Prentice-Hall.

Feldman, Richard (1993). *Reason and Argument,* 2nd ed. Upper Saddle River, NJ: Prentice-Hall.

Fisher, Alec (2001). *Critical Thinking, An Introduction.* Cambridge: Cambridge University Press.

Fisher, Alec and Scriven, Michael (1997). *Critical Thinking, Its Definition and Assessment.* Point Reyes, CA: EdgePress; Norwich, UK: Center for Research in Critical Thinking.

Fogelin, Robert and Sinnott-Armstrong, Walter (2001). *Understanding Arguments, An Introduction to Informal Logic,* 6th ed. Belmont, CA: Wadsworth.

Freeman, James B. (1988.) *Thinking Logically, Basic Concepts of Reasoning.* Englewood Cliffs, NJ: Prentice-Hall.

Grennan, Wayne (1984). *Argument Evaluation.* Lanham, MD: University Press of America.

Govier, Trudy (2001). *A Practical Study of Argument,* 5th ed. Belmont, CA: Wadsworth.

O'Keefe, Daniel J. (1977). Two concepts of argument. *Journal of the American Forensic Association, 13,* 121-128.

O'Keefe, Daniel J. (1982). The concepts of argument and arguing. In J.R. Cox and C.A. Willard (Eds.), *Advances in Argumentation Theory and Research,* pp. 3-23. Carbondale, IL: Southern Illinois University Press.

About the author:

J. Anthony Blair has published extensively in informal logic, critical thinking and argumentation. A selection of his papers appeared in his *Groundwork in the Theory of Argumentation* (Springer, 2012). He is presently a Senior Fellow at the Centre for Research in Reasoning, Argumentation and Rhetoric (CRRAR) at Windsor.

9

The Concept of an Argument

David Hitchcock

1. Introduction[1]

The concept of an argument for which I propose an analysis is the reason-giving sense in which one speaks, for example, about Daniel Kahneman's argument (2011, pp. 334-335) that the tendency of most people to be risk averse about gains but risk-seeking about losses is irrational. This sense of the word 'argument' should be sharply distinguished from the disputational sense in which one speaks about two people having an argument, discussed in Chapter 8. That these are two different senses is clear from the fact that languages other than English use two different words for the two senses. For example, in French, 'to argue' in the sense of quarrelling is '*disputer*', whereas 'to argue' in the sense of giving reasons for or against is '*argumenter*'.

We could give a rough lexical definition of the word 'argument' in this sense by quoting the definition by the Hellenistic Stoics of an argument as "a system composed of premisses[2] and a conclusion" (*systêma ek lêmmatôn kai epiphoras*, Diogenes Laertius 1925/ca. 210-240, 7.45). Aside from its idiosyncratic failure to recognize one-premiss arguments, this definition is an acceptable starting point for a conceptual analysis. That analysis would need to answer a number of questions raised by the lexical definition. What is a premiss? What is a conclusion? What sorts of entities can function as a pre-

---

[1] This chapter uses material from "The concept of an argument" (Hitchcock 2017, pp. 518-529; © Springer International Publishing AG 2017), with the kind permission of Springer.

[2] I use the spelling 'premiss' and 'premisses' rather than 'premise' and 'premisses', following the usage of such prominent logicians as Charles Sanders Peirce and Bertrand Russell. The spelling 'premiss' is peculiar to the original logical sense of the word, whereas the plural 'premises' can be used also for houses, buildings and land specified in a deed.

miss? What sorts can function as a conclusion? How do premisses and a conclusion form a unified system? Does such a system have an intrinsic function or purpose, or on the contrary can it be used for various purposes? What about complex arguments?

We should recognize that arguments are not necessarily the content or product of argumentation—that is, of communications in which arguments are exchanged. One can consider an argument for a certain position or policy even if nobody has ever used that argument. One can imagine crazy arguments that no sane person would ever put forward. One can apply the term 'argument' to unified stretches of solo reasoning where some conclusion is reached on the basis of reasons, as when one considers mentally various aspects of a situation and then describes "the argument that finally convinced me". Indeed, it seems consistent with our ordinary use of the term 'argument' in its reason-giving sense to say that there are arguments that nobody has ever thought of and nobody ever will. The most we can demand is that an argument must be thinkable and expressible. Arguments as a class thus have no common function or purpose. They are not necessarily used to justify or establish something. Nor are they necessarily used to persuade anybody.

Thus, critical thinking textbooks that define 'argument' as "rational persuasion—an attempt to influence another or others using reasons" are actually describing one use of arguments, not the concept itself.

2. Simple arguments

Begin by considering simple arguments, in the sense of single-inference systems that consist of one or more premisses and one conclusion. Of what sorts of entities are such arguments composed? That is, what kind of object can function as a premiss, and what kind can function as a conclusion? A common answer is that these components are propositions, in the sense of postulated timeless and non-located entities that can be expressed linguistically (or in some other way) and that can be objects of belief or knowledge. Propositions however are not the right candidates to be premisses or conclusions.

As to premisses, consider the following two arguments:

(1) *Suppose that there is life on other planets in the universe. Then it makes sense to look for it.*
(2) *There is life on other planets in the universe. So it makes sense to look for it.*

These arguments have the same conclusion, but different premisses. But both premisses express the same proposition, that there is life on other planets in the universe. The difference is in the illocutionary act performed by someone who utters the premiss in standard contexts. In uttering argument (1), the author *hypothesizes* the propositional content of the premiss. In uttering argument (2), on the other hand, the author *asserts* the proposition. The difference makes a difference to the evaluation of the two arguments: argument (2) requires a stricter condition of premiss adequacy than argument (1).

If arguments need not be expressed but their premisses are illocutionary acts, the premisses must be illocutionary act-types rather than illocutionary act-tokens. Sometimes the type may have no actual tokens. Someone can use the same argument on different occasions, and different people can use the same argument. A premiss can be a supposition or an assertive or any other member of the class of illocutionary acts that Searle (1976) grouped under the label 'representatives', and which he defined (p. 10) as acts whose point is to commit the speaker, perhaps hypothetically or guardedly, to something's being the case. It cannot be any other kind of illocutionary act, as we can see by noting the peculiarity of putting examples (taken from Hitchcock 2006, pp. 103-104) of the other kinds of illocutionary acts in premissary position before an inferential 'therefore':

(3) * *What time is it? Therefore, you must go home.*
(4) ? *I promise to pick up some milk on the way home. Therefore, you don't need to get it.*
(5) * *Congratulations on your anniversary. Therefore, you are married.*
(6) * *I hereby sentence you to two years less a day. Therefore, the guards will now take you to prison.*

In standard contexts, the utterances in the premissary position are respectively (3) a directive (in particular, a request for information), (4) a commissive (in particular, a promise), (5) an expressive (in particular, a congratulation), and (6) a declarative (in particular, a judicial verdict). The inappropriateness of these pairings reveals the general inability of illocutionary acts other than representatives to function as premisses. The premiss in (4) is a borderline case, because a promise can be taken to imply a prediction (that the promise will be kept) and a prediction is a kind of assertion. It is the implicit prediction rather than the commitment that makes it possible to construe example (4) as an argument.

Among conclusions, we find a greater variety of illocutionary acts than among premisses. We have already seen two examples ((1) and (2) above) in which the conclusion is a representative. Conclusions (and premisses too) can be hedged by such qualifiers as 'probably', 'presumably', 'possibly', and the like, which are best given a speech-act interpretation.[3] Thus a wide range of

---

[3] As Toulmin (1958, pp. 47-62) and Ennis (2006, pp. 145-164) have argued.

representatives can be conclusions of arguments. But the other main kinds of illocutionary acts can also be conclusions, as we can see from the following examples (taken from Hitchcock 2006, p. 105):

(7) *There is a forecast of thundershowers, so let's cancel the picnic.*
(8) *I know how difficult it will be for you to get the milk, so I promise you that I will pick it up on the way home.*
(9) *My conduct was inexcusable, so I apologize most sincerely.*
(10) *The evidence establishes beyond a reasonable doubt that you committed the crime of which you are accused, so I hereby find you guilty as charged.*

When these arguments are expressed in standard contexts, their conclusions are respectively (7) a directive, (8) a commissive, (9) an expressive, and (10) a declarative. Thus the conclusion of an argument can be an illocutionary act type of any kind: a representative, a directive, a commissive, an expressive, or a declarative.

A reason can be advanced as a reason against some claim as well as a reason for it. Consider the following example:

(11)
Proponent: *We need a concerted global reduction of greenhouse gas emissions to mitigate future climate disruption.*
Opponent: *A cost-benefit analysis needs to be done first to determine whether it makes more sense to adapt to future climate disruption rather than to mitigate it.*

Here the opponent's reason is put forward as a reason against the proponent's claim. The exchange has an inferential structure that is quite parallel to that in which a reason is put forward in support of a claim. In general, objections and criticisms seem to have just the same inferential structure as supports. In other words, there can be arguments against something as well as arguments for something. Consider an example. In the 11th century the monk Gaunilon objected to Anselm's ontological argument for the existence of God that by the same reasoning one could prove the existence of a perfect island (Anselm 1903/1077-78). Gaunilon's objection is an argument against the cogency of Anselm's argument. It would involve needless and misleading subtlety to recast his objection as an argument in support of some claim. It is better to follow a number of authors who have recognized that there can be arguments against as well as arguments for (Johnson 2000; Rahwan et al. 2009; Freeman 2010; Wohlrapp 2014/2008; Blair this volume, Ch. 8; Davies et al. this volume, Ch. 10; Goddu this volume, Ch. 16).

In fact, the same reason can be adduced for a claim by one person and against the same claim by another person. For example, some people use the principle of self-determination as a reason for legalizing voluntary euthanasia, whereas others use it as a reason against legalizing voluntary euthanasia (Wohlrapp 2014/2008, pp. 264-265[4]). Each group advances an argument, and the two arguments clearly differ from each other. Thus it makes sense to add to the conception of an argument as a premiss-conclusion or claim-reason complex a third component indicating whether the reasons are to count for or against the claim. Further, to accommodate the existence of arguments against as well as arguments for, I shall hereafter use the term 'target' rather than 'conclusion' or 'claim' for the part of an argument to which its reasons are directed.

We are now in a position to say what a simple argument is:

A simple argument *consists of one or more of the types of expression that can function as reasons, a "target" (any type of expression), and an indicator of whether the reasons count for or against the target.*[5]

There may be no tokens of the component illocutionary act types. In other words, simple arguments as just defined are abstract structures that are not necessarily actually realized. We need impose no further restrictions on what can count as a simple argument, thus widening the class of arguments to the craziest combinations that one can imagine.

What gives such a set unity as a single argument is that someone puts forward or entertains–that is, adduces—its reasons as support for or opposition to its target. In doing so, the person ordinarily claims or thinks that the reasons, if true or otherwise acceptable, provide grounds for accepting or rejecting the target (to an extent indicated). A common motivation for adducing the reasons as counting for or against the target is the belief that the person addressed by, or considering, the argument did not previously think that the reasons provide the claimed support for, or opposition to, the target.

---

[4] Wohlrapp argues that if voluntary euthanasia becomes legal on the basis that self-determination requires it, those whose condition might qualify them for approval to be euthanized but who want merely to live out the remainder of their natural lives are pressured by appeals to self-determination to submit to euthanasia. The supposedly liberating value becomes coercive.

[5] More precisely: A simple argument is a triple whose first member is a set of one or more representative illocutionary act types (called 'the reasons'), whose third member (called 'the target') is an illocutionary act type of any kind, and whose second member is an indicator of whether the reasons are to be taken as counting for or against the target.

Goddu (2018) has objected to this way of securing the unity of an actualized argument. He contends that a person can entertain an argument mentally without supposing that its reasons support (or oppose) its target. One can for example wonder whether the reasons in an argument one is considering actually support the target. This is true, but in such a case the person considering the argument is viewing it as an argument that someone might or could adduce, i.e., as a hypothetical argument, a possible complex of reasons, indicator, and target.

Someone who adduces reasons as counting for or against a target must be the author of either the reasons or the target. But such an adducer need not be the author of both. One can draw a conclusion from something someone else has said, in which case the person who draws the conclusion adduces what the other person said as supporting the conclusion drawn. One can provide reasons against someone else's claim, in which case the person who provides the reasons adduces them as opposing the other person's claim. In any situation where an argument is expressed, the adducer is the person who articulates the inferential claim conveyed by the (possibly implicit) indicator that points to the argument's target.

3. Complex arguments

So far this conception of an argument accommodates only simple arguments, i.e., single-inference arguments with a set of one or more reasons, a target, and an indication of whether the reasons count for or against the target. We need to allow as well for complex arguments that involve a chain of reasoning or embedded suppositional reasoning.

3.1 Chain of reasoning arguments

In chained arguments, a reason of one argument (which I will call 'the superordinate argument') is the target of another (which I will call 'the subordinate argument' or 'sub-argument'). Since only representatives can be reasons, the target of any subordinate argument must be a representative. There is no limit to the depth of chaining. The ultimate target in a chain of reasoning is supported or opposed by one or more reasons, each of which may be the target of one or more reasons in a sub-argument, each of which in turn may be the target of one or more reasons in a sub-sub-argument, and so on indefinitely. In an expressed sub-argument at any level, the reasons must be adduced in support of the target. Otherwise the target would have to be the complement of the reason in the superordinate argument to which it was linked. But it is hard to define the complement of a representative illocutionary act. What, for example, is the complement of a hedged assertion of the form 'probably p'?

Representatives incompatible with 'probably p' include 'definitely p', 'probably p''', and 'definitely p''', where p' is a contradictory of p. An argument against some target that was used to support a reason of the form 'probably p' would therefore need an unwieldy disjunction as its target, for which it would be difficult if not impossible to formulate a set of reasons that successfully opposed each disjunct simultaneously. Since subordinate simple arguments in an expressed complex argument make sense only if their reasons are presented in support of their target, it makes sense to limit unexpressed subordinate simple arguments in the same way.

The natural way to accommodate the indefinite complexity of chained arguments is to use an inductive clause[6] that can be applied again and again so as to build up arguments of increasing complexity. The process is analogous to that by which one defines what a person's ancestor is by saying that a parent of a person is an ancestor of that person and that a parent of any ancestor of that person is also an ancestor of that person. This definition allows one to construct the class of a person's ancestors, starting with the person's parents, then adding the grandparents, then the great-grandparents, and so on without end.

In defining inductively what an argument is, one needs to take some care in constructing the inductive clause for chained arguments. The most sensible way to do so seems to be to add one at a time a simple argument for a reason in an already constructed argument. One can conceive of a simple argument, which is a triple, as a unit set, a set with one member. One can combine it with a simple argument whose target is a reason in the first argument by taking the union of the two sets, i.e., the set whose members are all the triples that are members of either set. And then one can combine this set of two triples with a third simple argument whose target is a reason in one of the first two triples. And so on. Let us call a reason in any triple in a set of such triples a 'reason in the argument'. The inductive clause might then read as follows:

If in an argument something is a reason but is not a target, then the union of that argument with a simple argument whose target is that reason and whose indicator is positive is also an argument.

As with the definition of simple arguments, this clause allows that the most fantastic and crazy combinations are arguments in the abstract sense. The

---

[6] In the first edition of this book, I called this clause a "recursion clause". The phrase "inductive clause" is more accurate, since it applies to the building up of a domain of objects step by step. Recursive definitions, strictly speaking, define terms that apply to a domain that has already been constructed; an example is the recursive definition of the plus symbol '+' as applied to the previously constructed domain of natural numbers.

condition that the reason is not already a target is meant to exclude from being a single argument structures in which a reason is the target of more than one simple argument. Just as multiple arguments for or against the same ultimate target do not constitute a single argument, so too multiple arguments for the same intermediate target cannot be components of a single complex argument.

3.2 Embedded suppositional reasoning

Chaining is one of two ways to construct complex arguments. The other is embedding, where suppositional reasoning is used to support or oppose a target, with one or more of its suppositions being "discharged" in the process. (E.g., "Suppose the U.S. did not use the atomic bomb in WWII. Had that been the case, then probably…" or "Suppose we take on the debt of a big mortgage and buy a house. If we were to do that, then …".) Any line of suppositional reasoning is an argument according to the inductive definition of argument developed so far. To allow for embedding one or more such lines of suppositional reasoning, we need to allow that a line of suppositional reasoning can count as something like a reason.[7] One way to do so is to take the line of suppositional reasoning as an implicit assertion that the ultimate target of the line of suppositional reasoning follows from its ultimate supposition in combination with any other ultimate reasons used in derivation of the ultimate target. (The assertion may be qualified, if either an inference or an ultimate reason in the suppositional reasoning is qualified.).

When the suppositional reasoning is embedded in a larger context, the target external to this line of reasoning is a representative, which in the case of nested suppositional reasoning may itself have a suppositional status. The inductive clause allowing embedding of suppositional reasoning thus needs to allow for the dual complexity of chains of reasoning from suppositions and nesting of suppositional reasoning inside suppositional reasoning. It also needs to allow that a line of suppositional reasoning can be used in opposition to a target as well in support of one. If the target of a line of suppositional reasoning is a reason in a sub-argument, however, then the expression of such a complex argument makes sense only if the suppositional reasoning is adduced in support of the target, for the same reason that an expressed chained simple sub-argument makes sense only if its reasons are adduced in support of its target: an opposed target would have to be too complex to count as the com-

---

[7] It won't do, however, to count it as a reason in the same sense as that in which a representative is a reason. Otherwise the inductive clause for chaining would allow for arguments that are subordinate to a line of suppositional reasoning, which makes no sense.

plement of the reason in the superordinate argument that is being indirectly supported by opposition to the target of the suppositional reasoning.

In general, too, it makes sense to use a line of suppositional reasoning only if its internal ultimate target is argued for rather than against, since all the recognized legitimate ways of discharging a supposition assume that the supposition is used to support the ultimate target. Similar restrictions to arguments with a positive indicator are therefore appropriate for abstract arguments that need not be expressed. It seems an unnecessary further complication, however, to incorporate in a clause allowing embedding the specific ways in which a supposition in a piece of suppositional reasoning may legitimately be discharged.[8] The abstract definition of an argument will thus allow for embedding pieces of suppositional reasoning in totally illegitimate ways.

The following is a possible inductive clause allowing embedding;

A triple is an argument if its first member is a set whose members include at least one argument with a suppositional ultimate reason, whose third member (the target) is an illocutionary act of any kind, and whose second member is an indicator of whether the members of the set count for or against the target.

As is usual with inductive definitions, there needs to be a final closure clause to the effect that nothing is an argument unless it is an argument

---

[8] One way of legitimately discharging a supposition is conditional proof, in which one derives a conditional from a line of suppositional reasoning that starts from the supposition of the conditional's antecedent and ends with the conditional's consequent. A variant form of conditional proof starts from the supposition of a contradictory of a conditional's consequent and ends with a contradictory of its antecedent. Another way to legitimately discharge a supposition is reductio ad absurdum, in which one uses a line of reasoning from a supposition to some absurdity as a reason for denying the supposed proposition. Another is argument by cases, in which one considers an allegedly exhaustive set of possible cases, deriving the same ultimate target from the supposition of each case, and then drawing this ultimate target as a conclusion. Another is to argue for a proposition in a proof by mathematical induction by supposing at the inductive step that the proposition holds for the number n (or for every number up to and including n) and deriving from this supposition that then it also holds for the number n + 1. Another is universal generalization, in which one derives a universal generalization about a kind by reasoning from the supposition that some individual is of that kind to the conclusion that the generalization holds for this individual, without using any other assumption about the individual.

according to the base clause and the inductive clauses.[9] One can illustrate and test the resulting definition by using its clauses to construct complex arguments as they appear in argumentative texts.

As with the abstract concept of a single argument, we need a basis for the unity of an expressed complex argument. An expressed chaining of two arguments is a complex illocutionary act of adducing the resulting chain of reasoning as supporting or opposing the ultimate target of the superordinate argument in the chain (i.e. the argument that has a reason which the subordinate simple argument targets). The essence of adducing in this case is that the utterance of the adducer counts as a claim that in each link of the chain the reasons if true or otherwise acceptable would provide epistemic support for the target or as a claim that the reasons if true or otherwise acceptable would provide epistemic opposition to the target. An embedding of an argument is a complex act of adducing the embedded suppositional reasoning, possibly along with one or more reasons, as support for or opposition to the target of the argument in which the suppositional reasoning is embedded. The essence of adducing in this case is that the utterance of the adducer counts as a claim that the suppositional reasoning would if the additional reasons (if any) were true or otherwise acceptable provide epistemic support for the target or as a claim that the suppositional reasoning would if the additional reasons (if any) were true or otherwise acceptable provide epistemic opposition to the target. The content conditions, preparatory conditions and sincerity conditions for these more complex acts of adducing are a function of the content, preparatory and sincerity conditions for the simple acts of adducing from which they are constituted.

As with simple expressed arguments, we can accommodate merely entertained complex arguments by a hypothetically possible act of adducing. If one is entertaining mentally a complex abstract argument as a whole that could be used to adduce the reasons as supporting or opposing its ultimate target, then one is considering an argument.

---

[9] One can express the inductive definition in the customary form of a statement in which there appears in the first part the term to be defined, in the last part the defining part of the definition, and in between these two parts an indicator (such as 'means', '=df', 'if and only if', or 'is a') that the defining part states the meaning of the defined term. For example, one could say that something is an argument if and only if it belongs to every set that includes everything that satisfies the base clause, as well as everything that can be constructed from its members using the inductive clauses for chaining and embedding.

4. Summary

The conception of an argument that I propose has the following distinctive features:

- It takes the ultimate constituents of arguments to be illocutionary act types rather than propositions, statements, utterances, and the like.

- It allows for arguments against something as well as arguments for something.

- It allows the reasons in an argument to be any kind of representative illocutionary act.

- It allows arguments to have as their target any kind of illocutionary act.

- It distinguishes arguments as abstract structures that may never be expressed or even thought of from expressed arguments.

- It locates the unity of an expressed or mentally entertained argument in a second-order illocutionary act of adducing, which may be actual or merely hypothetically entertained.

- It allows for a variety of uses of arguments, since neither the abstract conception of an argument nor the act of adducing that constitutes a complex of illocutionary act types as a single argument includes any conception of the purpose or function of an argument.

- It provides explicitly for complex arguments to be constructed inductively by steps of chaining and embedding.

References

Anselm, Saint (1903/1077-78). *Proslogium; Monologium: An appendix in behalf of the fool by Gaunilo; and Cur deus homo*, translated from the Latin by Sidney Norton Deane, B.A. with an introduction, bibliography, and reprints of the opinions of leading philosophers and writers on the ontological argument. Chicago: Open Court. Latin original of the *Proslogium* written in 1077-78.

Diogenes Laertius (1925/ca. 210-240). *Lives of eminent philosophers*, with an English translation by R. D. Hicks, 2 vols. Loeb Classical Library 184 and 185. Cambridge, MA: Harvard University Press. First published ca. 210-240 CE.

Ennis, Robert H. (2006). 'Probably'. In David Hitchcock and Bart Verheij (Eds.), *Arguing on the Toulmin model: New essays on argument analysis and evaluation* (pp. 145-164). Dordrecht: Springer.

Freeman, James B. (2010). Commentary on G. C. Goddu's "Refining Hitchcock's definition of 'argument'". In Juho Ritola (Ed.), *Argument cultures: Proceedings of OSSA 09*, CD-ROM (pp. 1-10). Windsor, ON: OSSA. Available at http://scholar.uwindsor.ca/cgi/viewcontent.cgi?article=1141&context=ossaarchive.

Goddu, G.C. (2018). Against the intentional definition of argument. In Steve Oswald and Didier Maillat (Eds.), *Proceedings of the Second European Conference on Argumentation, University of Fribourg, Switzerland, 20-23 June 2017*, Vol. II (pp. 337-346). London: College Publications.

Hitchcock, David (2006). Informal logic and the concept of argument. In Dale Jacquette (Ed.), *Philosophy of logic*, volume 5 of Dov M. Gabbay, Paul Thagard and John Woods (Eds.), *Handbook of the philosophy of science* (pp. 101-129). Amsterdam: North Holland.

Hitchcock, David (2017). The concept of argument. In David Hitchcock, *On reasoning and argument: Essays in informal logic and on critical thinking* (pp. 518-529). Dordrecht: Springer.

Johnson, Ralph H. (2000). *Manifest rationality: A pragmatic theory of argument*. Mahwah, NJ: Lawrence Erlbaum Associates.

Kahneman, Daniel (2011). *Thinking, fast and slow*. New York: Farrar, Straus and Giroux.

Rahwan, Iyad and Chris Reed (2009). The Argument Interchange Format. In Guillermo R. Simari (Ed.), *Argumentation in artificial intelligence* (pp. 383-402). Boston: Springer.

Searle, John R. (1976). A classification of illocutionary acts. *Language in Society*, 5(1), 1-23.

Toulmin, Stephen Edelston (1958). *The uses of argument*. Cambridge: Cambridge University Press.

Wohlrapp, Harald R. (2014/2008). *The concept of argument: A philosophical foundation*. Dordrecht: Springer. German original first published in 2008.

About the author:

David Hitchcock is emeritus professor of philosophy at McMaster University in Hamilton, Canada, where he taught service courses in critical thinking over a span of 40 years. He is the author of *Critical Thinking: A Guide to Evaluating Information* (Methuen, 1983) and co-author with Milos Jenicek, MD, of *Evidence-Based Practice: Logic and Critical Thinking in Medicine* (AMA Press, 2005). He co-edited with Bart Verheij *Arguing on the Toulmin Model: New Essays in Argument Analysis and Evaluation* (Springer, 2007). His *On Reasoning and Argument: Essays in Informal Logic and on Critical Thinking* (Springer, 2017) brings together 25 previously published sole-authored articles, along with seven new chapters updating his views on their topics: deduction, induction and conduction; material consequence; patterns of reasoning; interpersonal discussion; evaluation of reasoning; fallacies; and informal logic and critical thinking. He is the author of the entry on critical thinking in *The Stanford Encyclopaedia of Philosophy*.

10

Using Computer-aided Argument Mapping to Teach Reasoning

Martin Davies, Ashley Barnett, and Tim van Gelder

1. Introduction[1]

Argument mapping is a way of diagramming the logical structure of an argument to explicitly and concisely represent reasoning. (See Figure 1, for an example.) The use of argument mapping in critical thinking instruction has increased dramatically in recent decades. A brief history of argument mapping is provided at the end of this chapter.

Pre- and post-test studies have demonstrated the pedagogical benefit of argument mapping using cohorts of university students and intelligence analysts as subjects, and by comparing argument mapping interventions with data from comparison groups or benchmarks from other meta-analytic reviews. It has been found that intensive practice mapping arguments with the aid of software has a strong positive effect on the critical thinking ability of students. Meta-analysis has shown that high-intensity argument mapping courses improve critical thinking scores by around 0.8 of a standard deviation—more than twice the typical effect size for standard critical thinking courses (van Gelder, 2015). This strongly suggests that argument mapping is a very effective way to teach critical thinking.

The process of making an argument map is beneficial because it encourages students to construct (or reconstruct) their arguments with a level of clarity and rigor that, when divorced from prose, often goes unnoticed. The shortcomings of a badly-constructed map are plain to see. This is not the case with dense blocks of written prose, which can give an impressionistic sense of rigor to the reader.

---

[1] The colored versions of the argument maps in this chapter are available only in the open-access Ebook edition of this book at: https://windsor.scholarsportal.info/omp/index.php/wsia/catalog

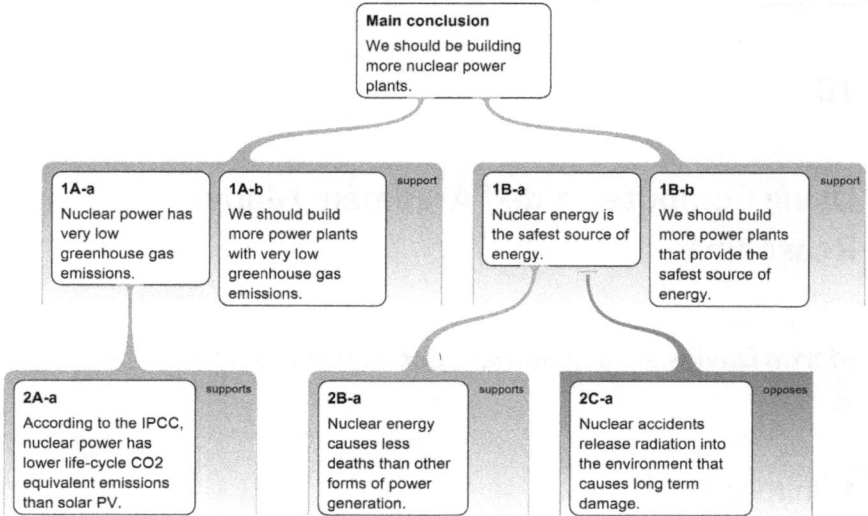

Figure 1. A short argument showing the main conventions used in argument mapping. The main conclusion is placed at the top of the map. The reasons for the main conclusion are identified by green shaded areas connected by lines to the main conclusion. The main conclusion in this example has two reasons, 1A and 1B. Inside the green shaded areas white claim boxes are used to display individual premises. Premises are placed in separate premise boxes because each premise needs its own justification. The surrounding green reason envelope effectively groups together linked premises working together to form a reason for the conclusion. Argument maps clearly show which premises of a reason are supported by further reasoning. For example, 1A-a is a premise, which is itself supported by a reason, 2A-a. As claim 1A-a is both a premise in one inference and a conclusion in another it sometimes called an 'intermediate conclusion' or lemma. Objections to claims are identified by a red shaded area. In the map above, there is only one objection, 2C-a. NB: When colour cannot be used, the labels to the right of the shading helps to designate reasons and objections (i.e., the words 'supports', 'opposes').

Argument maps can also help students evaluate reasoning because they can easily focus on evaluating each inferential step of an argument. These inferential steps are indicated by the green and red connecting lines in the example provided. Students using argument mapping software can easily see how their evaluation of each step affects the conclusion. For example, in the argument in Figure 1, suppose the objection in red is strong enough that we can no longer accept claim 1B-a in the reason above it. That would mean that the second reason given for the contention (formed by claims 1B-a and 1B-b) no longer offers any support for the conclusion. However, the first reason (formed by claims 1A-a and 1A-b) is unaffected by the objection and may still be strong enough to establish the conclusion. A map makes this very intuitive. It is much harder to see the implications of changing premises using prose alone and without the visual markers provided by mapping software.

One of the main pitfalls when using argument mapping in teaching is that students may find the level of rigor and clarity encouraged by the technique to be onerous. However, using interesting examples that increase the demands of the argument mapping course gradually and incrementally allows students to have fun exploring how different arguments work. In most argument mapping software students can freely move the parts of an argument around and experiment with different logical structures. This ability to "play around" with an argument allows students, over time, to gain a deep and practiced understanding of the structure of arguments—an important aim of any critical thinking course. Anecdotally, it also helps with student engagement: by manipulating parts of a map using a software, participants more actively engage with critical thinking tasks than they would do otherwise (i.e., if maps were not being used).

From an instructor's point of view, adapting a classroom to teach critical thinking using argument mapping requires flexibility, and a willingness to experiment and try out new methodologies and principles. Some of these are covered in this paper. Fortunately, a variety of software and the exercises needed to run an argument mapping course are available for free online. We return to these later.

2. Computer-aided argument mapping

Computer-aided argument mapping (CAAM) uses software programs specifically designed to allow students to quickly represent reasoning using box and line diagrams. This can, in principle, be done without software (Harrell, 2008), but the software makes it much easier. Boxes are used to contain claims and lines are used to show which claims are reasons for others. The software does not itself *analyze* argumentative texts, or check the validity of the arguments, but by making argument maps students can, with practice, get better at argument analysis and evaluation.

In terms of entry-level skills required to use CAAM, little more is needed other than a solid understanding of the target language, basic computer skills, a broad familiarity with the importance of critical thinking, and a willingness to experiment with argument mapping software. In terms of achieving *expertise* in using CAAM, however, a rigorous approach to text analysis is involved, along with adoption of a number of CAAM methodical principles, and of course, the help of a dedicated and experienced instructor. Lots of argument mapping practice (LAMP) is also recommended (Rider and Thomason, 2008).

The theoretical basis for argument mapping *improving* critical thinking skills is based on two principles:

1. It takes for granted the well-established notion of dual coding as it is understood in cognitive science. Human information processing is enhanced by the use of a number of sensory modalities. Diagrams and words allow better cognitive processing of complex information than words alone.

2. It assumes the not unreasonable point that cognitive processing capacity in humans is limited, and that understanding complex arguments is enhanced by "off-loading" information as visual displays (in other words, it's easier to remember and understand information if one can draw a diagram).

Argument mapping is similar to other mapping tools such as mind mapping and concept mapping. All attempt to represent complex relationships. However, there are also important differences. Unlike mind mapping, which is concerned with associational relationships between ideas, and concept mapping, which is concerned with relational connections between statements and events, argument mapping is principally concerned with inferential or logical relationships between claims (Davies, 2011). There is a difference between argument mapping and various diagrammatic representations in formal logic too. Argument mapping is concerned with representing informal, i.e., "real world", or natural language argumentation. It thus contrasts with the use of diagrammatic techniques such as Venn diagrams as used in formal logic. In an important sense, argument maps should make intelligible what is going on in arguments as they are (imperfectly) expressed in prose.

As noted, argument mapping software provides several benefits in the classroom. The software makes building argument maps easy, so teachers can provide their students with many practical exercises to work on. Because the software allows the students to edit their maps freely, they can engage in self-directed exploratory learning as they try out different argument structures to see what works best.

Argument maps also show the anatomy of an argument more clearly than can be done in prose. By seeing models of well-constructed maps, students can appreciate how all arguments are made up of claims and how some of these work together as co-premises. They can see at a glance how claims belong to separate lines of reasoning, and can see why some claims are necessary for an argument to succeed and why some are not.

For example, often when students are presented with a range of reasons for a conclusion in prose, they will focus on counting the mistakes and erroneously think that the side of the debate that made the most number of outrageous mistakes must be wrong about the conclusion. But by presenting the argument in the form of a map illustrates the point that these bad reasons neither increase or decrease the reliability of a conclusion, and hence are irrelevant to our final evaluation. Instead, attention needs to be focused on the strongest reasons, not the number. It is possible that the side of an argument that presented the worst reasons for a given conclusion also provided the most conclusive reason (see Figure 2).

Argument maps can make discussing complicated arguments in a classroom much easier too. The number of reasons or objections to a contention can be easily "read-off" an argument map (this is difficult to do with a prose equivalent). Example arguments can be displayed on the projector and the teacher can point precisely to the part of the argument that he or she wants to discuss. When debating issues in a classroom, using argument maps can help externalize and depersonalize the debate so that the students are no longer arguing with one another in a competitive way but are collaborating on mapping an argument together in an attempt to construct the best argument for or against the conclusion. This promotes a sense of involvement in a joint scholarly enterprise.

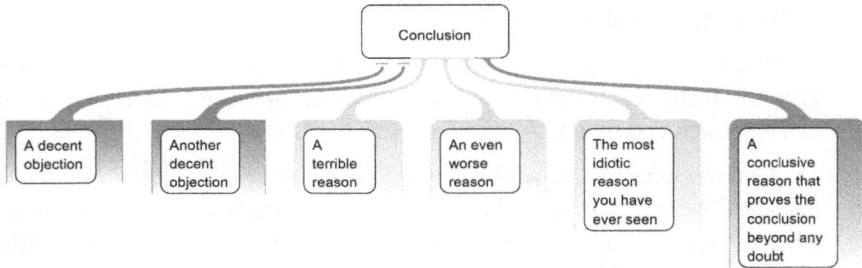

Figure 2. Argument maps clearly distinguish between separate reasons, so it easier to focus on the logical implications of the good reasons and not get distracted by the bad reasons that should just be ignored when it comes to evaluating the conclusion.

An additional benefit is this: Maps also make assessing student's reasoning skills much easier in assignments, because the teacher can clearly see what his or her students had in mind without the confounding variables to be found in an argumentative essay (Davies, 2009). Also, asking the students to make an argument map prior to writing an argumentative essay can also help ensure that the basic structure of the argument is adequate before they start writing. For a number of reasons, this can assist in the process of essay writing.

3. Teaching using computer-aided argument mapping

Let us now look at how to teach critical thinking using argument mapping. Some of these points apply to any informal logic or critical thinking class, but they are particularly relevant to any class intending to use argument mapping as a teaching tool.

3.1 The parts of an argument

In teaching students about argument mapping it is helpful to first distinguish the following component parts of an argument and to provide examples of each:

- *Contention/conclusion* (a singular claim being argued for);
- *Reasons* (a set of claims working together to support a conclusion or sub-conclusion);
- *Objections* (a claim, or set of claims working together to oppose or undermine a conclusion, another reason, or an inference);
- *Inference* (a logical move or progression from reasons to contention);
- *Inference indicator words* (a word or phrase that identifies a logical progression from reasons to a contention, such as 'because', 'therefore' or 'it can be concluded that');
- *Evidential sources taken as the endpoint of a line of reasoning* (arguments must end somewhere, and often this will be a source of information, e.g., a media report, or an expert opinion, that we expect people to accept without the need for additional argument).

3.1.1 Claims

Argument mapping concerns itself with relationships between claims or propositions. The first main challenge is to discuss with students the nature of claims. Experience in teaching argument mapping has shown us that students find this concept problematic, and, if students are unclear about claims, they cannot easily create argument maps.

How can the notion of a claim be taught to students? One might start with definitions such as:

- *A claim is a declarative sentence that has a truth value;* or
- *A claim is an assertion that can be agreed with or disagreed with (or partly agreed with).*

Often, however, students find such definitions difficult to grasp. It is best to start with examples of simple empirical statements using the first definition above. Model claims can be instructive here, along with a discussion about the states of affairs that can establish if and whether certain sentences can be said to be true or false (or empirically uncertain):

- *The door is shut.* (This might be true, false, or empirically unclear, i.e., when viewed from an angle).

- *Donald Trump was elected President of the United States.* (This is clearly true, and there are a number of facts that make it so.)

- *Sally is at McDonald's.* (This could be determined by observational evidence and perhaps knowledge of Sally dining habits.)

- *Acid turns blue litmus paper red.* (This could be determined by various procedures used in the science of Chemistry.)

Students should then be encouraged to find similar claims in published literature. They should practice reading passages from texts, paying attention to whether the claims meet the standard criteria. The criteria are as follows.
Claims should be:

- Singular declarative sentences (i.e., not making more than one point);

- Complete sentences (not fragments);

- Precisely expressed with a potential truth value (not vague or ambiguous);

- Free of inference indicator words.

Once simple empirical claims are successfully used to clarify the notion of the claim, instructors can begin to use examples less reliant on a truth value, i.e., claims more subject to dispute and more likely to engender arguments. The second definition of a claim is apposite here: *an assertion that can be agreed with or disagreed with* (or partly agreed with). For example:

- *In a democracy, the poor have more power than the rich.*

This is not a simple empirical claim (there is no discoverable fact of the matter) yet it is a claim with a potential truth value—even if this is not easily ascertained. While not a claim with an empirical basis, the same criteria for claims still apply. Examples like this can lead to many useful departure points for instruction and debate.

Once appraised of the distinction between an empirical claim and a contestable claim, one can introduce the distinction between claims and reasons.

This is where inference indicator words become important. For example, it would be a mistake to include the following inference as a single claim in an argument map, because it contains two claims connected by the inference indicator 'because'.

- *In a democracy the poor have more power than the rich, because there are more of them.*

i.e., not:

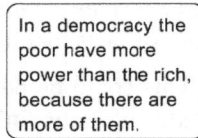

but instead:

Figure 3. A claim compared to a contention with a reason

It should be made clear to students that there should be no reasoning going on *inside* a claim box. Students should watch out for typical inference indicator terms that occur in passages of text such as: *so, since, consequently, therefore, as a result/consequence, in view of the fact that, as shown by* (see Table 2, p. 134). These terms are represented as relationships between the claims and their location in the map rather than in the premise boxes themselves. *Because* in this example becomes an inference indicator (not part of the statement), and any claims in boxes are rendered as complete sentences (not fragments). This is important to stress because the argument mapping software doesn't check what the students put into the claim boxes. Without instructor input, students can create unintelligible maps because they put either multiple claims into each box or ungrammatical or fragmentary sentences that don't have a potential truth value.

It is also important to make clear to students that claims are *not* questions, commands, demands, exhortations, warnings, and so on. *Shut the door!* (a demand) is not a claim as it is not potentially true or false. Similarly, interrogative forms such as: *Is Sally going to McDonald's?* is not a claim. (One cannot ask: Is the question: *"Is Sally going to McDonald's?"* true or false?) By contrast, one can establish the truth of the assertion: *Sally is at McDonald's.* Practice should be emphasised in establishing claims in key passages of text, identifying non-claims, and turning non-claims into claims.

It is generally helpful to make sure that claims are singular statements and do not include conjunctions (e.g., *and, but, moreover*) though there is nothing logically wrong with putting conjunctions into an argument map. Conjunctions are permitted in a single claim box if they *expand* or elaborate on a singular claim rather than add another. If they *add* another claim they must be treated differently. For example, take *Socrates is a man but he is not famous.* This is two separate claims: *Socrates is a man* AND *Socrates is not famous*—the first true; the second clearly false, and in an argument map we generally shouldn't conflate them. These would be represented in separate claim boxes.

It is also important to stress that claims are always complete sentences. They should also be *clearly* potentially true or false: *Reshine moisturiser may make you look better* is not even a potentially clear claim (how would one decide if it is true or false?) whereas the more precise *Reshine moisturiser will make all your wrinkles disappear from your face within 24 hours* is a claim that is much easier to verify or falsify. Moreover, it seems to beg a reason (e.g., that Reshine moisturiser might have exfoliate properties) and this suggests at least that there might be some science behind this. In the latter case, but not the former, there is—potentially at least—a fact of the matter that can be empirically determined. All claims can be mapped, but those with reasons and evidentiary support will inevitably be seen as much stronger—as they should.

The distinction between (a) simple empirical claims; (b) contestable claims that unclearly expressed; and (c) clearly expressed contestable claims which potentially admit of reasons that could be potentially true or false, is fundamental to argument mapping and time needs to be given to explore the differences.

These points are important to establish early in argument mapping as one of the ways in which students can fail to map arguments properly is either by (a) constructing a map without claims at all; (b) using unclear claims or truth-dubious claims; or (c) putting more than one claim inside a reason, objection or contention box. Any of these can lead to poorly constructed maps. Argument mapping can help students understand why these problems are important, but the software doesn't assess students' work for these problems. Some programs however offer online tutorials[2] that cover some of these points. Importantly, students should be given time to play around with the argument

---

[2] https://www.rationaleonline.com/docs/en/tutorials#tvy5fw

mapping software being used, and to practice putting claims into boxes. Simple examples of prose, e.g., from Letters to the Editor, advertising slogans, or extracts from academic texts can be used for this purpose.

4. Sources of evidence and the provisional endpoints of arguments

Arguments and argument maps need to stop somewhere and where possible it is good practice to finish a line of reasoning with an evidence source that is uncontentious and can be accepted without further debate. Evidential sources come in many forms. For example, a person might accept the claim that he or she has disease x because they trust the expert opinion of their doctor. Evidence sources include assertions, data, common belief, case studies, legal judgements, expert opinion, personal experience, quotes, statistics, and so on. The argument mapping software *Rationale*™ allows users to represent sources of evidence as unique claim boxes that can be used to clearly mark the current endpoint of a line of reasoning (see Figures 4 and 5 below).

Of course, whether a source of evidence is uncontentious or not is provisional, and this provisional nature make the notion of an endpoint to an argument difficult to teach to students. Teachers need to make the point clear to students that *context matters* when deciding if a particular source of evidence can be used as an endpoint in an argument. It is probably fine to take the testimony of one's housemate that there is no milk in the fridge, but it is not acceptable to take for granted the assertion that Donald Trump is a part of a conspiracy of reptilian space aliens trying to take over the planet. It probably helps to reassure students that deciding on an acceptable endpoint to their argument is a very difficult thing to do and they can always revise their argument map at a later point in time if they tied off a line of debate too quickly.

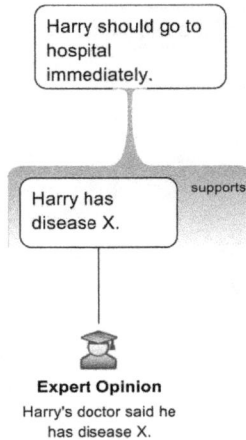

Figure 4. Example of source of evidence used to end a line of reasoning. The argument mapping software Rationale™ has unique icons for different sources.

5. Arguments

Once the notion of a claim is clear, the concept of an argument needs to be introduced and applied using CAAM software. The notion of an argument, like the notion of claim, may also need some explanation. An argument *qua* an unpleasant interpersonal quarrel between individuals, is in such common use that it can be hard for students to see the alternative. The philosophical concept of an argument is typically defined as *a connected series of claims intending to establish some conclusion,* or variations on this, e.g., *a sequence of claims with an inference i.e., a logical move, to a conclusion/contention.* Students should be taught to appreciate that while claims are singular propositions only, arguments are—by definition—claims for which reason(s) are given. [See Chapters 8 and 9.]

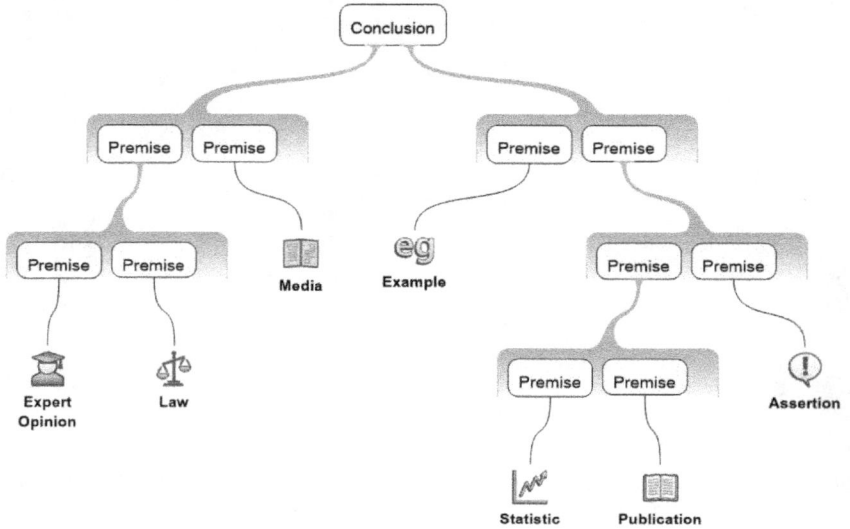

Figure 5. Ideally, a good argument map requires all premises to be either supported by further reasoning or provisional sources of evidence.

5.1 Simple, Complex and Multi-Layer Arguments

Early on, the distinction between *simple* and *complex* arguments should be made clear. A simple argument is one for which a single reason is given; a complex, or multi-reason argument—as the name suggests—is one with a set of reasons supporting a contention. Here is an example of each:

Figure 6. Simple argument with a single reason

Figure 7. Complex argument with more than one reason

A key pitfall for students is in telling whether an argument has separate reasons working independently (as in this last example) or whether the reasons work together as dependent *co-premises*. We return to this later.

As students advance their understanding of argument mapping, *multi-layer* arguments can be introduced. These arguments have primary reasons supported by secondary level reasons.

An example is provided below. Here it should be noted that the contention of one argument can become a premise of another argument (see Figures 9 and 10 on the next page):

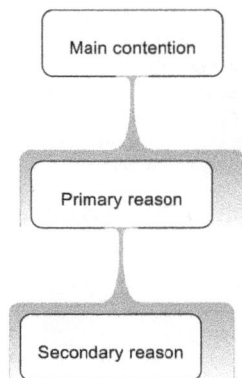

Figure 8. A multi-layer argument

It takes a great deal of practice for students to accurately reconstruct multi-layer arguments from a passage of raw text. Gratuitous assumptions are often made in authentic prose, premises are left out, and connections between premises and contentions are not clear. The job of the argument mapper is to make all connections between reasons and contentions, and between primary and secondary-level reasons very explicit. There is no substitute for a skilful pedagogy that builds student's skills from achieving competence in analysing and reconstructing simple and complex arguments, eventually to multi-layer arguments (naturally, mapping an argument does not imply one agrees with it):

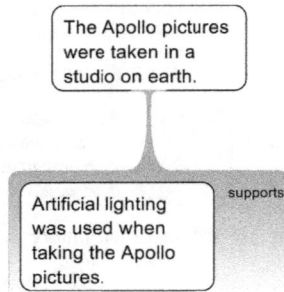

Figure 9. Example of a simple argument

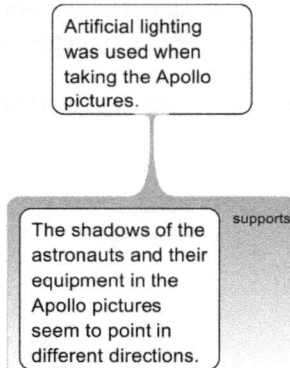

Figure 10. Using a premise in one argument as a contention in another

Expressed as a single multi-level argument, the two arguments in Figure 9 and Figure 10 become:

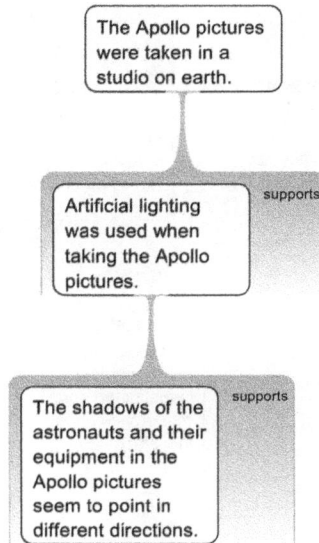

Figure 11. Example of a multilevel argument

6. Objections

The notion of an *objection* can be generally explained without difficulty as it mirrors the structure of reasons. Indeed, objections are simply reasons *against* something, and likewise, come in simple, complex and multi-layer variations.

When discussing objections, it should be made clear to students that objections can be supported by reasons—reasons here provide evidence that suggests an objection is a good one. For example, see Figure 12.

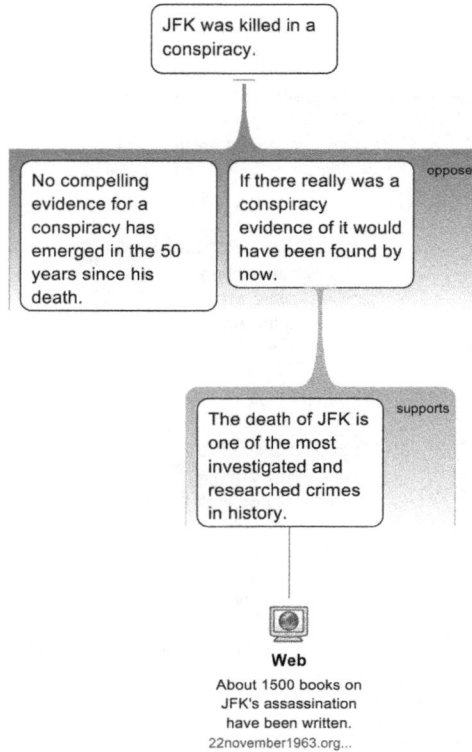

Figure 12. Supported objection

7. Ambiguity

Students should be made aware that very often passages of text are ambiguous. Argument mapping has to deal with such ambiguities. Is the following example a singular claim, or a claim for which a reason is given (an argument)? i.e., is it best rendered as a simple conditional claim?

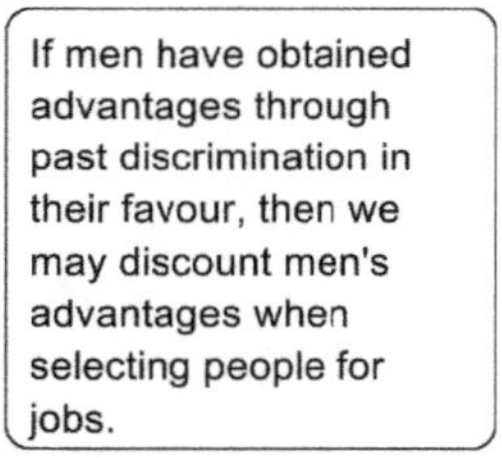

Figure 13. A conditional claim

Or should it be rendered as an argument (a contention with a premise offered in support of it)?:

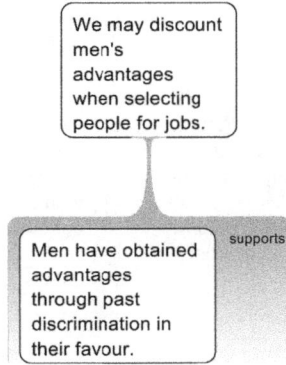

Figure 14. Example of a simple argument

Such examples are often context-dependent; a function of whether the author is trying to *convince* the reader of something, or whether they are merely asserting something. Class time should be devoted to looking at passages of text, establishing whether they are arguments or mere assertions and translating them into the argument mapping software.

As well as statements that could be arguments, there are also arguments that have implicit inferences that need elucidation. This phenomenon is very common. For example:

- *If you want a new car, now is the time and Hindmarsh is the place.*

This advertising slogan for a Building Society money-lender is probably best interpreted (charitably) as an argument, not merely a conditional statement. It is trying to convince us of something. Context, and knowledge of the role of money-lenders in society can help interpret it. A moment's reflection will tell us that the passage is trying to convince us that *we should borrow money from Hindmarsh*. Unfortunately for students, this contention is not present in the passage but must be gleaned from it. Indeed, the passage also intimates *we want a new car!* What seems like a simple conditional assertion appears to be a subtle argument with an intermediate conclusion and number of assumed premises. A possible interpretation of the argument is represented using the argument mapping software *Rationale*™ in Figure 15 on the next page.

No argument software can assist on its own with the interpretation of difficult passages of text like this, and an instructor's role is essential (Note that argument mapping convention requires that implicit or hidden claims, when explicated, are expressed in square brackets […].).

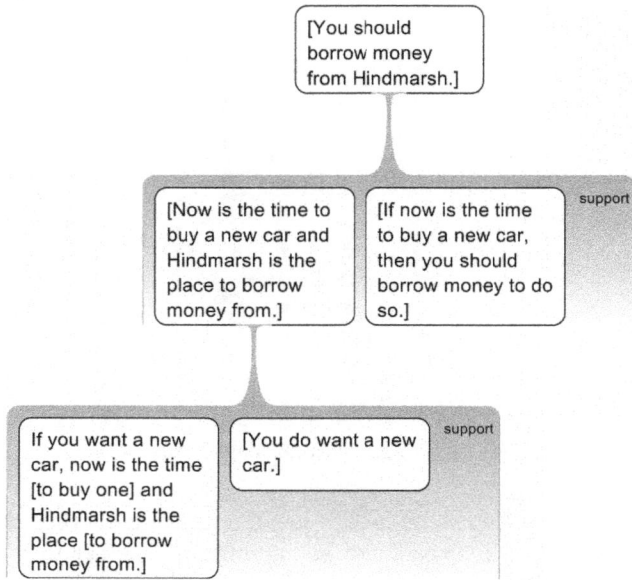

Figure 15. Complex enthymematic argument

Exposure to many different texts, and teaching sensitivity to argument context, can help. For example, the following advertising slogan:

• *The bigger the burger the better the burger, and the burgers are bigger at [Hungry] Jack's.*

conceals an implicit conclusion: *So/Therefore the burgers are better at [Hungry] Jack's.* Not including the contention renders the passage as a simple assertion rather than what it really is, namely, an argument with an implied contention—and *a non-sequitur* at that!

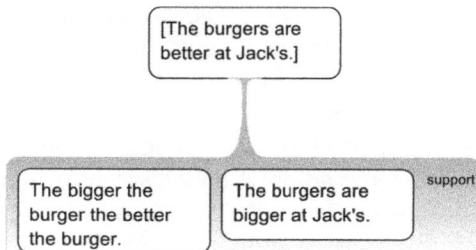

Figure 16. Simpler enthymematic argument

Enthymematic arguments (with suppressed claims) are difficult for students, and are commonplace in reasoning. In this example, these premises work together as co-premises to support the (implied) contention. We shall discuss how to deal with these below.

As well as dealing with enthymematic arguments, mapping is also helpful in clearly identifying and exposing instances of circular reasoning—where question-begging supporting reasons are provided, as Figure 17 indicates.

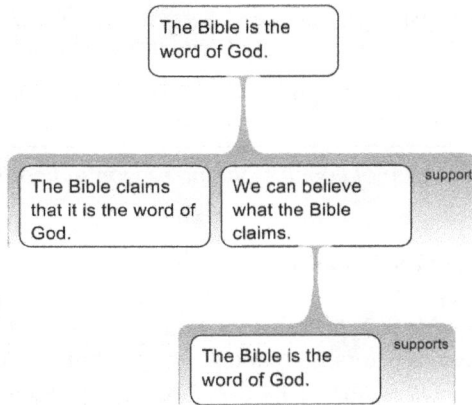

Figure 17. Example of a circular argument

8. Inference indicators

Early in class instruction it is important to introduce the idea of an *inference indicator.* There are two types: (a) reason indicators and (b) conclusion indicators. The difference between them is the role they play in an argument. It should be demonstrated how these words and phrases have different grammatical roles too. Reason indicators such as *because* point to the reason in a grammatical construction; conclusion indicators (like *so* and *therefore*) point to the contention. The role they play in sentence construction can be introduced and it can be shown how they can be transposed (see Tables 1 and 2 below).

Students should learn the different kinds of indicators to help determine what a reason is and what a conclusion is. They should be given practice in translating passages like these into simply box and arrow diagrams, or—if they are confident—into argument maps. A table showing how the indictors work can be helpful here (the examples provided below are not exhaustive).

Conclusion indicator pointing to a conclusion	...can be transposed to a reason indicator pointing to a reason
The crops failed [implies] the Sun God is angry.	*The Sun God is angry [since] the crops failed.*
He had a low mark [consequently] he failed.	*He failed, [as shown by] his low mark.*
A strong work ethic [strongly suggests that] one will be successful.	*Success in life is [strongly suggested by] one's work ethic.*
You want to get a High Distinction [therefore] you should study hard.	*You should study hard [because] you want to get a High Distinction*

Table 1. Transposition of conclusion and reason indicator words within sentences

At present, CAAM software has a limited range of inference indicators mostly using *because* or the neutral term *supports* exclusively (i.e., premise X *supports* contention Y; or X *because* Y). Students need to be able to translate the many inference indicators used in text into the blunt categories offered by CAAM software. This is one of its drawbacks. Future developments might address this. Given present limitations, it is important that students understand how to interpret ordinary language arguments replete in inference indicators of different kinds. Nothing substitutes for class work using passages of text that illuminate the many examples of indicator words in use.

Conclusion indicators	Premise indicators
Implies	Since
Therefore	As shown by
Hence	For
Thus	As
As shown by	In view of the fact that
So	Because
Consequently	Seeing that
It can be seen that	Is strongly suggested by
Strongly suggests that	

Table 2. Commonly-used conclusion and reason indicator words

9. Over-interpretation of inference indicators

When students are sufficiently informed about inference indicators, they can be prone to overuse their relevance and see arguments when they are not there. This is something the instructor needs to be wary of as well. Take, for example, the sentence: *Sally said she was hungry before, so that is why you can see her eating a sandwich now.* This appears to have an inference connector, "so", but the "so" functions grammatically to connect an explanation to an observation, not as an inference indicator. The passage is not *concluding* that you can see Sally eating a sandwich. Similarly, *Synonyms are good servants but bad masters, therefore select them with care.* This is not proffering a contention; it is best interpreted as a subtle piece of advice. Inference indicator words are thus not always indicating an inference (neither is the indictor word *thus* in that sentence). There is a difference between their use in inference-making and their use in grammatical construction. Again, lots of text-based practice is needed.

10. Tiers of Reasons/Objections: A procedural approach to argument mapping

We have mentioned that arguments can be represented in terms of tiers of reasons and objections in the form of multi-layered arguments. It is very easy for students to become overwhelmed by the difficulty of this task. How is this best taught and what are the things to watch out for?

As always, it is best to start with simple examples and then attempt more complex examples. The following example, the kind of thing to be found in a 'Letter to the Editor', provides an instructive case.

* *Dogs fetch balls and cats don't, so you can play with dogs. I mean, who'd disagree with that? It's obvious isn't it? You can't play with cats, of course. They are too stuck up. Dogs clearly make better pets.*

It is clearly an argument. How can one map it to clearly display the reasoning? To establish this, it is best to ask students to follow a series of steps. This is important as there is a strong tendency for students to jump into the task of mapping a passage without clearly thinking through the text, nor establishing the connections between the component parts of an argument.

Here is a suggested step-by-step approach that could be used with students to help them understand arguments. It is a good idea to ask students to follow these steps for any argument under consideration:

Step 1: Number the independent claims in any passage of text, ensuring that each claim is a singular statement or proposition. Assess each claim dispassionately. Ignore filler words like "Also", "however", or "clearly" which are not germane to the argument.

Upon completing this it is useful to:

> *Step 2:* Establish the conclusion, which often needs to be ascertained without the help of inference indicators. Ask yourself: *What's the point?* Say *Convince me!* The contention being argued for will typically emerge naturally. Place this at the top of the map in a contention box (Note: it is possible to invert argument maps in some software, displaying contentions horizontally.)

This step is followed by:

> *Step 3:* Eliminate redundancy. Ensure that each claim is a complete sentence and the text under consideration consists of stand-alone claims.

Eliminating the redundant expressions not germane to the argument, and the questions (non-claims), we get the following:

> *<1>Dogs fetch balls and cats don't, so <2>you can play with dogs. I mean, who'd disagree with that? It's obvious isn't it? <3>You can't play with cats, of course. They are too stuck up. <4>Dogs clearly make better pets.*

The claims are as follows:

1. Dogs fetch balls and cats don't
2. You can play with dogs
3. You can't play with cats
4. Dogs make better pets

Using the *What's the point?* test mentioned above, the conclusion reveals itself to be the last claim <4>. This is placed at the top of the map, but how are the reasons supporting it to be arranged? The temptation might be that there are two independent reasons supporting the contention: *You can play with dogs* and *You can't play with cats.*

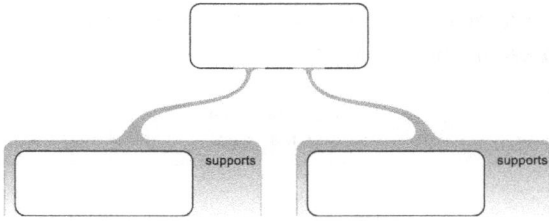

Figure 18. Complex argument

But this representation of the argument is missing something. What is to be done with claim <1> *Dogs fetch balls but cats don't?* At this point attention should be drawn to the inference indicator "so" that seems to draw a conclusion, i.e., it is not merely functioning grammatically in the sentence. But this "so" is clearly not an inference to claim <4>; it appears to be an inference to an intermediate conclusion that consists of claim <2> and thus should thus be represented in a multi-level argument like the maps below (Figures 19 and 20).

On reflection, it can be seen that that the two supporting reasons <2> and <3> are best rendered as a single claim—an intermediate conclusion (they are both making a point about "playing")—and the claim about "fetching" can be seen as reasoned support for this. This captures the intended use of the connector word "so" linking <1> to <2>.

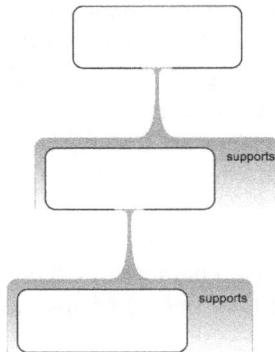

Figure 19. Multi-level argument

There is thus another rule to consider:

Step 4: Combine like claims into a single claim if they are making the same point.

The resulting argument map provides a clear example of serial reasoning that accurately represents the case being made:

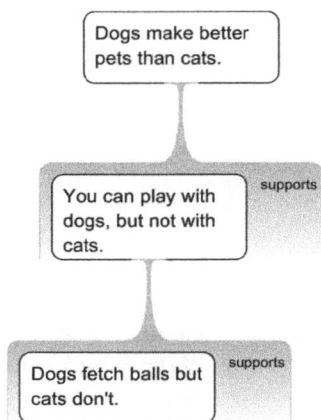

Figure 20. The argument exposed

In the case of more complex arguments additional principles need to be followed.

11. The principle of abstraction

A very useful guideline for argument mapping is the *principle of abstraction*. In many cases, the higher the claim in a multi-layered argument the greater the degree of abstraction; or to put it differently, the lower the claim the more specific it should be. In the above example, "playing" is more abstract than "fetching balls", and both claims are less abstract than "better pet". They provide serial support for each other. Students should be guided in how to apply this principle, as without this, maps can become a jumble of disorganized claims with no clear hierarchical structure. Once again, this requires practice and students should be given a number of exercises where they are required to rank claims in terms of their degree of abstraction. To our series of rules we can add the following:

> *Step 5:* Generally try to ensure that higher-level claims are more abstract than lower-level claims

12. The principle of level consistency

Complex arguments have both a vertical and a horizontal axis. Arguments can be multi-layered along the vertical axis (as we have just seen), but premises are present along a horizontal axis as well. Insofar as many premises can be brought to bear in an argument it is important to stress another principle, the *principle of level consistency.* Within each horizontal level, reasons or objections should be approximately of equal weighting in terms of their abstraction or generality. In the argument below this rule is not adhered to and is consequently hard to interpret.

The argument is improved by subordinating lower-level claims to a more general claim at the middle-level, and ensuring level consistency at the lower level, as shown on Figure 22.

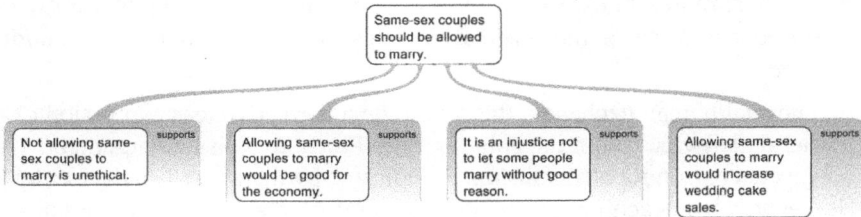

Figure 21. Lack of level consistency

Paying attention to the principle of level consistency we get:

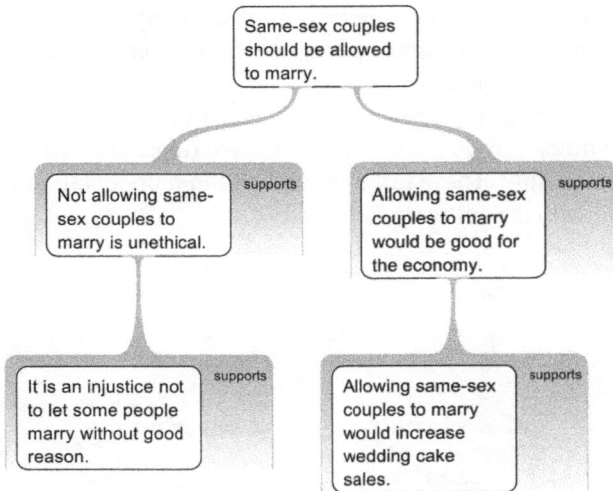

Figure 22. Applying level consistency

We can thus add another guideline:

Step 6: Aim for an equal weighting of premises in terms of level of generality across the horizontal axis of a multi-premise argument.

13. Missing Premises

Teaching students how to look out for missing premises is complex, but there are strategies that can help. It is difficult because reasoning is often replete in missing premises. Indeed, it is *very rare* that all premises are made explicit in reasoning. This is due to the implicit reliance of speakers or writers on the background beliefs assumed to be shared in any argumentative exchange. Here is a simple example.

- *Art must represent the world if it is to appeal to a broad audience for generations to come. So that's why* Blue Poles *will not appeal to a broad audience.*

In a normal human exchange, this would be a perfectly clear expression of a (rather dated) view about the painting *Blue Poles*. It is also an argument. We are given a reason for a conclusion, as indicated by the words "so that's why". However, when teaching argument mapping it is an example of an argument with a missing premise; a premise that needs to be exposed, and made clear. What, precisely, is being argued?

In this case, it is easy to see what is missing. It is the assumption that *Blue Poles does not represent the world.* Exposing this missing premise allows it to be evaluated, confirmed or rejected. In this example, the missing premise can stated quite easily; in simple passages, this is often the case. But for more complex reasoning a series of steps need to be followed to ensure all missing premises are catered for. Fortunately, there is a very simple way to establish missing premises. This is done by applying two rules: *the Rabbit Rule* and *the Holding Hands Rule*. These rules are outlined in more detail in online tutorials available with the software *Rationale*™.

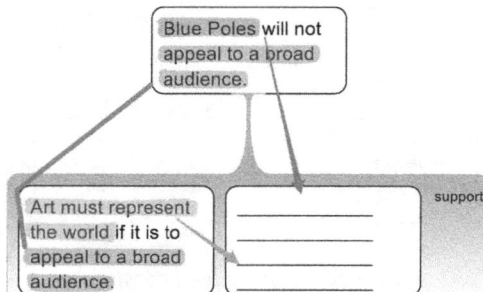

Figure 23. Determining a missing premise

14. Assumptions and how to find them using the Rabbit Rule and Holding Hands Rule

The Rabbit Rule is applied (vertically) to the inferential link between conclusion and the premises. This rule states that no conclusion should come out of thin air. (No rabbits out of hats!) The conclusion terms *appeal to a broad audience* appears in the available premise. We therefore know that *Blue Poles* must be supplied to the missing premise.

The Holding Hands Rule is applied horizontally between premises to any remaining terms after the Rabbit Rule has been applied (that is, if a term is not already supplied by means of the Rabbit Rule). The remaining terms must "hold hands" with another premise. No term can appear in one premise alone—there is always a companion term "holding hands". In this example, we can see that *Art must represent the world* appears in the one premise, so too it must be present in the missing premise (see Figure 23). As the argument is *negating* something about *Blue Poles,* we similarly apply a corresponding negation to the terms of the missing premise. So *Blue Poles does not represent the world.*

We can add the following to our list of procedural rules to establish missing premises:

Step 7: Apply the Rabbit Rule and the Holding Hands Rule to make missing premises explicit in an argument map.

The argument can be expressed as follows:

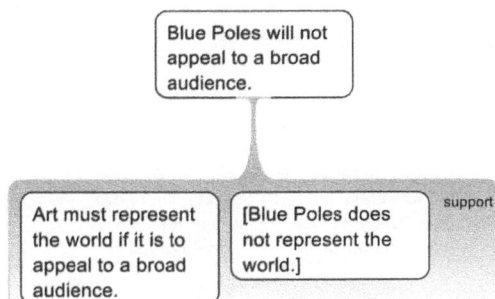

Figure 24. The argument exposed

It may not have escaped notice that the two claims that support the above contention are *jointly* necessary for the conclusion to follow. Strictly speaking they are not two *independent* reasons supporting the conclusion, but are co-premises that jointly support the conclusion. This raises the important issue of co-premises or "linked" premises. This is another crucial methodological principle that students find difficult. Consider the following example:

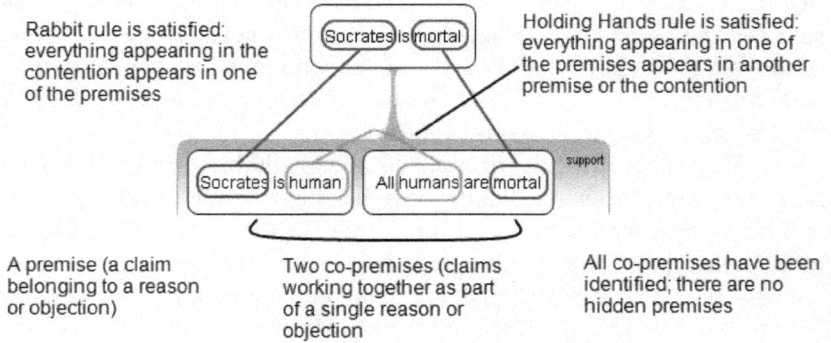

Figure 25. The Rabbit and Holding Hands rules

The above example (Figure 25) of a famous deductively valid argument in Philosophy demonstrates how both the Rabbit Rule and the Holding Hands Rule are satisfied. It also demonstrates an example of co-premises in action.

A co-premise is when two or more premises are jointly necessary for the truth of the conclusion. Co-premises are often enthymematic and sometimes a co-premise is trivial. For example, a person who reasons that they should rent a house because they should find a place to live as quickly as possible, tacitly assumes that renting a house is quickest way of finding a place to live.

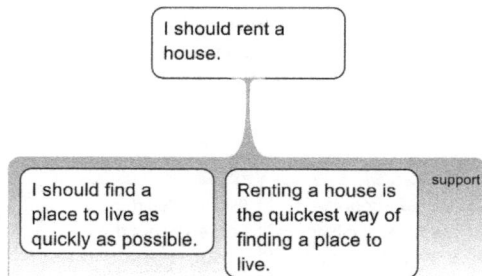

Figure 26. Example co-premise

Such assumed claims are often tacit in arguments in both writing and speech, and are often so trivial they do not need to be stated. However, they are an important feature of arguments. Indeed, every argument has at least two of them. In CAAM this is often the called "The Golden Rule": *every argument has at least two co-premises.* In the example in Figure 27, we have extended the argument in Figure 20 by the addition of enthymematic co-premises.

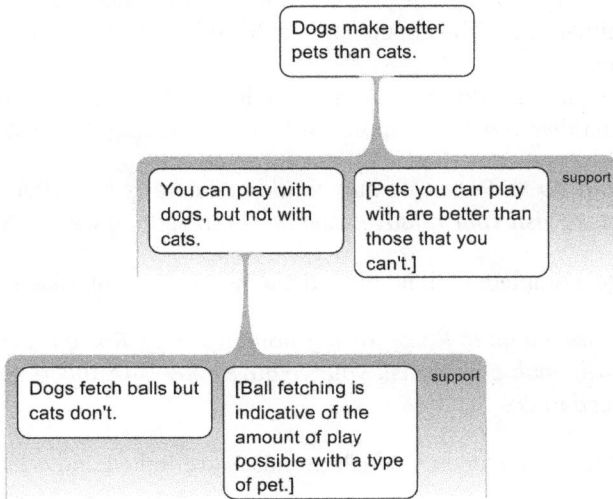

```
                    ┌─────────────────┐
                    │ Dogs make better│
                    │ pets than cats. │
                    └─────────────────┘
```

┌──────────────────┐   ┌──────────────────┐ support
│ You can play with│   │ [Pets you can play│
│ dogs, but not with│ │ with are better than│
│ cats.   │   │ those that you   │
└──────────────────┘   │ can't.]   │
                       └──────────────────┘

┌──────────────────┐   ┌──────────────────┐ support
│ Dogs fetch balls but│ │ [Ball fetching is │
│ cats don't.   │   │ indicative of the │
└──────────────────┘   │ amount of play   │
                       │ possible with a type│
                       │ of pet.]   │
                       └──────────────────┘

Figure 27. The Golden Rule applied

While ubiquitous in reasoning, co-premises are not always uncontroversial. Often, co-premises conceal hidden assumptions that are false or misleading. This is why it is good argument mapping practice to expose them. For example, it need not be accepted (without evidence—or even intuitively) that *Pets that you can play with make better pets than those you can't [play with]* (elderly people, the infirm or disabled, for example, like more docile pets). Being able to expose hidden assumption clearly for the purpose of critiquing them is a major advantage of argument mapping. Argument mapping software makes identification and representation of hidden claims easier by using color conventions and shading; however, this does not help students deciding how to determine how to locate a co-premise in a passage of text. Clear instruction and LAMP is needed. Probably the best way to approach co-premises in the classroom is to begin by discussing the differences between complex reasoning and linked reasoning.

15. Co-premises (Linked reasoning)

Students find the distinction between linked reasoning (dependent premises) and complex reasoning (independent premises) hard to grasp. It is best taught by showing students a number of multi-premise arguments and asking them to classify examples of complex and linked reasoning. In the "same sex" example given earlier (Figure 22, p. 139), it is fairly easy to see that the supporting premises are independent and not necessary for each other.

Plausibly, neither premise could be true or both could; or one could be true, and the other false. If any one premise was true the conclusion could sensibly follow in either case. The conclusion could follow even if one of the claims was missing.

In other examples, co-premises are needed as the claims are not independent of each other and are examples of linked reasoning. For instance:

- *We should go to Rome for our holidays. Rome is beautiful. Also it will enable us to visit your relatives and this is something we really need to do.*

The passage, complete with numbered claims, would look like this:

- *<1> We should go to Rome for our holidays. <2> Rome is beautiful. ~~Also~~ <3> it will enable us to visit your relatives ~~and~~ <4> this is something we really need to do.*

How can one teach students which premises are linked and which are independent?

To our set of suggested procedural rules discussed earlier, we can add another step:

Step 8: Establish if any of the claims are linked or whether they stand-alone. Do this by assessing whether the conclusion can follow if any one of the claims was missing or false.

In convergent (or divergent) reasoning, none of the claims are dependent on any other claim; either one of the claims might support the conclusion alone. By contrast, in linked reasoning, the claims are not independent; they are necessary for each other for the conclusion to follow.

In the example above the claim *Rome is beautiful* is an independent reason (it does not depend on visiting relatives) and the contention *We should go to Rome for our holidays* can be supported by it. The contention can follow from *Rome being beautiful* regardless of the other claims provided. However, the claims about visiting the relatives appear to be linked. The claim: *This is something [Visiting your relatives] we really need to do* will not alone support the conclusion without including the claim *It [Visiting Rome] will enable us to visit your relatives*. Note however, this relationship is not symmetrical. Premise <3> *can* support the contention without premise <4>. However, <4> can't without <3>. If one premise can't support a conclusion without another premise, they can be said to be "linked".

With <2> as an independent premise, and<3> and <4> being linked premises, the map would appear as in Figure 28.

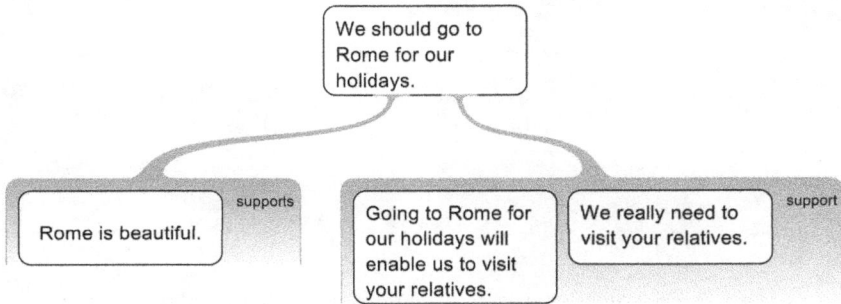

Figure 28. Example of linked reasons

A useful feature of argument mapping is the capacity to display linked premises in an intuitive visual way. Like other software, the software *Rationale*™ (used here) uses the color green for reasons and the color red for objections (the color orange is used exclusively for rebuttals, i.e., objections to objections). Co-premises are indicated by an umbrella shading that fades to white. This is a subtle visual indication that no argument is ever complete and more premises could potentially be added.

Objections too can be linked as co-premises as the following extension to the argument indicate. We have added a rebuttal against an objection (in orange) to demonstrate their use.

- *On the other hand <5> travelling to Rome is very expensive, primarily because <6> flights are so expensive. And <7>don't have a lot of money at the moment. But then again, <8> there is plenty of money in the children's bank account we could use.*

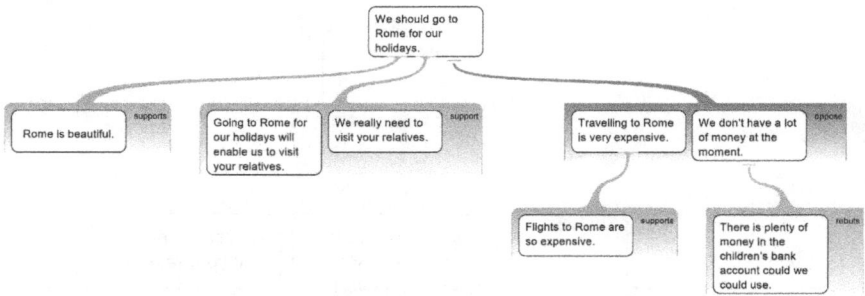

Figure 29. The argument exposed (with linked reasons and linked objections)

Note here that the claim that *Travelling to Rome is very expensive* could well object to the conclusion alone, but premise <7> could not (without premise <6>). The premises under consideration must *independently* support the conclusion to stand as independent reasons. If this is not the case, the premises are said to be linked.

16. A brief history of argument mapping

Argument mapping can be traced to the work of Richard Whately in his *Elements of Logic* (1834/1826) but his notation was not widely adopted. In the early twentieth century, John Henry Wigmore mapped legal reasoning using numbers to indicate premises (Wigmore, 1913; Wigmore, 1931). Monroe Beardsley developed this, and it became standard model of an argument map (Beardsley, 1950). On this approach, premises are numbered, a legend is provided to the claims identified by the numbers, and *serial, divergent and convergent* reasoning can be clearly represented. An example of each of these forms of reasoning using the standard model is provided below.

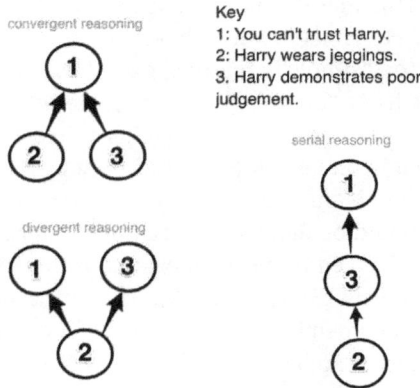

Figure 30. Serial, divergent and convergent maps using the Beardsley model

This model is still widely used and is advantageous in contexts where students are required to produce argument maps without access to software (e.g., in paper-based logic and reasoning exams under timed conditions).

In 1958, Stephen Toulmin devised another model of an argument map that included the notion of a "warrant" (which licenses the inference from the reasons, which he called "data", to the claim), "backing" (which provides the authority for the warrant), modal qualifiers (such as "probably"), and "rebuttals" (which mention conditions restricting the inference) (Toulmin, 1958).

An example of a Toulmin map is provided in Figure 31.

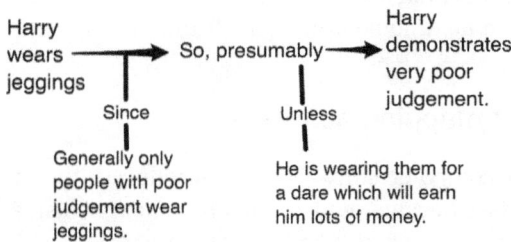

Figure 31. Example of a Toulmin map

In 1973, Stephen N. Thomas refined Beardsley's approach (Thomas, 1997/ 1973). Thomas included in his approach the important notion of "linked" arguments where two or more premises work together to support a conclusion (the distinction between dependent and independent premises having being described earlier). This innovation made it feasible for arguments to include "hidden" premises. He is also said to have introduced the terms "argument diagram", "basic" (or "simple") reasons, i.e., those not supported by other reasons (as distinct from "complex" reasons). He also made the distinction between "intermediate" conclusions (a conclusion reached before a final conclusion) and a "final" conclusion (not used to support another conclusion). Thomas also suggested including objections as reasons *against* a proposition, and that these too should be included in argument maps.

In 1976, Michael Scriven proposed a procedure for mapping that could be recommended to students (Scriven, 1976). This involved a number of steps: (1) writing out the statements in an argument; (2) clarifying their meaning; (3) listing the statements, including any hidden claims; and (4) using numbers for premises along the lines of the Beardsley-Thomas model. In the case of hidden assumptions, Scriven's notation used an alphabetical letter to distinguish hidden assumptions from explicit reasons. Scriven also emphasized the importance of a rebuttal in argument mapping, a notion identified earlier by Thomas.

In the 1990s a number of innovations occurred. Robert Horn helped popularize the notion of an argument map by producing idiosyncratic, large-format argument diagrams on key issues in philosophy such as "Can Computers Think?" (Horn, 1999; Horn, 2003). These maps did not adopt either the standard model or Toulmin-style notation for mapping arguments, but did use arrows and pictures to make the content clear, making it obvious for the first time that argument maps could be visually interesting as well as informative. These were distributed widely and used in class teaching. In addition, computer software programs began to be developed. This was important, as dedicated argument mapping software allowed premises to be composed, edited and placed within an argument map, as distinct from a legend alongside the map.

17. Argument mapping software

Once dedicated computer software was introduced, the standard model of numbered premises became outdated in all contexts outside its use in examinations. Several iterations of mapping software were developed in Australia and the U.S.A. with increasingly greater levels of sophistication. Tim van Gelder developed *Rationale*™ and *bCisive*™, the former designed as a basic argument mapping software, the latter designed for business decision-making applications (van Gelder, 2007, 2013). Both were later purchased by Dutch company Kritisch Denken BV.

A variety of argument mapping packages are now available, including *Araucaria, Compendium, Logos, Argunet, Theseus, Convince Me, LARGO,*

Athena, Carneades and *SEAS*. These range from single-user software such as *Rationale™, Convince Me* and *Athena*; to small group software such as *Digalo, QuestMap, Compendium, Belvedere,* and *AcademicTalk*; to collaborative online debating tools for argumentation such as *Debategraph* and *Collaboratorium*. Enhancements to argument mapping software proceed apace. For example, there are moves to introduce a Bayesian network model to *Rationale™* to cater for probabilistic reasoning.

Rationale™ or *bCisive* are perhaps the easiest programs to use for teaching argument mapping, but they require a subscription. Excellent free alternatives include the Argument Visualization mode in the online *MindMup*: https://www.mindmup.com/tutorials/argument-visualization.html and the cross-platform desktop package iLogos: https://oli.cmu.edu/courses/argument-diagramming-open-free/ and new-comer: Kialo: https://www.kialo.com/

18. Argument mapping class room examples

There are a number of free argument resources available online.

- The designers of *Rationale™* made tutorials to be used with their software. https://www.rationaleonline.com/docs/en/tutorials#tvy5fw

- Simon Cullen, who helped design the *MindMup* argument visualisation function, has posted some of the activities he uses for teaching philosophical arguments using argument maps. http://www.philmaps.com

19. Conclusion

In this chapter we have covered some of the basic concepts and considerations that teachers need to be aware of when using CAAM in the classroom. A set of procedural steps was suggested that is recommended for use with students. Understanding claims and arguments and how they are structured is only the start. Students should also be aware of how to interpret inference indicators, construct and analyse simple, complex and multi-layer arguments, and be able to integrate objections and rebuttals. They should be wary of misusing inference indicators, confusing reasons with evidence for reasons, and misinterpreting independent reasons for co-premises. There is much more we could have discussed. We have not touched on the use of inference objections (in contrast to premise objections). We have not mentioned argument webs or chains of reasoning, nor have we discussed in detail the appropriate ways to integrate evidence into an argument. However, it should be clear from this brief outline how CAAM can assist students in disentangling arguments in everyday prose—replete, as it often is, with non-sequiturs, repetition, irrelevancies, unstated conclusions, and other infelicities.

References

Beardsley, M.C. (1950). *Practical logic*. New York: Prentice-Hall.

Davies, M. (2009). Computer-assisted argument mapping: A rationale approach. Higher Education, 58, 799-820. *Higher Education, 58*(6), 799-820.

Davies, M. (2011). Mind Mapping, Concept Mapping, Argument Mapping: What are the differences and do they matter? *Higher Education, 62*(3), 279-301.

Gelder, T. van (2007). The rationale for Rationale™. *Law, Probability and Risk, 6*, 23-42.

Gelder, T. van (2013). Rationale 2.0.10. Retrieved from http://rationale.austhink.com/download

Gelder, T.J. van (2015). Using argument mapping to improve critical thinking skills. In M. Davies and R. Barnett (Eds.), *The Palgrave Handbook of Critical Thinking in Higher Education* (pp. 183-192). New York: Palgrave MacMillan.

Harrell, M. (2008). No Computer program required: Even pencil-and-paper argument mapping improves critical-thinking skills. *Teaching Philosophy, 31*(4), 351-374.

Horn, R. (1999). *Can Computers Think?* : Macrovu.

Horn, R.E. (2003). Infrastructure for navigating interdisciplinary debates: Critical decisions for representing argumentation. In P.A. Kirschner, S.J.B. Shum and C.S. Carr (Eds.), *Visualizing argumentation: Software tools for collaborative and educational sense-making*. New York: Springer-Verlag.

Rider, Y. and Thomason, N. (2008). Cognitive and pedagogical benefits of argument mapping: L.A.M.P. guides the way to better thinking. In A. Okada, S. Buckingham Shum and T. Sherborne (Eds.), *Knowledge Cartography: Software Tools and Mapping Techniques* (pp. 113-130): Springer.

Scriven, M. (1976). *Reasoning*. New York: McGraw-Hill.

Thomas, S.N. (1997/1973). *Practical reasoning in natural language* (4th ed.). Upper Saddle River, NJ: Prentice-Hall.

Toulmin, S.E. (1958). *The uses of argument* (1st ed.). Cambridge: Cambridge University Press.

Whately, R. (1834/1826). *Elements of logic: comprising the substance of the article in the Encyclopædia metropolitana: with additions, &c.* (5th ed.). London: B. Fellowes.

Wigmore, J. (1913). The problem of proof. *Illinois Law Review, 8*, 77.

Wigmore, J. (1931). *The Science of Judicial Proof as Given by Logic, Psychology and General Experience and Illustrated in Judicial Trials* (2nd ed. Vol. Little, Brown and Co.): Boston.

About the authors:

Martin Davies is Principal Fellow in Higher Education in the Graduate School of Education at the University of Melbourne. He received the H. J. Allen Prize in Philosophy from the University of Adelaide in 2002. His work intersects philosophy and education, in particular, researching better ways of teaching critical thinking. He has a particular interest in computer-aided argument mapping. His most recent book is the edited collection (with Ronald Barnett): *The Palgrave Handbook of Critical Thinking in Higher Education* (2015). http://www.martindavies.com.au

Ashley Barnett has worked on several projects funded by the Intelligence Advanced Research Projects Activity (IARPA), including the design and evaluation of critical thinking and argument mapping courses for intelligence analysts. He enjoys making free online critical thinking and argument mapping courses.

Tim van Gelder is a Melbourne Enterprise Fellow in the School of Bio-Sciences, University of Melbourne, Australia. He is a Principal Investigator on the SWARM Project, a major effort to develop a cloud platform for collaborative analytical reasoning. He has contributed to the development of argument mapping tools and methods and research on the impact of their use on the development of critical thinking skills. His work has been funded by the Australian Research Council, including a Queen Elizabeth II Fellowship, and (currently) by IARPA, the US Intelligence Advanced Research Projects Activity. In addition to his academic activities he has considerable experience providing consulting and training services to large public and private sector organisations in areas such as reasoning, estimation, and decision making. He also keeps bees.

11

Argumentation Schemes and their Application in Argument Mining

Douglas Walton

Introduction

One aim of this chapter is to survey the resources available for the project of building a method using argumentation schemes that will be helpful for the purpose of identifying arguments in natural language discourse. A second aim is to formulate some specific problems that need to be overcome along the way to building the method. It is argued that such a method would be useful as a tool to help students of informal logic identify arguments of the kind they encounter in natural language texts, for example in newspapers, magazines or on the Internet.

The project is related to the development of argumentation systems in artificial intelligence. One of these technical initiatives, outlined in Section 7, is the project of building an automated tool for argument mining. The idea is that this tool could go onto the Internet and collect arguments of specifically designated types, like argument from expert opinion for example. These technical initiatives are connected to the aim of finding an exact method for argument identification in informal logic, because the most powerful method would likely turn out to be to combine both tasks. The most powerful method would have human users apply the automated tool to identify arguments on a tentative basis in a text, and then correct the errors made by the automated tool. It is not hard to see how even a semi-automated procedure of this kind would be extremely helpful for teaching courses in informal logic.

As teachers of logic courses well know, judging whether an argument in a given text of discourse fits some abstract form of reasoning is a sophisticated task that many beginning students in courses in argumentation and informal logic have recurring problems with. Such courses are based on the identification, analysis and evaluation of examples of arguments found in magazines, newspapers, and the Internet, or whatever other sources of text materials are available. It is necessary, in order to do an adequate job of teaching an informal logic course, to have access to examples of commonly used arguments, and especially types of arguments that tend to be associated with common fallacies, like arguments from expert opinion, *ad hominem* arguments, appeals to force and threats, and so forth. To improve informal logic methods, we need to have systematic criteria for identifying a particular type of argument, like an argument from expert opinion, as found in a natural language text of discourse. For as we all know, natural language discourse is full of vagueness and ambiguity, and it can be very hard to pin down a real instance of some text to see whether it fits any abstract structure like a form of argument. Having a procedure for assisting with this task is simply a continuation of the kind of work that is being done every day in teaching courses and writing textbooks in the field of informal logic. However, more exact methods would enable us to find new examples more easily, and to document and store them so they could be easily re-used

1. Teaching Students to Identify Arguments

At the beginning, there are two specific tasks that need to be separated. One is the task of identifying arguments as entities that are distinct from other kinds of entities that occur in natural language discourse, such as explanations. This is the task of distinguishing between arguments and non-arguments. This task is far from trivial, as verbal indicators are often insufficient to distinguish between something that is supposed to be an argument and something that is supposed to be an explanation (van Eemeren et al., 2007). The other task is that of identifying specific types of arguments. In an earlier book on argumentation schemes (Walton, 1996) I identified and described twenty-nine commonly used schemes that represent types of arguments familiar to anyone with a beginner's knowledge of informal logic.

1. Argument from Analogy
2. Argument from a Verbal Classification
3. Argument from Rule
4. Argument from Exception to a Rule
5. Argument from Precedent
6. Practical Reasoning
7. Lack of Knowledge Arguments
8. Arguments from Consequences
9. Fear and Danger Appeals
10. Arguments from Alternatives and Opposites

11. Pleas for Help and Excuses
12. Composition and Division Arguments
13. Slippery Slope Arguments
14. Arguments from Popular Opinion
15. Argument from Commitment
16. Arguments from Inconsistency
17. Ethotic *Ad Hominem*
18. Circumstantial *Ad Hominem*
19. Argument from Bias
20. *Ad Hominem* Strategies to Rebut a Personal Attack
21. Argument from Cause to Effect
22. Argument from Effect to Cause
23. Argument from Correlation to Cause
24. Argument from Evidence to a Hypothesis
25. Abductive Reasoning
26. Argument from Position to Know
27. Argument from Expert Opinion
28. The Sunk Costs Argument (a.k.a. Argument from Waste)

Later work (Walton, Reed and Macagno, 2008) presented a compendium of ninety-six argumentation schemes, depending on how the subtypes are classified.

For example, argument from expert opinion is a common type of argument that we are often interested in for argumentation studies. It is made up of two distinctive premises and a conclusion. Basically it says: so-and-so is an expert, so-and-so says that some proposition is true, therefore (defeasibly) this proposition is true. Identifying this particular type of argument would seem to be simple. For example, the method could use keywords, like the word 'expert'. However, from experiences with teaching informal logic methods to students, there is a problem that occurs with some students who will immediately go to the Internet when asked to find examples of this kind of argument, and pick the first text they find containing the word 'expert'. Of course, many of these examples are not instances of argument from expert opinion. Keywords that occur in standardized forms of arguments, like the word 'expert', can be useful in helping a student to find examples of a specific type of argument. But they are crude tools, because their use without further refinement results in many errors.

This kind of work represents a more systematic continuation of the kind of practice that is carried out in teaching courses on argumentation or informal logic. Over many years of teaching courses of this type, I always used basically the same method of starting to teach the students through the use of examples. I searched through magazines, newspapers, and the Internet, or whatever other sources of material were available, to find interesting examples of arguments from expert opinion, *ad hominem* arguments, cases of equivocation, and so forth. From building up stocks of these cases and discussing and analyzing them with my classes, I started to compile accounts of each of the types of arguments, the kinds of premises they have, and the different varieties of them.

However, I didn't do this collecting in any systematic way. The examples I found initially came from the news magazine I usually read, or from the sections on informal logic in the many logic textbooks that use such examples. Eventually the wealth of experience that came from studying these examples led to the formulation of argumentation schemes, forms used to represent the basic structure of each type of argument. The schemes turned out to be very helpful as I continued to teach courses on argumentation, because they gave students some guideposts to use in their attempts to identify, analyze and evaluate arguments.

There were two kinds of assignments I used to typically give to my students in these courses. In the one type, I gave them each the same text of discourse containing an interesting argument, say a one page magazine opinion editorial. In the other type of assignment, I asked the students themselves to find an interesting example of one of the arguments we were concerned within the class, like argument from expert opinion, and analyze and evaluate their example. These tasks correspond to what the method to be built in this project is designed to help with. So it is easily seen how such a method would be helpful for teaching courses of this sort. It would also have a much wider use, however. For example, it would be an extremely powerful tool for researchers in fields like argumentation and informal logic. They could collect masses of interesting data on particular types of arguments that have long been studied in a more anecdotal way, and make the findings of the field of argumentation study much more powerful, because they would then be based on documented data of a comprehensive sort.

Another example that illustrates how the project will work is the *ad hominem* type of argument. The way I defined this type of argument and crafted the argumentation schemes for it, there has to be more than just a personal attack. For something to be a genuine *ad hominem* argument, four requirements have to be met. First, there have to be two arguers who are engaging in some sort of argumentation with each other. Second, one of the arguers has to have put forward an argument. Third, the other arguer has to be attacking the first party's argument. And fourth, the other arguer has to be using personal attack for this purpose. Very often I found that if I asked students to go and collect an interesting example of an *ad hominem* argument, they would find some instance of name-calling or personal attack, "Bob is a liar", and label that as an instance of an *ad hominem* argument. But if the instance of name-calling was not being used to attack somebody's argument, according to the argumentation scheme for the *ad hominem* argument, it should not correctly be so classified. Of course, one can debate the classification system, and there has been plenty of that going on in the field of informal logic, but to carry out a systematic study of any domain, one has to start with some initial hypotheses, definitions and classifications of the things being studied. Hence it is most useful, and in my opinion even necessary, to start with a well-defined set of argumentation schemes, even if the definitions of them are only regarded as tentative hypotheses that are subject to modification and revision as the project processes more and more real examples of a given type of argument.

2. Introducing Argumentation Schemes

Argument from expert opinion is a subspecies of position to know reasoning, based on the applicability of the assumption that the source is in a position to know because she is an expert. In trying to apply these schemes to real cases of argumentation, it can sometimes be easy to get them mixed up. Here is a typical example of argument from position to know.

> If one is trying to find the best way to get to City Hall in an unfamiliar city, it may be helpful to ask a passer-by. If it looks like this passer-by is familiar with the city, and she says that City Hall is 12 blocks east, it could be reasonable to accept the conclusion that City Hall is 12 blocks east.

This form of reasoning is called position to know argumentation.

Where a is a source of information, the following argumentation scheme represents the form of position to know argumentation (Walton, Reed and Macagno, 2008, 309).

Scheme for Argument from Position to Know

MAJOR PREMISE: Source a is in position to know about things in a certain subject domain S containing proposition A.
MINOR PREMISE: a asserts that A is true (false).
CONCLUSION: A is true (false).

Such an argument can be reasonable in many instances, but it is also defeasible. It can be critically questioned by raising doubts about the truth of either premise, or by asking whether a is an honest (trustworthy) source of information. The following critical questions match the scheme for the position to know argument:

CQ₁: Is *a* in position to know whether *A* is true (false)?
CQ₂: Is *a* an honest (trustworthy, reliable) source?
CQ₃: Did *a* assert that *A* is true (false)?

The second critical question concerns the credibility of the source. For example, a lawyer cross-examining a witness in a trial is allowed (within controlled limits) to raise critical questions about the character of the witness for honesty. If a witness has been known to lie in previous cases, a cross-examiner is allowed to ask such *ad hominem* questions, as an exception to the general rule against prejudicing the jury, by attacking the ethical character of a defendant.

Consider once again the case of asking the passerby where City Hall is located in a city one is not familiar with. Such a case is clearly an instance of position to know reasoning, but is it also an instance of the scheme for argument from expert opinion? Students in a critical thinking course are often inclined to think so, because it may seem to them reasonable to say that the passerby is being consulted as an expert on the city streets. After all, if she is very familiar with them, she might be said to have a kind of expert knowledge of them.

The argumentation scheme for argument from expert opinion is different from the one for argument from position to know, because it is required that the source who is in a position to know be an expert. For example, ballistics experts and DNA experts are often used to give expert testimony as evidence in trials, but they must qualify as experts. The basic version of this scheme for argument from expert opinion is given in (Walton, Reed and Macagno, 2008, 310) as follows.

MAJOR PREMISE: Source *E* is an expert in subject domain *S* containing proposition *A*.
MINOR PREMISE: *E* asserts that proposition *A* is true (false).
CONCLUSION: *A* is true (false).

It is rarely wise to treat an expert as an infallible source of knowledge, and taking that approach makes argumentation susceptible to the fallacious misuse of argument from expert opinion. Generally this form of argumentation is best treated as defeasible, subject to failure under critical questioning. The six basic critical questions matching the appeal to expert opinion (Walton, 1997, p. 223) are the following.

1. *Expertise Question*: How credible is *E* as an expert source?
2. *Field Question*: Is *E* an expert in the field *F* that *A* is in?

3. *Opinion Question*: What did *E* assert that implies *A*?
4. *Trustworthiness Question*: Is *E* personally reliable as a source?
5. *Consistency Question*: Is *A* consistent with what other experts assert?
6. *Backup Evidence Question*: Is *E*'s assertion based on evidence?

If the respondent asks any one of the six critical questions a burden of proof shifts back to the proponent's side to respond appropriately.

On this interpretation, the argument would fit the major premise of the scheme for argument from expert opinion. But in the absence of further evidence, can it be correctly said that she is an expert? Unless she is a cartographer, or an expert on city planning, or has some qualification of that sort, she would not qualify as an expert in the primary sense in which the term is used here (as in law). But we can draw a distinction between having a working or practical knowledge of some area, and having expert knowledge of it (Godden and Walton, 2006).

It might be noted here as well that many arguments that occur in real argumentation texts, whether in law or everyday conversational argumentation, have implicit premises or conclusions (Walton and Reed, 2005). Consider the example, "Markley lives in California and says the weather is fine there". An implicit premise is that Markley is in a position to know about the weather in California, based on the explicit premise that he lives in California. Another implicit premise is the defeasible conditional that if a person lives in a place, he is in a position to know about the weather there. The implicit conclusion of the argument is the statement that the weather is fine in California. At present, such implicit premises and conclusions can only be found by having a human analyst dig them out as best explanations of the meaning of the text. It should be noted that argumentation schemes are very helpful for this purpose in many instances. In the Markley example, the scheme for argument from position to know can be applied to extract the missing premise and conclusion.

Argument from ignorance, or lack-of-evidence reasoning as it is often called, is another scheme that is so common and natural to use that it is hard to identify. We use it all the time, but are scarcely aware we are doing so. This scheme is hard for students to grasp at first and to identify in natural language discourse, because it is subtle, and because it involves negation. The scheme for argument from ignorance is based on both what is known and what is not known to be true at some point in a sequence of argumentation (Walton, 1996, p. 254). The major premise is a counterfactual.

MAJOR PREMISE: If *A* were true, *A* would be known to be true.
MINOR PREMISE: *A* is not known to be true.
CONCLUSION: *A* is false.

The major premise is based on the assumption that there has been a search through the knowledge base that would contain A that has supposedly been deep enough so that if A were there, it would be found. The critical questions include considerations of (1) how deep the search has been, and (2) how deep the search needs to be to prove the conclusion that A is false to the required standard of proof in the investigation. In typical instances of the argument from ignorance, the major premise of the argument is not explicitly stated. It has to be extracted from the text by applying the argumentation scheme. It is perhaps also for this reason that students tend to overlook this type of argument and have a hard time identifying it in a given text.

3. More Schemes: Practical Reasoning and Arguments from Consequences

There are variants of the scheme for practical reasoning, but the simplest one (below) is called practical inference. In the scheme below, the first-person pronoun 'I' represents a rational agent of the kind described by Woodridge (2000), an entity that has goals, some (though possibly incomplete) knowledge of its circumstances, and the capability of acting to alter those circumstances and to perceive (some of) the consequences of so acting. The simplest form of practical reasoning is the following fast and frugal heuristic for practical inference (Walton, Reed and Macagno, 2008, 323).

> MAJOR PREMISE: I have a goal G.
> MINOR PREMISE: Carrying out this action A is a means to realize G.
> CONCLUSION: Therefore, I ought (practically speaking) to carry out this action A.

Below is the set of critical questions matching the scheme for practical inference (Walton, Reed and Macagno, 2008, 323).

> CQ_1: What other goals do I have that should be considered that might conflict with G?
> CQ_2: What alternative actions to my bringing about A that would also bring about G should be considered?
> CQ_3: Among bringing about A and these alternative actions, which is arguably the most efficient?
> CQ_4: What grounds are there for arguing that it is practically possible for me to bring about A?
> CQ_5: What consequences of my bringing about A should also be taken into account?

The last critical question, CQ_5, is very often called the side effects question. It concerns potential negative consequences of a proposed course of action. Just asking about consequences of a course of action being contemplated could be enough to cast an argument based on practical reasoning into doubt.

Another possibility is that an argument based on practical reasoning could be attacked by the respondent claiming that there are negative consequences of the proposed action. This move in argumentation is stronger than merely asking CQ5, as it is an attempted rebuttal of the original argument. There is a specific argumentation scheme representing this type of argument. Argument from negative consequences cites the consequences of a proposed course of action as a reason against taking that course of action. This type of argument also has a positive form, in which positive consequences of an action are cited as a reason for carrying it out. These are the two basic argumentation schemes for arguments from consequences (Walton, Reed and Macagno, 2008, 332), where *A* represents a state that could be brought about by an agent.

Argument from Positive Consequences
PREMISE: If *A* is brought about, good consequences will plausibly occur.
CONCLUSION: Therefore *A* should be brought about.

Argument from Negative Consequences
PREMISE: If *A* is brought about, then bad consequences will occur.
CONCLUSION: Therefore *A* should not be brought about.

Argumentation from consequences offers a reason to accept a proposal for action tentatively, subject to exceptions that may arise as new circumstances become known. An instance of argument from consequences can be stronger or weaker, depending on its initial plausibility and the critical questions that have been used to attack it.

The scheme for argument from positive value (Walton, Reed and Macagno, 2008, 321) takes the following form.

PREMISE 1: Value *V* is *positive* as judged by agent *A*.
PREMISE 2: If *V* is *positive*, it is a reason for *A* to commit to goal *G*.
CONCLUSION: *V* is a reason for *A* to commit to goal *G*.

The scheme for argument from negative value (Walton, Reed and Macagno, 2008, 321) takes the following form.

PREMISE 1: Value *V* is *negative* as judged by agent *A*.
PREMISE 2: If *V* is *negative*, it is a reason for retracting commitment to goal *G*.
CONCLUSION: *V* is a reason for retracting commitment to goal *G*.

Argument from negative consequences is a form of rebuttal that cites the consequences of a proposed course of action as a reason against taking that course of action.

Another type of argument widely used in argumentation is the variant of practical reasoning called value-based practical reasoning (Bench-Capon, 2003). The version of this scheme below is from (Walton, Reed and Macagno, 2008, 324).

PREMISE 1: I have a goal *G*.
PREMISE 2: *G* is supported by my set of values, *V*.
PREMISE 3: Bringing about *A* is necessary (or sufficient) for me to bring about *G*.
CONCLUSION: Therefore, I should (practically ought to) bring about *A*.

Another version of the scheme for value-based practical reasoning (Atkinson, Bench-Capon and McBurney, 2004, 88) unpacks the notion of a goal into three elements: the state of affairs brought about by the action, the goal (the desired features in that state of affairs) and the value (the reason why those features are desirable).

In the current circumstances *R*
Action *A* should be performed
To bring about new circumstances *S*
Which will realize goal *G*
And promote value *V*

Note that value-based practical reasoning can be classified as a hybrid scheme that combines argument from values with practical reasoning.

In some cases, it may be hard to identify the type of an argument, because it is not obvious what scheme it fits, because some elements of the argument are not explicitly stated. However, in such cases, clues from the context of dialogue can help. Consider the following blood pressure dialogue (Restificar, Ali and McRoy, 1999, 3).

Proponent: Have you had your blood pressure checked?
Respondent: There is no need.
Proponent: Uncontrolled high blood pressure can lead to heart attack, heart failure, stroke or kidney failure.

The respondent's reply, 'There is no need', could be seen as a way of attacking the second premise of the simplest version of the scheme for argument from practical reasoning. He is saying, in effect, that having his blood pressure checked is not a necessary means to maintain his health. This move illustrates the type of rebuttal that is an attack on a premise of an argument. As noted above, the fifth critical question is associated with argument from negative consequences.

It may be possible to reconstruct the proponent's reaction at his first move by using this clue. It could be interpreted as an instance of the scheme for practical reasoning if we insert an implicit premise. Restificar, Ali and McRoy (1999, 3) offer no further information about the context of the argumentation in their example, but it seems reasonable to presume that the proponent is concerned about the respondent's health. If so, one could insert as an implicit premise the statement that a goal for the respondent is his health. If this is a reasonable assumption, the proponent's argument could be reconstructed as follows:

Implicit Premise: Your goal is to maintain your health.
Explicit Premise: Having your blood pressure checked is a necessary means to maintain your health.
Conclusion: You should have your blood pressure checked.

On this interpretation, the scheme for practical reasoning can help to reconstruct the argumentation sequence, as one can see as follows. The proponent made an argument from practical reasoning. The respondent questioned the major premise of this practical argument. He doubts that having your blood pressure checked is necessary to maintain your health. The proponent then provided an argument to support the major premise of his practical argument. The above analysis of the example is meant to be simple, for purposes of illustration. A fuller analysis would show how another scheme, value-based practical reasoning, is involved, and also how it is the necessary condition variant of the scheme for practical reasoning that is involved.

4. The Sunk Costs Argument

Argument from waste is a kind of argument where one party is thinking of discontinuing some course of action she has been engaging in for some time, and another party argues, "If you stop now, all your previous efforts will be wasted". It is also called the sunk costs argument in economics, where it has traditionally been regarded as a fallacy, even though more recently, it has been thought to be reasonable in many instances. It is typified by the following kind of case (Walton, 2002, 473).

Someone has invested a significant amount of money in a stock or business. Decreasing value and poor performance suggest it might be a good time to pull out and invest the remaining money elsewhere. But because the person has already invested so much in this venture, and would lose so much of it by pulling out now, she feels that she must stay with it rather than take the loss. To abandon the investment would be too much of a waste to bear, given all the money that has been sunk into it at this point. Reasoning on the basis of sunk costs, the person concludes that she must stay with this investment, even though she is convinced that the prospects for its rising in value are not good.

It is not hard to see why the sunk costs argument is often regarded as fallacious in economics and in business-decision-making generally, where an investor needs to think of the future, and should not be emotionally tied to previous commitments once circumstances change. However, there are other cases where the sunk costs argument can be reasonable (Walton, 2002), especially those where one's commitments to something one has put a lot of effort into are based on one's values. The sunk costs argument appears to be a species of practical reasoning that is also built on argument from consequences and argument from values. It is a composite argument built from these simpler schemes. So it is a classic case raising the problem of how this cluster of schemes should be structured in a classification system for argumentation schemes.

The sunk costs argument is a subtype of argument from negative consequences, as can be seen by putting it in this form.

If you stop doing what you are doing now, that would be a waste.
Waste is a bad thing (negative consequence).
Therefore you should not stop doing what you are doing now.

More precisely, the sunk costs argument has the following argumentation scheme, where A is an outcome of an action, and a is an agent (Walton, Reed and Macagno, 2008, 326)

PREMISE 1: If a stops trying to realize A now, all a's previous efforts to realize A will be wasted.
PREMISE 2: If all a's previous attempts to realize A are wasted, that would be a bad thing.
CONCLUSION: Therefore, a ought not to stop trying to realize A.

In (Walton, 2002) it is shown that the sunk costs argument can be a reasonable form of argument, but also that it is defeasible, and open to the following critical questions.

CQ$_1$: Is bringing about A possible?
CQ$_2$: If past losses cannot be recouped, should a reassessment be made of the cost and benefits of trying to bring about A from this point in time?

A failure to address a critical question appropriately during changing circumstances, due to an attachment to previous commitments and efforts, is associated with fallacious instances of argument from sunk costs.

As indicated above, the sunk costs argument needs to be built on argument from negative consequences and argument from negative values. This takes us to the problem of classifying schemes, by building classification trees showing one scheme is a subspecies of another. This problem will be taken up in Section 6.

Another problem we now need to address is of a different sort, although it is related to classification as well. It has to do with recognizing an instance of a scheme in a natural language argument in a given text of discourse. In some instances, a given argument may look like it should be classified as an instance of the scheme for argument from waste, but there may be questions about this classification. An example can be found in an opinion article in the *Western Courier*, October 25, 2008.[1] The article advocates the use of embryonic stem cells for the advancement of medicine, and claims that the technology exists for deriving human embryonic stem cells without harming the embryo. The argument opposes the position of conservative groups, who are unwilling to support any kind of embryonic research, regardless of whether or not it destroys the embryo. One of the main arguments appears to be an instance of argument from waste, as indicated in the part of the article quoted below.

The Stem Cell Example

This [position—i.e. opposition to any kind of embryonic research] is short-sighted and stubborn. The fact is, fetuses are being aborted whether conservatives like it or not. Post-abortion, the embryos are literally being thrown away when they could be used in life-saving medical research. It has become a matter of religious and personal beliefs, and misguided ones at that. Lives could be saved and vastly improved if only scientists were allowed to use embryos that are otherwise being tossed in the garbage.

The argument in this article could be recast in a format that makes it appear to fit the scheme for argument from waste.

Premise 1: The embryos could be used in lifesaving medical research.
Implicit premise 1: Lifesaving medical research is a good thing.
Premise 2: The embryos are being thrown away.
Implicit premise 2: Anything being thrown away that could be used is a waste [a bad thing].
Conclusion: The embryos should be used in medical research.

Putting the argument in this format makes it appear that it is an instance of argument from waste. But is it? This question is puzzling, and opinions on both sides can be found. The word 'waste' is used, and waste is taken to be a bad thing. Also, that some action is classified as a "waste" is taken as a reason

[1] www.westerncourier.com/news/2006/09/01/Opinion/Stem-Cells.Are.Going/To.Waste-2255161.shtml -40k -

against it. However, what appears to be missing is that in a proper argument from waste, as required by premise 1 of the scheme, the agent was making some previous efforts to do something, and if he stops now, his efforts will be wasted. In the stem cell example, there were no previous efforts of this sort. Instead, what is said to be a waste are the embryos that are "thrown away". Premise 2 of the scheme for argument from waste also requires that if previous attempts to realize something are wasted, that would be a bad thing. There seems to be nothing fitting this premise in the stem cells example. Nobody was doing anything with the stem cells previously. No effort or commitment was being put into doing something with them.

The problem with this kind of case is one of matching the premises of the scheme with the premises of the argument given in the text of discourse. If a required premise of the scheme is not found in the argument in the discourse, we need to look and see if there is evidence that it is an implicit premise. If there is no such evidence we need to conclude that the given argument is not an instance of this particular scheme. In the present example, we need to conclude that the given argument is not an instance of the scheme for the sunk costs argument.

5. Slippery Slope Arguments

Finally we need to consider the scheme for the slippery slope argument, a highly complex form of argument composed of the other simpler schemes we have so far studied. It is a common problem in teaching critical thinking skills to students that once they are taught a structure for the slippery slope argument, they tend to apply it to cases where the evidence does not really justify classifying it under this category. For example, they typically find cases of argumentation from negative consequences and leap to the conclusion that it must be a slippery slope argument because some bad outcome is being cited as a reason for not carrying out a particular course of action. Strictly speaking, however, to be a slippery slope, an argument has to meet a number of requirements

It is an important requirement for this scheme that the recursive premise be present. Without that premise, the argument clearly is simply an instance of argument from negative consequences. It is the presence of the recursive premise that enables us to distinguish any given case whether the argument is a slippery slope argument as well as being an argument from negative consequences (Walton, Reed and Macago, 2008, 339):

Scheme for the Slippery Slope Argument

FIRST STEP PREMISE: A_0 is up for consideration as a proposal that seems initially like something that should be brought about.

RECURSIVE PREMISE: Bringing up A_0 would plausibly lead (in the given circumstances, as far as we know) to A_1, which would in turn plausibly lead to A_2, and so forth, through the sequence $A_2, \ldots A_n$.

BAD OUTCOME PREMISE: A_n is a horrible (disastrous, bad) outcome.

CONCLUSION: A_0 should not be brought about.

The following example is a genuine slippery slope argument. It concerned the burning of an American flag by Gregory Lee Johnson during a political demonstration in Dallas to protest policies of the Reagan administration. Johnson was convicted of "desecration of a venerated object", but the Texas Court of Criminal Appeals reversed the ruling, arguing that Johnson's act was "expressive conduct", protected by the First Amendment of the United States' Constitution. This decision was reaffirmed by the U.S. Supreme Court in the case of Texas v. Johnson (1989 WL 65231(U.S.), 57 U.S.L.W. 4770). In delivering the opinion of the Court, Justice William Brennan cited the precedent case of Schacht v. United States, where it was ruled that an actor could wear a uniform of one of the U.S. armed forces while portraying someone who discredited that armed force by opposing the war in Vietnam.

> We perceive no basis on which to hold that the principle underlying our decision in Schacht does not apply to this case. To conclude that the Government may permit designated symbols to be used to communicate only a limited set of messages would be to enter territory having no discernible or defensible boundaries. Could the Government, on this theory, prohibit the burning of state flags? Of copies of the Presidential seal? Of the Constitution? In evaluating these choices under the First Amendment, how would we decide which symbols were sufficiently special to warrant this unique status? To do so, we would be forced to consult our own political preferences, and impose them on the citizenry, in the very way that the First Amendment forbids us to do.

The argument in this text can be identified as an instance of the slippery slope argument. A first step is said to lead to a series of unclear decisions (whether to prohibit the burning of state flags, copies of the Presidential seal, the Constitution, and so forth), which would in turn lead to the outcome of individual justices imposing their own political preferences on the citizens. This is said to be an intolerable outcome in a free country, a violation of the U.S. First Amendment. In this instance, clearly the recursive premise is present.

The problem with many examples is that the argument does appear to be of the slippery slope type, but the series of intervening steps required to get from the premises to the conclusion is not made explicit. The following excerpt from a letter written by Richard Nixon in *The New York Times* on October 29, 1965, has been taken as an example of a fallacious slippery slope argument in logic textbooks (Walton, 1992, 97), but it is hard to tell whether it really fits the scheme for slippery slope argument. Nixon's letter warned about consequences of the fall of Vietnam in the following terms.

> ... would mean ultimately the destruction of freedom of speech for all men for all time not only in Asia but the United States as well. ... We must never forget that if the war in Vietnam is lost ... the right of free speech will be extinguished throughout the world.

This argument certainly looks like a classic case of the slippery slope argument, but where is the recursive premise? The intervening steps are missing. Presumably what Nixon was claiming is that the fall of Vietnam would lead to the fall of other neighboring countries to communism, and these events in turn would cause a chain reaction with the final disastrous outcome that the whole world is taken over by undemocratic countries. The problem is that Nixon did not fill in all these intervening steps, and so how can we prove that the recursive premise requirement is really meant by the argument, as stated in the example above? One option that needs to be looked at is whether these intervening claims can be taken to be implicit premises. In other words, is the argument an enthymeme? There is evidence for this contention, and thus by marshalling the textual evidence, a case can be made that the argument should properly be classified as a slippery slope. However, the contention that this argument fits the scheme for the slippery slope argument needs to be argued for. If it cannot be sustained by the marshalling of the textual and contextual evidence in the case, the argument should only be classified as an argument from negative consequences that is not also a slippery slope argument.

The slippery slope argument does occur in everyday and legal argumentation, but it is not nearly as common as other schemes mentioned above, such as argument from negative consequences and practical reasoning. As shown by the example above, it is a substantial task to properly identify an argument in a given case as fitting the slippery slope scheme, because the scheme is so complex, with so many prerequisites, and because it is a composite, made up of other simpler schemes. It is argued in (Walton, 1992) that the slippery slope scheme can be analyzed as a complex chain of subarguments each having the defeasible modus ponens structure, but there is insufficient space to discuss this interesting analysis here.

6. Classification of Schemes

The project of automatic identification of arguments in a text using schemes would greatly benefit from a classification system showing which schemes are subschemes of others. The subject of classification schemes is a topic for another paper, but it will help to make a few comments on this related project here, since it is so obviously important in the schemes and examples studied above. So far there is no generally accepted system of classification for argumentation schemes. Walton, Reed and Macagno (2008, 349-350) surveyed several different approaches, and concluded that it appears that at the present state of development of schemes, the general system summarized below is the easiest to apply. In it, there are three main categories, and various schemes under each one.

REASONING

1. *Deductive Reasoning*
   Deductive *Modus Ponens*
   Disjunctive Syllogism
   Hypothetical Syllogism
   Reductio Ad Absurdum
   Etc.

2. *Inductive Reasoning*
   Argument from a Random Sample to a Population
   Etc.

3. *Practical Reasoning*
   Argument from Consequences
   Argument from Alternatives
   Argument from Waste
   Argument from Sunk Costs
   Argument from Threat
   Argument from Danger Appeal

4. *Abductive Reasoning*
   Argument from Sign
   Argument from Evidence to a Hypothesis

5. *Causal Reasoning*
   Argument from Cause to Effect
   Argument from Correlation to Cause
   Causal Slippery Slope Argument

(For details see chapter 5 of Walton, Reed and Macagno, 2008 on causal argumentation).

SOURCE-BASED ARGUMENTS

1. *Arguments from Position to Know*
   Argument from Position to Know
   Argument from Witness Testimony
   Argument from Expert Opinion
   Argument from Ignorance

2. *Arguments from Commitment*
   Argument from Inconsistent Commitment

3. *Arguments Attacking Personal Credibility*
   Arguments from Allegation of Bias
   Poisoning the Well by Alleging Group Bias
   Ad Hominem Arguments
   Etc.

4. *Arguments from Popular Acceptance*
   Argument from Popular Opinion
   Argument from Popular Practice
   Etc.

APPLYING RULES TO CASES

1. *Arguments Based on Cases*
   Argument from Example
   Argument from Analogy
   Argument from Precedent

2. *Defeasible Rule-Based Arguments*
   Argument from an Established Rule
   Argument from an Exceptional Case
   Argument from Plea for Excuse

3. *Verbal Classification Arguments*
   Argument from Verbal Classification
   Argument from Vagueness of a Verbal Classification

4. *Chained Arguments Connecting Rules and Cases*
   Argument from Gradualism
   Precedent Slippery Slope Argument
   Slippery Slope Argument

This classification system is very helpful for the purpose of orienting students taking an informal logic course, because it helps group some of the most commonly used schemes into categories. But as shown in the instances of the slippery slope argument and argument from sunk costs, the relationship of these more complex schemes to the simpler schemes that compose them, like practical reasoning, argument from consequences and argument from values, requires a deeper analysis.

Prakken (2010) has given another example of how two schemes are structurally related in an interesting way. He studied the structural relationship between argument from expert opinion and argument from position to know, and showed that the former scheme can be classified as a special instance of the latter scheme. He also showed how argument from evidence to a hypothesis can be analyzed in a manner showing that it is a species of abductive reasoning, often called inference to the best explanation. [But *cf*. Woods, Chapter 17 in this volume. –Editor] These findings confirm the hypothesis that many of the most common schemes have an interlocking relationship with other schemes so that one scheme can be classified as a subspecies of another, but only in a complex manner. This complex manner needs to take into account structural relationships between the schemes.

What has been shown here is very important for not only developing a precise system of classification of schemes, but also for the overarching project of developing a system for argument mining. What has been shown is the there are some simple and basic schemes, and there are some highly complex schemes that are built up as complexes from the simpler schemes. Among the most important simple schemes are practical reasoning, argument from position to know, argument from commitment, and argument from values. Argument from consequences is also a simple scheme, but it has an interesting relationship to the scheme for practical reasoning. Argument from negative consequences corresponds to one of the critical questions matching the scheme for practical reasoning.

There is not sufficient space in this chapter to take up the problem of how to provide a deeper classification of argumentation schemes of a kind that would be useful for argument mining and other informal logic tasks. It must be left as a problem for future research. In the next section, it is shown that there has been some groundbreaking work in artificial intelligence on taking the first steps in building systems of argument mining. It is very useful for those of us in the informal logic field to know about this research.

7. Research on Argument Mining in Artificial Intelligence

It is encouraging that there are already some systems applying argumentation schemes to legal texts that have been implemented and the results of this experimental work are very interesting so far (Mochales and Leven 2009, 27). Discourse theories assume that the structure of a text is that of a graph or a tree, and that the elementary units of complex text structures are non-overlapping spans of text. Moens, Mochales Palau, Boiy and Reed (2007) conducted experiments directed towards the ultimate aim of developing methods for automatically classifying arguments in legal texts in order to make it possible to access and search types of arguments in such texts conveniently. They build on recent work in legal argumentation theory as well as rhetorical structure theory. They look for prominent indicators of rhetorical structure expressed by conjunctions and certain kinds of adverbial groups (2007, 226). They identify words, pairs of successive words, sequences of three successive words, adverbs, verbs and modal auxiliary verbs. Rhetorical structure theory defines twenty-three rhetorical relations that can hold between spans of a text. Most hold between two text spans called a nucleus—the unit most central to the writer's purpose—and a satellite, which stands in a relation to the nucleus. For example, the evidence relation links a nucleus like 'Bob shot Ed' and a satellite like 'Bob's fingerprints were found on the gun'. Their experiments offer an initial assessment of types of features that play a role in identifying legal arguments and single sentences. In future work, they also hope to focus on the classification of different types of arguments.

This work has been applied to legal argumentative texts (Mochales Palau and Moens 2007; Mochales and Leven, 2009; Mochales Palau and Moens, 2009, 100). In this research the sentences are classified according to argumentation schemes, and the aim is to build a system for automatic detection and classification of arguments in legal cases (Mochales and Moens, 2008). The project has built a corpus from texts of the European Court of Human Rights that was annotated by three annotators under supervision of a legal expert (Mochales and Leven, 2009). This task was made easier by the fact that the court documents that provided their corpus were already classified using subheadings into different parts of the text that had different functions. So, for example, there is one section of the text where the arguments of the judges are presented. Using a limited number of argumentation schemes, for example the 26 or so identified in (Walton, 1996) would be a way to start identifying the different types of arguments. This research opens up opportunities for applying artificial intelligence research to informal logic.

It is interesting to note that there were no identifications of instances of argument from ignorance in the corpus, and very few instances of argument from commitment were identified. Practical reasoning was not used as a scheme in this study. 80 instances of argument from position to know were found. 2099 instances of circumstantial argument against the person were found. 10744 instances of argument from evidence to a hypothesis were found. 2385 instances of argument from expert opinion were found. 12229 instances of argument from precedent were found. 1772 instances of arguments that fitted no scheme were found.

These results are interesting, but Mochales and Leven (2009, 27) noted a number of problems. To improve the usefulness of systems for automated

argument text mining, several research topics are acutely in need of exploration. These observations suggest that what is needed, in addition to the more
precise definitions of the schemes themselves for use in automated argument detection (Rahwan et al., 2008), is the provision of additional criteria
that can be of assistance in determining in problem cases whether a scheme
applies to a given argument in a text of discourse or not. Sources for collecting such criteria can already be found in work in AI (Moens, Mochales-
Palau, Boiy and Reed, 2007; Mochales-Palau and Moens 2007; Mochales and
Leven 2009; Mochales-Palau and Moens, 2009) and in argumentation theory
(van Eemeren, Houtlosser and Snoeck Henkemans, 2007). The blood pressure example showed that the context of the dialogue in a case needs to be
taken into account, as well as the indicator words, in the task of detecting a
scheme in discourse. The clue to determining that practical reasoning was the
scheme fitting the argument in this case was the critical questioning matching
the proponent's use of practical reasoning.

The Amsterdam School has been conducting research for some time on the
task of identifying arguments in a text of discourse using so-called argumentative indicators like 'thus', 'therefore' and 'because' (van Eemeren, Houtlosser and Snoek Henkemans, 2007). A large part of this research has focused
on the task of distinguishing between an item in a text of discourse that may
properly be taken to represent an argument, as opposed to some other speech
act, like the putting forward an explanation or the making of a statement.
Only a few argumentation schemes have been studied so far. These include
argument from analogy, argument from sign and causal arguments.

Another approach (Wyner and Bench-Capon, 2007) reconstructs legal
case-based reasoning in terms of argumentation schemes. This approach uses
a set of cases, factors, and comparisons between cases to instantiate argumentation schemes from which justifications for an outcome of the case at issue
can be derived. These include argument from precedent and argument from
analogy. Cases have a plaintiff, a defendant, a set of factors present in the
case, and an outcome for the plaintiff or defendant (2007, 139). The authors
identify and define what they call the main scheme in a case, including its
premises and conclusion (143). One premise of this main scheme is called
the factors preference premise, which states that one factor was preferred to
another in a previous case decided in the plaintiff's favor. They then introduce a new argumentation scheme they call the preference-from-precedent
scheme, that is used to support the factors preference premise of the main
scheme. In the general literature on argumentation schemes, this legal scheme
would be at a particular species of the scheme called argument from precedent (Walton, Reed and Macagno, 2008, 344). They identify other schemes
as well, showing how arguments fitting schemes on both sides can be used to

support or attack other arguments used in the case at issue. There are some features of their approach that are especially significant. They use an applicability assumption, which arises because there might be a number of reasons why an argument put forward in a case is not a suitable precedent for that case. They also distinguish between three different kinds of premises in schemes, called ordinary premises, assumptions and exceptions (Gordon, Prakken and Walton, 2007). This approach is especially significant because it shows how schemes can be used within the framework of legal case-based reasoning (Ashley, 2006), and especially because it shows how factors can be used to define legal schemes and apply them to argumentation a legal case.

Rahwan et al. (2011) have advanced research on the automated identification of particular schemes by building the first ontology of argumentation schemes in description logic, showing how description logic inference techniques can be used to reason about automatic argument classification. An OWL-based system is implemented for argumentation support on the semantic web. At the highest level, three concepts are identified, called statements, schemes describing arguments made up of statements, and authors of statements. Different species of schemes are identified, including rule schemes, which describe the class of arguments, conflicts schemes and preference schemes. The schemes are classified by classifying their components: their ordinary premises, assumptions, exceptions and conclusions. Statements may be classified as declarative or imperative. For example, in the scheme for argument from position to know (see Section 1 above), the class of statement *PositiontoHaveKnowledgeStmnt* is defined as a species of declarative statement associated with the property *formDescription*, "agent *a* is in a position to know whether statement *A* is true or false", that describes its typical form (Rahwan et al., 2011, 8). Using these categories, it is possible to fully describe a scheme, like the scheme for argument from position to know, by stating the necessary and sufficient conditions for an instance to be classified as falling under this type. Special types of schemes called conflict schemes are identified. The method of identifying schemes is implemented in a web-based system called *Avicenna* (2011, 11-13). A user can search arguments on the basis of keywords, structural features and other properties (Rahwan et al., 2011, 12).

It is clear even from this brief description of current work on argument mining in the field of computing, that this technical initiative would benefit greatly from more work on refining argumentation schemes. It is also clear that, even though this technical work is only a first step towards the development of useful argument mining technology, there are already interesting implications on how the methods currently being used can be adapted to the needs of informal logic.

8. Argument Mining as an Informal Logic Method

How could we use these results to develop argument mining methods that could be used to help students of informal logic identify arguments—for example, arguments of the kind they encounter in natural language texts in newspapers, magazines or on the Internet, and want to analyze using standard methods of informal logic? We already have some methods helpful for this sort of task. They include, for example, the use of argument mapping tools to identify the premises and conclusions of arguments, and to show how one argument is connected to another in a chain of argumentation [see Chapter 10 in this volume. –Ed.]. A second, and more ambitious project, is to develop an automated argumentation tool for argument mining. The idea is that this tool could go onto the Internet and collect arguments of specifically designated types, like argument from expert opinion for example. Of course, these two tasks are connected, because the most powerful method would likely turn out to be to combine both tasks by having trained human users apply the auto-mated tool to identify arguments on a tentative basis in the text of discourse, and then correct the errors made by the automated tool.

There are six distinct tasks in this endeavor.

The first task is the identification of arguments in a text of discourse, as opposed to other entities, like statements, questions or explanations. Carrying out this task requires some definition of what an argument is as opposed to the speech acts that can often be confused with putting forward an argument, like offering an explanation. Part of this task is the identification of broad types of argument, like deductive and inductive arguments, as opposed to the third category sometimes called plausible arguments. [Note Goddu's objection to these as types of argument, in Chapter 19.]

The second task is the identification of specific, known argumentation schemes. The principal way of recognizing a particular argumentation scheme is to be able to identify the premises and the conclusion that make up that scheme. What is required is a parser that can recognize that not only the individual units of speech in one of these premises or conclusions, like nouns and verbs, but also recognize particular nouns can occur in a scheme, like 'expert', or particular phrases like 'position to know'.

The third task is the deeper classification of argumentation schemes.

The fourth task is the more precise formulation of schemes. This can be carried out a number of ways. One way is to formulate schemes that can be applied in particular field. For example, the scheme for argument from expert opinion needs to be formulated in a more precise way in law than it is for pur-poses of analyzing ordinary conversational argumentation, because specific criteria for argumentation from expert opinion as a kind of evidence have already been established in law through legal precedents and court judgments.

The fifth task is to develop criteria to enable the differentiation between schemes that appear similar to each other or closely related to each other. The sixth task is to develop techniques for minimizing errors in the identification of schemes in natural language text of discourse. As shown above, in some cases it is easy to mix up one scheme with another. Part of the task here is to develop a corpus of borderline problem cases of this sort, and work on criteria that can be used to solve the problem. An important part of this fifth task is to develop a deeper classification system for argumentation schemes.

There is much work to be done before any useful system of argument identification based on argument mining can be implemented in an informal logic setting. What is needed is to encourage those in the field of informal logic to carry out research projects on the subject. An initial problem for anyone setting up this kind of research project is to decide what kind of natural language texts of discourse should be used as the database. Textbooks in informal logic often take their examples from magazine and newspaper articles, but they sometimes include examples of legal arguments as well. One project would be to take a particular newsmagazine and try to identify instances of arguments found in it, as well as trying to identify the type of argument. A second project would be to use examples of legal argumentation of some sort. A third project would be to use the database of arguments in Debatepedia, or some similar online source that contains lots of interesting arguments pro and contra on controversial issues at any given time.

9. Conclusions

The work using schemes for argument mining in legal discourse suggests that in addition to the schemes themselves, additional information that cites specific requirements an argument has to meet to qualify as instance of a particular scheme would be extremely useful. For example, to help tell whether an argument in a text should best be classified under the heading of argument from position to know or argument from expert opinion, some requirements telling the argument annotator what kind of source qualifies as an expert source, like those discussed in section 1, would be useful. The way to build up such additional resources is to better integrate theoretical research on schemes with the work of testing its application to texts of discourse.

Even though the research work in artificial intelligence offers grounds for optimism about the feasibility of the project of automated argument detection using schemes, the harder problem cases posed above concerning argument from position to know, argument from expert opinion, the sunk costs argument and the slippery slope argument are reasons for concern. It needs to be noted that this task is related to another problem, the problem of enthymemes, or arguments found in a natural language text of discourse that have implicit premises or conclusions. As we saw in tackling the problem of differentiating between slippery slope arguments and arguments from negative consequences, much often depends on implicit premises, like the recursive premise, which the classification of the argument requires, but that were not explicitly stated in the given text of discourse. This kind of problem is a central one for argumentation studies. Would it be possible to build an automated system that could detect enthymemes and fill in the missing premises or conclusions so that an analysis of the argument with its missing premises indicated could be provided by an argument visualization tool? The short answer is that it might be a lot more difficult to build such a useful tool of this kind than one might initially think (Walton and Reed, 2005), but the employment of schemes will very definitely be helpful as part of the tool. So the project is worth doing for purposes of informal logic, and is closely related to the underlying problem of developing a deeper classification system for argumentation schemes.[2]

Acknowledgments

The work in this chapter was supported by a Standard Research Grant from the Social Sciences and Humanities Research Council of Canada. For comments received when an earlier version was presented at a meeting of the Centre for Research in Reasoning, Argumentation and Rhetoric at the University of Windsor, I would like to thank J. Anthony Blair, Marcello Guarini, Hans V. Hansen, Catherine Hundelby, Ralph Johnson, Robert C. Pinto and Christopher Tindale.

References

Ashley, Kevin (2006). Case-Based Reasoning, *Information Technology and Lawyers*, A. R. Lodder and A. Oskamp (Eds.). Dordrecht, Springer, 23-60.

Atkinson, Katie, Bench-Capon, Trevor and McBurney, Peter (2004). Justifying Practical Reasoning, *Proceedings of the Fourth International Workshop on Computational Models of Natural Argument* (CMNA 2004), ECAI 2004, Valencia, Spain, 87-90.

Bench-Capon, Trevor (2003). Persuasion in Practical Argument Using Value-based Argumentation Frameworks, *Journal of Logic and Computation*, 13, 429-448.

Eemeren, Frans H. van, Houtlosser, Peter and Snoeck Henkemans, Francisca (2007). *Argumentative Indicators in Discourse*, Dordrecht, Springer.

[2] Originally published as Douglas Walton (2011). Argument Mining by Applying Argumentation Schemes, *Studies in Logic*, 4(1), 38-64.

Godden, David M. and Walton, Douglas (2006). Argument from Expert Opinion as Legal Evidence: Critical Questions and Admissibility Criteria of Expert Testimony in the American Legal System, *Ratio Juris*, 19, 261-286.

Gordon, Thomas F., Prakken, Henry and Walton, Douglas (2007). The Carneades Model of Argument and Burden of Proof, *Artificial Intelligence*, 171, 875-896.

Moens, Marie-Francine, Mochales Palau, Raquel, Boiy, Erik and Reed, Chris (2007). Automatic Detection of Arguments in Legal Texts, *Proceedings of the International Conference on AI and Law* (ICAIL), Stanford, California, 225-230.

Mochales-Palau, Raquel and Moens, Marie-Francine (2007). Study on Sentence Relations in the Automatic Detection of Argumentation in Legal Cases, *Legal Knowledge and Information Systems: JURIX 2007, The Twentieth International Conference*, ed. Arno R. Lodder and Laurens Mommers, Amsterdam IOS Press, 89-98.

Mochales, Raquel and Moens, Marie-Francine (2008). Study on the Structure of Argumentation in Case Law, *Legal Knowledge and Information Systems: JURIX 2008, The Twenty-First International Conference*, ed. Enrico Francesconi, Giovanni Sartor and Daniela Tiscornia, Amsterdam IOS Press, 11-20, 89-98.

Mochales, Raquel and Leven, Aagje (2009). Creating an Argument Corpus: Do Theories Apply to Real Arguments?, *Proceedings of the 12th International Conference on Artificial Intelligence and Law*, New York, Association for Computing Machinery, Inc., 21- 30.

Mochales-Palau, Raquel and Moens, Marie-Francine (2009). Argumentation Mining: The Detection, Classification and Structure of Arguments in Text, *Proceedings of the 12th International Conference on Artificial Intelligence and Law*, New York, Association for Computing Machinery, Inc., 98-107.

Prakken, Henry (2010). On the Nature of Argument Schemes, *Dialectics, Dialogue and Argumentation: an Examination of Douglas Walton's Theory of Reasoning and Argument*, London, College Publications, 167 -185

Rahwan, Iyad, Banihashemi, Bita, Reed, Chris and Walton, Douglas (2011). Avicenna: Argumentation Support on the Semantic Web, *Knowledge Engineering Review*.

Restificar, Angelo, Ali, Syed S. and McRoy, Susan W. (n.d.). ARGUER: Using Argument Schemas for Argument Detection and Rebuttal in Dialogs, *UMP99: International Conference on User Modeling*, ed. Judy Kay, New York, Springer-Wien, 315-317.

Walton, Douglas (1992). *Slippery Slope Arguments*, Oxford, Oxford University Press.

Walton, Douglas (2002). The Sunk Costs Fallacy or Argument from Waste, *Argumentation*, 16, 473-503.

Walton, Douglas (1996). *Argumentation Schemes for Presumptive Reasoning*, Mahwah, New Jersey, Erlbaum.

Walton, Douglas (1997). *Appeal to Expert Opinion*, University Park, Pennsylvania, Penn State Press.

Walton, Douglas and Reed, Chris (2005), Argumentation Schemes and Enthymemes, *Synthese: An International Journal for Epistemology, Methodology and Philosophy of Science*, 145, 339-370.

Walton, Douglas, Reed, Chris and Macagno, Fabrizio (2008). *Argumentation Schemes*, Cambridge, Cambridge University Press.

Wooldridge, Michael (2000). *Reasoning about Rational Agents*, Cambridge, Mass., The MIT Press.

Wyner, Adam and Bench-Capon, Trevor (2007). Argument Schemes for Legal Case-Based Reasoning, *Legal Knowledge and Information Systems: JURIX 2007, The Twentieth International Conference*, ed. Arno R. Lodder and Laurens Mommers, Amsterdam IOS Press, 139-149.

About the author:

Douglas Walton (1942–2020) (Ph.D. University of Toronto, 1972) was the Distinguished Research Fellow of CRRAR (Centre for Research in Reasoning, Argumentation and Rhetoric) at the University of Windsor. During 2008-2013 he also held the Assumption Chair of Argumentation Studies at UWindsor. He had been a Visiting Professor at Northwestern University, at University of Arizona, and at University of Lugano (Switzerland). In 2009 he received the Faculty of Arts and Social Sciences Dean's Special Recognition Award of the University of Windsor, in recognition of excellence in research, scholarship and creative activity. In the area of argumentation studies he published 50 books, as well as 350 refereed papers, and had well over 20,000 citations of his writings (Google Scholar).

12

Constructing Effective Arguments

Beth Innocenti

1. The problem: How can speakers construct effective arguments?

Social actors make arguments for a range of purposes, such as to reflect on their own reasoning (Hoffmann 2016), to induce audiences to perform cognitive activities that may be precursors to belief or action such as wondering, considering, and looking for evidence (Pinto 1991), to accept accountability for a position (Andone 2015), to display identity (Hample and Irions 2015), and more. In this chapter I focus on making arguments for a proposal in order to influence audiences to consider the merits of the proposal.

By "making arguments" I mean the strategy of communicating linguistically explicable premise-conclusion units (O'Keefe 1982), distinguishable from other strategies such as using vivid descriptions, marching in protest, or drawing a border around some text that includes arguments (Jacobs 2000). When constructing effective arguments, social actors need to consider the full range of rhetorical strategies, in addition to making arguments, that they can use to get audiences to reason well (Jacobs 2006). Rhetorical traditions show that social actors have been inventing ways of managing disagreement in reasonable manners for centuries (Jackson 2015).

Proposing is a widespread illocutionary act—an act performed just by saying something (Austin 1962). Social actors propose in a range of contexts: proposing a policy at a school board meeting, proposing a topic for a research paper, proposing to a committee that a project receive funding, proposing a destination for a family vacation, and more. To address the range of contexts in which social actors make proposals and the various design options that contexts present, such as school board meeting procedures or the parameters of a research paper assignment, I limit the discussion to communication design strategies, or how social actors design contexts just by saying something (Goodwin 2007; Jackson and Aakhus 2014). What strategies can social actors use to construct effective arguments for a proposal, where "effective" arguments are arguments that audiences are influenced to scrutinize?

Social scientific researchers have identified factors that may influence the likelihood that audiences will scrutinize arguments. For example, on one hand, if personal involvement in an issue is low, then even if a social actor designs a proposal that includes many strong arguments to show why the matter is relevant to the audience, audience members may simply assume that the high number of arguments means the proposal was well-researched, and warrant their attitude about the proposal by that assumption rather than think carefully about the merits of the arguments (Petty and Cacioppo 1984). On the other hand, undistracted audiences who are knowledgeable, have a high need for cognition and high personal involvement with an issue, may scrutinize arguments by assessing the relevance and sufficiency of evidence, considering counter-proposals, playing devil's advocate, and so on (O'Keefe 2013). Many of these factors are beyond the proposer's ability to address directly, and focus on human cognition to the exclusion of actual circumstances of people's lives—their race, class, gender, ability, and more (hooks 2015). How can social actors construct effective arguments for proposals to influence even reluctant audiences to make special efforts, such as finding a quiet location or acquiring background knowledge, to scrutinize them?

Textbooks typically cover communication strategies proposers may use to construct effective arguments: undertaking and discharging a burden of proof, addressing stock issues, adapting to the audience, and using style and broader language strategies. In what follows I introduce argumentation theory developed by Communication Studies researchers (e.g., Goodwin 2011; Innocenti and Miller 2016; Jacobs 2000; Kauffeld 1998; van Eemeren et al. 2014) that explains why these strategies may reasonably be expected to influence audiences to scrutinize arguments for a proposal. The theory is called "normative pragmatic theory" because it accounts for the persuasive force of strategies social actors actually use ("pragmatic") by the norms that strategies bring to bear in the situation ("normative"). The theories hold that strategies influence because they bring to bear norms that audiences presumably want to enact, such as acting prudently, holding well-informed opinions, living up to the "golden rule," and more. To avoid criticism for ignorance, holding double-standards, and so on, audience members can be influenced by the strategies.

2. Undertaking and discharging a burden of proof

Textbooks typically discuss making arguments for proposals in terms of presumptions and burdens of proof. Students may be familiar with a presumption of innocence: a defendant is presumed innocent until proven guilty; the prosecution has the burden of proof. In the context of a policy debate, students or instructors may assign the burden of proof to those proposing changes to the status quo; the status quo has the presumption. But why do social actors in a range of more or less formal, institutional through interpersonal contexts, willingly undertake a burden of proof when making a proposal, even in contexts where a burden of proof is not simply assigned by, say, the forms of process in a legal institution or an instructor assigning a research paper?

The answer involves describing presumptions and burdens of proof in terms of the kinds of responsibilities incurred just by the act of proposing. A presumption may be described as an inference or a kind of reason based on what social actors believe someone would not risk doing due to the resentment it could occasion (Kauffeld 2001). For example, statements designed to get audiences to believe something engage a presumption of veracity: audiences can presume that a proposer would not risk their resentment for lying or ignorance unless she had made a responsible effort to ascertain the truth of what she was saying. Statements made for a proposal engage a presumption of veracity, but ordinarily just a presumption of veracity is not sufficient to influence audiences to give a proposal serious consideration (Kauffeld 1998; Pinto 2007). To construct a proposal that influences audiences to scrutinize arguments for its merits, typically a social actor needs to say more than "I propose *x*."

One strategy proposers use is deliberately, openly undertaking and discharging a burden of proof. In fact, ordinarily proposers are not simply advised but in fact are obligated to be able to give reasons why a proposal deserves consideration (Kauffeld 1998). First, it would be incoherent for a proposer to say, "I propose *x*, but I cannot give you any reasons why we ought to *x*." Second, a proposer who says, "I propose *x*," but gives few or poor reasons why the audience ought to *x*, risks the audience's resentment for wasting their time. Just saying "I propose *x*" licenses audiences to presume the proposer has good reasons in support of the proposal; audiences can presume the proposer would not risk their resentment for wasting their time unless she could show the merits of her proposal (Kauffeld 1998). A proposer can forestall the risk of resentment by making good on that presumption—by showing that she has good reasons for making the proposal. Moreover, a proposer can make further efforts—undertake additional burdens—to license audiences to presume that her proposal merits attention and scrutiny. For example, she can show that she has taken into account doubts and objections that may be raised by the audience. By bringing to bear a norm that prudent people attend to messages that take their interests into account and display hallmarks of rationality, a proposer makes it risky for audiences who want to lay claim to acting prudently to ignore or perfunctorily dismiss the proposal. Undertaking and discharging a burden of proof influences audiences to scrutinize arguments for a proposal in order to avoid criticism for acting imprudently.

3. Addressing stock issues

What kinds of reasons can a proposer give to an audience to make good on the obligation to have reasons? Again, textbooks typically suggest an effective strategy: addressing stock issues. Different textbooks may express stock issues in somewhat different ways. One possible list of stock issues for making a case that problems or needs ought to be addressed is the following:

- Conditions exist.
- The conditions result in harmful consequences.
- The harms are significant.
- The conditions are inherent to the system.

One possible list of stock issues for making a case for a solution or remedy is the following:

- The solution is possible.
- The solution will address the problem.
- The solution will produce additional benefits.
- The solution will not introduce new problems.
- The advantages of the solution outweigh the disadvantages.
- The solution is the best alternative.
- The solution is legal, fair, just, moral.

By addressing stock issues, a proposer can show that the proposal is well-researched, carefully-considered, and the like, and takes into account objections, queries, doubts, and so on that audiences may raise. So the strategy of addressing stock issues engages the presumption of veracity as well as a presumption that the proposer would not risk criticism for wasting the audience's time, misleading them, and the like, unless she had made a responsible effort to think carefully about the issues, collect evidence, consider its sufficiency and relevance, and so on. These presumptions are reasons the audience now has to scrutinize arguments for the proposal. To avoid a risk of criticism for ignoring, disregarding, dismissing a well-researched proposal that takes their queries, doubts, and so on into consideration—to continue acting in accord with a norm that prudent people attend to messages that display hallmarks of rationality—they can scrutinize the arguments.

Addressing stock issues may not be a straightforward task in actual situations where issues are indeterminate or social actors clash about whether something is an issue or what the issues ought to be. For example, proposers may need to make statements about what the "real" issues are and show that particular issues must be addressed to avoid future criticism for "wishful thinking" in case audience members refuse or fail to see that some matter is an issue (Goodwin 2002). Making arguments is a strategy for showing that some matter is an issue at all and worth arguing about. In short, constructing effective arguments for proposals involves making situated judgments to decide and then special efforts to show that something is an issue at all and to show that it is worth arguing about.

4. Adapting to the audience

The situated judgments that social actors need to make in order to decide how to design effective arguments for a proposal include deciding how to adapt to audiences. Typically textbooks suggest collecting different kinds of information about the audience in order to tailor arguments to the audience. For example, proposers may be able to collect demographic information about audience members' ages, races, ethnicities, genders, nationalities, and more. In addition, proposers may survey audience members about their attitudes, beliefs, and values. As with other topics typically covered in textbooks, this is good information to consider when designing arguments for a proposal for a specific audience. Deploying that information in a proposal shows that the proposer has made special efforts to take into account the audience's interests, so brings to bear a norm that prudent people will attend to messages that take their interests into account (Kauffeld 1998). To avoid a risk of criticism for acting imprudently, audiences can scrutinize the arguments for the proposal.

Perhaps proposers may easily collect that sort of information if they are constructing arguments for persons with whom they are familiar and have ongoing arguments (Gilbert 2014). But scenarios may present for which proposers do not know or are mistaken in their assumptions about the attitudes, beliefs, values, or demographics of persons with whom they are familiar. The difficulty of collecting that sort of information at all, or of using it to construct a coherent case for a proposal, is even higher in circumstances where an audience comprises diverse groups, and diverse groups comprise diverse individuals, or where a proposal may reach unintended audiences or unknowable future audiences (Tindale 2013). What general, theory-based advice can be given to proposers who want to adapt their arguments to their audience? How can proposers address the challenge of adapting to diverse audiences in their particularity?

Proposers can use strategies that bring to bear in the situation norms that involve the audience members acting as the kinds of persons they want to claim to be. Making arguments—stating claims and giving reasons—brings to bear norms of acting reasonably, so people who live up to the norms—who are influenced to scrutinize the arguments—can lay claim to acting reasonably. Other strategies such as using humor can bring to bear other kinds of norms that enable audiences to act as the kinds of persons they want to claim to be. For example, in the case of an historical argument that women in New York State ought to have the right to vote, if audiences "get" a humorous refutation of the serious claim that giving women the vote would lead to domestic strife—one that humorously predicts domestic harmony because when men solicit each other's votes, they buy each other drinks and smokes—then they can lay claim to being informed, unsentimental, politically savvy (Innocenti and Miller 2016).

Further, proposers can make these norms determinate to structure the interaction (Tracy 2010). For example, they can make statements about what reasonable, tolerant, thinking, open-minded people would do. Or they can narrate personal experiences that display these kinds of norms. For example, they can say that at one time they acted out of ignorance or fear, but now, in light of their own efforts to collect information and experiences, have changed their minds. These kinds of strategies hold both proposers and audiences accountable for living up to the norms or risking criticism for failing to live up to them. The strategies can be used to construct effective arguments for proposals, because the norms they bring to bear in the situation provide grounds for action and are sources of influence.

5. Using style and language strategies

Constructing effective arguments for a proposal involves attending to style. Analytically it is possible to separate arguments from style. Reconstructing arguments as premise-conclusion units to assess the acceptability, relevance, and sufficiency of premises does just that, and is a fundamental skill of critical thinking. When constructing effective arguments for proposals, it is possible to model the style on a reconstruction such that a reconstruction would look exactly like the argument as presented. Ordinarily actual arguments do not take the pristine shape of a reconstruction. In constructing effective arguments, proposers make stylistic choices from word choice to sentence structure to broader units of discourse, so making arguments is inseparable from style (Fahnestock 1999, 2011). In addition, proposers make other stylistic choices as they supplement the strategy of making arguments with other kinds of strategies that can enhance people's capacity or ability to choose when to scrutinize arguments (Jacobs 2000, 2006; O'Keefe 1995).

One way of explaining the effectiveness of particular language strategies is cognitively. For example, clarity is necessary for message comprehensibility and increases the likelihood that audiences will scrutinize arguments

(Petty and Cacioppo 1986). Normative pragmatic theory explains why clarity is typically foregrounded in discussions of style from some of the earliest reflections on style and argument such as in Aristotle's *Rhetoric*. Effective arguments that generate persuasive force require that social actors openly, deliberately intend to influence audiences, so proposers cannot plausibly deny their intent to influence audiences to seriously consider the merits of the proposal (Kauffeld 1998, 2001). As a result, proposing openly, with clarity, stylistically creates conditions that reduce the proposer's "wiggle room", constraining her from dodging obligations she incurs just by proposing, as discussed in the "Undertaking and discharging a burden of proof" section. Clarity makes vivid a presumption that the proposer would not risk the audience's resentment for wasting their time unless she had good reasons for proposing.

When constructing effective arguments for proposals, proposers can consider the obligations and responsibilities they are willing to undertake and discharge, and make stylistic choices accordingly. For example, they may choose to use vivid descriptions to display the adequacy of a premise and, by doing so, hold both themselves and audiences accountable for seeing, say, the nature and significance of a problem (Manolescu 2005). Or they may choose to make powerful emotional appeals that license presumptions such as: the proposer would not risk criticism for manipulation unless she had made efforts to ascertain the high stakes of the situation (Jacobs 2006; Manolescu 2006).

6. Conclusion

In summary, it is possible to provide theory-based rationales for the kinds of actions typically recommended for constructing effective arguments for proposals: undertaking and discharging a burden of proof, addressing stock issues, adapting to the audience, and using style and other language strategies. In all cases, these actions may be designed by proposers to influence audiences to scrutinize arguments for a proposal by making it risky not to. Strategies bring to bear different norms—acting prudently, holding well-informed positions, possessing political savvy, living up to the "golden rule", and more—that are designed to structure the interaction by pressuring audiences to act in accord with them. As it turns out, one of the best strategies a proposer can use to display these qualities and thereby pressure audiences to act in accord with them is making arguments.

References

Andone, Corina (2015). Pragmatic argumentation in European practices of political accountability. *Argumentation* 29 (1), 1-18.

Austin, J.L. (1962). *How to Do Things with Words.* Cambridge: Harvard University Press.

Eemeren, Frans H. van, Garssen, Bart, Krabbe, Erik C.W., Snoeck Henkemans, A. Francisca, Verheij, Bart and Wagemans, Jean H.M. (2014). *Handbook of Argumentation Theory.* Dordrecht: Springer.

Fahnestock, Jeanne (1999). *Rhetorical Figures in Science.* New York: Oxford University Press.

Fahnestock, Jeanne (2011). *Rhetorical Style: The Uses of Language in Persuasion.* New York: Oxford University Press.

Gilbert, Michael A. (2014). *Arguing With People.* Peterborough: Broadview Press.

Goodwin, Jean (2002). Designing issues. In F.H. van Eemeren and P. Houtlosser (Eds.), *Dialectic and Rhetoric: The Warp and Woof of Argumentation Analysis* (pp. 81-96). Dordrecht: Kluwer.

Goodwin, Jean (2007). Argument has no function. *Informal Logic* 27(1), 69-90.

Goodwin, Jean (2011). Accounting for the appeal to the authority of experts. *Argumentation* 25(3), 285-96.

Hample, Dale and Irions, Amanda L. (2015). Arguing to display identity. *Argumentation* 29(4), 389-416.

Hoffmann, Michael H.G. (2016). Reflective argumentation: A cognitive function of arguing. *Argumentation* 30(4), 365-397.

hooks, bell (2015). *Feminist Theory: From Margin to Center.* New York: Routledge.

Innocenti, Beth and Miller, Elizabeth (2016). The persuasive force of political humor. *Journal of Communication* 66(3), 366-385.

Jackson, Sally (2015). Design thinking in argumentation theory and practice. *Argumentation* 29(3), 243-263.

Jackson, Sally, and Aakhus, Mark (2014). Becoming more reflective about the role of design in communication. *Journal of Applied Communication Research* 42(2), 125–134.

Jacobs, Scott (2000). Rhetoric and dialectic from the standpoint of normative pragmatics. *Argumentation* 14(3), 261-86.

Jacobs, Scott (2006). Nonfallacious rhetorical strategies: Lyndon Johnson's Daisy ad. *Argumentation* 20(4), 421-42.

Kauffeld, Fred J. (1998). Presumptions and the distribution of argumentative burdens in acts of proposing and accusing. *Argumentation* 12(2), 245-66.

Manolescu, Beth Innocenti (2005). Norms of presentational force. *Argumentation and Advocacy* 41, 139-151.

Manolescu, Beth Innocenti (2006). A normative pragmatic perspective on appealing to emotions in argumentation. *Argumentation* 20(3), 327-343.

O'Keefe, Daniel J. (1982). The concepts of argument and arguing. In J. Robert Cox and Charles Arthur Willard (Eds.), *Advances in Argumentation Theory and Research* (pp. 3-23). Carbondale: Southern Illinois University Press.

O'Keefe, D.J. (1995). Argumentation studies and dual-process models of persuasion. In F.H. van Eemeren, R. Grootendorst, J.A. Blair and C.A. Willard (Eds.), *Perspectives and Approaches: Proceedings of the Third ISSA Conference on Argumentation* (Vol. 1, pp. 3–17). Amsterdam: Sic Sat.

O'Keefe, D.J. (2013). The elaboration likelihood model. In J.P. Dillard and L. Shen (Eds.), *The SAGE Handbook of Persuasion: Developments in Theory and Practice*, 2nd ed. (pp. 137-149). Los Angeles: SAGE.

Petty, R.E. and Cacioppo, J.T. (1984). The effects of involvement in responses to argument quantity and quality: Central and peripheral routes to persuasion. *Journal of Personality and Social Psychology* 46(1), 69-81.

Petty, R.E. and Cacioppo, J.T. (1986). *Communication and Persuasion: Central and Peripheral Routes to Attitude Change*. New York: Springer-Verlag.

Pinto, Robert C. (1991). Generalizing the notion of argumentation. In F.H. van Eemeren, R. Grootendorst, J.A. Blair and C.A. Willard (Eds.), *Proceedings of the Second International Conference on Argumentation*, vol. 1 (pp. 137-146). Amsterdam: SIC SAT.

Pinto, Robert C. (2007). Burdens of rejoinder. In Hans V. Hansen and Robert C. Pinto, (Eds.), *Reason Reclaimed: Essays in Honor of J. Anthony Blair and Ralph H. Johnson* (pp. 75-88). Newport News: Vale.

Tindale, Christopher W. (2013). Rhetorical argumentation and the nature of audience: Toward an understanding of audience-issues in argumentation. *Philosophy and Rhetoric* 46(4), 508-532.

Tracy, Karen (2010). *Challenges of Ordinary Democracy: A Case Study in Deliberation and Dissent*. University Park: Pennsylvania State University Press.

About the author:

Beth Innocenti has authored numerous essays on contemporary and historical argumentation theory and the entry "Argumentation" in *Oxford Bibliographies in Communication*. Her research has been published in journals such as *Argumentation, Philosophy and Rhetoric,* and *Journal of Communication,* and explains how social actors design speech acts and strategies—such as demanding, using humor, and making fear appeals—to influence addressees as openly intended. She has also published accounts of historical theories of argument proffered by eighteenth- and nineteenth-century writers on rhetoric. She serves as Editor of *Argumentation and Advocacy* and on the editorial board of *Philosophy of Rhetoric.* She is currently Professor in the Department of Communication Studies at the University of Kansas and has served as Department Chair, Director of Graduate Studies, and Director of Undergraduate Studies. The department houses faculty and graduate students who coach one of the best collegiate debate teams in the United States.

13

Judging Arguments

J. Anthony Blair

1. Introduction

This chapter reviews what is involved in identifying, interpreting, displaying, evaluating and responding to arguments that people make—O'Keefe's "argument$_1$" discussed in Chapter 8. The term 'judging' encompasses all these activities, since all of them call for judgment. Most critical thinking textbooks focus on arguments that are reason-claim complexes. These are arguments about what is claimed to be true or reasonable to believe or to do. Their conclusions are either propositions—sentences with truth values (i.e., are true or false, probable or improbable, plausible or implausible)—or else they are prescriptions—recommendations or imperatives, (which are not true or false, but rather are sensible or ill-advised, wise or foolish, virtuous or vicious, and so on). It might turn out that different kinds of judgment are appropriate for these two kinds of aims of argument.

In this chapter, "judging arguments" includes: (1) judging that a particular text of discourse is or contains an argument, (2) judging just what the contents and structure of each such arguments consist of, (3) judging the strengths and weaknesses of each such argument, and (4) judging how best to respond to the argument(s). Correspondingly, judging arguments in this sense will have these four components, in this order: (1) argument identification, (2) argument analysis or mapping, (3) argument evaluation, and (4) responding to an argument.

The order matters, because each successive judgment presupposes the successful completion of its predecessor(s). Also, the judging can break off at any point. Obviously if it is determined that there is no argument, the exercise ends at (1). But sometimes although it is clear that someone is trying to argue, their communication can be so unclear that it is impossible to decide just what the argument is supposed to be, so the exercise ends at (2). Furthermore, it's often the case that there is no response to make beyond registering and defending one's assessment of the argument, so the exercise ends at (3).

Additionally, while these four judgments can be distinguished, in practice there is usually interaction among them. For instance the presence of illatives such as 'since' and 'therefore' can indicate (among other things) both (1) the presence and (2) the structure of an argument. Also, often the analyst's attribution of (2) one structure instead of another can depend on which of the two renders (3) the more plausible or stronger argument.[1] And (4) what response to make to an arguer depends partly on (3) how one assesses the merits of the argument, and perhaps even on (2) how one has analyzed the map of the argument.

2. Identifying arguments

Sometimes a writer will identify his or her contribution to a discourse as an argument:

"My argument for this claim is this:...."
"There are several reasons for adopting this view. First, ..."
"Not everyone agrees with this claim. Here is why I think it is true. ...."

And so on. (Such self-identifications will be mistaken if what the speaker or writer has produced is not an argument, but, for example, merely an assertion, or an explanation.)

Critical thinking textbooks almost invariably point out that people use *semantic cues* to make clear that they intend to be communicating an argument. Words such as 'therefore,' 'since,' 'because' and 'so' can mark the illative relation of support or consequence, and thereby be signs of the presence of argument. Unfortunately, they are not foolproof signs, for all of the so-called illatives can be and often are used to perform other speech functions besides signaling the premise-conclusion relation indicative of an argument. So additional cues need to be considered.

Arguments can be anticipated in a variety of *contexts*. Disagreements typically give rise to arguments, so discourse in a context of disagreement can be expected to be argumentative. Some venues are institutionalized to require

---

[1] Taking an author to intend the interpretation that yields the best argument from among the possible interpretations of a text that is unclear or ambiguous is an employment of the Principle of Charity as it applies to argumentation. One justification for invoking such charity is that the stronger argument puts the position in a better light, and both because she wants to put forward the best case for her position; the critic the arguer and the critic want to deal with the stronger argument: the arguer, because he doesn't want to waste time critiquing the weaker argument only to have the arguer withdraw it and replace it with the stronger one.

arguments. In criminal and civil trials, lawyers are expected to argue, and judges are expected to give arguments for their rulings. Even when doubt has not been expressed, there can be informal customs or institutionalized norms that place the burden of proof on anyone who would assert a claim, as in the case of scientific reports, scholarly articles in the humanities, or the afore-mentioned judges' rulings. The so-called "editorial" pages of newspapers, which contain *editorials* by the paper's editors, *opinion pieces* by regular or occasional columnists, and *letters to the editor*, are places where controversies are addressed (or initiated), and so where any "side" needs to be backed up by the reasons that its advocate thinks support it and that might persuade others to accept it.

Experienced speakers or authors speak and write with the audience they are addressing or hope to reach in mind. If you can anticipate the kinds of doubts or questions the likely or intended audience will harbor about the claims asserted, you can identify where the writer or speaker needs to be providing arguments. This can help to identify their presence in parts of the text that otherwise are hard to account for.

Yet another indication of the presence of an argument in a stretch of discourse is that some of the assertions "make sense" as support for one of the others. That is, even if there are no semantic clues, if some of the assertions were to be taken as support for another one and that would be a plausible argument, then the discourse may reasonably be taken as containing a plausible argument, if there are no contrary indications.

3. The structure of arguments: Argument mapping

Since the reason a critical thinker attends to arguments is to judge whether they provide the support that they're alleged to for their claims, the critical appraiser needs to understand accurately just what that support is supposed to be. That means getting a clear picture of the route that the author's reasons take in providing that support. Maps or diagrams showing the structure of an argument's reasoning can be drawn by hand; they can also be displayed on a computer's monitor. Drawing a diagram, or fashioning one on a computer monitor, that displays the route(s) the reasoning taken is called "argument mapping". In either case, sets of conventions have to be adopted (and learned by the reader or viewer). Thus any argument-mapping program will need what old-fashioned geographical maps used to call a "Legend". [Argument mapping, including computer-assisted argument mapping, is discussed in detail in Chapter 10.]

The analyst faces several choices when dealing with arguments "on the hoof"—i.e., in their native habitats", "as found" or "in the wild". Below are described various aspects of an argument's structure. It should not be overlooked, however, that these structural properties are determined by functional properties of the discourse. For instance, what counts as a premise or a conclusion is determined by the functions of the sentences in the discourse. Does *p* serve as support for *q*? If so, then *p* is a premise and *q* is a conclusion; or does *q* serve as support for *p*? If so, then *vice versa*.

3.1 Ordering

There is no convention in English composition for the order in which premises and conclusions appear in a text containing an argument, and in practice any order may be found. Thus, it's to be emphasized that 'conclusion', when used to refer to the claim being defended in an argument, has a different meaning than when it is used to refer to the final section of a text.

The analyst will have to identify which assertion states the conclusion, and decide on a convention for organizing the premises spatially on the page.

3.2 Deletion

In addition to the sentences expressing the premises and conclusion of an argument, typically there are parts of the discourse that are not elements of the argument. They might be performing other functions, such as clarifying, or explaining, or they might be simply irrelevant to the argument. Such material can be set aside, not to appear on the map of the argument.

3.3 Multiple-arguments

Frequently single arguments are combined in various ways. There can be a single main conclusion, but one or more of the premises directly supporting it are themselves the conclusions of other arguments. Or there can be more than one line of reasoning supporting the same conclusion. Some theorists hold that meta-arguments are supplied because arguments are always occasioned by doubts, disagreements, questions or challenges, either from an actual interlocutor or from one imagined or anticipated by the arguer. If so, the arguer who inserts a meta-argument must have anticipated some challenge. Other theorists, while they grant that this is often or even usually the case, hold that arguers can offer additional arguments to cement their case, whether that's needed to answer doubts or not.[2] Yet others hold that, at least in some special

---

[2] For instance: "You can't have seen Aunt Muriel in the Hudson Bay store in Windsor last week: there is no Hudson Bay store in Windsor any more, and anyway, Aunt Muriel died a year ago." Here the arguer gives two reasons for accepting the conclusion, each one of which is by itself decisive. So why offer both if one alone

fields if not generally, there are conventions that require every assertion to be defended unless one of the standard exemptions applies (e.g., it is self-evident, or in some sense primitive, or defended elsewhere) even if there are no actual or anticipated doubts.

Here is a simple example, in this case an argument about what to do, taking **1** to be meant to convey that the addressee should take her raincoat.

> **1**You'll be wanting to take your raincoat. **2**It might rain this afternoon. **3**At least, that was the forecast on this morning's news. **4**You won't want to get your new dress soaked.

Here, **2** and **4** combine to support **1**, and **3** supports **2**.

3.4 Addition

Consider simple arguments like these. "You should take your raincoat. It's going to rain." Or "He'll be late for dinner. His train's been delayed." In each case, how does the reason offered provide grounds for the conclusion? In each case there's an understood connection. If you'll want to have your raincoat if it rains, then if it's going to rain, you should take your raincoat. In the other case, if his not arriving at the regularly scheduled time will cause him to be late for dinner and if the train's being delayed means he'll arrive later than scheduled, then he will be late for dinner. By adding an obviously true piece of unexpressed information, the analyst can make the reasoning of the argument more perspicuous.

How does one know what to add? One approach is to add the associated conditional (AC) of the argument as a new premise. The associated conditional is the conditional statement former by taking the conjunction of the stated premises as its antecedent and the conclusion as its consequent. For the above examples, this advice would yield these reconstructions:

A.
1. It's going to rain.
2. If it's going to rain, you should take your raincoat. (AC)
3. You should take your raincoat.

B.
4. His train has been delayed.
5. If his train has been delayed, he will be late for dinner. (AC)
6. He'll be late for dinner.

is sufficient to establish the conclusion? There can no longer be reasonable doubt that the conclusion is true after just one of the reasons was mentioned.

Adding the associated conditional renders the argument deductively valid (by *modus ponens*), but it does so often at the cost of adding a questionable new premise. In arguments about what to do, like A, it overlooks the possibility of contrary considerations. If you are going to be indoors the whole time and/or if your raincoat would be an unwanted encumbrance, 2. is ill-suited advice. In arguments about what to believe like B, it overlooks possible conditions of rebuttal. If dinner will be delayed too, for some other reason, 5. might be false; or if the delay is too long he will miss dinner altogether, and 5. would be false. If any of such arguments' premises is false, the conclusion is not supported. This result has led some theorists to call for a modification of the associated conditional, and sometimes of the conclusions too, to make the argument plausible, consistent with the known commitments of the arguer. Accordingly, the first argument might be restated as:

C.
1. It's going to rain.
2. You'll want your raincoat if it rains.
3. You should take your raincoat.

And the second might be restated as:

D.
4. His train has been delayed.
5. The train delay will probably delay his arrival until after dinner begins.
6. He'll probably be late for dinner.

As Hitchcock (2017, p. 60) has noted, the traditional treatment of such arguments has variants:

> Ennis (1982), for example, distinguished two types of what he calls 'gap fillers': used assumptions and needed assumptions. Govier (1987, 1992) favours a policy of 'no supplementation without justification' (1992. p. 50), which leads her to focus on the first of these types, what the arguer implicitly accepts or can reasonably be assumed to accept; she does however allow that one may supply a 'missing premise' which is implied by 'the direction of the reasoning', a notion for which she gives no theoretical analysis. Van Eemeren and Grootendost (1984, 1992) regard the unexpressed premiss as implicit in the argument, thus focusing on the second of Ennis's two types. Anderson and Belnap (1961, p. 719) treat the task of evaluating the inference of an enthymeme neither as one of discovering some unstated claim which the arguer accepts nor as one of discovering some further premiss which is implicit in the argument, but rather as one of discovering an additional true sentence from which in combination with the stated premise the conclusion follows logically.

Hitchcock himself objects to the notion that it is necessary to supply unexpressed premises. He argues that every argument assumes a general conditional that its proponent thinks warrants the inference from the stated premises to the conclusion. Some such conditional inference license is presupposed by every argument. It is not another premise, just unexpressed, for if it were, the argument would require yet another inference license warranting the new set of premises as adequate support for the conclusion. But then the new inference license would have to be treated as another unexpressed premise to be added to the premise set, giving rise to the need for yet another inference license, and so on ad infinitum.

3.5 Restatement

Most theorists of argument analysis allow for restating the arguments in a text in order to make the reasoning of the arguments more perspicuous. For instance, arguers will use pronouns to refer to people and objects in their arguments, and when arranging the premises in an order that exposes their steps towards the conclusion there can be a number of 'he's and 'she's and 'it's that are confusing. It doesn't change the sense of the argument if these are replaced by their referents. Arguers employ synonyms for stylistic variation, but it can be clearer if the same term is used for a given referent throughout the reconstructed argument.

However, there are limits to restatement. Often the associations of given words lend force to the argument, and if a particular term used by the arguer is substituted by the analyst when reconstructing the argument, the argument can lose some of its persuasive power. Also, if question-begging value-laden terms are replaced during reconstruction, possible illicit devices will be cleansed and the argument can be made to appear less specious than it is.

On balance, probably a good rule of thumb is, as far as possible leave the language of the original argument untouched, and make changes only if the argument is otherwise unintelligible.

4 Evaluating arguments

This topic turns out to be more complicated than many textbooks seem to assume. Many suggest that to evaluate an argument one needs to determine whether its premises are true, and if so, whether they support its conclusion. An argument is thus to be accepted or rejected, on these grounds. But think of D. J. O'Keefe's distinction between an argument that someone **makes** (argument₁), and an argument that two (or more) people **have** (argument₂) (see Chapter 8). An argument that people are *having* can possess a number or virtues, or their corresponding vices. It can be judged to be friendly or unfriendly, sympathetic or hostile, constructive or destructive, pig-headed or accommodating, personal or detached, and so on. These and similar qualities do not apply to an argument that someone *makes*. Arguments of the latter sort are more or less convincing, provide strong or weak support, and so on.

Arguments about what to do introduce further complications. For while the audience might agree with the values and goals and the means-ends relations appealed to in the argument in support of the prescription, and thus grant that they constitute good reasons for it, its members might at the same time espouse other values and goals that weigh against the prescription and that in their judgment carry more weight. Thus, while granting the merits of the argument as far as it goes, they do not agree that it provides adequate support for its conclusion. To be decisive, such arguments need to include a premise to the effect that the audience will find no overriding contra-considerations, and such a premise is likely to be difficult to defend.

Scholars grounded in different fields tend to work with different conceptions of argument, and as a result, to evaluate arguments differently. Communication theorists tend to focus on argu*ing*—the characteristics of the communicative exchange in various kinds of arguments that people *have* with one another. Theorists from linguistics backgrounds tend to focus on the pragmatics of argu*ing*—the different uses to which arguments are put, the way language works in arguings, and the practical functions of arguing. Philosophers tend to be interested in the logic of the argu*ments* used in arguing and the conditions under which such arguments contribute to justified belief and knowledge acquisition. Rhetoricians tend to focus on arguments about what to do (Kock 2017).

4.1 Soundness

There have been various approaches to determining what makes for a good argument—"good" in the sense that its audience should either be convinced by it or in the sense that it should influence the audience to be inclined towards accepting its conclusion.

As 'sound' is often used in logic, a "sound" argument has *true premises* and they either logically *entail the conclusion or* they provide *strong inductive grounds* for accepting the conclusion. Some would both strengthen and weaken the truth condition here, so that a "sound" argument's premises are either *known* (by arguer and target audience) to be true, or else are *reasonably believed* (by them) to be true.

Some regard these two criteria—combinations of premise truth or reasonable believability with inferential deductive validity or with inductive strength—as exhaustive. "A good argument is either deductively valid or inductively strong", it is said. That view is true by definition of you define 'inductively strong' to cover any argument that has a good inference that is not deductively valid. "Inductive strength" thereby becomes a catch-all, to denote a property of any good argument that is not deductively valid. Others recommend distinguishing a wider variety of ways non-deductively valid arguments can be good arguments nonetheless.

Many theorists today classify logically good arguments as either deductively valid or *defeasible*. An argument that is rationally compelling but not deductively valid is said to be defeasible. Thus a strong inductive argument is defeasible, but so are some arguments that aren't typical inductive arguments. An appeal to authority would be an example. Moral arguments that appeal to rules that can have exceptions are defeasible. The premises of a strong but defeasible argument provide good reasons for accepting the conclusion, even though a situation is conceivable in which some additional statement that is consistent with the premises but inconsistent with the conclusion is also true.

Two approaches to determining whether an argument is good side-step the dispute over whether "deductively valid and inductively strong" exhaust the class of rationally compelling arguments. One approach is to check to see whether the argument scheme employed is appropriate and correctly used; the other approach is to employ the criteria of acceptability, relevance and sufficiency.

4.2 Argument scheme assessment

Here is how Walton, Reed and Macagno (2008, pp. 1-2), leading theorists of this approach, introduce the idea of argument schemes:

> Argumentation schemes are forms of argument (structures of reasoning) that represent common types of arguments used in everyday discourse, as well as in special contexts like those of legal argumentation and scientific argumentation. They include the deductive and inductive forms of argument that we are already so familiar with in logic. However, they also represent forms of argument that are neither deductive nor inductive, but that fall into a third category sometimes called defeasible, presumptive, or abductive. Such an argument can rightly carry weight, or be a plausible basis for acceptance.

Walton et al. include a compendium of 60 schemes representing "the most commonly used forms of argument" (2008, p. 308; see pp. 308-346).[3] To each scheme is attached a set of "critical questions" (*ibid.*, p. 3). These are

---

[3] Argument scheme theory is still under development. For instance, the Pragma-dialectical school holds that all schemes are variations of three basic types: symptomatic argumentation, similarity argumentation and instrumental argumentation (van Eemeren and Grootendorst 1992), whereas Walton et al. (ibid.) acknowledge no such classification.

questions that test an argument instantiating such a scheme in any circumstance and which, if answered satisfactorily in any particular case, authorize the argument as holding, at least tentatively.

Walton, who is recognized world-wide as an authority on argument scheme theory, introduces it thoroughly in Chapter 11, above. The reader who wants to know about it can turn there for a detailed account.

Using argument schemes to assess arguments does not require having on hand a list of schemes with their accompanying critical questions and looking these up, like checking in a book of recipes. Instead, the assessor can formulate the pattern of reasoning that the argument in question exhibits and then sketch the conditions that would have to be satisfied for any argument of this pattern to be plausible, thereby creating the pertinent critical questions. If the use of the argument in question on this occasion satisfies those conditions, it can be judged to be plausible; otherwise, not.

4.3 Checking Acceptability, Relevance and Sufficiency

Another general method of assessment is to use the criteria triad of Acceptability, Relevance and Sufficiency—ARS. The contention is that an argument is good if, but only if, its grounds are acceptable, relevant and sufficient. Govier (e.g., 1992) uses "adequacy of grounds" in place of "sufficiency". What constitutes each of these elements needs to be specified.[4]

Here is a sketch of an analysis of the acceptability of premises as a criterion of argument cogency. Being acceptable is a property of a sentence, p, in relation to a person, S. In this method of argument assessment, however, acceptability is the special case of a criterion for the adequacy of unsupported premises in an argument, A. A premise of an argument, A, is unsupported if no reasons are offered as part of A in its support. Such premise acceptability is relative to any person, S, who is a member of, or joins, the audience to which A is addressed. A premise is acceptable to S if S is entitled to accept it.

S is entitled to accept an unsupported premise, p, of an argument, A, addressed to S or to an audience of which S is a member, or that S entertains, and:

1. S knows that p, or S believes that p and is entitled to believe that p, or;
2. p is known to be true or reasonable to believe in S's cognitive environment, or;
3. p follows from assertions S is entitled to accept.

---

[4] Johnson and Blair 2006 is the *locus classicus* for an earlier version of the test. What is proposed here is slightly different.

The idea is that an arguer does not have to defend premises that the interlocutor and members of the audience know to be true, or that they believe on good grounds, or that are matters of common knowledge that the arguer can reasonably take them to know or reasonably believe, or that are implied by any of these.

For S to accept a premise, p, of A is for S to act in assessing A as if p is true. S can be entitled to accept a premise but not accept it. That is, a person might fail or refuse to accept a premise he or she ought to accept. And S can accept a premise that S is not entitled to accept.

Relevance and sufficiency are criteria for the adequacy of the link between the acceptability of the premises and the acceptability of the conclusion. The reasons offered must be *probatively* relevant to the acceptability of the conclusion for S. They have a bearing on the acceptability of the conclusion for the interlocutor or audience. Their truth would, in the absence of any other grounds, make it more likely or more plausible that the conclusion is true than would be the case if they were not true. (A *reason*, as the term is used here, is not identical to a *premise*, although a single premise can be a reason. Usually reasons consist of sets of two or more premises that are only jointly relevant.) Note that this "bearing" concept does not allow for degrees of relevance. Offered grounds either have a bearing, or they don't. There is another concept of relevance according to which evidence can be more or less relevant. According to this latter, "weight", concept, relevance signifies strength of support, and using the distinctions I am making here, this latter kind of relevance bears on the sufficiency of the grounds.

It has been argued that relevance is redundant, since sufficiency already presupposes it. You can't have enough evidence unless what you count as evidence is already relevant. That is true. However, people's arguments sometimes include irrelevant reasons. Those have to be identified and set aside before judging the sufficiency of the relevant ones that remain.

Sufficiency is the requirement that the relevant reasons offered supply enough of the right kinds of evidence to entitle the interlocutor or members of the audience to accept the conclusion as it is qualified. In many cases one example constitutes anecdotal evidence, and bears hardly any weight in supporting a conclusion that generalizes to all or even most members of a class. In others, one example can suffice as proof, e.g., that something is possible. In many cases, the findings from a well-drawn stratified random sample of 2000 people can justify a probabilistic generalization applying to 350 million people (see Chapter 18, on generalizing). So both the quantity and the quality of the evidence are important for assessing its sufficiency as support for a conclusion. Whether the reasons in support of a claim count as sufficient also depends on whether alleged reasons for not accepting the claim, or alleged reasons for rejecting any of those arguments, have been successfully refuted. What counts as "enough" will vary with the precision and the generality of the argument's conclusion. If no direct evidence for the conclusion at issue is given, it can be independently supported by arguments for rejecting alternatives to it.

These sketches of the modified ARS criteria need to be filled in, but they too are general in the respect that deductively valid and inductively strong reasoning and arguments, as well as those with other kinds of good consequence relations, all will pass their test.

The argument scheme approach and the ARS approach both assess the argument as a whole. A couple of other well-known approaches assess just the adequacy of the inference from the premises to the conclusion, and come into play independently of whether the premises are known to be true, or are reasonable to accept.

4.4 Testing by possible counter-examples

Testing by possible counter-examples is a way of assessing the strength of the link between reasons and conclusion. The reasons have to be appraised separately. The method is this: Step 1: think of considerations that are consistent with the given reasons but inconsistent with the claim being argued for (i.e., think of counter-examples). Step 2: Decide how likely or plausible are the possible counter-examples. Step 3: Draw the appropriate conclusion about the strength of the inference in the argument. Depending on whether any such counter-examples are conceivable, and if so, either probable or plausible to some extent, the reasoning can be determined to be deductively valid, or invalid but with some degree of inductive strength, or invalid but more or less reasonable.

norm	nature of counter-examples	premise-conclusion link
Deductive validity	no counter-examples can be conceived	possibly deductively valid
Inductive strength	the few counter-examples conceivable are unlikely	inductively strong
	the many counter-examples conceivable are likely	inductively weak
Plausibility	the few counter-examples conceivable are implausible	highly plausible
	the many counter-examples conceivable are plausible	highly implausible

Table 1: Testing by counter-example

Table 1 does not depict it, but likelihood (and unlikelihood), and plausibility (and implausibility) here name continuums, ranging from probability or plausibility that run so high as to be treated as certainties, at one extreme, down to, at the other extreme, improbability or implausibility that run so high as to be unquestionably false, utterly improbable, or wildly implausible. (See Pinto, Blair and Parr 1993, Ch. 6.)

4.5 Assessing the warrants of inferences in arguments

Under the influence of Stephen Toulmin's (1956) suggestion that arguments are more like legal briefs than mathematical proofs, some theorists hold that in arguments the inferential step is authorized by a presumed warrant. This warrant is not another premise; it is an assumption that is supposed to entitle one to draw the conclusion in question from the premises claimed to support it. Here is a statement of this view by David Hitchcock, its originator and most prominent advocate:

> A conclusion follows from given premises if and only if an acceptable counterfactual-supporting generalization rules out, either definitively or with some modal qualification, simultaneous acceptability of the premises and non-acceptability of the conclusion, even though it does not rule out acceptability of the premises and does not require acceptability of the conclusion independently of the premises. ... An inference claim is thus the claim that a counterfactually-supporting covering generalization is non-trivially acceptable. (Hitchcock 2017, p.180 quoting Hitchcock 2011, p. 209)

Applying this warrant-defining statement to an example, we get:

1st *premise*: My coach says I have great promise to make the national team but I need more coaching and training, which a particular summer soccer school would provide.

and

2nd *premise*: My coach is in a position to know such things [e.g., she has the experience and the expertise to be a reliable judge of soccer ability, national team standards, and so on]

So

Conclusion: I have a chance to make the national team if I get the coaching and training this summer soccer school would provide.

Warrant: If someone in a position to know such things were to say of a young soccer player that she has great promise to make the national team if but only if she obtains more coaching and training, then if that

young soccer player were to get more coaching and training, she probably would have a reasonable chance to make the national team.

Given the premises, the conclusion follows if, but only if, the warrant is
"non-trivially acceptable". If the warrant is acceptable and the premises are
true or otherwise acceptable, it is a good argument: one is entitled to accept
the conclusion.

4.6 Evaluating arguments about what to do

In argument about what to do – so-called "practical arguments" – the conclusion is not that some proposition is true or probable or otherwise acceptable, but that some action or policy should be chosen, or that some decision
should be made. Its conclusion will be supported by appeals to ideals, or goals
or other values and by claims about how the recommended action will bring
about or reflect these goals or ideals. Any disagreement might be about what
values are relevant, or, when there is agreement about what values are applicable, the disagreement might be about how to weigh them. For instance, many
Americans might agree that peace, order and good government are important
values, but many might weigh life, liberty and the pursuit of happiness more
heavily if the latter values came into conflict with the former. To be sure, one
can argue for the greater importance of, say, liberty over order in a given case,
or vice versa, but this argument too will turn on values or goals. At certain
point, disputants might have to agree to disagree.

In light of this kind of disagreement, two kinds of critical questions can be
raised in assessing practical arguments. One is whether all the values or ideals
bearing on the disagreement have been mentioned. It might turn out that some
overlooked value will change the argument. Another question is whether the
means-ends arguments being used are correct. Is the action being argued for
really required to reach that objective? In the end, however, the critic's objections will often come down to a difference in values deemed relevant, or to
a difference in the weighting of the values agreed to be relevant. When there
has been a thorough and open-minded discussion of the issues, the verdict
might have to be that the disputants simply weighted the values differently.

Notice that when a decision in the end comes down to subjective preferences and these clash, "sufficiency" can apply only as a criterion of whether
the best case for each side has been made. By hypothesis, once the best case
for each side has been argued and these have been understood and appreci-
ated by each side, the final decision is not the outcome of further argument.

4.7 Checking for fallacies

Many textbooks include lists of fallacies judged to trip up arguers or to be used by unscrupulous arguers to disguise poor arguments or shore up a weak case. Presumably textbook publishers include this material to meet a demand.

The current scholarly literature on fallacies, however, is not always reflected in these textbook treatments. For instance, it used to be held that a fallacy was a misleading pattern of argument, one designed to look valid and sound sound but that in fact was neither. Fallacies were thus viewed as counterfeit arguments as Fearnside and Holther's (1959) titled asserted: *Fallacy, The Counterfeit of Argument.* Today, the dominant view in the philosophical literature, following Walton (1995), is that fallacies are mis-deployments of otherwise innocent and useful argument schemes. In the speech communication literature, many follow van Eemeren and Grootendorst (1984) and van Eemeren (2010), who argue that fallacies are best conceived as violations of the rules for reasonable discussions designed to resolve a difference of opinion, occurring when a desire to win the argument overrides the commitment to reasonableness that engaging in argumentation presupposes. It's not clear that a fallacy-free argument is thereby a good argument, but a fallacious argument is flawed. Hence, checking for fallacies might be treated as a preliminary assessment—rooting out the worst arguments.

In light of the continuing interest in fallacies as a tool for argument appraisal, and with a view to offering an up-to-date picture of fallacy theory to instructors, this book includes a separate chapter, Chapter 13, devoted to the topic, "Introduction to the study of fallaciousness", by Christopher Tindale, taken from his book *Fallacies and Argument Appraisal* (2007).

5. Responding to arguments

What is the appropriate way to respond to an argument that one has assessed and made a considered judgment of its strength? It is useful at this point to keep in mind that our evaluations are judgment calls. Not that they are subjective intuitions (although we do form quick initial opinions). There are criteria for logically good, rhetorically good, and dialectically good arguments. But there can be and often are reasonable disagreements over whether a criterion has been met and over whether the standards being invoked for each criterion are appropriate in kind and rigor. Argument assessments may have to be defended by further arguments and are always subject to reappraisal. Hence it is wise to express one's verdict about an argument with a healthy dose of humility. The arguer, or other critical reviewers of the argument, might well have good rejoinders to your critique—points that had not occurred to you and that on reflection have both merit and implications requiring you to modify your initial judgment.

It's often a good idea to distinguish between one's judgment as to how good the argument is and one's judgment as to how best to respond to the arguer, if you are conversation partners. Suppose you find the evidence offered to be woefully weak. It might be more productive not to say that, but instead to suggest that the argument would be a lot stronger if evidence such as X, or Y, could be added. The point is that how you communicate your judgment of the argument should depend on what you hope to achieve by what you say. Do you want to help the arguer produce a stronger argument? If so, obviously avoid insulting criticism of the argument as it stands. Do you want to convince the arguer that the argument is fatally flawed (e.g., if it is circular or question-begging)? In that case, there's no avoiding pointing out how it is, though it might be possible to do so without using offensive labels. For instance, instead of labeling (e.g. "You've set up a Straw Man!"), being conciliatory (e.g., "That would be a good objection if that were my view, but my view is different, namely ...."). In short, think of the effect of your critique on the author and think of your objective in communicating with the author, and make your comments serve your objective.

6. Summary

This chapter has introduced four aspects of judging arguments in texts of discourse: determining whether there is any argument in the discourse, analyzing the structure of the argument, different ways of evaluating the logic of the argument, and various ways of responding to it. Soundness, appropriate use of an argument scheme and the ARS approach were reviewed as methods of overall argument appraisal. Testing for counter-examples and assessing the argument's warrant were discussed as ways of assessing the merits of the reasons-conclusion link in an argument. Fallacy identification was listed separately because some fallacies involve problems with the reasons and others problems with the reasoning. The possibility was raised that arguments about actions or policies (what to do) are to be assessed differently from arguments about propositions (what to believe).

References

Anderson, Alan Ross and Belnap, Nuel D. Jr. (1961). Enthymemes. *Journal of Philosophy* 58(23), 713-723.

Eemeren, Frans H. van and Grootendorst, Rob (1984). *Speech Acts in Argumentative Discussions*. Dosrdrecht: Foris.

Eemeren, Frans H. van and Grootendorst, Rob (1992). *Argumentation, Communication and Fallacies*. Hillsdale, NJ: Lawrence Erlbaum.

Eemeren, Frans H. van and Grootendorst, Rob (2004). *A Systematic Theory of Argumentation, The Pragma-Dialectical Approach*. Cambridge: Cambridge University Press.

Eemeren, Frans H. van (2010). *Strategic Maneuvering in Argumentative Discourse*. Amsterda: John Benjamins.

Ennis, Robert H. (1996). *Critical Thinking*. Upper Saddle Rivere, NJ: Prentice Hall.

Fearnside, W. Ward and Holther, William B. (1959). *Fallacy, The Counterfeit of Argument*. Englewood Cliffs, NJ: Prentice-Hall.

Hitchcock, David (1987). Enthymematic arguments. In *Argumentation, Across the Lines of Discipline. Proceedings of the Conference on Argumentation 1986*, Frans H. van Eemeren, Rob Grootendorst, J. Anthony Blair and Charles A. Willard (Eds.), pp. 289-298. Dordrecht: Foris.

Hitchcock, David (2011). Instrumental rationality. *Argumentation in Multi-Agent Systems. 7th International Workshop, argMAS 2010 Revised Selected and Invited Papers*, Peter McBurney, Iyad Rahwan and Simon Parsons (Eds.), pp. 1-11. Heidelberg: Springer.

Hitchcock, David (2017). *On Reasoning and Argument, Essays in Informal Logic and on Critical Thinking*. Cham, Switzerland: Springer.

Govier, Trudy (1987). *Problems in Argument Analysis and Evaluation*. Dordrecht: Foris.

Govier, Trudy (1992). *A Practical Study of Argument*, 3rd ed. Belmont, CA: Wadsworth.

Johnson, Ralph H. and Blair, J. Anthony (2006). *Logical Self-Defense*. New York: IDEA Press.

Kock, Christian (2017). *Deliberative Rhetoric, Arguing About Doing*. Windsor, ON: Windsor Studies in Argumentation.

O'Keefe, Daniel J. (1977). Two concepts of argument. *Journal of the American Forensic Association* 13(3), 121-128.

O'Keefe, Daniel J. (1982). The concepts of argument and arguing. In J.R. Cox and C.A. Willard (Eds.), *Advances in Argumentation Theory and Research*. Carbondale, IL:Southern Illinois University Press.

Pinto, Robert C., Blair, J. Anthony and Parr, Katharine E. (1996). *Reasoning, A Practical Guide for Canadian Students*. Scarborouogh, ON: Prentice-Hall Cana

Sperber, Dan and Wilson, Diedre (1986). *Relevance: Communication and Cognition*. Cambridge, MA: Harvard University Press.

Tindale, Christopher W. (2007). *Fallacies and Argument Appraisal*. Cambridge: Cambridge University Press.

Tindale, Christopher W. (2015). *The Philosophy of Argument and Audience Reception*. Cambridge: Cambridge University Press.

Toulmin, Stephen, N. (1956). *The Uses of Argument*. Cambridge: Cambridge University Press.

Walton, Douglas (1995). *A Pragmatic Theory of Fallacy*. Tuscaloosa: University of Alabama Press.

Walton, Douglas, Reed, Chris and Macagno, Fabrizio (2008). *Argumentation Schemes*. Cambridge: Cambridge University Press.

About the author:

J. Anthony Blair has published extensively in informal logic, critical thinking and argumentation. A selection of his papers appeared in his *Groundwork in the Theory of Argumentation* (Springer, 2012). He is presently a Senior Fellow at the Centre for Research in Reasoning, Argumentation and Rhetoric (CRRAR) at Windsor.

14

An Introduction to the Study of Fallaciousness

Christopher W. Tindale

1. Strong and weak arguments[1]

Arguments come in a range of types and employing a diversity of devices, from those that press a historical case using causal reasoning to those that recommend an economic course of action by appealing to an authority in the field. They will be characterized by a particular structure where one or more statements (premises) are given in support of a conclusion, and a range of intentions: to persuade an audience, to resolve a dispute, to achieve agreement in a negotiation, to recommend an action, or to complete an inquiry. Because of these different intentions, arguments arise in different contexts that are part of the argumentative situation. Arguments also come in a range of strengths, from those that conform to the principles of good reasoning, to those that commit some of the more abysmal errors that occur with some regularity. In between, are degrees of strength and weakness. In fact, many arguments of a more extended nature will admit of merits and demerits that can make our judgment about the overall quality of the reasoning quite difficult. A fallacy is a particular kind of egregious error, one that seriously undermines the power of reason in an argument by diverting it or screening it in some way. But a more precise definition is difficult to give and depends on a range of considerations.

One famous definition of 'fallacy' that C.L. Hamblin (1970, p. 12) derives from the Aristotelian tradition states: "A fallacious argument, as almost every account from Aristotle onwards tells you, is one that *seems to be valid* but *is not* so." This raises three central questions: Are fallacies all and only argu-

---

[1] Editor's Note: This chapter is an adaptation by Christopher W. Tindale of the introductory chapter of his textbook, *Fallacies and Argument Appraisal* (Cambridge University Press, 2007), reprinted here with the kind permission of the author and Cambridge University Press.© Copyright Christopher W. Tindale

ments, because Hamblin's definition is, strictly speaking, a definition of 'fallacious argument'? Are fallacies all a matter of validity, which seems to restrict attention to the relations between the parts of an argument? And are fallacies detected through their psychological effect, because if they *seem* valid they must seem so to someone?

To consider these questions and the kinds of problematic reasoning that may be elevated (or demoted) to the status of "fallacy" we will explore the following two cases:

Case A: This is from a letter sent to *Scientific American* (January 2, 2002) and it concerns the so-called Lomborg affair, a controversy that erupted in major scientific publications after Bjørn Lomborg published his book, *The Skeptical Environmentalist*, in which he challenged many "orthodoxies" of the environmental movement.

> In the 1970s there was a lot of excitement over two books: one theorized that our planet had been visited by friendly aliens who had helped our ancestors with all kinds of "impossible" achievements, including the building of the pyramids; another proposed paranormal explanations for the Bermuda Triangle, complete with "irrefutable" evidence. I can't remember the titles of these books or the authors' names, but I do remember watching one of them being interviewed on television. Although the interviewer was definitely hostile, the author remained confident and self-assured. After 15 minutes or so of well-informed questioning, however, the interviewer had effectively boxed his guest into a corner. At which point the still smiling, recently successful author finally stated, "If I'd said it that way, I probably wouldn't have sold many books."
>
> As far as Lomborg and his book go, I don't think we need look any further than the above statement. Also, growing up and going to school in Cambridge, England, I am extremely disappointed that Lomborg's book was published by Cambridge University Press. I just hope they realize how they have tarnished their reputation by publishing such a work. I think a more suitable vehicle would have been the checkout stand at the local supermarket, which thrives on misinformation and distorted facts.

While the author addresses his letter to "the editor" of the periodical, his audience will be the general readership. In general when assessing such texts, we will want to think about the kinds of beliefs and expectations audiences hold and how they may be predisposed to receive or challenge the ideas presented to them. Here we are primarily interested in the position or thesis that the author is promoting and the case he is making for it, because it is in the case that we see a strategy of argument being employed.

Clearly, the writer is antagonistic toward Lomborg's book. He is dismissing it as a serious work, judging it rather as a sensationalistic book. He makes this point implicitly rather than explicitly by associating it with two earlier sensationalistic books that made claims about aliens and about the Bermuda

Triangle. So the case for dismissing Lomborg's work involves associating it with two works that have already been dismissed. They have been judged, we might say, as guilty of being non-serious, unscientific work, and the present writer's strategy is to transfer this guilt to Lomborg and his book. Now, sometimes associations do exist and what holds for some partners in an association can be reasonably transferred to others. But we must be given reasons for believing both that an association exists and that a transfer of guilt is relevant. In this argument, no such attempt is made. Thus, the reasoning is weak and the conclusion is not supported. Moreover, in this case we have an identifiable strategy of argument that analysts have judged to be fallacious. The fallacy in question is Guilt by Association. You can see further that the same strategy is employed in the second paragraph. This time the claim is made that Cambridge University Press has tarnished their reputation. But the support for this is the transfer of guilt from the association with Lomborg's book. This time, the association clearly exists, but since the previous guilt was never established, there is nothing to transfer.

Case B: This is a letter to the Canadian newspaper, *The Globe and Mail* (June 19, 2003, p. A16), contributing to the debate over same-sex marriage in Canada. (Ontario is a Canadian province; "Ottawa" is a reference to the federal government, which sits in Ottawa, Canada's capital city, and at the time was headed by the Liberal Party; the Charter of Rights and Freedoms is part of the Canadian constitution.)

> The liberal government plans to endorse same-sex marriage based on a lower-court ruling in Ontario (Ottawa Backs Gay Marriage – June 18). Once it does, the well-defined definition of traditional marriage in Canada will be forever altered.
>
> If we allow people to marry without regard to their sex, who is to say that we can't discriminate on the basis of number? It is a small step then to legalizing polygamy.
>
> Once we open up marriage beyond the boundary of one man and one woman only, there will be no difference based on the Charter of Rights and Freedoms between gay marriage and polygamous marriage. Do we want to erode our societal values based on the whims of a small minority? I hope not, and let's not abuse the Charter in this way.

There is much happening in this argument that a full analysis would identify and evaluate, but we are again interested only in the primary strategy the writer employs in opposing this government initiative. The primary reason given for not allowing same-sex couples to marry is that this will lead to undesirable consequences because similar cases, here polygamous marriage, would have to be accorded the same right. The writer believes that same-sex marriage will set a precedent for legalizing polygamy. The Appeal to

Precedent[2] is another argument form that must meet strict conditions in order to be legitimate. Where such conditions are not met, we would judge the argument to again have the kind of serious weakness that warrants the label "fallacy". A precedent is set only if the cases are sufficiently analogous in relevant respects such that what holds for one will hold for the other. One weakness in this argument is that the writer fails to meet a burden of proof to provide the grounds for such analogical reasoning. More specifically, relevant *dissimilarities* between the two cases tell against the belief that legalized polygamy would have to follow. Discrimination on the basis of sexual orientation is a specific concern of the Charter and those involved are recognized as a historically disadvantaged group. No such beliefs or recognition holds for polygamous relationships. More significantly, legislation to permit same-sex marriage is giving gays access to something that everyone else has a right to, a legally recognized "traditional marriage." No advocate of polygamous marriage could insist that they were being denied such rights.

These cases reveal two preliminary things about the evaluation of fallacious arguments. In the first instance, it is not a matter of simply applying a fallacy label to a piece of text and then moving on. What is involved is a careful sifting of claims and meanings against a backdrop of an ongoing debate, and within a wider context. In evaluating the second example, we had to bring information into the discussion in order to fully appreciate the problem involved. At the same time, each piece involved the employment of an identifiable strategy. Or, perhaps we should say a misemployment, since in each case the argumentative strategy could possibly have provided a fitting vehicle to make the writer's point if the appropriate conditions had been met. Hence, when considering the potential existence of various fallacies it is important to ask whether they are the countersides of legitimate argument forms, but where the appropriate conditions have simply not been met or have been specifically violated. This will force us to be clear about what has gone wrong in each case, and why, and whether the mistake could have been avoided.

2. Some historical conceptions of fallacy

Having this preliminary sense of how we might approach fallacious reasoning has taken us closer to understanding how the term 'fallacy' should be used. It is worth our time, though, to look briefly at something of the history of this

---

[2] This argument is also a candidate for the fallacy called "Slippery Slope", where one action is advised against because it will lead (downward) toward other undesirable consequences. The Slippery Slope involves a causal relationship between cases (see Chapter 11, above); the Appeal to Precedent involves an analogous relationship between cases.

field and the controversies it has engendered in order to fully appreciate some of the difficulties that are involved.

The story really begins with Aristotle. While there was certainly an appreciation of such mistakes in reasoning earlier, Aristotle was the first one to begin categorizing them in a systematic way, first under the title of "sophistical refutations", in a work of that title, and later with a revised list in the *Rhetoric*.[3] The *Sophistical Refutations* provides a list of thirteen errors. To understand what he meant by a sophistical refutation we need to appreciate something of the dialectical reasoning that was popular with Aristotle and his contemporaries. Many may be familiar with Socrates' famous way of proceeding in Plato's *Dialogues*. In search of some important definition, like the meaning of 'courage' or 'friendship', Socrates would seek out alleged experts who could provide the information required and engage them in discussion. These discussions would have a structure to them whereby a definition or thesis was put forward by the "expert" and Socrates would then ask questions by means of which he gradually demonstrated that the definition failed, or "refuted" the definition. In Plato's Academy, where Aristotle received his formal training, this model was the basis of a number of structured games or exercises that involved one disputant trying to refute the thesis put forward by another. The inquiry would follow certain accepted patterns and be governed by rules. If the right processes were followed, then any resulting refutation would be judged a real one. But Aristotle also recognized that there could be refutations which appeared real but were not so. These he called "sophistical", thereby associating them with the argumentative practices of the Sophists.[4]

The first six members of the list of thirteen in the *Sophistical Refutations* belong to his classification of refutations that depend on language: Equivocation, Amphiboly, Combination of Words, Division of Words, Accent, and Form of Expression. The remaining refutations are placed in a category that does not depend on language: Accident, *secundum quid*, Consequent, Noncause, Begging the Question, *ignoratio elenchi*, and Many Questions.

To illustrate the treatments of this list, we can take as an example the fallacy of Amphiboly, or "double arrangement". As generally interpreted, this

---

[3] There is also a treatment of fallacy in the *Prior Analytics*, although scholars find no clear doctrine there, nor much that is new (Hamblin, 66).

[4] The Sophists were itinerant teachers in fifth century Greece. Various doctrines and practices are attributed to them, but the picture is less than clear due in part to our need to rely on the testimonies of Plato and Aristotle (both firm opponents of the Sophists) for much of our information about them. It does seem, though, that to consider all of their reasoning fallacious would be doing a great injustice to the complexity of their thought.

fallacy involves an ambiguity arising from the way language is structured. So, a sign in a shop window reading "Watch repairs here" would seem to qualify as an amphiboly since it is unclear whether the reader is being invited to leave a watch to be repaired, or to observe repairs taking place. Hence, the double arrangement. While some modern and contemporary accounts retain this fallacy, it is difficult to find examples of it that arise in arguments, and the kinds of ambiguity involved can be covered in a broader treatment of Equivocation.

Aristotle's list in the *Rhetoric* still retains some of the original thirteen, but since his goals were different in that work, other fallacies are introduced. Here he provides nine candidates, all judged "spurious enthymemes" rather than sophistical refutations. A problem may (1) arise from the particular words used; (2) involve an assertion of the whole what is true only of the part, and vice versa; (3) involve the use of indignant language; (4) involve the use of a "sign", or single instance, as certain evidence; (5) represent the accidental as essential; (6) involve an argument from consequence; (7) involve a false cause; (8) omit mention of time and circumstance; (9) confuse the absolute with the particular. We will see vestiges of some of these in the accounts ahead; others have dropped by the wayside.

As a tradition of fallacy developed out of the Aristotelian account, scholars and teachers have struggled to fit Aristotle's original fallacies into their own discussions. In many instances, such attempts were unsuccessful because the nature of Aristotle's insight arose from the original context of a dialectical debate. Outside of such a context, the "fallacy" and its description made little sense. Thus, while contemporary accounts retain some of Aristotle's fallacies, they often take on much different descriptions. Our understanding has simply changed too much for the original description to be completely applicable in modern contexts.

Twenty-three centuries after Aristotle, C. L. Hamblin reports the sad state of affairs that "we have no *theory* of fallacy at all, in the sense in which we have theories of correct reasoning or inference" (1970, p. 11). Nor do we have any agreement on how a "fallacy" should be defined. In spite of Hamblin's subsequent claim that "almost every account from Aristotle onwards" identifies a fallacious argument as "one that *seems to be valid* but *is not* so" (p. 12), the weight of recent scholarship would tell against both the claimed tradition and the alleged definition (see Hansen 2002). In short, this standard treatment provides no standard at all. What it does do is emphasize the problems associated with the three central questions raised earlier.

Hamblin implied that all fallacies are arguments. But some candidates from among Aristotle's original list, like "Accent" and "Many Questions", are not arguments at all, or, at least, not arguments in the sense that the tradition has tended to give to that term, as a collection of statements, one of which is a conclusion and others of which are premises for it.[5] We have already accounted for this concern in the definition given earlier, looking at reasoning within argumentative discourse rather than just arguments per se. This allows us to accommodate Many Questions and other concerns like Vagueness.

Secondly, it is asked, are fallacies to be restricted to a failure of validity? Even if this is understood in its widest sense to include both deductive and inductive validity, there still remains the stark fact that a traditional fallacy like the *petito principii*, or begging the question (again from Aristotle's list) is not invalid. Hence, we have the strange situation where Aristotle himself is not committed to the definition ascribed to him. The simplest way to respond to this concern in an introductory treatment of fallacies is to employ a wider criterion than validity. Since a problem such as Begging the Question is a violation of correct procedures even though it is valid, we can speak of fallacies as arguments or reasonings that appear correct when they are not.

Perhaps most problematic of all is the final aspect of Hamblin's definition: the *seeming* validity. This vestige of Aristotle's concern between truth and appearance shifts attention from the argument to the audience that considers it and deals with its potential to deceive. Many of the examples favoured by textbook authors, and by Aristotle himself, are not particularly deceptive, conveying an obviousness that amuses more than it concerns. This, though, may be more a problem with the examples than with the idea behind them. As we look to the importance of contextual features in identifying and assessing many of the fallacies, we will see that this audience-related feature cannot be avoided and so "seeming correctness" will be an important consideration not just in identifying the presence of a fallacy but also explaining how it has come about and why it is effective if it is so.

As befits its dialectical origin, one clear sense of fallacy that we can encounter involves a shift away from the correct direction in which an argumentative dialogue is progressing. By various means, an arguer may impede the other party from making her point, or may attempt to draw the discussion off track. In fact, one popular modern approach to understanding fallacious reasoning is to see it as involving violations of rules that should govern disputes so as to ensure that they are well conducted and resolved. This approach, put forward by van Eemeren and Grootendorst in several works (1984, 1992, 2004), goes by the name of pragma-dialectics. Not only is each of the traditional fallacies understood as a violation of a discussion rule, but new fallacies emerge to correspond to other violations once we focus on this way of conducting arguments.The tradition canvassed by scholars like Ham-

---

[5] Both qualified, of course, under Aristotle's original concern with dialectical arguments, where what matters are the exchanges that go on in a dialogue.

blin and Hansen also gives rise to other interesting problems determining the nature of fallaciousness, two of which are the following.

The first of these involves the relationship between truth and correctness. For some writers (e.g., Black 1952) a failure of an argument's premises to be true is sufficient to render that argument fallacious. Whereas other authors (e.g., Salmon 1963; Carney and Scheer 1964) insist that the correctness or incorrectness of an argument has nothing to do with the truth of the premises. Salmon, for example, writes: "*logical correctness or incorrectness is completely independent of the truth of the premises.* In particular it is wrong to call an argument 'fallacious' just because it has one or more false premises" (p. 4). To a certain degree, this is a useful move because it avoids the quagmire of deciding what we mean by a premise's "truth", and in particular, what theory of truth is intended.[6] But it is still a disagreement that warrants further investigation, particularly considering that the origins of the problem are integral to how Aristotle identified fallacies with sophistical reasoning.

The other concern worth noting is one that arose in the previous section of this chapter. This is the question of whether a form of argument must always be fallacious in order for it to count as a fallacy, or whether fallacies are problematic variants of arguments that can have quite legitimate instantiations. The arguments "ad" are obvious candidates here. While the *ad hominem*, which involves an attack against the person delivering the argument rather than the position argued, was long considered a clear fallacy and all instances of it dismissed as such, more recent work has concluded this not to be the case. There are examples where an *ad hominem* attack, as a strategy in a court of law or political debate, is perfectly warranted. The challenge to the theorist, as we have already anticipated, then becomes identifying the conditions under which the fallacious instances do arise.

With respect to this last problem the tradition of fallacies gives us both possibilities. Some cases, like the *ad hominem* or *ad verecundiam* (appeal to authority), can have both legitimate and illegitimate variants depending on whether they meet certain conditions. But not all identified fallacies fit this explanation. A counter example is the Straw Man or Straw Person. This involves the misrepresentation (deliberate or accidental) of a person's position, a subsequent attack on the misrepresentation, and the conclusion that the person's position has been refuted. There seems no clear way that we can judge this the counter-side to some legitimate argumentative strategy, unless

---

[6] For argumentation theorists who take this route, the preferred theory seems to be the correspondence theory (Ralph Johnson, *Manifest Rationality* (Mahwah, NJ: Erlbaum, 2000), but this leads to a host of problems traditionally associated with that theory (see Christopher W. Tindale, *Rhetorical Argumentation* (Thousand Oaks, CA: Sage Publishing, 2004, Chapter 7).

we conjure up something trivial like "Real Man". A Straw Man argument would seem to be always incorrect and have no redeemable instances. This means that we cannot define 'fallacy' as the misuse of a legitimate argument strategy because, as with Aristotle's definition, there are recognized fallacies that do not fit. While many fallacies will be counter-sides of legitimate argument schemes, some will have no correct variant.

3. Approaching fallacies

Because many fallacies are incorrect versions of good argument strategies and because arguments themselves are so embedded in the contexts that create them, identifying and evaluating fallacious reasoning will never be a matter of simply applying a label from a list that can be learned. We will need to consider each case carefully and decide what is involved, whether something has gone wrong and, if so, what it is that has gone wrong. That is, we need to learn not just how to identify fallacies but also to clearly explain what is fallacious about them. This identification and explanation will then form the basis of a clear and thorough evaluation.

The identification of fallacious arguments is aided by the fact that we are dealing with traditional (and modern) patterns of argument that provide specific characteristics in each case. As explained, these patterns will often cover both good and bad instances of the argument type in question, that is, they are value-neutral in terms of the correctness of the argument. Good basic texts in argumentation will assist you in recognizing these patterns or schemes, and having this general background before you turn to the study of fallacies will help you. What distinguishes the good from the bad will depend upon whether certain conditions have been met, and that will be our major interest.

To help us consider such conditions and develop our evaluations of specific cases, we adopt a set of critical questions for each "fallacy", based on what our discussions tell us goes wrong in each case. Armed with these questions, we can then consider a range of arguments in their contexts and evaluate them appropriately.

Our earlier, very preliminary discussion of the fallacy "Guilt by Association" indicated how there is a specific pattern for the reasoning which will recur in other such cases, and it also demonstrated what it is that goes wrong when the fallacy arises. This recognition allows us to adapt critical questions that we develop for *ad hominem* arguments, where a person's position is dismissed because of their character or circumstance (like their associations). In such instances we ask, for example, whether the material about the person that is introduced in the premises is relevant to our appraisal of the position or claim, and whether there are grounds for believing the material is factually correct. Our answers to such questions form the core of evaluating fallacies in argument appraisal.

A further feature of our approach in many cases involves raising the question of where the burden of proof lies. This has been an important feature of fallacy analysis since the contributions of Richard Whately (1787–1863). Prior reasoning and understanding will form a presumption in favour of a proposition until sufficient reasons have been brought against it. This is an important consideration when we are considering the basic premises in an argument (those that are not themselves supported). Where there is such a presumption in favour of such premises, then the onus or burden of proof lies with any one who would dispute it. As we will see, one way in which a fallacious move in argument can be made is when someone tries to shift their burden of proof onto the other person. As Hamblin (p. 173) points out, we see this particularly in the case of "*ad*" arguments. Indeed, this works with fallacies like the *argumentum ad ignorantiam* (appeal to ignorance) or the *argumentum ad populum* (appeal to popularity). It matters when evaluating the latter, for example, whether the popularity premise has a presumption in its favour or whether the burden of proof lies with the arguer who introduces it.

4. Why arguments go wrong and how they fool us

In spite of the best intentions of arguers, some arguments do go wrong. Human reason, as a tool, is not perfect, particularly during the period when we are learning to use it. And since most of us are learning to use it throughout our lives, the opportunities for error never seem to wane. You may not have really thought about this, but you probably have experienced something similar on a physical level. Our bodies are not perfect either and if we want to improve them then a lot of hard work is required. Physical excellence comes naturally to few people, and something similar holds for mental excellence. So we should take the study of fallacious reasoning seriously because we can easily fall into such errors if we are not careful.

One obvious occasion when the possibility of fallacious reasoning arises is when we are closely attached to an issue that is being argued. Full detachment from issues, or complete objectivity, is not possible, so that is not what is being suggested. But we should try to monitor our attachments so that we avoid falling into error. When we feel strongly about a topic we may rush hastily to defend it, drawing a conclusion that is not fully warranted; or we may not listen carefully to what another person is saying and assume that their position is something it is not; or we may be inclined to engage in personal attacks on the one who holds a contrary view to our own.

Just as we may fall into logical error, so might those around us. None of this is deliberate fallaciousness, and so we should not take deception to be part of the definition of 'fallacy'—at least not as this describes the intent of an arguer. Deception may be an appropriate description of how we come to mistake incorrect arguments for good ones. We have been deceived, not necessarily by the cleverness of an arguer, but perhaps by the closeness in similarity between good and bad arguments of the same form. As Aristotle pointed out back in the *Sophistical Refutations*, people do have a tendency to confuse parts of their experience, and since they see that the ground is wet after it rains, they mistakenly assume that it has rained when they see the ground is wet. This is the kind of error we can all appreciate, and it is not difficult to imagine how such "deceptions" can build into arguments.

Of course, it could also be the case that people do set out to deceive us, that some fallacies are deliberate rather than accidental. If people know what issues we feel strongly about, for example, they may choose to exploit that knowledge by offering arguments that we might quickly adopt although they are fallacious. Sometimes the misreading of others' arguments in political debate seems to be a deliberate attempt to sidetrack or derail discussions. But, in spite of these deliberate cases, the fact that fallacies can arise unintentionally shows that deception cannot be part of the definition itself

5. Avoiding fallacious reasoning

It follows from what was said in the previous section that most of the ways to avoid fallacious reasoning, whether on our own part or directed at us, reduces to some kind of education. In the earliest textbook on fallacies, if we can call the *Sophistical Refutations* that, Aristotle points to inexperience. Inexperienced people, he tells us, do not get a clear view on things and so confuse the appearance with the reality. And the key way we can overcome such inexperience is by training ourselves to see the counterfeit against the real. This extends from Aristotle's general interest in refutations to the fuller modern-day treatments of argument forms that have good and bad varieties, according to whether specific conditions have been met.

Learning about these and identifying them as they arise is the first step in avoiding them ourselves. The next step involves evaluating them fairly and thoroughly. This will give us a further appreciation for why things go wrong and how we might correct them.

6. Summary

We have gathered, then, a set of ideas about fallacies and what to expect of them. A full understanding of "fallacy" arises once we have a deeper experience of the matter and better appreciation of the complexities involved. We are looking for arguments, and we do expect them to have a surface correctness about them, so we might avoid simple examples, which are hardly likely to deceive anyone. On the question of deception, we have seen that no intention to deceive should be part of the definition. But that fallacies have the power to undermine reason and deceive us seems clear.

Furthermore, some fallacies will be counterfeits of good argument forms, thus adding to their deceptiveness. But, again, this cannot be a part of our definition, because other fallacies have no correct form to which to correspond. A further major division suggested in the discussions of this chapter concerns fallacies that express interior errors and fallacies where the problems are exterior. The first class involves arguments where problems arise in the relations between the parts. The second class, and here we can think of arguments like the "*ad*" arguments, involve problems between parts of the argument and contextual features like those involving the audience. Whether there are characteristics that connect these two categories is something to be explored in a further discussion. For now, we have uncovered the basic ideas involved with fallaciousness and how to approach it.

References

Aristotle. *Rhetoric*.

Aristotle. *Sophistical Refutations*.

Black, Max (1952). *Critical Thinking*. Englewood Cliffs, NJ: Prentice-Hall.

Carney, James D. and Scheer, Richard K. (1964). *Fundamentals of Logic*. New York: Macmillan.

Eemeren, Frans H. van and Grootendorst, Rob (1984). *Speech Acts in Argumentative Discussions*. Dordrecht: Foris.

Eemeren, Frans H. van and Grootendorst, Rob (1992). A*rgumentation, Communication and Fallacies*. Mahwah, NJ: Erlbaum.

Eemeren, Frans H. van and Grootendorst, Rob (2004). *A Systematic Theory of Argumentation*. Cambridge: Cambridge University Press.

Hamblin, C.L. (1970). *Fallacies*. London: Methuen.

Hansen, Hans V. (2002). The straw thing of fallacy theory. *Argumentation* 16, 133-155.

Johnson, Ralph H. (2000). *Manifest Rationality*. Mahwah, NJ: Erlbaum.

Lomborg, Bjørn (2001). *The Skeptical Environmentalist: Measuring the Real State of the World*. Cambridge: Cambridge University Press.

Salmon, Wesley (1963). *Logic*. Englewood Cliffs, NJ: Prentice-Hall, 1963);

Scientific American (2002). Letter to the editor. January 2nd.

The Globe and Mail (2003). Letter to the editor. June 19th.

Tindale, Christopher W. (2004). *Rhetorical Argumentation*. Thousand Oaks, CA: Sage Publishing.

Tindale, Christopher W. (2007). *Fallacies and Argument Appraisal*. Cam bridge: Cambridge University Press.
Whately, Richard (1826). *Elements of Logic*.
Whately, Richard (1828). *Elements of Rhetoric*.

About the author:

Christopher W. Tindale is Director of the Centre of Research in Reasoning, Argumentation, and Rhetoric, and Professor of Philosophy, at the University of Windsor, where he is also co-editor of *Informal Logic* and the book series Windsor Studies in Argumentation. His textbook authorship includes *Good Reasoning Matters* (with Groarke, 5th edition, Oxford 2013) and *Fallacies and Argument Appraisal* (Cambridge 2007). He is the author of many papers in argumentation theory, and his most recent books include *Reason's Dark Champions* (USC Press 2010), *The Philosophy of Argument and Audience Reception* (Cambridge 2015), and a series of essays in Spanish, *Retórica y teoría de la argumentación contemporáneas: ensayos escogidos de Christopher Tindale* (EAFIT 2017).

IV

Other Elements of Critical Thinking

Introduction to Part IV

Useful background for critical thinking

Since critical thinking requires background knowledge, a further seven chapters were commissioned to provide it, in Part IV, on topics that are widely addressed in critical thinking courses and textbooks.

The web is today the dominant venue for the practice of critical thinking, and Sally Jackson's timely Chapter 15, offers advice about how someone who thinks critically uses the web—and includes ways to avoid being used by the web. The different forms and purposes of definition are covered in Robert Ennis's Chapter 16, along with advice about how to select the best kind of definition for your purposes. How to recognize unwarranted generalizations and distinguish them from legitimate ones is laid out in Dale Hample and Yiwen Dai's Chapter 17. In our everyday thinking we rely on the authority of various alleged sources of belief and knowledge, including experts. Mark Battersby, in Chapter 18, discusses how the critical thinker distinguishes reliable from unreliable authorities: experts and other sources. While logic is not equivalent to critical thinking and while there is little evidence that learning formal logic transfers to critical thinking ability, a number of logical concepts do play key roles in critical thinking—as becomes clear in G. C. Goddu's essay, Chapter 19, on logic and critical thinking. "Abduction" and "argument to the best explanation" are bandied about as forms of reasoning. John Woods, in Chapter 20, makes crystal clear Peirce's concept of abduction and its connection to argument from the best explanation. Critical thinking entails evaluation, and evaluation theory pioneer, Michael Scriven, discussed the logic of evaluation in Chapter 21.

The reader whose thinking practices are informed by the contents of these seven chapters will be capable of subtle and complex critical thinking analysis over a wide range of subject matters.

15

How a Critical Thinker Uses the Web

Sally Jackson

The web, or Worldwide Web as it was first known, is all of the services and content that a person can access using a web browser like Google Chrome, Firefox, Internet Explorer, Safari, or any of a number of less familiar products. My task in this chapter is to explore how critical thinkers use the web, but it is impossible to do this without also speculating about how the existence of the web may change what it means to think critically. Since the late 19th Century much of the world has gone through two media revolutions: from a media environment dominated by print to an electronic broadcast environment, and from an electronic broadcast environment to a digital networked environment (Finneman, 2011). The sum of available communication media at any point in time is sometimes called a "media ecology" (Postman, 2000), and media theorists who think in ecological terms believe that social practices, especially communication practices, reshape themselves to adapt to a change in environment of this kind. The central insight of media ecology has been that new technologies do not just add to prior technologies. They change the environment so that even older technologies get used differently. Habits formed under one configuration of communication technologies may or may not make sense when the configuration changes.

There is no guarantee that the tools and skills long associated with critical thinking will transition smoothly from one media ecology to another. It is altogether possible that the rise of a new media ecology may require not just new tools and new skills but also abandonment of some of the habits and assumptions associated with centuries of reliance on information appearing in print. A thoughtful discussion of how a critical thinker uses the web must be open to these possibilities.

I begin by offering a brief overview of certain features of the web that are especially significant for critical thinking. I then turn to a core set of web-related practices that demand either new critical thinking skills or new perspectives on critical thinking. Finally, I return to the speculation raised briefly above, that critical thinking itself may need to be reconceptualized in terms that are less tightly tethered to individual thinkers, and more tied to social arrangements in which societies delegate some responsibility for critical thinking to institutions, to specialized professions, and even to machines.

1. The web as information environment

The Internet (not the web) began in the 1960s as a US Defense Department project. First used to connect major computing resources across the US (Abbate, 1999), the Internet expanded rapidly as a tool for human communication. By the mid-1980s Internet services were available (via telephone infrastructure) to ordinary households in many countries, though these services bore little resemblance to what soon developed. The most common Internet application at that time was email, presented as a screenful of text navigated through keyboard interaction with a menu of options.

Today's web is a global software system of platforms, applications, and data operating on the Internet and growing autonomously in interaction with billions of human users. Its core technology was invented by Tim Berners-Lee in 1989 and successfully prototyped in 1990 at CERN. Like email, the web was first presented to users as text menus on computer screens. But graphical web browsers appeared a few years later (starting with Mosaic, created by the National Center for Supercomputing Applications in 1992), making the web accessible to the general public. By the time the web was invented, a considerable amount of index-type material was already available over the Internet, sufficient to allow people to search online for information about offline resources (such as library collections or business directories). The rise of the web stimulated a burst of activity to digitize vast stores of print information that could be both located and consumed online, as well as a variety of service transactions performed entirely online.

From its beginnings, the web was designed to ingest new content from any of its endpoints (users and their devices), but it took more than a decade for this idea to take hold widely enough to expose the fundamentally participatory nature of the web. The web is not (and never was) just an online repository of information, but a platform for transactions of all kinds, including communication. At the time of this writing, the web has existed for less than 30 years, but it has infiltrated virtually every important domain of human experience, fundamentally altering many practices (such as news production and consumption) that are central to any discussion of critical thinking.

Both the design ideas behind the web and the technical components built from these ideas have consequences for critical thinking. From these ideas and the technologies they have inspired, three characteristics have emerged as especially relevant: accumulation of unreviewed content; algorithmic search; and personalization of the information environment.

1.1 Unreviewed content

The web was invented to allow for collaborative creation of content by an arbitrarily large set of creators. As explained by the web's inventor (Tim Berners-Lee, 1996), "The intent was that this space should span . . . from high value carefully checked and designed material, to off-the-cuff ideas which make sense only to a few people and may never be read again." Unreviewed content is a design feature of the web, not an unintended consequence.

For a very short time, the computer programming skills needed for publishing content to the web limited the number of people who could contribute, and during this short period, most individuals experienced the web simply as content available for consuming. But programmers, including many self-taught amateurs, quickly began inventing platforms that would allow other people without programming skills to contribute content, whether as personal "home pages," as sites for groupwork, or as some other kind of content. Some platforms emerged to support large collaborative writing projects—highly imaginative experiments in collaborative writing as well as visionary knowledge repositories.

The speed with which all of this occurred was dizzying. The wave of participatory web applications invented in the 2000s, known collectively as social media, included social networking platforms (such as Facebook, invented in 2004), blog platforms (such as WordPress, available as a service since 2003), a massively successful microblogging platform (Twitter, invented in 2006), plus several platforms for rapid dissemination of image data, several platforms for distributing user-made video, platforms for citizen science and citizen journalism, book publishing platforms, and much more. These were not the first participatory media, but their clustered appearance created a sense that the web itself was changing (from "Web 1.0" to "Web 2.0" as the shift was described in industry news).

The significance of social media for critical thinking is mostly in the way they have affected the status of published information, including what is found in "old media." Print technologies and broadcast technologies both restricted the ability to publish to those who controlled production and distribution resources. A certain level of thoughtfulness was a natural practical consequence of the costs and effort associated with print and broadcast media. The web too is dependent on material technologies, and building the web has required massive worldwide investment. But for the content producer, there is no cost other than one's own labor for publishing an idea on the web; publishing is an immediate result of interacting with social media. Information on the web can be completely unreviewed, and it can also be published with little or no information on its own provenance.

One challenge this presents to critical thinking seems rather obvious: Much of the information a person can find on the web has no serious claim on anyone's attention or belief, and quite a lot of it is false. Bad information can circulate easily on the web, and it is not always easy to track down its source. But there is a second risk for critical thinking: the categorical rejection of information that does not satisfy the standards associated with earlier media ecologies. Unreviewed content is not necessarily poor quality content, and it is a mistake to reject it categorically.

An instructive example is Wikipedia, the free online encyclopedia launched by Jimmy Wales in 2007, during the great wave of social media inventions. The premise behind Wikipedia is that allowing everyone to contribute and everyone to edit will produce high quality information that can expand without limit (in a way that print encyclopedias cannot). The fact that an article can be written or edited by anyone in the world was regarded at first as a fatal flaw. Experience has shown that for topics that matter, communities form around curating the content of Wikipedia, reversing edits that are outright errors and engaging in lengthy behind-the-scenes argumentation over content that is in any way controversial. Wikipedia has evolved a style, a "neutral point of view" that handles unresolved controversy within an editing group by *presenting arguments without arguing*.

As Wikipedia has developed, it has acquired some of the attributes of review, but reviewing means something different for Wikipedia than for a traditional publication process. Nothing prevents an author from publishing in Wikipedia, but scrutiny follows immediately and does not end until an article arrives at a form that no one sees a need to edit further. Articles do not have authors; to see who participated in any way requires going behind the article (to its revision history or to its discussion pages), and even then the authors' identities and credentials are rarely available. It is a participant-administered system in which abuse is controlled only through tireless vigilance and enforcement of evidence standards.

For sensibilities trained by print and broadcast eras, unreviewed content is immediately suspect. In a desire for simple rules to guide reliance on the web, one might suggest that users rely only on trusted websites, rejecting information that cannot pass tests for conventional legitimacy. This would be a mistake, though. The web allows for accumulation of new *kinds* of information, information that in earlier media configurations would not have been considered worth saving, let alone publishing. One important category of such information is individual reports of experience. These range from satisfaction ratings that are central to the business models of e-commerce platforms like eBay, to observational data collected by citizen scientists, to self-observation related to health and medicine. To take just health as an example, no sensible person relies on web discussions to learn whether the rash on the bottom of her foot is shingles, but if (having been properly treated by a doctor) that person needs to know how to get along for a week or two with shingles blisters on the bottom of her foot, there is nothing quite as useful as the ideas of the very small fraction of other humans who have actually had this experience.

A critical thinker will certainly not believe everything found on the web, but it is equally uncritical to reject all unreviewed content out of hand. Distinguishing between experience and expertise as bases for knowledge and appreciating when content gains credibility through some form of expert review are new skills needed by everyone who uses the web, a point to which I return in the second section of this chapter.

1.2 Algorithmic search

In the context of the web, an algorithm is a bit of computer programming that performs some task. Algorithms can cooperate with other algorithms, especially if one algorithm can take another's output as its own input. Algorithmic search means a search conducted by a computer program in response to a user's query—the leading example being a Google search. The user enters a query, and Google's army of algorithms combine this user input with both stored and transactional data (such as the user's current location) to decide what the user is looking for and deliver a list of results. Google maintains a good general explanation [1] of the many individual algorithms that are required for its search engine to cater to our needs. What a user experiences as a simple query/response transaction is a set of powerful tools that maintain comprehensive, continuously updated index information that can be combined with rapidly improving methods for inferring users' intentions and calculating which of the items in the index are most likely to satisfy the needs of particular users.

In the very early days of the web, efforts were made to provide guides to the web modeled on a library catalogue, with hierarchies of categories such as "Art" and "Travel," through which a user could browse. Yahoo! started out in this fashion, trying to curate web pages using methods that had worked well for physical collections of books and other objects. All such efforts at curation were immediately and completely obsolesced by the invention of search engines. Without algorithmic search, most of the content on the web would be undiscoverable.

---

[1] https://www.google.com/search/howsearchworks/

In principle, everything in a physical library can be found by simply being thorough, moving along item by item and inspecting each one. The same is not true for web content, because an item on the web has no fixed physical location in a space navigable by a human. But algorithmic search is not just a virtualized form of library search. It is a different kind of search based on different principles.

To get a sense of the difference between physical browsing and searching, imagine a library where, as you walk through the bookstacks, certain titles push themselves out, some pushing out just a little and others pushing themselves all the way out so they cannot be ignored. Imagine further that these pushy books recede until they are flush with their shelf-mates when you have walked on, and that when your colleague walks through the same stacks, different books push out. Imagine still further that your actions, and those of your colleague, affect future pushing-out. If you or your colleague remove a book from the shelf, an invisible mechanism records that action. If you finger a book but do not remove it from the shelf, that is recorded too. A book that pushes out over and over without being selected becomes less pushy, and what is more, other books that share any commonality with that book also become less pushy.

Information retrieval tools of the past relied on the codable characteristics of the items to be located (such as topic, author, date of publication, and so on). Web search differs in relying on social and relational data as well. Algorithms deliver information in response to queries, but they also continuously collect data on what is being searched for and how people react to what is delivered. This means that the curation of the information environment is delegated to computer programs whose outputs are not controlled even by the programmers. A new area of scholarly inquiry has emerged around this fact known as algorithm studies. Critical algorithm studies (e.g., Introna, 2006; Introna and Nissenbaum, 2000) problematize the delegation of so many matters of importance to systems that are subject to no governance by their users. For example, scholars working on algorithms have already shown how the behaviour of an algorithm like Google's PageRank can be shaped to reproduce biases and prejudices present within a population of users (Noble, 2013).

For teaching critical thinking there is very little point in focusing on any particular algorithm, such as Google's PageRank algorithm or Facebook's news feed algorithm. The instructional goal should be creating an intuitive foundation for reasoning about algorithms in general, including those that will emerge in the future. The ones that matter most (MacCormick, 2012) are changing constantly as their programmers try to make them better in some sense.

Any individual algorithm should be examined and critiqued in such a way as to focus on the more abstract point that algorithmic search and many other algorithms that control other web business introduce their own poorly understood influence on the information environment. Section 2 offers some suggestions for how to apply this abstract lesson both to search strategies and to the management of one's overall relationship with the web.

1.3 Personalization

Mass media deliver the same message content to all who choose to pay attention. The web takes note of its interactional partner and personalizes information in myriad ways. Users seek this as a convenience, and it is widely regarded by web developers as a competitive advantage for any product or service offered on the web. In the early days of the web, personalization meant that users could affect the content displayed by entering data, such as a bit of personal information or as a choice from a menu of options. Early online courses could personalize lessons by creating multiple paths through content based on a student's responses to quiz questions (or to instruments designed to measure preference in "learning style"). Personalization has since become ubiquitous on the web, operating below the level of the user's awareness and beyond the user's control.

Personalization in the context of the web means that the web itself remembers users and exploits all of what it *knows* about the user. The technologies that are most important to personalization are changing rapidly, so in trying to work out implications for critical thinking, it is not worthwhile to focus on any particular example. A critical thinker needs to understand personalization as a broad media trend and to grasp intuitively its consequences for personal point of view.

At the time of this writing, personalization has two expressions that are of central importance to critical thinking: filtering of information to fit a model of the user's interests, and deliberate targeting of content to particular users.

1.3.1 Filtering and feeding

Eli Pariser (2011) first called attention to what he called the "filter bubble": the tendency of people getting most of their information from the web to see only information that confirms their prior expectations. As noted earlier, many algorithms that deliver web content take the user's prior behaviour into account in guessing what the user would like to see. Google's search engine may rank results one way for one user and a different way for another user, leading to dramatic differences in what the two users see when making the very same query. Each choice a user makes from a list of search results is captured as data that can be used to better personalize future search results. One way to look at this is as the user "training" the algorithm to deliver a certain kind of content. But that would be a very misleading view, because users typically have no idea that they are in this way limiting their own access to information.

Fig. 1. Screenshot of "Blue Feed Red Feed" from September 23, 2017

The 2016 U.S. Presidential election exposed a fact that should have been widely known but that was not: Facebook's news feed algorithm was discerning users' political tastes and introducing dramatically different views of the world for those on the left and those on the right. The filtering of content affects not only the political information that a user sees, but also what social information a user sees (that is, whose status updates are called to the user's attention). *The Wall Street Journal* produced a powerful infographic demonstration of this, showing side-by-side "red feed" and "blue feed" content updated in real time (http://graphics.wsj.com/blue-feed-red-feed/; as of this writing, the infographic remains visible in archival form). One screenshot from the site is shown in Figure 1.

Filtering and feeding are output from automatic processes. Add human intentionality and strategic thinking to these processes and the result is a form of highly individualized persuasion known as behavioral targeting (common in product advertising) or micro-targeting (when applied in political campaigning).

1.3.2 Behavioral targeting

Behavioural targeting is a technique for individual-level tailoring of message content. Originally developed to improve the return on investment from product advertising (Turow et al., 2009), behavioural targeting is now being used more and more extensively in political campaigning and other forms of noncommercial persuasion, where it is often called micro-targeting (Turow et al., 2012).

A well-known peculiarity of the American electoral system (the Electoral College) has made it essential for every candidate for national office to design campaigns around the prospects of winning particular states. Since the invention and institutionalization of public opinion polling, campaigns have been able to engage in geographic targeting of campaign messages, with heavy investment in battleground states to the neglect of states considered safe for one party or the other. From the perspective of political theorists (e.g., Gimpel et al., 2007), this is a matter of concern for the health of democracy, with possible harmful consequences for "political socialization." Without exposure to candidates' arguments, citizens can still vote, so they are not exactly disenfranchised; but they have been excluded from a discourse that might have been helpful to them in other contexts (such as reasoning about the Affordable Care Act also known as Obamacare).

In the American presidential campaigns of 2008, 2012, and 2016, not only did geographic targeting achieve higher levels of precision, but behavioral targeting emerged at the individual level, with likely supporters receiving intense attention while likely opponents received none. Behavioural targeting is a creature of the new media environment: it is not simply a shift from mass media to social media platforms, but is much more importantly an exploitation of the rise of powerful algorithms for profiling consumers and voters based on increasingly detailed information about their behaviour. The first Obama campaign, in 2008, used social media extensively to concentrate on known supporters; the second Obama campaign, in 2012, introduced an unprecedented reliance on Big Data and algorithmic techniques for targeting particular voters with messages tailored to their profiles (Jamieson, 2013; Murphy, 2012; Tufecki, 2012). In the 2016 presidential campaign, these techniques were taken to a new and frightening level, with targeted delivery of fake news aimed at harming a candidate (Calabresi, 2017). Though exactly who was responsible remains a matter of inquiry at the time of this writing, it is highly likely that future campaigns will find more-or-less legitimate ways to target opponents' supporters (with conventional attack messages). A looming threat is the possibility of tailoring messages based not just on political leaning but on "psychographics" inferred from massive datasets of personal information stored on the web (Confessore and Hakim, 2017).

The importance of this for critical thinking is to realize that persuasive messages directed to one's email and other personal accounts may have been crafted quite purposefully to exploit knowledge about the recipient that is growing ever more specific. A candidate for political office will have positions on many issues, only some of which will be a match with a particular voter's views. Rather than presenting campaign messages that disclose an array of policy positions, candidates using micro-targeting technologies can send an environmentally engaged voter information on the candidate's views on climate change but omit information on any other issues on which the voter might disagree. Or, if targeting an opponent's supporters, a micro-targeted message might focus on a single issue on which the voter can be assumed to disagree with the opponent. Every individual should try to notice when messages appear to have been targeted—being especially alert to messages with uncanny personal relevance. Playing on specific fears of specific individuals appears to be possible.

To whatever extent these technologies confer competitive advantage to candidates, candidates can be expected to use them aggressively. Setting aside what this will mean for winning and losing, political micro-targeting can affect the overall health of a democracy. Elections have outcomes beyond who wins and who loses, such as political participation, belief polarization, and contempt for those who disagree. One difficulty in anticipating serious societal consequences of this emerging practice is that consequences of this kind unfold very slowly, over multiple election cycles. Denying candidates the competitive advantage that motivates micro-targeting is one way to push back against these damaging effects. Others will be described in Section 2.

2. New expressions of critical thinking

Earlier chapters have thoroughly discussed both the evaluation of individual arguments a person may encounter and the construction of strong arguments, so there is no need to repeat here that a critical thinker will approach the web with many of the same skills and dispositions that apply wherever argumentation occurs. But as argued above, the web is a new and still evolving ecology of data and applications, a new communication environment that transforms humanity's relationship with information. In this section, I explore a small set of new critical thinking skills and dispositions that have already become important for using the web. These often involve either reflection on the communication environment itself or meta-cognitive skills related to the limits of one's own knowledge and judgment.

2.1 Acknowledging the vulnerabilities of algorithmic search

The unwarranted confidence people have in their own web searches is a new threat to critical thinking. Algorithmic search is a powerful resource for locating information on any issue of interest, but it is also a potent source of bias. Being critical of specific information encountered on the web is not enough, if what is selected for you by algorithms is already a slanted view of the world.

Search engines do not deliver the same information in response to the same query by different people; they use social and behavioral data to tailor results to what are assumed to be the user's interests and preferences. A critical thinker aware of this fact will not only evaluate the content returned by a search, but will also take into account that algorithmic search may filter out content that would challenge the searcher's sense of what is true. In other words, in using web search to form an impression of a person, an event, or an issue, a critical thinker will not assume that the results of this search are an accurate representation of what there is to know about the subject. In particular, a critical thinker will be conscious of the filter bubble and cautious about relevance ranking.

To avoid the filter bubble, a web user can choose incognito browsing, accomplished by installing a browser that allows incognito mode. Fully anonymized browsing is also possible. But although incognito and anonymized browsing eliminate personalization of the results list, they cannot eliminate the influence of social information, such as data on other searchers' choices of which search results to select. Safiya Noble (2013) reported that querying for "black girls" returned large amounts of sexualized and even pornographic content, exposing the fact that many people in the past have searched for "black girls" intending to find pornography; going incognito will not prevent these past searches from affecting the results of any new search, even one motivated by an interest in how to parent a black girl.

Search results have the capacity to mislead in other ways even when the content returned, taken item by item, is pretty good. One error to avoid is thinking that the best items appear at the top of a list of results. Recall the metaphor of the library whose items push out to attract attention of passers-by. Items found in a search push themselves toward the top of the list, and their success in reaching the top is not an assurance of quality. Users may assume that position in a results list indicates information quality. This is false. In a study of search designers' own rationale for search algorithms, van Couvering (2007) found little interest in values like source credibility. Commercial goals drive most design decisions.

Good search techniques mitigate some of the effects of filtering, and one good general practice is to look (far) beyond the first page of results returned from a search to see results that might be ranked highly for other users. Humility is a useful disposition for a critical thinker: The goal is to avoid placing more confidence than is warranted in the competence and completeness of one's own searching. Search makes it easy to find information; it does not make it easy to master the subject of the search, nor to spot the gaps in one's own understanding.

2.2 Respecting both expertise and experience as sources of knowledge

A considerable amount of work on digital literacy has focused on how to discriminate between credible information and the vast bodies of false or unfounded information that can be found on the web (see, e.g., Rheingold, 2012, Ch. 2). Students are often urged, when writing academic papers, to use specific databases (such as EBSCO or ProQuest) or specific search tools (such as Google Scholar) to locate credible information. They may also be taught to seek curated information sources for their non-academic purposes, preferring government sponsored sources for public health information over popular sources like WebMD, and avoiding altogether sources that are maintained by uncredentialed health advocates.

As I have already suggested in Section 1.1, there is reason to worry that advice of this kind may be ill-adapted to the new media. Information curated by experts is certainly to be preferred when a question is one that can be answered only with the judgment and research resources of experts. But experts take no interest in many matters of importance, and their special skills are not needed for many questions ordinary people may ask. The web encourages sharing of information among members of the public who share an interest or a life circumstance, and rejecting this for lack of expert authority is a waste of an important new possibility for extending human knowledge. Rather than building critical thinking skills around a preference for credentialed information over uncredentialed information, an approach more suited to the web cultivates at least general understanding of the myriad ways in which knowledge can be produced. A critical thinker should be able to reflect on what basis there *could be* for answering any question and should have a flexible repertoire of tools for assessing the quality of all kinds of information.

Evaluating the credibility of information that has been assembled from contributions of many ordinary people is a new problem for critical thinking. However, this new problem does not have to be entrusted to the forms of individual analysis that have been taught as critical thinking skills. Thinking ecologically, humanity can choose to develop new roles and resources for sharing the work of evaluating credibility. Many resources of this kind are already familiar, especially those that have emerged around the problem of fact-checking. Well-established resources provided by trusted investigative agencies include (among many others) factcheck.org, snopes.com, and verificationjunkie.com.

In addition to resources built around trusting human investigators, certain problems can be addressed algorithmically. Customer reviews are one important and pervasive form of web content requiring an ability to discriminate between authentic and inauthentic reviews. It is possible that assessing authenticity will require tools that bear no resemblance to critical thinking skills as they have been taught in the past. For example, detecting inauthenticity may be impossible when examining an individual bit of content like a product review, but possible when comparing the content with large collections of other content. Credible scholarly research has demonstrated that fake content can be identified algorithmically (see Heydari et al., 2015, for a useful survey and assessment of many different approaches). Websites like fakespot.com offer analysis of reviews for selected sites (Amazon and Yelp at the time of this writing). Figure 2 shows output from an algorithmic analysis of all of the 338 customer reviews of a Chinese restaurant posted to Yelp, with the overall conclusion that the reviews can be trusted. In the rapidly changing information environment, tools that operate above the level of individual judgment of individual texts may become important accessories for critical thinkers.

> 🔍 **You can trust the reviews.**
>
> ---
>
> **Analysis overview**
>
> - Our engine has discovered that over **90%** high quality reviews are present.
>
> - Our engine detects that in general the reviewers have a **positive** sentiment.
>
> - Our engine has profiled the reviewer patterns and has determined that there is **minimal deception** involved.
>
> - The most used word by reviewers is **food.**

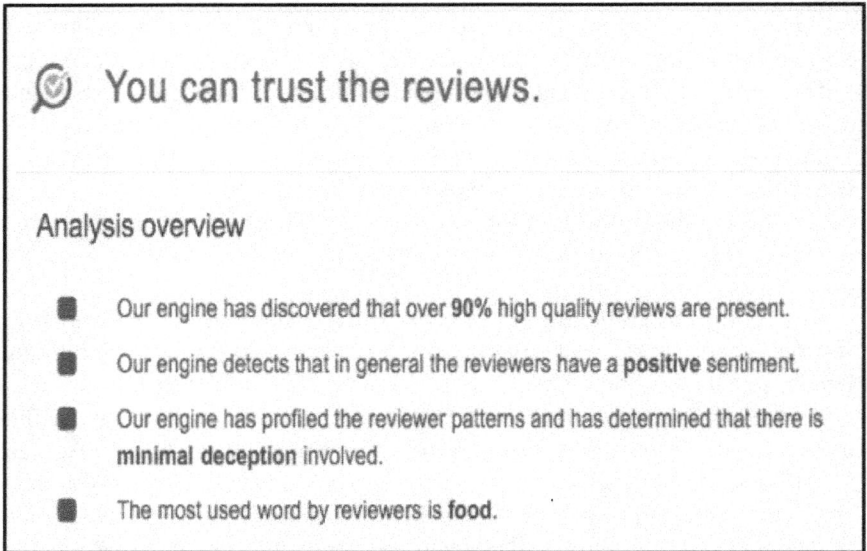

Fig. 2. Results from a fakespot.com analysis of Yelp reviews

Other novel features of the web environment make it worthwhile to reconsider even instruction in the use of expertise-based knowledge. Before digitization and algorithmic search, encounters with primary research reports involved exposure to at least some of the social context for scholarly research. Expert writing is discoverable through algorithmic search and increasingly accessible to the public as more resources shift to digital open access. But context is degraded in this environment. When primary research reports of experts are as easy to find as blog columns by non-experts, there may be as much threat to critical thinking in the one source as in the other. Theoretical explorations of the nature of expertise (notably Collins and Evans, 2007) make clear that exposure to the primary literature of an expert field, without appreciation of the tacit knowledge possessed by all contributors to that field, does not necessarily provide knowledge of the field. Critical thinking instruction should take into account how easily nonexperts can misinterpret what an expert, writing for other experts, is actually saying.

A well-documented metacognitive bias is the Dunning-Kruger effect, a tendency for people with poor skills in an area to greatly overestimate their skills (Dunning, 2011). This effect occurs when the skills needed to perform a task are the same as the skills needed to evaluate the performance. If the Dunning-Kruger effect occurs for interpretation of expert opinion, a person who misunderstands what an expert is saying is unlikely to accurately assess his or her own understanding. A critical thinker should be able to question, and even doubt, his or her own ability to make sense of what experts say about a question.

In the changed information environment of the web, a critical thinker should have an open mind about potential sources of information, paired with strategies for assessing the quality of the new kinds of information found on the web. A critical thinker will try to cultivate good individual judgment, but will also know its limits and rely when possible on tools developed to augment individual judgment.

2.3 Managing the cognitive environment

As the web becomes ever more fully integrated into daily life, its influence becomes less noticeable. It becomes an invisible part of the environment. Information flows whether or not a person has turned on the tap, and this flow of information shapes what a person experiences as familiar, as plausible, and as natural. Allowing the flow to be controlled by algorithms optimized for commercial value or political success is a danger to critical thinking, both at the individual level and at the societal level. To begin with, it is likely to involve systematic overexposure to information biased in one way or another (the filter bubble problem), and in the extreme, it opens the door to large-scale manipulation by micro-targeters.

The societal level effects are beyond the scope of this chapter, and managing these effects depends on developments in new areas of inquiry like critical algorithm studies and value-centered design. But it is possible to mitigate the individual level effects by managing one's own cognitive environment—the part of the information environment that any individual inhabits. To manage the cognitive environment means, first, making a deliberate decision about how to allocate one's attention. For news, having a set of reliable news sources to review daily is far better than absorbing news from Facebook or other social media. Giving attention to social media is fine, so long as that is not a person's primary (or only) source of news. Choosing multiple news sources is preferable to a single source, and deliberately introducing diversity of political slant is even more preferable. The goal is to avoid a view of the world that is chosen by algorithms designed to cater to the user's known preferences.

Convenient ways to routinize a decision like this include bookmarking the websites of several good newspapers or using a smartphone app that delivers news daily from the same selected sources. Carefully choosing and curating social media sources is another good practice (e.g., on Twitter, "unfollowing" sources that routinely retweet suspect material).

Another issue to consider is how aggressively to resist personalization. Personalization is a source of bias, but also a very handy feature of the web.

Managing one's cognitive environment includes balancing the value of personalization against its biasing effects. Various browser extensions are available for pushing back against tracking and targeting. For example, Ghostery (http://www.ghostery.com) is a web privacy tool that can detect efforts to track a person's movements on the web and can block those the user does not want. (For up-to-date options, search for "browser extensions that block tracking"). Preventing collection of data on one's behavior gives targeters (whether commercial or political) less to work with. Going incognito is a more drastic alternative, but it involves sacrifice of all personalization (at least while remaining incognito). More difficult but also more impactful are various resources for controlling what the web knows about the user. Users of Google can log in to https://myactivity.google.com to review and edit data Google uses to deliver personalized content. For example, Google invites users to fine-tune the product classes of ads they are interested in seeing, allows users to delete items from their search history, and so on. Choosing a personalized environment is not wrong, but because it means handing over control to algorithms, it is a choice that should be made deliberately.

New resources for management of the cognitive environment may be invented at any time. Eslami et al. (2015) have developed a piece of software, called FeedViz, that allows Facebook users to see what Facebook chooses not to include in their news feeds. FeedViz assembles all items generated by a user's social network and presents these in direct comparison with the items selected from this pool by Facebook's news feed algorithm. Users may or may not prefer the algorithm-curated news feed, but by allowing users a choice, FeedViz could be considered a tool for managing the user's cognitive environment.

In the same spirit, the artist Ben Grosser has focused on Facebook's penchant for quantification and how that might affect users' evaluations of particular items viewed on Facebook. He created a browser extension, Facebook Demetricator[2], to strip quantitative information from a user's view of Facebook (so that items are not accompanied by counts of people who "liked" the item or counts of people who commented on the item). In terms of legacy critical thinking concepts, Facebook feeds the user a steady stream of information on popularity, constantly whispering the message that what is popular is also valuable. One way to address this is to train people to resist these whispered messages; Grosser's work illustrates another, completely new way to address the problem, giving the user a tool for control of the cognitive environment.

One point to take from this discussion is that individuals have more control over their cognitive environments than they suppose they do, and this means

---

[2] http://bengrosser.com/projects/facebook-demetricator/

that a person can choose whether or not to live in a personalized filter bubble and whether or not to go with the flow of suspect information. Those who aspire to critical thinking can start by pushing back against distortion and manipulation that have been designed into the information environment under the guise of providing a more satisfying online experience.

3. Critical thinking about the web

Part of what is necessary for critical thinking in *use* of the web is critical thinking *about* the web as an information environment. Neil Postman (2000) argued for a certain kind of critical assessment of media themselves in a keynote address to the Media Ecology Association, saying "I believe that rational thinking is one of humanity's greatest gifts, and that, therefore, any medium that encourages it, such as writing or print, is to be praised and highly valued. And any medium that does not, such as television, is to be feared." He proposed a number of critical questions to ask about any medium of communication, the most relevant being "To what extent does a medium contribute to the uses and development of rational thought?" Postman (who died just as the web was exploding with new social media platforms) would have us ask, what kind of medium is the web, taken as a whole? Does it encourage or inhibit rational thinking? Should it be valued for the vast stores of information it contains, or feared for its shallowness and defiance of intellectual standards?

As should be clear, these questions cannot be answered straightforwardly, or at least not just yet. Postman's case against television was that regardless of content, the medium itself was dangerous, putting entertainment and distraction at the center of human existence. He would surely note similar tendencies in the web if writing today. But along with the web's infinite capacity for distraction and disinformation, its capacity for reorganizing human experience must be considered. For human rationality, the web enables new arrangements for shifting responsibility for critical thinking from individuals to various kinds of sociotechnical systems, ranging from algorithms that perform human decision-making tasks more dependably than humans themselves do, to institutions that conduct the work of critical thinking on behalf of an entire society. There is little point for now in trying to guess whether this will degrade rational thought or greatly enhance it.

The future of the web, and especially its longterm impact on human rationality, is unknowable because it is undetermined. Postman and other media ecologists (such as Marshall McLuhan) were often criticized for the technological determinism they embraced, but this sort of thinking has fallen out of fashion, in part because it so badly underestimates human inventiveness. Nowadays, instead of asking Postman's question (does the web contribute to rational thought?), theorists would be more likely to pose a design-oriented question: How *can* the web contribute to rational thought? Put just a little differently, we might ask how the deepest insights of critical thinking can be designed into the new media ecology.

Explorations of this reframed question are already well underway. Closest to the field of critical thinking are the many argumentation support systems that have flourished online (Schneider et al., 2013). Some of these systems, such as debate.org and debatewise.org, rely on disagreement to force arguers into deeper thought, providing little else in the way of intervention. Others, such as Carneades (Walton and Gordon, 2012) and Agora (Hoffman, 2016a), attempt to support critical thinking by encouraging reflection on the quality of the individual arguer's own reasoning. For example, Agora asks users to input a claim and prompts for what grounds can be advanced in support of those claims. The system then supplies a linking premise (generated automatically to assure a valid argument) and lets the user decide whether this linking premise is true. In theory, a linking premise that is obviously not true should alert the user to grounds that are insufficient to justify the claim (but see Hoffman, 2016b, and Jackson, 2016, for discussion of the limitations of this form of support for critical thinking).

An idea mentioned earlier has broad possibilities for designing an information environment that supports critical thinking: the idea that critical thinking can be accessorized with online tools that perform certain parts of the assessment of an argument. Certain difficult information assessment problems that cannot be solved by humans are more easily solved by algorithms. Spotting fake product reviews and other fake opinion content is not a matter of knowing what to look for in an individual message, but a matter of searching for anomalous patterns in large bodies of messages. Something similar is true for detecting bias. It is often impossible to detect bias in a single evaluation, while patterns observable in large numbers of assessments may be incontrovertible evidence of bias. An important and unanswerable question this raises is whether it is better to keep trying to rid human reasoning of bias or to search for inventions that ingest biased human reasoning and deliver unbiased results.

4. Conclusion

As observed very early in this chapter, a new media ecology can challenge old assumptions and old habits of thought while requiring new skills and new tools. What have we observed so far, in the very short time since the intention of the web?

To begin with, the web (or the new media ecology generally) does not make critical thinking irrelevant, but it does change the relevance of some component skills associated strongly with prior media ecologies, and it does seem to call for some entirely new skills. For example, skill in reconstructing and evaluating what is argued in a particular text has long been considered a central component of critical thinking. The web changes the scale of this task, as can be seen by considering the effort required to reconstruct and evaluate any fraction of the information returned by algorithmic search. New parents searching for authoritative content on whether to vaccinate their baby, for example, will find an overwhelming amount of information, including an overwhelming amount of content produced by indisputable experts and an equally overwhelming amount of content produced by other parents who have had the same question. Deciding what deserves any attention at all is as much a matter of critical thinking as is the detailed assessment of items that manage to claim some share of attention. Preferring authoritative sources becomes a rule of thumb that applies in many cases, but not all.

As argued earlier, when large bodies of experience-based content are being examined, new skills are needed for evaluating the body of content as a whole. The authenticity of product reviews, for example, cannot be judged reliably by applying tests to an individual review, but the overall trustworthiness of a collection of reviews can be assessed algorithmically. The search for patterning in large bodies of content requires an ability to zoom out from any one bit of argument. The meta- cognitive lesson of this applies broadly, not only to collections of product reviews, but also to collections of much more serious content, including medical advice extracted from primary research literature. Too much focus on evaluating one such text can produce unwarranted confidence in one's own grasp of a subject (Jackson and Schneider, 2017). Learning to investigate the provenance of evidence (roughly, where it comes from and how it has "traveled" through cyberspace) is a subtle transformation of skill in evaluating the credibility of the person who states (or re-states) a claim. As the web becomes more and more integrated into daily life, many such transformations are to be expected.

Earlier in the chapter I pointed out the value of delegating some kinds of critical questioning to algorithms that can improve on individual judgment. In an information environment like the web, it is well worth considering what other cognitive work can be better done by new inventions that might truly augment human reasoning. The web's most lasting effect on human reasonableness is likely to come from *tools* invented to improve on human reasoning—that is, tools that lead to better inferences than humans can draw without the aid of the tools. These can include not only the sort of workaday algorithms that figure so heavily in selection and presentation of content, but also novel ways of aggregating the cognitive work of many individual humans (requiring other sorts of algorithms). New theorizing will be needed around what should count as an improvement over (or in) human reasoning. New methods will be needed for judging the overall dependability of tools that purport to extend or substitute for human reasoning, and new standards will be needed (such as overall track record) for deciding when unaided human reasoning really should *not* be trusted.

Ultimately, critical thinking is a means to an end, rather than an end in itself, inviting questions about whether humanity can seek the end served by critical thinking through new means. If the end served by critical thinking is greater reasonableness, depending on individuals trained in critical thinking techniques may need complementary strategies aimed at exploiting new possibilities presented by the web, including not only the new possibilities associated with computational tools but also the new possibilities associated with the web's ability to mobilize human effort at massive scale. What might be possible for humanity now that has never been possible before? How might new tools be designed to meet Postman's standard of contribution to rational thought? As Shirky (2010, p. 162) put it, "Upgrading one's imagination about what is possible is always a leap of faith." The web itself is such a leap, and its long-term contribution to human reasonableness is yet to be determined.

References

Abbate, J. (1999) *Inventing the Internet*, Cambridge, MA: MIT Press.

Berners-Lee, T. (1996). The Worldwide Web: Past, present, and future. https://www.w3.org/People/Berners-Lee/1996/ppf.html

Calabresi, M. (2017, May 18). Inside Russia's social media war on America. *Time*. Retrieved from http://time.com/4783932/inside-russia-social-media-war-america/.

Collins, H.M. and Evans, R.J. (2007). *Rethinking expertise*. Chicago: University of Chicago Press.

Confessore, N. and Hakim, D. (2017, March 6). Data firm says 'secret sauce' aided Trump; many scoff. *New York Times*. Retrieved from https://www.nytimes.com/2017/03/06/us/politics/cambridge-analytica.html

Dunning, D. (2011). The Dunning-Kruger effect: On being ignorant of one's own ignorance. In *Advances in Experimental Social Psychology, 44*, 247-296. doi: 10.1016/B978-0-12-385522-0.00005-6

Eslami, M., Aleyasen, A., Karahalios, K., Hamilton, K. and Sandvig, C. (2015) FeedVis: A path for exploring news feed curation algorithms. In *Proceedings of the 18th ACM Conference Companion on Computer Supported Cooperative Work & Social Computing* (CSCW'15 Companion). ACM, New York, NY, USA, 65-68. doi:10.1145/2685553.2702690

Finneman, N.O. (2011). Mediatization theory and digital media. *European Journal of Communication, 36*, 67-89. doi:10.1515/COMM.2011.004

Gimpel, J.G., Kaufmann, K.M. and Pearson-Merkowitz, S. (2007). Battleground states versus blackout states: The behavioral implications of modern presidential campaigns. *The Journal of Politics, 69*(3), 786–797.

Heydari, A., Tavakoli, M. ali, Salim, N. and Heydari, Z. (2015). Detection of review spam: A survey. *Expert Systems with Applications*, 42(7), 3634-3642. doi:10.1016/j.eswa.2014.12.029

Hoffman, M.H.G. (2016a). Reflective argumentation: A cognitive function of arguing. *Argumentation, 30*(4), 365–397. doi:10.1007/s10503-015-9388-9

Hoffman, M.H.G. (2016b). Collaborative reframing: How to use argument mapping to cope with 'wicked problems' and conflicts. In D. Mohammed and M. Lewinski (Eds.), *Argumentation and Reasoned Action: Proceedings of the First European Conference on Argumentation, Lisbon, 9-12, June 2015, Vol. 1.* College Publications (Studies in Logic and Argumentation), pp. 187-215.

Introna, L.D. (2016). Algorithms, governance, and governmentality. *Science, Technology & Human Values, 41*(1), 17-49. doi:10.1177/0162243915587360

Introna, Lucas D. and Nissenbaum, Helen (2000). Shaping the web: Why the politics of search engines matters. *The Information Society, 16*(3), 169-185.

Jackson, S. (2016). Comment on Hoffman's "Collaborative reframing: How to use argument mapping to cope with 'wicked problems' and conflicts." In D. Mohammed and M. Lewinski (Eds.), *Argumentation and Reasoned Action: Proceedings of the First European Conference on Argumentation, Lisbon, 9-12, June 2015, Vol. 1.* College Publications (Studies in Logic and Argumentation), pp. 217-220.

Jackson, S. and Schneider, J. (2017). Cochrane Review as a "warranting device" for reasoning about health. *Argumentation.* doi:10.1007/s10503-017-9440-z.

Jamieson, K.H. (2013). Messages, micro-targeting, and new media technologies. *The Forum: A Journal of Applied Research in Contemporary Politics, 11*(3), 429-435. doi:10.1515/for-2013-0052

MacCormick, J. (2012). *Nine algorithms that changed the future: The ingenious ideas that drive today's computers.* Princeton, NJ: Princeton University Press.

Murphy, T. (2012, September/October). Harper Reed's machine can't read your mind—yet. *Mother Jones, 37*(5), 42-47.

Noble, S.U. (2013). Google search: Hyper-visibility as a means of rendering black women and girls invisible. *InVisible Culture: An Electronic Journal of Visual Culture.* http://ivc.lib.rochester.edu/google-search-hyper-visibility-as-a-means-of-rendering-black-women-and-girls-invisible/

Pariser, E. (2011). *The filter bubble: How the new personalized web is changing what we read and how we think.* New York: Penguin Press.

Postman, N. (2000). The humanism of media ecology. *Proceedings of the Media Ecology Association, 1,* pp. 10-16. http://media-ecology.org/publications/MEA_proceedings/v1/postman01.pdf

Rheingold, H. (2012). Crap detection 101: How to find what you need to know, and how to decide if it's true. *Netsmart: How to thrive online*, ch. 2. Cambridge, MA: MIT Press.

Schneider, J., Groza, T. and Passant, A. (2013). A review of argumentation for the Social Semantic Web. *Semantic Web, 4*, 159–218 159. doi:10.3233/SW-2012-0073

Shirky, C. (2010). *Cognitive surplus: Creativity and generosity in a connected age*. New York: Penguin Press.

Tufekci, Z. (2012, November 16). Beware the smart campaign. *The New York Times*. http://www.nytimes.com/

Turow, J., King, J., Hoofnagle, C.J., Bleakley, A. and Hennessy, M. (2009). Americans reject tailored advertising and three activities that enable it. Available at SSRN: https://ssrn.com/abstract=1478214 or http://dx.doi.org/10.2139/ssrn.1478214

Turow, J., Delli Carpini, M.X., Draper, N.A. and Howard-Williams, R. (2012). Americans roundly reject tailored political advertising. Annenberg School for Communication, University of Pennsylvania. Retrieved from http://repository.upenn.edu/asc_papers/ 398.

Van Couvering, Elizabeth (2007). Is relevance relevant? Market, science, and war: Discourses of search engine quality. *Journal of Computer-Mediated Communication, 12*, 866–887. doi:10.1111/j.1083-6101.2007.00354.x

Walton, D.N. and Gordon, T.F. (2012). The Carneades model of argument invention. *Pragmatics & Cognition, 20*(1), 1–31. doi:10.1075/pc.20.1.01wal

About the author:

Sally Jackson is best known for her work on naturally occurring argumentation, an area of research opened by her collaborative work with Scott Jacobs. Her writings (mostly notably her co-authored book *Reconstructing Argumentative Discussion* and her early articles on conversational argument) have been recognized with multiple awards from the (US) National Communication Association and the American Forensic Association. In 1997 she received the Distinguished Research Award from the International Society for the Study of Argumentation for career achievement. She is currently Professor of Communication and Informatics at the University of Illinois at Urbana-Champaign, and has also held professorial appointments at the University of Nebraska, Michigan State University, Oklahoma University, and the University of Arizona. She served as Chief Information Officer at both the University of Arizona and the University of Illinois, assuming responsibility for each institution's communication technology strategy during the rise of the World-wide Web.

16

Definition

Robert H. Ennis

1. Introduction[1]

Definition, though often neglected, plays an important role in critical thinking by helping us make our positions, inquiries, and reasoning clear.

Every definition has three dimensions: *form, action,* and *content.* The *form* of a definition is essentially the structure of the definition. An example of form is definition by synonym, a simple form of definition in which the word being defined is equal in meaning to one other word.

Three definitional *actions* that can be performed with any form of definition are *reporting* a meaning, *stipulating* a meaning, and *advocating* a meaning that incorporates a *position* on an issue.

This chapter focuses on these first two dimensions, form and action.

The third dimension, *content,* deals with the meaning conveyed by the definition. The content dimension is enormous because it involves the definitional content of all subject matter areas, as well as all other areas of human life. Attention to the content dimension will here be exemplified only in a discussion of a case of probable equivocation with the term 'reliability'.

To the extent possible, a definition should be clear, brief, efficient, informative, responsive to background information, and easy to remember and understand. It should be at an appropriate level of sophistication and difficulty for the situation. It should employ an appropriate form and have a reasonable amount of vagueness and specificity. Because so much depends on the situation, and because these general criteria overlap to some extent, informed cautious judgment is required.

---

[1] I deeply appreciate the help and advice of Jennie Berg, David Hitchcock, and Kevin Possin in the development of this chapter.

There has been little recent work with practical application in the area of definition. I hope that in the future there will be more explicit attention given to this topic than has been afforded it so far.

2. Common forms of definition

Full-definition forms to be presented are: (1) classification, (2) equivalent-expression, (3) range, (4) synonym, (5) extended-synonym, (6) antonym, and (7) operational. Partial-definition forms to be considered are (8) giving examples, non-examples, and borderline cases (all three either verbally or ostensively), as well as using the term in a sentence.[2] There is much to consider in a given context in choosing what form is more successful in specifying the meaning of a term. It is often helpful to compare a definition with another definition of the same word in the same form or in a different form.

2.1 Classification definition

Classification definition is a very common form of definition of nouns. Here is one of a number of possible classification definitions of the noun, 'argument' (Example 1):

> **E1** *An argument is a reason-based attempt to justify a conclusion.*

I have called this popular type of definition "classification definition" because things labeled by the term being defined (in this case, 'argument') are *classified* as the members of a general class (e.g., *reason-based attempts*) and then further classified under one or more distinguishing features (e.g., *to justify a conclusion*).

In definition lore, classification definition is often called "genus-differentia definition", with the word 'genus' referring to the *general class* and the word 'differentia' referring to the *distinguishing features*.[3] I prefer the label "classification definition" over the label "genus-differentia definition" primarily because the words 'classification definition' are more user-friendly for beginners than 'genus-differentia'. Another reason is that in 'genus-differentia' terminology the differentia must be treated as one thing because the word, 'differentia' is singular. Even though there are ways around this, I usually find

---

[2] Recursive definition is not included because it is used too rarely by expected readers to warrant explaining its complexities. Those who need it will have good sources for it.

[3] Copi (1953 and later editions), in a popular book, used the label "genus-difference" definition (rather than "genus differentia"). He stated that by "difference" he meant "differentia".

it easier to develop and work with definitions that make it easy to treat multiple distinguishing features separately.

In logical terms the components mentioned in the defining part of a simple classification definition (the *general class* and the *distinguishing features*) are each necessary and jointly sufficient for something to be what is labeled by the term being defined. Most other definition forms do not have the strictness of 'necessary' and 'sufficient'.

2.1.1 Flexibility in offering and selecting the general class

In this classification definition of 'stapler', 'a *device* for fastening two or more pieces of paper together', *device* is the general class. In this classification definition of 'automobile' (adapted from *Dictionary.com*, accessed Sept. 5, 2017), 'a *vehicle* designed for operation on ordinary roads, able to carry passengers, and typically having four wheels and a gasoline or diesel internal-combustion engine', *vehicle* is the general class. In a classification definition, there must be a general class.

However there is often more than one legitimate choice of the general class for any given meaning of a term. One way to look at Example 1 (above) is to consider *reason-based attempt* as the general class and *to justify a conclusion* as a distinguishing feature. A different way to analyze this meaning of 'argument' is to treat *attempt* as the general class and the rest (*based on reasons* and *to justify a conclusion*) as the distinguishing features, as is explicitly exemplified in Example 2.

> **E2** *An argument is an attempt based on reasons to justify a conclusion.*

Such variations in general class and accompanying variations among the distinguishing features often are possible without changing the meaning of the term being defined. Note that in Example 3 (below), the same meaning of 'argument' is captured, though there is a considerably different general class, *set of reasons and a conclusion offered by the arguer,* and different distinguishing features, *in an attempt* and *to justify a conclusion*:

> **E3** *An argument is a set of reasons and a conclusion offered by the arguer in an attempt to justify a conclusion.*

One should be flexible in choosing the general class because one choice is often better than the others, so we should not hastily accept the first to occur to us. This flexibility calls for paying attention to the general criteria for a definition mentioned earlier.

Of the three general classes so far considered (each of which introduces what is basically the same meaning of 'argument'), the one that I prefer is *reason-based attempt.* I choose it over *attempt* because *attempt* seems to be too broad a category; it does not rule out enough things; that is, it does not give much guidance. Furthermore, I prefer *reason-based attempt* over *set of reasons and a conclusion offered by an arguer* as the general class, because the definition in Example 1 using *reason-based attempt* seems to satisfy more of the above-mentioned criteria for a definition than Example 3. Example 1 seems clear, brief, efficient, easy to remember, and easy to understand.

One important thing to be learned from these examples is that there can be explicitly different definitions of a term, each of which defines the term adequately without changing the basic meaning. Elsewhere (2016), I have gathered fourteen definitions of 'critical thinking' by leaders in the field, starting with John Dewey (1933, first ed., 1910), who inspired the current critical thinking movement under the label "critical thinking". Most of these fourteen definitions are classification definitions They are essentially in agreement with each other about the meaning of 'critical thinking', even though they use different words and cite different features. Each one seems essentially right. This sort of occurrence is an interesting content-dimension fact about a number of concepts and definitions. Many concepts have more than enough necessary and/or sufficient conditions to identify them uniquely. And different definitions have different amounts of informative but not logically necessary material.

2.1.2 Imprecision

Ordinary language being what it is, we often must accept some imprecision, which often depends on the context. For instance, Example 3 does not tell us whether a pair of people working together can constitute an *arguer*. But specifics like that might not matter at all, given the context in which the term is being defined. Also the first three examples above do not specify what kind of justification is involved (for example, deductive validity, or validity in its non-technical sense, meaning roughly 'correctness'), but the context might settle that. If the context were a course in deductive logic, the "necessary-follows" sense of 'validity' would probably be appropriate.

In these cases, given that the context is the field of critical thinking, the three definitions are concerned with all kinds of justification, and are not limited to deductive validity.

The range definition form, which is soon to be considered, explicitly makes imprecision evident when defining obviously imprecise terms. But at some level of elaboration, most everyday terms have a degree of possible imprecision, and the definer must decide how much precision is available and desirable, given the context and the ordinary meaning of the term in the context, and implement that decision with appropriate wording.

2.1.3 Nouns and Non-nouns

Classification definition and genus-differentia definition require that the term being defined be a noun. If some other part of speech, for example, a verb (an example being 'argue') is to be defined using the classification form, perhaps because of familiarity with classification definition, or its completeness, the term 'argue' can be converted to a noun (possibly 'argument') and defined as a noun. From this definition the receiver must infer what the original word ('argue') means. If an expected audience can infer the meaning of 'argue' from Examples 1, 2, and/or 3, then these examples of classification definition might well be used to define 'argue' in this manner, that is, indirectly. But there are other definition forms, especially the equivalent-expression form, which might work as well or better in some cases.

2.2 Equivalent-expression definition

When the term we want to define is not a noun, another form, equivalent-expression definition might be appropriate. Equivalent-expression definition does not require that we convert the term to be defined to a noun, which can make problems, as I shall later show. Instead the term to be defined remains unchanged and is put in a larger expression that is equated with an equivalent expression. This type of definition, which I call "equivalent-expression definition", is called "contextual definition" by Hempel (1952, p. 5), and *Dictionary.com* (August, 2017). Example 4 is an equivalent-expression definition of the verb, 'argue':

> **E4** *'To argue in support of a conclusion' is 'to attempt to justify it'.*[4]

The expressions on each side of the word 'is' are claimed to be equal in meaning to each other, giving us a good idea of the meaning of 'argue' in the sense in which I believe it is usually used in the field of critical thinking.

The adjective 'biased' can be handled the same way, as shown in an equivalent-expression definition in Example 5:

> **E5** *To say "a person is biased" is to say "the person lets his or her prejudices influence his or her judgment".*

---

[4] Notes about punctuation of definitions: Equivalent-expression definitions equate expressions, so the things equated are in quotes. Classification definitions are about classes, so the items in the definition are not in quotes. Similar ideas apply to other definitions in this chapter. If the verb in the definition is 'means', the subject of the definition sentence is a word and is in quotes, and the part after 'means' is not in quotes. If the equating verbal phrase in the definition is 'means the same as', both sides of it are in quotes. The basic idea is that references to words are in quotes; other references are not.

However, if we try to convert the non-noun ('biased' for example) to a noun, such as 'bias', as we might in trying to make a classification definition for 'biased', the task might become difficult. I invite you to ask yourself, "What general class could one use to give a classification definition of the noun, 'bias'?" After rejecting a number of candidates that occurred to me, I chose 'disposition', resulting in Example 6:

> **E6** *A bias is a persistent prejudiced disposition toward issues and/or people.*

But it took me a while to come up with that. I considered 'quality', which is a common, but often not very informative, general class term, and feel it is too general to be of much help. The result in Example 6 is usable, but I prefer Example 5, the equivalent-expression definition. It seems more informative. Some readers might prefer Example 6. The important thing is that there are generally different alternatives in defining terms, and a definer should consider the alternatives and apply the general criteria for definitions. No one form is always best. Sometimes the classification form seems best, sometimes the equivalent-expression form, sometimes another form. This is a matter about which reasonable people can differ.

Another instructive example is the term, 'valid', as used by logicians. Although not a noun, its companion noun, 'validity' can be given a classification definition as a noun by introducing the very general noun, 'quality', followed by a user's inference back to the meaning of the adjective, 'valid' (assuming a logician's context). Here is such a classification definition:

> **E7** *Validity is the quality of an argument in which the conclusion follows necessarily from the premises.*

Here is an equivalent-expression definition of 'valid':

> **E8** *'An argument is valid' means the same as 'The conclusion follows necessarily from the premises.'*

The equivalent-expression form obviates the need to find a workable noun for a general class term, and generally provides a convenient definition, as noted in dealing with 'bias' (Examples 5 and 6), and 'valid' (Examples 7 and 8).

But the equivalent-expression form does not provide the general class and distinguishing features characteristic of the classification form, and so is not so clearly bounded as a classification definition of the term. For example, it does not necessarily provide an interpretation when the term being defined is not in the chosen context, and is in other contexts, or no context. Furthermore it does not require the necessary and sufficient condition guarantee provided by a classification definition.

One must decide, and not only between these two forms. There are other forms as well. In any case one must consider the definition criteria, the situation, and one's personal theoretically-motivated or pedagogically-motivated preferences.

2.3 Range definition

Range definition, a deliberately-vague form named by Max Black (1954), can be roughly a classification definition in form, specifying a general class and roughly distinguishing the term being defined from other members of the class. But it deliberately introduces explicit vagueness. Black likened the vagueness to that of a mountain range (hence the term "range"). The following range definition of 'scientific method', based on Black (1954), exhibits deliberate vagueness:

> **E9** *Scientific method is a method of investigation characteristically involving a substantial number, but rarely all, of the following characteristics: observation, generalization, experimentation, measurement, calculation, use of instruments, formulating and testing hypotheses that get support from their being able to explain the facts and their competitors' being inconsistent with the facts, and being more or less tentative when concluding.*

The general class is *method of investigation*. The vagueness is deliberately introduced by the terms 'characteristically', 'substantial number', 'rarely all', 'more or less', and 'tentative'. The definer should use such qualifiers as these to indicate when defining a term that is clearly vague in the situation. Although this particular definition of 'scientific method' is close to being in a classification form, range definitions need not approximate the classification form. They can be similar to other forms. But of course they should satisfy definition criteria, as is feasible, given their vagueness.

2.4 Synonym definition

The synonym form uses one word to define another word. One advantage of the synonym form is that it is suitable for non-nouns. Another advantage is its brevity. Here is an example:

> **E10** *'Biased' means the same as 'prejudiced'.*

Although convenient when time is short, synonym definitions often do not capture the full meaning of the word being defined, sometimes because they are made in a hurry, but often because there is no single word that is equivalent. Synonym form may not be the best way to define a term in a given situation because, although convenience and understandability are important, accuracy is often more important.

2.5 Extended-synonym definition

Instead of being limited to a one-word meaning as we are with a synonym definition, it is often helpful to add clarification to the defining component, producing an extended-synonym definition. This form does not embed the term being defined in a context, and thus is not the equivalent-expression form. Furthermore the extended-synonym form is useful for those terms that do not work well with the rigid necessary-and-sufficient-condition structure of a classification definition.

I think that 'objective' is such a term and suggest the following extended-synonym definition of 'objective' from *Dictionary.com* (2017):

> **E11** *'Objective' means not influenced by personal feelings, interpretations, or prejudice; based on facts; unbiased.*

The term 'objective' I believe loosely fits each part of the array of terms in Example 11. But it fits no one of these terms exactly, although as a group, they do a fairly good job, making the extended-synonym form appropriate for this term. Adding a use-in-a-sentence partial definition (see Example 17 below) to Example 11 provides what I believe is an even better grasp of the term, 'objective'.

I realize this is a somewhat subjective appraisal. But the principal goal of this chapter is to provide a choice of alternative forms that one can use. This requires using one's judgment (which often will be somewhat subjective) in each situation with due respect to the criteria for a good definition.

Example 12 is an unsuccessful attempt to convert Example 11 into a classification definition:

> **E12** *Objectivity is the quality of not being influenced by personal feelings, interpretations, or prejudice; being based on facts; being unbiased.*

Using *quality* as the general class does help in this case by somewhat narrowing down the alternatives. However, the rest of Example 12 does not provide a set of necessary-and-sufficient condition distinguishing features. So Example 12 is not a classification definition. It is basically another extended-synonym definition and, as such, is a helpful conveyor of the meaning of 'objective' and 'objectivity'. As I noted earlier for Example 11, it can helpfully be supplemented by Example 17, yet to be presented, which adds concreteness to this definition.

2.6 Antonym definition

In the antonym form the defining term is one that means the opposite of the term being defined, an antonym being the opposite of a synonym. According to *The Random House Dictionary of the English Language, College Edition* (1968) and *Dictionary.com* (August, 2017):

>   **E13** *'Fast' is an antonym of 'slow'.*

When the antonym is clear, well understood, and accurate (as it is in this case), the anonym form is quite useful.

2.7 Operational definition

The idea of operational definitions is often attributed to Percy Bridgman (1927) working in theoretical physics, where he suggested that the value of the term being defined is the reading on an instrument, assuming that the appropriate operation has been performed. An example in everyday life is the use of the basic fever thermometer to determine one's temperature, when the appropriate operation (including placing the tip of the thermometer under one's tongue for two minutes) has been performed. Using an operational definition, the operation and the reading on the instrument operationally define the meaning of the word 'temperature', by providing helpful concrete interpretation.

Roughly speaking there are two different directions of emphasis in implementing this basic operational idea: *strict* and *loose*. In the strict approach, the language does not leave room for human judgment. Here is an example of the strict approach:

>   **E14** *If student X is given the "Wechsler Intelligence Scale for Children", X has an IQ of Y if and only if X gets a score of Y.*

Note that there are no qualifications in this strict version. This definition does not allow for exceptions and unforeseen situations. If a person had been up all night with the flu and could hardly concentrate when taking the test, there is no leeway. The person's IQ is the score on the test, if the test is given and scored.

Strict operational definition was adopted by participants in the reductionist, behaviorist, logical-positivist tradition of the early part of the Twentieth Century, which equated the meaning of a theoretical concept (for example, IQ) with the use of a particular measuring instrument and the resulting score, as in Example 14 above. Especially in testing humans, precision is claimed at the cost of ignoring the obvious problems.

In the loose approach (Ennis, 1964), qualifying words are inserted in anticipation of possible problems. Human judgment is needed and accepted in order to apply the words of the loose operational definition of Example 15, which contains qualifying words like 'probably', 'roughly', and 'under standard conditions':

> **E15** *If a native-English-speaking college student is given the "Cornell Critical Thinking Test, Level Z" under standard conditions; then, if and only if that person gets a score of X, that person has probably mastered critical thinking roughly to the degree of X.*

Actually in my experience there never has been a complete precise list of standard conditions for any test, presumably because it is impossible to know everything that can go wrong. There is always some variation in conditions. Many people do not realize the looseness introduced by "standard conditions". Furthermore the causal relationships between a student's characteristics and a test score are a matter of continuing controversy. All this justifies the use of such terms as 'probably', and 'roughly' when the defined term applies to a human mental characteristic, such as "critical thinking" does in Example 15.

Operational definitions provide a basis for some of the current extensive school testing emphasis in United States schools, but so used should be of the loose interpretation form of operational definition because of reasons given in the previous paragraph.

Both Examples 14 and 15 apply to human mental characteristics. When the definitions apply to characteristics of physical objects (like the fever thermometer), at least a somewhat strict approach is generally appropriate. But watchfulness and care are still required.

Some people have totally abandoned both the strict and the loose interpretations of the original spirit of operational definition, and think of operational definitions as just examples, or alternatively, as criteria for good things like "walkable neighborhoods" (Moudon, *et al.*, 2006). I urge us not to abandon the loose spirit of operational definitions, because holding at least a loose connection among the meaning of a term, a test, and a test result is insightful. It is politically important in dealing with the current testing movement at all levels of education.

2.8 Partial-definition forms

Strictly speaking, examples, non-examples, and borderline cases, as well as the use-in-a-sentence form of definition, do not approximate being full definitions. So I call them 'partial-definition forms'.

2.8.1 Examples, non-examples, and borderline cases

Examples, non-examples, and borderline cases are partial forms of definition that can sometimes be especially helpful in providing meaning because they indicate crucial limits and provide helpful concrete elaboration. Often they can convey meaning to an extent that is sufficient for the situation, and can often do so even more effectively than, say, a classification definition that lacks concreteness. However, combining examples, non-examples, and borderline cases with full classification definitions can sometimes be even better.

The example, borderline-case, and non-example passages in Examples 16a and 16b below were useful to me elsewhere in introducing and clarifying a new meaning of the term '*subject-specific critical thinking ability*' (Ennis, 2018, p. 169):

> **E16a** *An example of a subject-specific critical thinking ability is the ability to plan, perform, and judge the results and relevance of **analysis of covariance** (used in several social and psychological sciences in order to judge the practical and statistical significance of a difference) with an understanding of the limitations involved. However, just understanding the concept of **statistical significance**, including sensitivity to its major strengths and weaknesses, is arguably a general ability.*

Analysis of covariance is not used in most fields and is totally unfamiliar to most educated people I know. So the example of doing analysis of covariance as a *subject-specific critical thinking ability*, which is specific to certain subjects or fields, should I believe help make this new meaning of the term 'subject-specific critical thinking ability' clear.

Statistical significance on the other hand is a borderline case. It is arguably general because most people have some sense of what it means. But most educated people I know do not really know what *statistical significance* is (in the social sciences), so it is arguably also subject-specific. It is thus a borderline case, and helps further to clarify 'subject-specific critical thinking ability'.

Example 16b, from a list of critical thinking abilities (Ennis, 2011, 2017), is a striking non-example of *subject-specific critical thinking ability*:

> **E16b** *Make and judge inductive inferences and arguments:*
> *Enumerative induction*
> *Argument and inference to best explanation*

'Inductive inferences and arguments', including the subcategories 'Enumerative induction' and 'Argument and inference to best explanation', are widely used in almost all fields (although perhaps not by those names), including such widely disparate fields as courtroom trials and Shakespearean criticism (Ennis, 1996, pp. 221-228). So they are helpful *non-examples* of 'subject-specific critical thinking ability'.

So because of their immediacy and concreteness, the example and the borderline case in Example 16a and the non-example in Example 16b can be helpful in introducing and clarifying a new and useful term, 'subject-specific critical thinking ability', a term that I have found helpful in advocating critical thinking across the curriculum (2018).

Examples, non-examples, and borderline cases need not be only verbally presented. They can be presented in part by physically pointing, as in for example pointing at an almost-leafless formerly-healthy grapefruit tree to show someone an example of citrus greening (a serious citrus tree disease). Such pointing is called "ostensive definition". Like most ostensive definitions, it usually requires some verbal supplementation as well as background experience on the part of the learner. In this example the learner must have some grasp of the appearance of a healthy grapefruit tree. Together the pointing and the background knowledge are helpful in understanding the ostensive act. This example shows that ostensive definitions can be quick and effective in the right conditions. Incidentally they are also helpful in teaching words to children.

2.8.2 Using the term in a sentence

Here is a helpful example of the use-in-a-sentence form of partial definition for the term 'objective', provided by *Cambridge Dictionaries Online* (October, 2016):

> **E17** *I can't really be objective when I'm judging my daughter's work.*

Example 17 recognizes the prohibition against being influenced by personal feelings when trying to be objective, and makes use of well-known strong feelings most people have about their offspring. By itself, the use-in-a-sentence form is often not sufficient to convey fully the meaning of a term. However, as noted earlier in discussing Examples 11 and 12, combining the use-in-a-sentence partial-definition form with some of the other definition forms I have described can contribute to a fuller understanding of the meaning of a term.

3. Three basic actions that definers perform: reporting a meaning, stipulating a meaning, and advocating a meaning that incorporates a position

The *form* of a definition is one basic dimension of defining. A second basic dimension is the *action* the definer is performing when offering a meaning of a term. When the definition's form and content are combined with the action, the result is part of an act of human communication.

There are three basic definitional actions: (1) the definer's *reporting* what the definer claims to be a meaning, (2) the definer's *stipulating* a meaning, and (3) the definer's *advocating* a particular meaning that incorporates a *position* on an issue. A definition such as Example 4, an equivalent-expression definition of 'argue', can be used to introduce the distinctions among these three actions.

Example 18 uses Example 4 in a reporting action, Example 19 uses it in a stipulating action, and Example 20 uses it in a positional action. The exact same words (Example 4) are used as the definition in all three contexts, but a different action is being performed in each case.

> **E18** *On the basis of my experience communicating with critical thinking experts, I report that the following definition states what the experts generally mean by 'argue' in the field of critical thinking: 'To argue in support of a conclusion' is 'to attempt to justify it'.* (reporting ameaning)

> **E19** *As the instructor of this critical thinking course in this institution, I stipulate that in this course we shall mean the following by the word 'argue': 'To argue in support of a conclusion' is 'to attempt to justify it'.* (stipulating a meaning)

> **E20** *As long-time members of this department, we advocate the following definition of 'argue' for use in the critical thinking course we are developing: 'To argue in support of a conclusion' is 'to attempt to justify it.' We believe that this sense of 'argue' is the appropriate one for a course in critical thinking, because* (their position) *the major concern in a critical thinking course is how to tell whether the conclusion of an argument is justified.* (advocating a particular meaning that incorporates a *position*)

3.1 Reporting a meaning

In reporting a meaning, the reporter (the definer) claims that the reported meaning is a meaning of the term.[5] The definer in Example 18 claims the meaning in Example 4 to be a meaning of the term 'argue'. Such a report can be true or false, and thus requires critical thinking (including inference to best explanation, as well as observation and other data gathering) to judge its acceptability.

---

[5] By "a meaning" I mean a way the term has been used.

Note that Example 18 is a special case of reporting a meaning. It is also reporting *the* meaning held by a certain group of people. So it requires more information for its support than simply reporting *a* meaning.

The definition that results from reporting a (or the) meaning shall here be called a "*reportive* definition" a term suggested by David Hitchcock (personal communication).[6] If I used the label '*reported* definition' instead of '*reportive* definition', then according to the ordinary meaning of '*reported*', a *reported* definition could be a definition that the definer tells us about (reports) but does not claim to be a meaning of a term. This means that it would not necessarily be a product that the reporter (the definer) claims to be a (or the) meaning. I stipulate that a 'reportive definition' is one in which the definer claims that the meaning reported is a (or the) meaning of the term.

Although ordinarily we report a meaning that is widely used or at least used by a group, a specific person's meaning could be claimed in a reportive definition, as in Example 21:

E21 By 'silly', she means good.

3.2 Stipulating a meaning

Stipulating a meaning of a term is deeming that the meaning given is what the term shall be taken to mean in a given situation. Grammatically, the definer expresses the stipulation in the imperative mood, rather than the indicative mood. A stipulation of a meaning is neither true nor false.

In stipulating a meaning, a definer assumes that she or he has the right to determine what the term shall mean in the situation. As author, I have the right to stipulate the meaning of 'reportive' in this chapter. If the would-be stipulator does not have the right, then the stipulation fails, and the definition ordinarily would be considered a positional definition that incorporates a position on an issue (see next section), if the author desires to perform that action. A definer can choose both actions if the definer does have the right to stipulate. I treat my definition of 'reportive' not only as a stipulative definition, but also as a positional definition, because I advocate the theory of, and approach to, definition in which it is embedded.

In 2006, the International Astronomical Union reached a decision about Pluto that was implied by the following apparently stipulative classification definition of 'planet' (International Astronomical Union, 2006):

---

[6] Something like it is called "lexical definition" or "descriptive definition" by some other authors. I do not feel that these names are sufficiently descriptive of what this type of definition does.

E22 Planet: A celestial body that (a) is in orbit around the Sun, (b) has sufficient mass for its self-gravity to overcome rigid body forces so that it assumes a hydrostatic equilibrium (nearly round) shape, and (c) has cleared the neighbourhood around its orbit.

An implication of this apparently stipulative definition is that Pluto is not a planet, because it does not meet criterion (c). There is a nearby large mass called Eris.

Stipulating a meaning as part of a theory is a common occurrence. The International Astronomical Union, I suspect, has a right to stipulate a definition of a key term ('planet') that plays an important role in a theory it is advancing, but in this case the extent of this right, or its existence at all, is a matter of some controversy.

Former NASA scientist Phil Metzger provided conflicting usage rejecting the apparent stipulation: "We are free to call it a planet right now. The planetary science community has never stopped calling bodies like Pluto 'planets'" (Wiener-Bronner, 2015). So, given this description of the situation, it is not clear that the International Astronomical Union has the authority to stipulate the meaning for 'planet' in Example 22. If it does not have the right, the definition cannot be considered a stipulative definition, and in this case would be considered a positional and reportive definition that conflicts with Metzger's positional and reportive definition, and so must be defended by critical thinking evidence and argument.

3.3 Advocating a meaning of a term incorporating a position on an issue (positional definition)

Sometimes definers advocate a meaning for a term that incorporates a position on an issue. Scheffler (1960) has given this topic a thorough treatment under the label, "programmatic definition". I will use the topics of segregation and marriage to exemplify definitions that take a position.

3.3.1 Segregation

School segregation was judged unconstitutional (but was not defined) by the United States Supreme Court (1954). Since it was not defined, it was too vague to provide specific guidance to a school system, which was needed. Then a possible result was that a superintendent in a large school system would propose to the governing board the following equivalent-expression positional definition of 'segregated':

E23 To say 'a school is segregated' is to say 'it has a population more than 80% of which is of a given minority race.

Example 23 advocates the position that a school with more than 80% of its students of a given minority race, but not a school with 80% or fewer of its students of a minority race, is in violation of the segregation law. Thus it is a definition that expresses a position on an issue. Argument is needed to support that position in the ensuing discussion.

A desirable condition for success of a positional definition is that the position being taken be a clear position, the clearer the better. A further condition for its success is that the position be justified. Critical thinking is called for in making this judgment.

3.3.2 Marriage

Here is a positional definition of 'marriage':

E24 *Marriage is a legal, committed union of a woman and a man.*

Inherent in this classification definition, assuming the 'is' is the 'is' of equality, when it was presented, was the position that two people of the same sex cannot and should not be married, currently a controversial issue. In this case the position of the definer was opposition to same-sex marriage. So it was a positional definition.

Example 24 was also a reportive definition because the definer claimed that this was a common meaning of the word 'marriage', which it was. The definition of 'marriage' in Example 24 thus is another instance of a definer's performing more than one definitional action with the same definition, in this case, positional and reportive.

4. A glimpse of the content dimension: equivocation and impact equivocation with the term, 'reliability'

Because words in virtually any subject matter or area of interest are subject to definition, and all definitions have content, any fully-exemplified discussion of definition *content* would be huge in scope. So, at least to give the flavor of dealing with a content issue, I shall present one example, which deals with the ambiguity of a term, 'reliability', and its possible exploitation.

Exploitation of the ambiguity of a term is equivocation and is a significant critical thinking concern. When such equivocation is inadvertent, I call it "impact equivocation", because it has the impact of equivocation, though it is unintentional. Equivocation is a topic within the area of the third dimension of definition, content.

In what follows, I shall describe an occurrence of impact equivocation, explain why I think it occurred, and hold that such impact equivocation occurrences are likely to happen often if the field of psychometrics retains its meaning of 'reliability', given the ordinary-language meaning of 'reliability'.

Impact equivocation faced me when, inquiring of a school principal about the *validity* of the academic aptitude test taken by my then 5th-grade son, I was told that the test was quite valid because it had a "reliability" of 0.94. This rating was thought by the principal to be a high *validity* rating. This was a case of impact equivocation. The principal believed that this "reliability" meant *validity*, which it did not.

The psychometric definition of 'reliability' does not specify anything about the quality of a performance; it only indicates consistency and patterns of consistency. Psychometric 'reliability' is defined as follows in the fourth edition of *Educational Measurement* (Haertel, 2006, p.65): Reliability is "concerned solely with how the scores resulting from a measurement procedure would be expected to vary across replications of that procedure". In simpler terms, 'reliability' in psychometrics basically means 'consistency'.

On the other hand, the ordinary meaning of 'reliability' incorporates consistency, but also requires good quality performance. Here are the two definitions of 'reliability' in *Oxforddictionaries.com* (accessed September 8, 2017):

1. The quality of being trustworthy or of performing consistently well.

2. The degree to which the result of a measurement, calculation, or specification can be depended on to be accurate.

Here is the definition of 'reliability' in *Dictionary.com* (accessed August 22, 2017):

the ability to be relied on or depended on, as for accuracy, honesty, or achievement.

These dictionary definitions of 'reliability' are in accord with the ordinary meaning of 'reliability': 'dependability in getting things right'; more briefly, 'consistency plus quality'.

Furthermore, correlations of aptitude tests with later grades or other indicators of success (validity correlations) are only "modest" (Thorndike, 1971; Linn, 1982, p. 287, two major leaders in psychometrics over the years). For example, an analysis of the validity of the *Graduate Record Exam* (GRE) in predicting graduate school success found correlations of .30 to .45 between the GRE and both first year and overall graduate GPA. Correlations with faculty ratings ranged from .35 to .50 (Kunzel and Hazlett, 2001). Because validity correlations are generally "modest", and because the correlation of 0.94 on my son's test was called "reliability" in a psychometric publication, the 0.94 correlation clearly was not a validity correlation.

So given that psychometric reliability does not imply quality, which an inference to validity would require; given that ordinary reliability does require good quality; and given that the correlations for validity run much lower than the 0.94 that was reported, the principal's reporting the 0.94 as indicating validity depended on a shift from the psychometric meaning of 'reliability' to the ordinary meaning of 'reliability'. So the principal was impact equivocating. I say "impact equivocating" rather than "equivocating" because it appeared that the principal did not realize that she was not answering my question about validity.

In view of the widespread ordinary meaning of 'reliability', I suggest that the field of psychometrics consider changing the label 'reliability' in their vocabulary to 'consistency' in order to minimize such impact equivocations. The ordinary-language meaning of 'reliability' is not likely to change.

This suggestion and accompanying discussion fit within the content dimension of definition. The meanings discussed here and their interaction are matters of content.

5. Summary: A three-dimensional theory of definition, encompassing form, action, and content

A variety of possible forms and variations thereof are available for defining terms, *form* being a first dimension of definition. Three different *actions*, reporting, stipulating, and advocating a position, comprise the second dimension of defining, *action*. And the broad area of *content* provides the third basic dimension of definition. In this chapter I have focused on the two dimensions, form and action, and provided one case of attention to content, a concern about equivocation.

To the extent possible, a definition should be clear, brief, efficient, informative, responsive to background information, and easy to remember and understand. It should be at an appropriate level of sophistication and difficulty for the situation. It should employ an appropriate form and have a reasonable amount of vagueness and specificity. Because so much depends on the situation, and because these general criteria overlap to some extent, informed cautious judgment is required.

The maker of a definition should be flexible in selecting an appropriate form for defining the term, given the situation. The *classification* form is used often, because it offers completeness in a simple structure, specifying a set of necessary and jointly sufficient conditions for the use of the term being defined. But it has the disadvantages of needing the term being defined to be a noun, or be convertible into a noun, a process which is not always easy to perform, leading on occasion to the use of the rather broad and often uninformative general class, *quality*. Furthermore classification definition generally lacks the helpful concreteness of some of the other forms of definition.

The *equivalent-expression* form puts the term to be defined in a larger expression, which is equated with another expression. It is often easier to construct than a classification definition, and usually provides sufficient coverage of the meaning, although it does not provide the clear necessary-and-sufficient boundaries of a classification definition.

The *range* form has the advantage of making vagueness quite explicit, a characteristic that we should acknowledge when it exists. *Synonym* and *antonym* definitions provide quick equivalence and the opposite when available, but are often overly simple. The *extended-synonym* definition provides more detail in the defining part of the definition than a pure synonym definition. Although it does not provide the precision of a classification definition, it can be quite useful, especially for terms that seem not to have exact equivalents.

The *operational* form provides a connection among the meaning of a term, a test, and a test result. Strict operational definition allows no exceptions in application, and is not generally suited to defining human characteristics. Loose-form operational definition loosens the connection among its elements with the use of such terms as 'generally' and 'probably' and is better suited for use when discussing human characteristics.

While *partial definitions*, such as example, non-example, borderline case, and the use-in-a-sentence form, are not full-blown definitions, they are often useful and can sometimes be sufficient to define a term. They can also be helpful as supplements to other forms of definition to provide better understanding of a term.

A definition in a form but not yet offered in an action is inert. The action of the definer transforms an inert definition into part of an act of human communication. The three major definer actions are: (1) reporting a meaning that the definer claims to be a meaning, (2) stipulating a meaning that the definer deems shall be the meaning of the term in some type of circumstance, and (3) advocating a meaning that incorporates a position on an issue. The results of these actions are reportive, stipulative, and positional definitions.

The result for the first action, reporting, can at least in part be judged by critical thinking criteria, including truth. The second action, stipulating a meaning, can be judged by its convenience in dealing with the situation, but not for its correctness, which in pure examples it is not claimed to possess. It is stated in the imperative mood. Stipulating can only be successfully done by someone who has the right to stipulate in the situation. Positional definitions are successful in part to the extent that the position they advocate is clear, and even more successful if their positions are justified. Critical thinking is relevant here. Care and sensitivity to the situation are crucial throughout.

Because many crucial terms have more than one meaning, there is often danger of equivocation and impact equivocation for which we must be on guard. The example used here is 'reliability'. I thus give some attention to the content dimension, which, because of its immensity, must be treated elsewhere, at greater length.

Language and its meanings are crucial aspects of critical thinking. Defining terms cannot be neglected. I hope that the ideas about definition in this chapter will contribute to more critical thinking.

References

Black, Max (1954). The definition of scientific method. Definition, presupposition, and assertion. Both in Max Black (Ed.), *Problems of Analysis: Philosophical Essays* (pp. 3-23; pp. 24-45). Ithaca NY: Cornell University Press.

Bridgman, Percy (1927). *The Logic of Modern Physics*. New York: Macmillan.

Cambridge Dictionaries Online (2016). Examined April 2, 2016, at http://dictionary.cambridge.org/us/dictionary/english/objective

Copi, Irving (1953). *Introduction to Logic*. New York: Macmillan.

Cronbach, Lee (1971). Test validation. In R.L. Thorndike (Ed.), *Educational Measurement*, 2nd ed. (pp. 443-507). Washington, DC: American Council on Education.

Dewey, John (1933; original edition, 1910). *How We Think*. Boston: D. C. Heath.

Dictionary.com (2016, 2017), http://www.dictionary.com, definition of 'objective', April 9, 2016; definition of 'contextual definition' Aug.14, 2017).

Ennis, Robert H. (1964). Operational definitions. *American Educational Research Journal, 1*, 183-201. (Reprinted in L.I. Krimerman (Ed.), (1969), *The Nature and Scope of Social Science: A Critical Anthology*. New York: Appleton-Century-Crofts (pp. 431-444). (Title as reprinted: Operationism can and should be divorced from covering law assumptions.)

Ennis, Robert H (1996). *Critical Thinking*. Upper Saddle River, NJ: Prentice Hall.

Ennis, Robert H (2011). Critical thinking: Reflection and perspective—Part I. *Inquiry: Critical Thinking Across the Disciplines* 26(1), 4-18.

Ennis, Robert H. (2016). Definition: A three-dimensional analysis with bearing on key concepts. OSSA Conference Archive. http://scholar.uwindsor.ca/ossaarchive/OSSA11/papersandcommentaries/105

Ennis, Robert H (2017). The nature of critical thinking. Viewed April 12, 2017, at http://criticalthinking.net/longdefinition.html.

Ennis, Robert H (2018, online first). Critical thinking across the curriculum: A vision. *TOPOI* 37(1), 165-184.

Haertel, Edward H. (2006). Reliability. In Robert L. Brennan (Ed.), *Educational Measurement*, 4th ed. (pp. 65-110). Westport, CT: Praeger Publishers.

Hempel, Carl (1952). Fundamentals of concept formation in empirical science. *Foundations of the Unity of Science, II 7.*Chicago: University of Chicago Press.

International Astronomical Union (2006). Pluto and the developing landscape of our solar system. Downloaded April 4, 2016, from http://www.iau.org/static/resolutions/Resolution_GA26-5-6.pdf

Kane, Michael (2006), Validation. In Robert Brennan (Ed.), *Educational Measurement,* 4th ed. (pp.17-64). Westport, CT: Praeger.

Kelley, Truman (1927). *Interpretation of Educational Measurements.* Yonkers-on-Hudson, NY: World Book.

Kuncel, N.R., Hezlett, S.A., Ones, D.S. (2001). "A comprehensive meta-analysis of the predictive validity of the Graduate Record Examination: Implications for graduate student selection and performance" (PDF). *Psychological Bulletin* 127(1), 162–181. doi:10.1037/0033-2909.127.1.162. (https://en.Wikipedia.org/wiki//GraduateRecoredExamination#Validity).

Linn, Robert (1982). Admission testing on trial. *American Psychlogist, 37* (3), 279-291.

Moudun, Anne, *et al.* (2006). Operational definitions of walkable neighborhood: theoretical and empirical insights. *Journal of Physical Activity and Health,* 3, Suppl 1, S99-S117.

Scheffler, Israel (1960). *The Language of Education.* Springfield, IL: Charles Thomas.

Thorndike, R.L. (1971). Concepts of cultural fairness. *Journal of Educational Measurement* (8), 63-70.

United States Supreme Court (1954). Brown v. Board of Education of Topeka. *347 US 483.*

Urdang, Laurence (1968). *The Random House Dictionary of the English Language.* New York: Random House.

Weiner-Bronner, Danielle (2015). Is Pluto a planet? The answer may surprise you. Examined March 28, 2016, at http://fusion.net/story/158379/is-pluto-a-planet-the-answer-may-surprise-you/.

About the author:

Robert H. Ennis has long been an innovator in critical thinking. He authored *Logic in Teaching, Ordinary Logic,* and *Critical Thinking*; co-authored *Evaluating Critical Thinking*; and co-edited *Language and Concepts in Education* and *Philosophy of Educational Research*. He also co-authored the two *Cornell Critical Thinking Tests (Level X* and *Level Z)* and several other critical thinking tests. He has over seventy publications dealing with critical thinking, nine of which were co-authored or co-edited. He is Professor Emeritus of Philosophy of Education at the University of Illinois, was Professor of Philosophy of Education at Cornell University, was a high school science teacher, and was a Fellow at the Center for Advanced Study in the Behavioral Sciences at Stanford. He received awards from the Ontario Society for the Study of Argumentation, the Network to Improve Thinking and Learning, the Sixth International Conference on Thinking, and the American Association of Philosophy Teachers.

17

Generalizing

Dale Hample and Yiwen Dai

1. Preliminaries

Arguments manage meanings. Normally an argument begins with something that is already known or agreed upon, and then proceeds to a conclusion that is "new" in some sense. This movement from given to new is characteristic of all social arguments. The only exception might be perfectly deductive arguments, where all the information is already understood to be contained somehow in the premises. Informal (or social) arguments involve some sort of inference, a going-beyond what is strictly expressed in the premises. By moving to a new proposition or thought, the argument can create a new meaning for someone, or reinforce an old meaning, or refute an inappropriate meaning. Arguments manage meanings.

One particularly valuable sort of meaning is a generalization. A generalization summarizes or characterizes material that is more singular than it is. If the singular things are few and straightforward, the generalization isn't especially useful (e.g., "My parents both like fruit pies" isn't much more convenient than "Mom and Dad both like fruit pies"). But the real value (and threat, but we will come to that when we discuss stereotypes) of a generalization is when it does a lot of work by summarizing too many things to think about at once (e.g., "Some thoughtful adults in nearly every human generation and culture have complained that younger people are lazy and self-centered").

Generalizations are often involved in arguments, and we can distinguish several kinds of such arguments. Some arguments move from singular premises to a more general conclusion. This involves arguing from examples or doing some approximation of scientific induction. For example, "In my survey, most people who were high on dogmatism were also high in authoritarianism; so dogmatism and authoritarianism are positively associated." We will call these *generalization-establishing* arguments. Other arguments have a generalization in the premises, but still move to a singular conclusion (you know one famous example like this: "All men are mortal; Socrates is a man; so Socrates is mortal"). We will call these *generalization-using* arguments. Finally, some arguments contain nothing but generalizations. For example, "everyone acts from self-interest; all self-interested actions damage social cohesion; therefore everyone damages social cohesion." We will call these *generalization-saturated* arguments. We will discuss all these, but will have the most to say (by far) about generalization-establishing arguments.

As for other social arguments, we have four measures of evaluation available to us. These are criteria that one can use to evaluate the argument's strength or cogency. The first three are the ARS considerations, originated by Anthony Blair and Ralph Johnson. The argument's premises must be *acceptable* (A). They must be true, or probable, or plausible, or agreeable in some respectable way. If at least one key premise fails this test, the argument is poor. The conclusion might still be true by accident, but that argument will not have supported it. Second, the premises must be *relevant* (R) to the conclusion. Relevance is a little hard to define precisely, but the idea is that premises must bear on the conclusion, so that if the premises are true a reasonable person becomes more comfortable with the conclusion. Relevant premises assert something that is an element of the conclusion or that implies something about the likelihood of the conclusion. S stands for *sufficiency*. The idea here is that *all the premises together* are enough to prove the conclusion. One can have what is called a convergent argument that contains perhaps four individually flawed reasons for the conclusion. One at a time each reason could be set aside, but when they are combined they make a jointly suitable case for the conclusion. Sufficiency and necessity are different, by the way, and they are sometimes confused. Sufficient premises are *enough* to prove a conclusion. Necessary premises are *required* for a conclusion to be so. A premise can be necessary without being sufficient ("You have to study a lot in order to graduate"). A premise can also be sufficient without being necessary ("People lucky enough to win the lottery end up being rich"). Sufficiency is the third criterion, not necessity.

The fourth criterion is what Ralph Johnson called the dialectical tier of argument. Acceptability, relevance, and sufficiency are all internal to the argument. They are about the premises and the argument scheme. The dialectical tier is external to it. "Dialectic" describes an exchange between two ideal arguers who marshal their reasoning skills, commitment to the truth, and their *knowledge of the world* to come to a conclusion. When thinking about the dialectical level of argument evaluation, we ask ourselves what else in the world—external to these premises—might bear on the conclusion. So someone might present us with an argument for Western European military intervention into Turkey. Even if the premises about Western Europe and

Turkey seemed acceptable, we would be entitled to object to the argument if it didn't take Russia into account at all. Refutative arguments, exceptions, and counter-examples take their place on the dialectical tier.

We will be using these four standards—acceptability, relevance, sufficiency, and dialectical quality—as we work through the various ways generalizations fit into arguments. Generalization arguments are as likely to go bad as any other kind of argument, but these also hold out the special danger of stereotyping. So as we move along we will pause to give particular attention to the possibility that arguments contain racism, sexism, religious intolerance, damaging views about other people's identities, and similar sorts of things. Stereotypes and generalizations can be hard to distinguish in a technical way. We will loosely say that stereotypes are generalizations that express unjustified hate, offense, or devaluing of some group of people, and not pursue definitions any further than that. (Actually, some stereotypes can be positive, as with a favorable view of everyone representing your political party, but we will neglect that possibility here.) As the United States Supreme Court ended up saying about pornography in the 1964 case *Jacobellis v. Ohio*, "I know it when I see it." We will organize the rest of the chapter by reference to the ideas of generalization-generating, generalization-using, and generalization-saturated arguments.

2. Generalization-establishing arguments

We begin with arguments that move from premises about specific cases to a summative conclusion that groups the cases together and offers some statement about the group. For example, "Uncle Ed is a schmuck; Aunt Raby is dumb; cousin Edward can't count yet and he is 8 years old; cousin Edie won't read a book unless you pay her; these are most of my relatives on my father's side; so my father's family is pretty hopeless." This argument moves from specifics (Uncle Ed, Aunt Raby, etc.) to a group (my father's family) and makes a remark about the group. Notice that the example also collects various descriptions (schmuck, dumb, can't count, won't read) and composes them into a summary (pretty hopeless) that is an idea that not only collects but also extends the implications of the specific descriptions. So there are actually two sorts of generalizing going on here. The first is like induction, where individual cases are examined and a probabilistic conclusion is drawn about the class of cases. The second is a kind of argument by composition, where attributes of some more general characteristic are sampled and a conclusion is drawn about the general characteristic. These two sorts of generalization don't always have to be present together, but they often are. They are quite likely to be involved in evidence offered for stereotypes.

Just by using common sense, we can immediately see opportunities to criticize this argument. We might think along these lines:

Acceptability: Are these attributes (schmuck, etc.) really true about each case (Uncle Ed, etc.)? Or are they perhaps just a series of poorly supported impressions? What's the evidence? Does everyone (or informed people, or smart people, etc.) see these people this way?

Relevance: Do these attributes (schmuck, etc.) really bear on the conclusion about the group (pretty hopeless)? Are these four people really "most of" the people in the group mentioned in the conclusion? Are these four people typical of everyone in your father's family? You are in your father's family, too, for instance.

Sufficiency: Is it possible for the attributes to be true and relevant, but the conclusion to be wrong? That is, does more need to be known before the conclusion can be fairly drawn? Are the named attributes (can't count, etc.) keys to the conclusion (pretty hopeless)? That is, do they "add up" to the conclusion?

Dialectical Tier: Do these people have other, more wonderful, attributes? Or even more awful characteristics? Is "pretty hopeless" too strong a characterization? Too weak? As a matter of fact, what could "hopeless" mean in this sort of context, and can we define and defend the core idea of "pretty hopeless?"

Perhaps you can immediately see the usefulness of our little system of four criteria for evaluating an argument. We had some trouble deciding where to put the question about what "pretty hopeless" means, by the way. The component meanings in an argument need to be clear before you can really think about any of the ARSD standards, so the question of clarity actually appears at any time you are trying to evaluate anything that bears on the term. We put it in Dialectical Tier mainly because it seemed a little philosophical. You don't need to do the ARSD thinking in any particular order anyway.

We started with what we thought might be a recognizable sort of example so that you can see where we are going with all this. But now we want to get a little bit more sterile in order to clarify some of the standards for this sort of argument. By looking at the most formally developed ways to establish a generalization, we should see the principles at work in more ordinary arguments too. We are going to abandon the argument-by-composition feature and just concentrate on induction-like sorts of generalization. You will encounter many examples of this when you read about public opinion or scientific investigation.

3. Surveys

Let's begin with public opinion polling. If you are interested in public affairs, nearly every week you will read about some poll that summarizes (i.e., makes a generalization about) public views of a politician or policy. Some of these polls are now labeled "unscientific" by the media that report them. Often the media also report that results have a "margin of error," perhaps plus or minus 5%. We will explain these things as we go. Younger readers may not appreciate that neither of these things—acknowledgement that a poll is unscientific, notice that the results are not precisely accurate—used to be done, and that these are improvements in journalism during the last half century. Even now, however, the media do not always report the exact question they are summarizing, which is really essential to evaluating their generalization.

Two of the key preliminary steps in conducting a poll are to write the questions and select the sample. The question needs to be such that it will get the pollster an accurate answer, and that means that it must address the subject matter without any imbalance. For example, you will get different answers to these pairs of questions:

- "Do you think that women have a right to choose what happens within their own bodies? / Do you think that women have a right to abort their fetuses?"
- "If a drug would save 200 lives out of 600 very sick people, should we administer it? / If a drug would kill 400 people out of 600 very sick people, should we administer it?"
- "Do you think that everyone, regardless of race or other identity, should have an equal chance to succeed in life? / Do you think that affirmative action programs are justified?"

It's possible that a particular person might think that the first question in each pair has the same meaning as the second one. (It's also possible that someone is trying to rig a poll to mislead the public into committing the bandwagon fallacy, or is actually using the poll as a persuasive device by getting people to agree to certain things out loud.) But the questions are probably going to register differently with people, emphasizing one element of the issue more than another or using some vague but hard to question phrase ("right to live," "equal chance," etc.). When the media report the question, viewers are better positioned to evaluate the poll. But often the media will "summarize" the question for their audience, reporting either half of the first pair as "attitudes toward abortion," or either half of the third pair as "approval ratings for affirmative action programs." Professional political pollsters have quietly decided to use the same question phrasing from poll to poll and from political party to political party, so that their clients can actually compare themselves to opponents and past results. Even if the standard question is flawed, at least the same flaw will be propagating through everyone's data, and that makes the results more useful. Data doesn't have to be perfect to be valuable: it merely has to have a known level of accuracy.

Oddly, that brings us to the second preliminary matter, selecting a sample. A perfect statement about what the citizens of Mexico think about Mexican tax rates would be to ask every single Mexican citizen, and report the answer. This would be a census, not a sample. Samples are used because they are cheaper and faster than taking a census. A sample of Mexican citizens imperfectly represents the whole population of Mexican citizens, but the degree of imperfection is known—provided that the sample is done in a particular way. This is where the "margin of error" comes from. To get a known margin of error, the pollster needs to collect a random sample of the population. A "random sample" means that every person in the population has an exactly equal chance to be in the sample. To assure this (well, to approximate it, really), polling firms might use lists of people (perhaps everyone who voted in the last Republican primary, or everyone living in an apartment building, or everyone with a driver's license in a particular state or province, depending on the population one wants to generalize to) and choose people for the sample by using a random number generator. If the random number generator's first result is 546, the 546th person on the list is contacted, and so on. The list is the population (technically, it is the "sampling frame"), and the sample result is intended to generalize to that population. Sometimes pollsters will just randomly generate telephone numbers within particular area codes so that they can cover cell phones and unlisted numbers. The size of the population is known, either from the list of voters or the number of possible phone numbers, and the size of the sample is also known. *Provided that the sample was drawn randomly,* we can calculate or just look up the margin of error.

On the next page is a standard table[1] that shows some benchmark values. The population size is the total number of people on the list, in the country, etc. It is how many people would be in a census of that sort of person. The sample size is the number of people who were actually polled. The margin of error is the plus or minus estimate of how accurate the poll's answer would be (e.g., "54% of people approved, plus or minus 5%"). The confidence in the margin of error is how sure you are that the true answer will actually be within 5% or whatever the margin of error is. (Technically the confidence statistic is not a summary of people's subjective feelings. It is a statistical calculation of how often the percentage of results would be within the margin of error if an infinite number of samples of that size were drawn from a population of that

---

[1] (http://research-advisors.com/tools/SampleSize.htm)

Population Size	Sample Size	Margin of Error	Confidence in Margin
100	80	5%	95%
100	89	3.5%	95%
100	87	5%	99%
100	93	3.5%	99%
1,000,000	384	5%	95%
1,000,000	783	3.5%	95%
1,000,000	663	5%	99%
1,000,000	1352	3.5%	99%
300,000,000	384	5%	95%
300,000,000	784	3.5%	95%
300,000,000	663	5%	99%
300,000,000	1354	3.5%	99%

size.) Media aren't to the point of reporting this fourth thing yet, but as more people become better educated, perhaps they will start.

The table's information is interesting, and runs counter to many people's intuitions. Sometimes people will hear about some poll (inevitably, one whose result is annoying), and will dismiss it, saying something like, "How can 400 answers tell us what two million people think?" The table is right and that intuition is wrong. With small populations (the example in the table is 100), you really do need to survey nearly everyone to get very close to an accurate answer. Just to get within an error margin of 5% (with 95% confidence in that 5% margin), you need to get 80 out of 100 people in your sample. If you wanted 99% confidence in a 3.5% margin of error, you would need 93 people. This is where people's intuitions come from, we suppose. But with larger populations, you need much smaller percentages. You would only need 384 people out of a million to have 95% confidence in a 5% margin of error (that's about .04% of the population). And with a population of 300 million (almost the whole population of the U.S.A.), you don't need any more people in your sample than you did for a one million population. So there are enormous economies of scale in doing this sort of sampling.

But we emphasize: the results in the table only apply to perfectly random sampling. We tend not to worry very much about tiny imperfections, like missing people who lost their cell phone that day or other little flukes of everyday life. Those are technical violations of random sampling but they probably have negligible effects on the results, because they are non-systematic. That is, we can assume for instance that an equal number of Republicans and Democrats probably lost their cell phone that day. But when the violations are systematic, that is when the media have to call the poll "unscientific." For example (this is the usual one), a TV network might put a poll up on the Internet during the newscast and invite people to respond. The only people who respond are those who are watching that network at that particular time, who have Internet access at that moment, and who are highly motivated. If the poll result is accurate that is purely by accident, and there is no way to calculate things like margin of error—because all the statistical theory requires random sampling to have been done.

So *random sampling* is the gold standard for *knowing how much inaccuracy there is*. It isn't necessarily the gold standard for getting the most accurate results or getting them most efficiently. At least two other sorts of sampling are common in scientific investigations and both should be respected provided that they are done properly. *Stratified random sampling* is done when the population is divided into strata (or subgroups), and each stratum is then sampled randomly. Suppose that your population was all the children in your community playing a youth sport. Your strata might be 6-9 year olds, 10-12 year olds, and 13-16 year olds, because that's how the sports are organized, and you know that these age groups of kids are very different in many ways. Within each age group you would sample randomly. The advantage of this is that, because you assume that the children's age will be important to their answer, you have made sure that each age group is properly represented in your sample. That makes your overall result more accurate. However, it sacrifices your ability to say that your overall result has a specific margin of error, because it is not a random sample of the *whole* population. *Cluster random sampling* is another high quality sampling procedure. This time instead of dividing your sample into some interesting strata, you divide them up, usually geographically. So you might get a map of your city, mark off and number all the city blocks, and then randomly choose a certain number of blocks. That makes it efficient to gather your data: you simply drive to one block, park your car, and go home to home (or you could randomly sample within each block), and then drive to the next block on your list. This efficiency is paid for by some possible sacrifice of accuracy, because you might miss some interesting city blocks this way (maybe many of the elderly people live in one section of the city that has retirement homes or some minority is clustered, and you under- or over-represent them). These two kinds of sampling are rarely mentioned in the media, and you are mainly likely to encounter them if you are reading original research papers. For public use, most of what is done and reported is simple random sampling, and you should pay attention for any indications that it has been done inappropriately.

Polls, as we said, are intended to produce some generalization about what the public thinks. They move from individual answers to a generalized summary. Let us consider some of the ways one might argue for such a generalized summary.

1. You could ask your best friend, who says taxes should be lowered, and then announce that the public thinks taxes should be lowered. This can actually happen if you were talking to someone you really respect, like a parent or professor, and you don't stop to think about what you're doing. It is a pretty bad argument. It might be called anecdotal evidence or overgeneralization. The problem is that the evidence in the premises isn't sufficient to support the conclusion.

2. You could interview a hundred people in the shopping mall, average their answers, and announce that 62% of all citizens think taxes should be lowered. This is "unscientific" because it isn't a random sample. You don't have any way to estimate margin of error. And you misstated your conclusion: you have no right to say anything about "all citizens" because your population was "people in the mall on Thursday night." And you didn't even randomly sample them. Your data is barely relevant to a conclusion about "all citizens," and certainly not sufficient to support any answer as specific as 62%.

3. You can do (or hire) a professional survey that starts with a good population list, samples it randomly, and obtains a large enough sample to report that 55% of the citizens think taxes should be lowered, plus or minus 4%. If the scientific procedures are followed properly, we really only need to worry about whether the question was neutrally worded.

To this point, we have been discussing public opinion polling, which is a way to generalize views (or habits, or intentions, etc.) of people. This is very common in political affairs and even has some prominence in economic news (consumer confidence, wholesale orders, etc.). It is also the source of many conclusions about correlations, for example, that extroversion is positively correlated with a satisfying social life. Polling—or to be more general, surveying—involves observation of what is naturally happening. Experiments, in contrast, intervene into what is naturally happening and make generalizations about what happens as a result.

4. Experiments

In the past decades we have seen more and more media reports about experiments, especially about medical things. As people have become more sensitive to the sources of medical and nutritional advice, they have wanted to know something about the research basis of recommendations about whether they should use butter or margarine, whether coffee is healthy or deadly, what pills to take for arthritis, and so forth. The media have obliged by summarizing experimental research and conveying its generalizations to us. As practicing social scientists who actually conduct and publish experiments, we are often upset at what gets left out of these journalistic reports and what phrasing is used to replace the scientists' careful statements. You should learn to read the original reports for yourself if you are truly interested in the topic. Here, let us outline some basic ideas that will help you evaluate the generalizations that are drawn from experiments. These are issues that you should deal with yourself when you are reading the original reports, or suspicions that you should have when you are reading a summary of the reports that does not mention these matters.

An experiment differs from a poll in several fundamental ways because an experiment is straightforwardly designed to discover causality. In polls and surveys, everything co-occurs: causes, effects, and epiphenomena are mixed together; one cannot discern what things changed first and what things changed later; and one can only see the detritus of causal processes but not the causal processes themselves.

Experiments address these issues with several design features. (1) There is always at least one comparison group. Two or more groups with different histories (histories that are hypothesized to differ in a causal-process-relevant way) can be compared on a key outcome measure. The outcome measure is often called the dependent variable because its value depends on earlier causal dynamics. Sometimes it is called the criterion variable. (2) The timing of events is known. This is because the experimenter initiates a key change for the "experimental" group. (3) This change is the experimental manipulation. The experimenter interferes with the usual order of events by changing something artificially. In most social sciences this is called the manipulation because the researcher manipulates the value of the causal (independent or predictor) variable. In economics this would be called a shock to the system, which is a nice metaphor for what the experimenter does to the otherwise stable causal field. (4) Membership in the two (or more) groups to be compared is determined by random assignment. Random assignment is different than random sampling. In random sampling, everyone in the population has an exactly equal chance to be in the sample. In random *assignment*, everyone in the sample has an exactly equal chance to be in group 1 or group 2, and so forth. Even if the sample was not drawn at random, a study can still have random assignment. So out of a group of volunteers (not a random sample of the population) an experimenter could randomly assign some to eat from one diet and the others to eat from another diet. Many descriptions of experimentation only emphasize two of these elements, manipulation and random assignment, but it is just as well to spell out the other items in order to appreciate how experiments generate generalizations.

For a simple design, an experimenter's argument goes like this. "I originally had two groups that were originally comparable in every important respect. I did not measure 'every important respect' because no one can think of all of them. Instead, I relied on random assignment to equalize the groups. With large enough sample sizes, random assignment will even out everything between the groups, even the things that aren't actually relevant. Then I intervened into the natural order of things by manipulating one of the groups' drug regimen (or their internet access, or the amount of sugar they ate, etc.). I then waited a scientifically justifiable length of time and accurately measured their health (or weight, or level of depression, etc.). I detected a difference between the two groups' average level of health (or weight, or depression, etc.) and applied proper statistical procedures to judge whether the difference was either dependable or so small that it might have occurred by chance. It was 'statistically significant,' meaning that it was large enough that it was unlikely to have happened by chance (this is the $p < .05$ standard). Since the difference between the two groups was statistically significant, I went on to calculate the effect size of this difference. This leads me to conclude that in this study, the experimental group (the one that got the manipulation) had X% better health. Therefore the manipulation causes better health to X degree."

In evaluating a study like this one, there are two categories of concern. These are internal and external validity. The classic treatment of these matters was written by Donald Campbell and Julian Stanley. These validity matters can be broken down into ARSD issues, and this would be an interesting exercise. But since there are well developed vocabularies for these two kinds of study validity, we will use those. Pure experiments are actually not vulnerable to internal validity problems because they were designed to avoid such critiques. But since every real-world experiment has some approximations and corner-cutting, we will cover those issues anyway.

For internal validity, the basic question is, "Are we sure that we understand the causal dynamics within the experiment?" In other words, if we observed a difference between the two groups, are we sure that the difference was due only to the experimental manipulation? Setting aside obvious impurities such as we see in movies (e.g., an evil doctor messing with the medicines, an unscrupulous Senator getting his daughter into the treatment group, etc.), here are the standard internal validity issues: history, maturation, testing, instrumentation, statistical regression, selection biases, experimental mortality, and selection-maturation interaction. History refers to outside events that might have affected results. For instance, during World War II sugar was not ordinarily available in England and that would have affected a diabetes experiment that began in 1935 and ended in 1945. Maturation refers to the natural growth and development of study participants due to time passage and time passage alone. For instance, in a long-term study of adolescent drug usage the participants would get older and perhaps wiser. Maturation could also happen in relatively short-term studies. For example, participants might become tired or hungry during a two-hour experiment. Testing refers to the possible effect of taking a test once on taking it again. For instance, if students are given the same math test at the end of every week they might eventually learn to answer those exact questions. Instrumentation has to do with inadvertent changes in the measurements. For instance, a new set of counselors might be brought in partway through a study to evaluate depression levels, and they could use different standards. Statistical regression happens when groups with extreme characteristics move toward more ordinary values. For instance, if a group of extremely obese people were in a weight-loss study, some of them might naturally lose some weight over time because there is not much room to gain more weight. Selection biases have to do with who gets assigned to the groups. In other words, participants in the experimental group may differ from those in the control group to begin with. For instance, if study administrators make sure their friends get into the treatment group, this would make the two groups incomparable. Experimental mortality refers to differing levels of dropout in the two groups. For instance, if everyone stays in the control group but half the people in the experimental group resign from the study, the groups are no longer comparable. And finally, selection-maturation interaction is the possibility that people selected for the two groups have different maturation experiences. For instance, if the control group had normally sized people but the experimental group were composed of people with dietary issues, the second group might get hungrier and react differently in the experiment. What all of these internal validity threats have in common is that each one of them points to a different causal explanation of why the two groups might have had different results in the study. Random assignment, perfectly executed, should protect against all of these threats. That is why the "gold standard" for medical research designs requires random assignment (and also that both participants and experimenters are blind to each person's assignment to one or the other group).

Assuming that these internal validity threats can be argumentatively nullified (or measured and accounted for), then we move to the question of external validity: "Given that we understand what happened within the study, can we be confident that it will also happen out in the real world?" In other words, external validity is concerned with the extent to which a study result can be generalized to a different population, a different context, and a different time. The issues here are reactive testing, interaction of the manipulation and selection, reactivity of the experimental circumstances, and multiple-treatment interference. Reactive testing refers to the possibility that the actual testing makes the participants unrepresentative of the general population. For instance, if people in the study have to weigh themselves every morning, that might make them more focused on their weight than the general population. Interaction of the manipulation and selection is the possibility that the people selected for participation in the study react differently to the manipulation than the population would. For instance, if the study consisted of people who are allergic to the ordinary medicine for some condition, their reaction to the new drug might not generalize to people who aren't allergic to the standard treatment. Reactive effects of the experimental circumstances is the chance that people act differently in the experiment than they would in ordinary life. For instance, if participants in a depression study were brought to a lab full of scientific equipment and were attended by considerate professional personnel, they might be so taken with their general treatment that they became more optimistic than they would ordinarily have been, and therefore reacted better to the drug or counseling than people in a non-experimental setting will. Finally, multiple-treatment interference happens when multiple treatments are used in the study. For instance, if people are first counseled and then given a drug, we could not be sure that the drug alone would have had the same effects. These external validity issues point to arguments that might justify setting aside the experiment's results when trying to understand how the overall population would react to the manipulation.

These issues summarize what might well be most of a course in study design, but what little we have said here should illustrate the kind of critical thinking that can be done about a study announcing some new generalization about diet, medicines, counseling, exercise, sleep patterns, or the many other things that journalists and bloggers are now reporting. These issues are likely to have been explicitly addressed in the original research report if the experimenters themselves were worried about the issue. Most experimenters are happy to do this because it justifies someone funding them for the next study. Corporations, however, might like their drug studies or other products never to be questioned so that they can persuade people to request the product. Therefore it is well to pay attention to who did the study, where it was published, whether there were conflicts of interest, whether the results can be replicated, and perhaps to wonder how that study out of all the studies on the topic was put in a journalist's hands to report on.

We do not mean to be encouraging cynicism about scientific experiments. Cynicism is when things are rejected out of hand ("All politicians lie all the time, so ignore anything Senator Smith says"). Skepticism, which we do encourage, is withholding judgment until the evidence and arguments have been carefully examined.

As with surveys, people can do little approximate experiments themselves. You can set out a piece of fruit and a piece of pie to see which one your nephew will take first. You can make hints for your boyfriend to see how he will react. You can organize a group of fellow students to laugh at an instructor's jokes only when she or he is looking at the ceiling. In each of these cases, you will have done a manipulation but you will be implicitly comparing your results to what you would have expected based on your experience, you will have a tiny sample size, you will not have a randomly assigned control group, and you will have taken many other huge shortcuts that would not be allowed in a real experiment. This doesn't mean that your results are useless, but you should have great reserve about trusting or generalizing them too far.

5. Meta-analyses

In the early 1970s, one of us was taught in graduate school that "One study never proves anything." By itself, this is an over-generalization. But as a guiding principle for reading individual studies it is a good impulse because it encourages reserve and proper skepticism. When evidence cumulates over many studies, generalizations from that data become increasingly reliable.

A meta-analysis is an "analysis of analyses." A standard survey or experiment gets its data from individual respondents. A meta-analysis gathers its data from the results of previous surveys or experiments. The outcomes of those studies are averaged and analyzed to produce conclusions that are based on many studies and large groups of respondents.

Meta-analyses became increasingly common in the last quarter of the 20th century. At first they were mainly offered as summaries of large research traditions and their merit was that they damped out the effects of occasional statistical flukes. But in the 21st century additional analytic methods have been developed to critique whole lines of research. We have recently become aware of "replication crises" in medical and psychological research. The problem is that certain results don't replicate—that is, that they can't be reproduced by studies that had a good chance to generate the original findings. The new techniques can detect if failed research has been withheld from the public record, so that only the glittery results-revealing studies are published. The likelihood of missing studies can now be detected by examining the patterns of studies that do make it into print. If—and this is sadly not rare—the meta-analysis discovers that the big effects are reported with small-sample studies and that large-sample studies show lesser (or no) effects, the meta-analysis will now show this clearly. In other words, statistical scrutiny of the research record can now predict pretty well whether results will replicate or not. The techniques for doing this are complex and the scientific community is still in the process of choosing which ones deserve to be standard.

Meta-analyses are not yet reported in the media as commonly as dramatic single studies, but we can hope that this will change. A good meta-analysis is more trustworthy than a good survey or experiment. You can even do informal meta-analyses yourself. Perhaps you notice that most of your friends believe in some generalization, and then take on that generalization yourself. Although this can be an instance of the bandwagon fallacy, it may also be more reliable than trusting only your own impressions, especially if you have some reason to respect the views of the people who are influencing you.

6. Summary about Generalization-establishing arguments

And that brings us to a key point about generalizations generated by arguments, whether the argument takes the form of a survey, an experiment, a meta-analysis, or some less disciplined real-life activity (such as noticing a couple of examples of something or feeding your dog weird food for a day). Unless your reasoning was just irredeemably ridiculous, the generalization you came to should have *some* argumentative value. The question is how much. Generalizations, like other conclusions, need to be qualified so that they fit the strength of their argumentative support. A generalization can be "maybe true," "occasionally true," "possible, at least for people with histories of psychiatric upset," "often true for men in Western cultures," or something along those lines. The worst reasoning about generalizations happens when people let the generalization get loose from the argument that produced it. The best thing you can do when thinking in general terms is to keep in mind the nature of the generalization's support and the inevitable flaws in those underlying arguments. Weigh the flaws properly and carry that weighing forward to the generalization.

So what about stereotypes? The nasty ones—remember, we are only claiming "to know them when we see them"—are based on terrible arguments. Often the evidence is biased. Perhaps you notice and remember every flaw in a postmodernist philosopher's life but ignore or forget the very same flaws in a logician's life. Or maybe there was no evidence at all. Perhaps your mother warned you against postmodernists before you set off for college, and you completely absorbed her warning that they are all pernicious, immoral youth-corrupters, without exception. Or perhaps you swallowed an unqualified generalization from your news feed without inquiring about the evidence that generated it. No one can investigate the basis for every opinion they hold—life is too short for that—but we are each responsible for what we believe and say. If you expose your generalizations to a good sample of the rest of the world, the world will let you know which of your opinions might actually be stereotypes, and those are the ones you need to investigate further. That is the nice thing about living in a civilly argumentative environment, rather than being completely self-enclosed or restricted to only like-minded familiars.

7. Generalization-using and Generalization-saturated arguments

To this point, we have been mainly considering arguments that conclude in a generalization. However, generalizations can appear elsewhere in an argument. An argument can *use* a generalization in its premises: Politicians say false self-serving things all the time; Prime Minister Cobbler says he is innocent of taking bribes; so Prime Minister Cobbler is lying. An argument can also be completely *saturated* with generalizations: Professors are all brilliant; brilliant people are all excellent friends; so professors all make excellent friends.

As far as we can tell, generalization-using and generalization-saturated arguments can take just about any form. They can be deductive, or causal, or practical, or many other things. Each of these other things is an argumentation scheme of its own. Every known argumentation scheme has its own form and its own associated critical questions. Douglas Walton, Chris Reed, and Fabrizio Macagno have written a book that details dozens of these schemes and lists their individual critical questions. All those critical questions, along with those you might generate if you were looking at an argument that didn't quite fit their typology, come down to the ARSD standards, one way or the other.

Our message about such arguments has to do with A, the acceptability standard. Every premise that expresses a generalization ought to have been established by some prior argument. Perhaps it is based on scientific methods such as those we have discussed. More probably, it is based on some informal approximation of those scientific forms of reasoning: intuition, impressions, life experience, something you tried once with success, and so forth. Scientific method and statistics are basically just codifications of the best and most reliable kinds of informal reasoning. After investigation of a generalization, you should be able to connect its basis to what the best possible standards for the argument that established that generalization ought to have been.

A flaw in an argument's premises interrupts the argument's movement toward its conclusion. However, "flaw" is a matter of degree. A premise would have to be astonishingly awful to have no value at all. Just as we have tried to show you how to weigh and qualify the generalized conclusions to arguments, you should be able to apply that advice to the premises of other arguments. If you encounter a generalization-using or saturated argument that contains generalizations that are unqualified, all or nothing, black or white, you should try to figure out what the qualification should have been. That qualification should propagate throughout the argument, so that a qualification attached to a premise should reappear somehow in the conclusion. An exaggeration in the premises should be edited so that the conclusion isn't exaggerated as well.

8. Conclusions

Generalizations are an inevitable and useful element of human thought and argument. It simply isn't possible to store every individual bit of data in our heads or list them all in an argument. Even if it were possible it would be boring and overwhelming. We need generalizations. By summing things up, generalizations allow us to estimate what is likely to happen, to appreciate what might be going on now, and to understand what occurred before.

Like other kinds of thought and expression, generalizations can be imperfect. We can have over-generalizations that lack proper qualifying, we can have under-generalizations that don't take proper account of important evidence, and we can have generalizations that are so poorly founded that they might as well be fictional. The essential way to evaluate and correct a generalization is to know where it came from, and to be able to evaluate its origins. Knowing the evidence for or against a generalization and the means that were used to generate that evidence, are essential to improving our own thought and our public discourse. The standards of acceptability, relevance, sufficiency, and dialectical quality can all be complex and challenging to apply, but they are essential in one form or another if we are to make and receive arguments as best we can.

Suggested Readings

Blair, J.A. and Johnson, R.H. (Eds.) (1980). *Informal Logic: The First International Symposium*. Inverness CA: EdgePress.

Campbell, D.T. and Stanley, J.C. (1966). *Experimental and Quasi-experimental Designs for Research*. Chicago: Rand McNally.

Cooper, H., Hedges, L.V. and Valentine, J.C. (Eds.) (2009). *The Handbook of Research Synthesis and Meta-analysis* (2d. ed.). New York: Sage.

Johnson, R.H. (2000). *Manifest Rationality: A Pragmatic Theory of Argument.* Mahwah NJ: Erlbaum.

Walton, D., Reed, C. and Macagno, F. (2008). *Argumentation Schemes.* Cambridge: Cambridge University Press.

About the authors:

Dale Hample has been publishing research on argumentation since the 1970s. He has written two advanced books on argumentation, *Arguing: Exchanging Reasons Face to Face* (2005) and *Interpersonal Arguing* 2018), and with William and Pamela Benoit has co-edited a book of essays, *Readings in Argumentation* (1992). He has published about 150 journal articles and book chapters. His discipline is Communication, which has led him to integrate quantitative social science with the humanistic traditions of rhetorical theory. He has given keynote addresses at argumentation conferences in the U.S., Canada, Chile, and the Netherlands. He is an Emeritus Professor of Communication at at the University of Maryland.

Yiwen Dai received her Ph.D. in Communication from the University of Maryland, College Park. Her research interests include argumentation and interactions in romantic relationships. She has published in *Argumentation and Advocacy* and *Western Journal of Communication* and presented her work at national and international communication conferences.

18

Appeals to Authority: Sources and Experts

Mark Battersby

1. Background

Assessing appeals to authority, including the evaluation of sources of information and the evaluation the opinions of experts, should be a central concern in critical thinking courses. Thanks to the Web and Google, practically everyone will spend their lives supplied with an abundance of putative information. Weeding the credible from the not credible will be crucial to leading a well-informed life. Students should be clear that the authority in question is not political moral or administrative authority, but rather *epistemic authority*.

Since the Enlightenment[1], the appeal to authority (*ad verecundiam*) has often been treated as a fallacy. Locke was the first to identify and name the *ad verecundiam* fallacy, noting that it involved taking advantage of the common habit of deference to authority to drive acceptance of a conclusion. Here is his argument for the classic Enlightenment negative view of appeals to authority.

> The floating of other men's opinions in our brains, makes us not one jot the more knowing, though they happen to be true. What in them was science, is in us but opiniatrety; whilst we give up our assent only to reverend names, and do not, as they did, employ our own reason to understand those truths which gave them reputation. Such borrowed wealth, like fairy money, though it were gold in the hand from which he received it, will be but leaves and dust when it comes to use. (Locke, 1948 Bk I, Ch 3, Section 24)

Locke (like other Enlightenment philosophers), inspired by the success of science, was concerned to liberate people from accepting hand-me-down claims that were untested and unquestioned by the recipient. Intellectual liberation meant the rejection of such claims and the move to establish independently

---

[1] For a comprehensive scholarly review of the fallacy and its history see (Walton, 2010).

and personally the truth of claims. While such advice was undoubtedly salutatory in its day where priestly authority tended to claim epistemic authority, the situation today is very different.

Despite Locke's claim, a little reflection of what we know reveals that most of what we know (or claim to know) is based on claims received from credible sources (i.e., belief-worthy sources). Even autobiographical knowledge, such as our birth date, is based on a trusted source—our parents or a birth certificate.

More generally, none of us is equipped to establish independently most of the claims that we depend on. In our own areas of expertise we may be able to verify claims, but as Steven Pinker recently stated, "Nowadays we specialists cannot be more than laypeople in most of our own disciplines, let alone neighboring ones" (Pinker, 1997). Outside of our own lives and our areas of specialty we are in a state of "epistemic dependency"—a lovely turn of phrase from John Hardwig (1985). This dependency is not necessarily bad; it means that we can know many more things than we could if left to our own investigations. It is part of the great power of society and language that such knowledge can be passed on.

Take the obvious example of the view that the sun is the centre of our solar system and the far from obvious claim that the earth is turning and the sun is not, as we still say, "going down." Few of us could prove either of these well-established claims that we may have learned even before going to school. Clearly we know these facts about the solar system, and the basis of this knowledge is primarily the credible sources (teachers, astronomers) who supplied us with the information. While knowledge transmission provides undoubted benefits, the problem is that erroneous beliefs can be passed on using the same powerful vehicles.

2. Evaluating credible sources

To start with we need to make a distinction between what I will call "credible claims" and "expert opinions." *Credible claims* are backed by disciplinary authority, not primarily the expertise of the informant, whereas *expert opinions* get their credibility primarily from the competence and presumed independently knowledge of the expert. Our belief in the heliocentric account of the solar system as explained by our first grade teacher does not get its credibility from the teacher, but from the scientific understanding and consensus which is the basis of the claim. The question about informants is not whether they have expert knowledge of the claim, but whether they are reliable transmitters of this type of information.

On the other hand, an expert's claim, such as a pathologist's claim that a biopsy reveals cancer, receives much of its credibility from the expertise of the pathologist. There is of course a scientific basis to determining whether a cell is cancerous, but the application of this knowledge requires a competency beyond simply knowing the science. Applied expertise is a combination of "know how" and factual and theoretical knowledge. The credibility of the claim depends on the knowhow of the expert as much as or even more than the credibility of the background scientific understanding.

To be clear: I am using the term 'credible' to mean "rationally worth of belief." That does not of course mean *certain*. Rather it means that the support for the claim meets the relevant criteria for claiming that a belief is rationally worthy of belief. In addition, like most rationally based beliefs, expert based beliefs come with degrees of reasonable confidence.

2.1 General argument model of Appeals to Authority

The logic of appeals to credible sources or expert opinions can be schematized as:

1. The source or expert states "P".
2. The source or expert meets the relevant criteria of credibility (to be discussed below).

Conclusion: P is a credible belief, or it is reasonable to believe that P.

The premises of this type of argument do not entail the conclusion nor is this argument a case of statistical induction. The premises, if satisfied, provide reasonable support for the conclusion—the inference is best described as "probative" (Scriven, 2009) .

2.2 Evaluating sources independently

A useful way to apply the relevant criteria of credibility to claims based on putatively credible sources is to subject them to the following critical questions:

Q1. Is the claim from an appropriate and reliable domain of knowledge?

Q2. Is there consensus among the relevant experts supporting the claim?

Q3. Has the claim in question been subject to peer review or is it from a peer reviewed source?

Q4. Is the claim supported by evidence?

The characteristics of a domain of inquiry in which credible appeals to the source can be made are:

1.1 The domain is not an area characterized by moral autonomy.

1.2 The domain has widely agreed-upon procedures and criteria for establishing claims.

1.3 The domain is generally characterized by a significant degree of expert consensus.

The issue of which domains of inquiry (e.g., history, psychology, economics, physics, newspapers, theology) are credible sources of authority is not without controversy, though for the purposes of critical thinking the domains to which appropriate appeals to authority can be made are those based on domains that have well established, consensually agreed upon proof procedures and reliably yield consensus based knowledge claims. The clear paradigm in this case is the natural sciences, such as physics and chemistry, which have a long history of being a reliable (though far from infallible) source of knowledge. On the other hand, certain kinds of claims are not appropriately settled or even well support by appeals to authority.[2] One of the most significant of these types of claims is moral claims. When people make moral decisions, they cannot say, as they often do about scientific claims, "I believe it because experts claim it." There are three reasons for this. First, as we will see below, a primary reason to trust expert judgment is that there is consensus among the experts. On many moral issues there is controversy among candidate experts (moral philosophers, theologians). They disagree not only about a particular moral judgment but also about what are the justifiable criteria for making a particular judgment. Arguably there is not even agreement about who are experts on moral judgment. These problems undermine any appeal to moral authorities to reliably adjudicate moral issues.

Second, in a secular society such as ours, the responsibility for a moral judgment or decision stops with the individual. Any of us can decide to follow the edicts of our church or the moral advice of a friend, but it is still *our* decision and belief, and the responsibility rests with us. This is not to say that we should not listen to people who study ethical questions. They may well have insights to share. The crucial point is that we cannot appeal to their expertise to claim moral knowledge (Hooker, 1998).

Third, there is no well-established epistemology for moral judgments. People not only disagree about moral judgments, they even disagree about how

---

[2] This position is of course that of the secular, post-enlightenment view, which is the basis of critical thinking instruction. In many traditions appeal to tradition, sacred texts, or the pronouncements of religious authorities is taken as "authoritatively" determining moral truth.

such judgments can be verified. There is even widespread disagreement about whether there is moral knowledge. This is in stark contrast to the physical sciences where there is objective knowledge and it is agreed that observation provides a crucial basis for verification. The uncertainly about criteria and objectivity also undermines appeals to authority about aesthetic judgments. Though again this is not to claim one should ignore that the arguments and opinions of experts in this domain.

The physical sciences provide a broad basis for appeal to authority because they have well-established procedures for verification and as a result have a large degree of consensus on most claims. If we want to know the speed of light or the molecular weight of oxygen, we can look them up in any text-book. There is virtual unanimity in these disciplines on these topics. But even these fields have their zones of dissensus, or disagreement. Any astrophysicists can tell us the speed of light and the approximate number of stars in our galaxy; however, only recently have they reached consensus on the issue of whether the universe is expanding, and at this point, there is no consensus on how to account for the rate of the universe's expansion. As a result, appeals to the claim that dark matter (or dark energy) is causing the acceleration of the expansion of the universe are necessarily low in credibility.

To take other areas of science, we know how old the earth is, although this question was settled only recently (EarthSky, n.d.), and still more recently, there is a general consensus that *homo sapiens* emerged out of Africa (Boyd and Silk, 2014). To the extent that experts in these fields (geology and paleoanthropology) agree, we, as laypeople, have grounds to believe their claims. We should also recognize, however, that, because of the challenges of doing research in disciplines such as paleoanthropology—even biological paleoanthropology, the discipline that studies human origins using physical analysis of human remains—do not yield the same degree of certainty that a discipline like physics does. In general, non-experimental sciences will always be subject to more uncertainty than experimental ones, as will disciplines that study human behavior. Sciences such as paleoanthropology that are also vulnerable to the "luck" of finding fossils, tools, and other artifacts are unlikely to achieve the level of certainty that other observational sciences such as geology or ecology might achieve. Different disciplines or areas of inquiry have demonstrated different degrees of epistemic reliability. As a result, an important consideration when evaluating sources is the reliability of the discipline based on its particular subject matter, methodology, and history.

While reliable consensus and agreed-upon procedures for assessing claims are the best guide to establishing the credibility of discipline- based claims, we should not ignore the fact that even the domains of inquiry which generally meet these criteria have often had consensus claims that later turn out to be false. Credible sources can be wrong. The history of science, especially some sciences, is littered with error and revision. But how do we know that? We know that because later science disproved the earlier claims/theories. To take two examples, plate tectonics refuted the stable earth theory, and the Michelson Morley experiment disproved the existence of "the ether"—the supposed medium of light waves. The history of self-correction in science is part of the basis for having a reasonable confidence in current scientific claims.

Even though science is self-correcting, the emergence of a consensus based on peer evaluation of a claim or theory takes time. New claims do not warrant the same credibility as those that have stood the test of time. "If it is in the news, it is probably not established science" is a good rule of thumb to use when evaluating claims reported in the media. On the other hand, that a theory/claim has been accepted for some time and has presumably survived ongoing scrutiny contributes to its credibility. In contrast, the notorious lack of long term consensus for many claims in the area of nutrition research weakens any appeal to authority in this area—even those claims supported by a current consensus (Freedman, 2010).

Given the importance of expert consensus in providing a basis for credibility it is important to establish the current state of a claim's status. Because many claims do get revised or rejected over time, the most credible belief is one supported by the current consensus.

If, on the other hand, there is no current consensus on a particular claim, then any appeal to disciplinary authority is weak.

By consensus, we do not mean complete agreement by all scientists. We cannot and should not expect this on many matters. But the degree of disagreement is relevant. If the number of dissenting voices is relatively small, this is not a reason for laypeople to give up relying on the general consensus (although understanding the basis of the disagreement can be relevant to evaluation). If the domain of knowledge is a relatively reliable one, then it is completely reasonable to trust the dominant view. If there is no such consensus, then one's belief cannot be reasonably based on an appeal to disciplinary credibility (Bailin and Battersby, 2016).

Another source of uncertainty when appealing to disciplinary sources is the fact that certain disciplines are characterized by divisions into "schools of thought". Within these schools there may be a consensus, but across the discipline as a whole there may be no consensus. Psychology and economics are particular examples of such disciplines with competing schools of the thought. So, for example, rather than saying economists believe, it is more accurate to say "supply side economists" believe or "Keynesian economist hold that", and these qualified references acknowledge the limits of such appeals.

Even within a relatively reliable discipline or profession, claims clearly come with degrees of credibility or belief-worthiness. While consensus is the primary criterion for assessing the appeal to credible disciplinary sources, there are other criteria that can be used to assess a scientific claim. It is beyond the limits of this chapter to explain these criteria in detail. They involve such factors as the size and type of studies (e.g., experimental vs. observational), the extent of replication, whether claims about humans are in fact based on animal studies, and whether studies were financed by interested parties. (For more details see Battersby, 2016.) As an example of the application of these type of criteria see the table on the next page, based on a table used by United States' Surgeon General assessing evidence about evidence for the carcinogenic effects of second hand smoke (Surgeon General of the United States, 2006).

Domains involving the study of human behavior are particularly prone to dissensus and a shifting consensus not only because of the great difficulty of studying humans but also of the intrusion of ideological bias. Not only are experiments limited, but they are difficult to generalize from because of cultural and other differences of the studied subjects from the target population, and studies of humans are also particularly vulnerable to political bias. In addition, most such studies are observational, making it difficult to identify and so to eliminate the problem of confounding factors. Predictions about future human behavior are especially uncertain and appeals to such claims have low epistemic worth.[3]

We can roughly think of four different levels of belief-worthiness of scientific claims concerning a causal relationship (see Table 1).

Given disciplinary uncertainty it is fortunate that on many matters we do not need to make up our minds. For example, we can leave the question about the existence of "dark matter" (which may explain why the expansion of the universe is not slowing but accelerating) to the experts to work out. But as citizens we need to make up our minds about appropriate economic policies. As parents we will have to make a decision about the dangers of violent video games. As individuals, we have to decide what to eat even if nutritionists disagree or exhibit a shifting consensus. Such decisions should not ignore expert views; rather the critical thinker's judgment should be based on an assessment of the competing arguments. Expert summaries written for laypeople are often available as "executive summaries" and can inform one of the var-

---

[3] Tetlock's study of the ineptitude of "pundits" to predict world affairs provides vivid examples (Tetlock, 2017)

ious arguments on an issue, providing the possibility of a rational decision based on an assessment of the best evidence available.

Hierarchy for classifying the belief-worthiness of scientific claims		
	Judgment	Evidence Quality
Strong	Highly credible	Extensive studies with appropriate size, duration and variety, including large prospective studies and if possible experimental studies. A convergence of study results. A credible causal explanation. Large effects or extensive evidence for reported small effect.
Weak	Evidence is suggestive but not sufficient; still uncertain.	Significant correlation evidence from credible studies with at least some prospective studies. Some experimental evidence if possible. Smaller size and fewer studies than above. Credible causal explanation.
Inconclusive	Evidence is inadequate to support claim	Evidence is sparse, of poor quality, or conflicting. Credible causal explanation may be lacking.
Negative	Evidence is suggestive of no causal relationship.	Extensive studies have failed to reveal a consistent correlation. The causal relationship seems implausible in view of current understanding.

Table 1

2.3 Is the claim in question from a peer-reviewed source?

Peer review is the gold standard for evaluating claims and arguments made in academic journals. The idea is that peers, people in the same field as the article is written, are best positioned to assess the credibility of the article. The process usually involves an editor sending an article submitted to a journal to two or three experts in the relevant field to review and assess the quality of the article and assess whether it is worthy of publication. The process is not without its weaknesses. Some concerns: (1) reviewers do not usually see the original data or primary material but just the summary in the article; (2) while reviews are done anonymously, reviewers can often tell who has written the article and be unduly influenced by such factors as the eminence of the author; (3) reviewers, being experts in the relevant field, may also reject articles to protect their own the theories (Freedman, 2010). But this process is still the best method we have for short-term evaluation of a claim or theory. Longer-term evaluation can be based on such things as successful or failed replication, scrutiny by other experts after publication, and results from application (e.g., results from drug usage that provides information on long-term effects).

Fallible as this review process is, it is still the main quality control on claims, and publication in a peer-reviewed journal, especially the more eminent ones, is a reasonable source of credibility. While the peer review process is a reasonable basis for a tentative acceptance of a claim, a claim is more credible if it has widespread peer acceptance and has survived years of peer scrutiny and other research efforts.

3. Assessing

As with the variety disciplines, not all experts are equally credible as sources of knowledge or practical advice.

In the case of assessing expert opinions, we use critical questions to evaluate both the claim itself, and the expertise of the expert.[4]

Regarding the claim

C1. Is the claim based on an appropriate and reliable domain of knowledge?

C2. Is there disciplinary/professional consensus that is the basis of the expert's opinion?

C3. Is the claim supported by evidence?

Regarding the expert

E1. Does the expert have expertise in the relevant domain of knowledge / expertise?

E2. Is the expert trustworthy?

E3. Has the expert properly attended to the question at hand?

E4. Is the expert's opinion backed by plausible arguments and evidence?

---

[4] In his most recent article on appeals to authority Douglas Walton recommends a similar list of critical questions (Walton, 2014):*Field Question*: Is *E* an expert in the field *F* that *A* is in? *Opinion Question*: What did *E* assert that implies *A*? *Trustworthiness Question*: Is *E* personally reliable as a source? *Consistency Question*: Is *A* consistent with what other experts assert? *Backup Evidence Question*: Is *E*'s assertion based on evidence?

3.1 Assessing the claim

Turning first to evaluating the claim:

C1. Is the claim based on an appropriate and reliable domain of knowledge?

This question illustrates a key idea about expert credibility: an expert's claim is grounded first on the reliability of the source discipline. Given that experts are usually called upon to give opinions involving the practical application of disciplinary or professional knowledge, the reliability of the discipline or profession as a source of practical knowledge must be considered. Advice based on fields with notoriously changing advice, has much weaker credibility than that based on more stable and reliable fields. For example, the ever-changing advice that emerges from management theorists reflects the weakness of research in that field and weakens the credibility of the expert advice based on this research. Similar cautionary advice applies to nutritionists (Freedman, 2010).

We have addressed the issue of moral expertise above; but leaving aside the notorious difficulties in the field of moral philosophy, it is widely recognized that some people are more thoughtful and wise about moral decisions. This is probably a case where the "expertise" of the individual transcends the credibility of the disciplinary basis.

C2. Is there disciplinary/professional consensus that is the basis of the expert's opinion?[5]

When there is no disciplinary or professional consensus, a significant part of our basis for believing an expert is undercut.

A classic example is the widespread theoretical disagreements in psychology. Despite these disagreements psychologists are often called on to make important judgment about such issues as criminal culpability, incarceration for mental illness, appropriate therapies, etc. In such areas, the expertise (experience, reputation) of the expert may provide a more significant basis of credibility than the disciplinary theories.

The problem of the lack of disciplinary consensus is compounded by the fact that areas of applied expertise are almost always less certain than more theoretical areas. Applying expertise in a real world situation requires the considering a wide range of relevant factors and knowing what is relevant;

---

[5] C2. also touches not only on the debate of objectivity, but also the particularism vs. general debate about moral judgment. Again, a Critical Thinking course is not the place to address these philosophical issues and any "appeal" to a morally wise person should be treated as "advice" not expert opinion (Dancy, 2013).

even knowing the limits of one's own expertise—all of which seriously complicates expert judgment.

Take the area of law. An experienced lawyer will know, or know how to find out, the relevant precedents and statutes for a case. But this knowledge does not guarantee that the lawyer will recommend or adopt the best legal strategy. For example, there is almost always a question of whether going to court or settling is the best strategy.

The choice of strategy goes beyond any legal facts and is a complex judgment which depends on the "expertise' of the lawyer, not just her knowledge of the law.

Given the challenges involved in such practical judgments it is also very likely that experts will disagree—even if there is disciplinary consensus on the underlying theory. This is why we are advised to seek a second opinion when getting medical advice.

Ideally in the situation of expert disagreement (as with lack of disciplinary consensus), the most reasonable position for a layperson is to just admit, "I don't know because they don't know". But most cases where we seek expert opinion are driven by a need to make a decision on the best information we can get. On these occasions, this will necessitate taking a (fallibilist) position in areas where there is no reassuring expert consensus. Dealing with such a situation will require assessing both the trustworthiness of the consulted expert(s) and the reasonableness of the arguments for their differing positions.

C3. Is the claim supported by evidence and cogent argument?

When seeking expert advice we do not want to simply be told "In my expert opinion you should do this" or "this is the case." We have a legitimate interest in knowing the basis of the expert's opinion, even if at the same time we recognize that an expert may not be able to fully articulate the entire basis of her judgment. It is legitimate for an established expert to make claims such as "in my experience such an approach is most effective" though the trustworthiness of that claims depends heavily on the track record of the expert—which is one reason why it is crucial to assess not only the claim of the expert, but the expert herself.

3.2 Assessing the expert

E1. Does the expert have expertise in the relevant domain of knowledge / expertise?

When we give epistemic weight to an expert opinion we do so not only on the basis of the knowledge contained in the discipline or profession, but also on an assessment of the expert's relevant expertise. Because of specialization that is common in many professions, the *specificity* of the expert's knowledge and experience is relevant. Being a general medical practitioner makes someone an expert in the area of medicine, but being an oncologist makes one more expert in the area of cancer, and being an oncologist specializing in prostate cancer makes one even more expert on questions of how to treat prostate cancer—though even in this narrower category there are differences in expertise and treatment strategies between radiologists and surgeons. When seeking expert opinion, the more the expert has the specialized knowledge, the more epistemic weight her opinion carries. The willingness to trust the judgment of people who may have expertise but not necessarily the relevant expertise in a particular area is one source of the fallacious acceptance of authoritative pronouncements. Living in a culture of media personalities we are subject to the views of both Nobel Prize winners and movie stars, who might offer all sorts of advice outside their domain of expertise. Being influenced by people making claims outside their area of expertise is to succumb to a *fallacious appeal to authority* Given the willingness of advertisers to pay large amounts of money for product endorsement by entertainment and sports personalities, it would appear that this type of fallacious appeal continues to have significant influence in our culture.

E2. Is the expert trustworthy?

Everyone understands that expert bias can be a problem in fields where financial incentives are influential. But even in such domains as basic research, the drive for personal success can lead individuals to fabricate data and mislead the public (see Freedman, 2010). The personal integrity of the expert therefore is relevant and can be evaluated in part by seeing if the expert demonstrates appropriate humility in areas of controversy, clarity in the presentation of reasons, a personal history of integrity, and reputation for integrity among peers. Unfortunately, pharmaceutical companies exploit these principles of expert respect by seeking to fund the well respected leaders in medical research and accepting such funding must call into question their trustworthiness (Goldacre, 2014).

E3. Has the expert properly attended to the question at hand?

The media is understandably fond of calling up experts to comment on newsworthy events. But such invitations often don't allow the expert to properly consider the matter. Opinions offered in this situation should be appropriately discounted. The same goes for discovering your doctor hasn't reviewed your file, and for comments by a professional at a social gathering.E4. Is the expert's opinion backed by intelligible arguments and evidence?

As argued above, for the recipient of an opinion to make any of kind of minimally autonomous judgment, the recipient needs the expert to provide intelligible case for her judgment. The haughty appeal to "I know and you should do or believe what I say" or an explanation shrouded in unintelligible jargon, undermines not only the autonomy of the recipient, but the reasonable confidence that one can have in the expert. While acknowledging that expertise involves tacit knowledge, the capacity to explain and justify is a key basis for being able to trust an expert's opinion.

To some extent such explanations may be generated after an opinion has been offered or a decision made. Chess masters often know what move to make based on just looking at the board, but nonetheless they can also give a rationale if pressed. If they could not, we would be dealing with a kind of idiot savant and not a true expert.[6]

3.3 The fallacy of Inappropriate Appeal to Authority

As can be seen from the discussion above, appeals to authority come in degrees of credibility, but an appeal that violates the following key criteria can be treated as simply fallacious.

1. The appeal is not in an appropriate domain of knowledge.
2. There is no expert consensus in a particular area.
3. The expert/source appealed to does not have the appropriate expertise.
4. The expert has not had the appropriate opportunity to review relevant information.
5. The expert is not trustworthy or has obvious biases.

4. Finding credible sources

Students need guidance not only on how to assess sources, but also what kind of information they need. Research is best started with overview articles that provide history and context. Well reputed popular media is usually an excellent place to begin. I suggest a tripartite categorization of credible print sources.

Level 1 is the popular and credible media that is indexed in various "periodical" indexes. Credible media such as the *Scientific American* or *Atlantic Monthly* or *The New York Times* and *The Globe and Mail* can be excellent sources of overview articles usually written by knowledgeable researchers. But this is still the tip of the information iceberg. The information presented by these sources is usually written by reporters who are not scientists and are far removed from the fundamental information.

---

[6] Interestingly, AI programs that learn to play games (as opposed to those that are programmed to play), are just such idiot savants—even the programmers often do not know what considerations caused the program's decision.

These media usually have websites with varying degrees of free availability. There are also websites in this category, often sponsored by government agencies or health agencies such as Cancer Agency, that supply responsibly digested information for the layperson. Unfortunately, many of these are "dumbed downed", assuming that the reader wants to know, e.g., "how to reduce the risk of colon cancer", not what the latest research is showing. They sometimes supply links to research but that is not their primary focus.

Level 1 material seldom provides enough evidence to support a well reasoned and confident belief. Personally-significant problems (e.g., medical decisions, lifestyle health choices) or significant public policy issues should be researched more deeply.

Level 2 sites and material are written for the sophisticated non-experts such as government policy makers. A classic example of such a site is the website of the *International Panel on Climate Change* (http://www.ipcc.ch). The site provides a range of information from fairly simple accounts of global warming, to extensive literature reviews written for policy makers, and finally, primary research written by and for researchers in the field. Many UN sites also have this range of information, as does the World Bank site.

Level 3. Lastly, there is Level 3 research. This is the level of primary research that is found published in peer-reviewed journals in all fields. While access to many peer-reviewed journals is not free, students can gain access to many of them through public and post-secondary libraries. *Google Scholar* can usually provide access at least to the abstracts of the articles. Articles in peer-reviewed journals are often technical and filled with jargon, making them difficult for a layperson to follow. But the articles usually come with an abstract and/or summary at the beginning and concluding discussion at the end. The abstracts often state the basics of the research and the conclusion in understandable terms. For most purposes, what a student needs, even from the peer reviewed journals, are reliable overview summaries that can give them an understanding of the direction of the research and the extent to which researchers feel confident about this direction. Literature reviews and meta-analysis, while not written for the non-expert, often provide overview discussions that are comprehensible to the non-expert. Most importantly, these reviews provide the crucial information about the direction of the research (consensus or dissensus) and how reliable it is.

4.2 Footnotes

Publishers generally exclude footnotes from popular and even credible popular journals; while peer reviewed journals often contain an overwhelming number of footnotes. Hostility to the tedium of footnoting when writing the academic essay often leads students to "footnote phobia"—they're too complicated, too tedious, and too academic.

But when researching, students need to realize that footnotes are their friend. When looking for information, a well-footnoted article is a kind of open-sesame into the literature. Quickly perusing the footnotes of a recent specialized journal article will often reveal crucial bits of information such as a key summary or a seminal article.

4.3 Using the Web

How to use the Web is discussed in much more detail in Chapter 15. Here is some additional advice.

Specialized Web sites from reputable institutions can also be a good initial source of information. With respect to health issues, for example, the Web sites of such well-known research centers as the Mayo Clinic and Harvard University are highly credible sources.

Another preliminary source of information is Web sites devoted to particular topics. Recognizing the bias of a site is important, but it is not a basis for ignoring the site if the site contains useful and credible information. Such sites may also supply useful footnotes to articles that one could then go to for further examination.

How do we evaluate information from a Web site? We evaluate it using questions that are very similar to those we use to assess claims from supposedly expert sources:

1. Is the claim from an appropriate domain of knowledge?
2. Are the site authors or sources competent in the domain of the claim?
3. Is the site relatively free from bias? What effect does the site's bias have on the credibility of its arguments and information?
4. Does the site refer to peer-reviewed sources for its claims?
5. Does the site supply plausible arguments or explanations for the point of view being presented?
6. What is the date of the information? Is it current and timely?

The web presents more of an assessment challenge than the library, but also considerably more convenience and frequently more timeliness. Books in libraries have the advantage that publishers usually make some effort to ensure the accuracy of claims in books. The mere fact that a book is published, though, does not provide adequate reason to trust its information. The evaluation of claims in books should be based on the criteria for evaluating any source.

Satirical websites present a particular challenge to the use of the web. Some of so-called fake news spread during recent American elections was the

result people treating claims from satirical websites as credible. The intrinsically outrageousness of the claims did not seem to stop people from believing
them. Slickness of appearance and political prejudice trumped common sense
(Murdock, 2017).

Wikipedia. While most academics frown on students citing Wikipedia,
most also use it, though not for academic citation. The key to making an intel-
ligent use of Wikipedia is to use it as a portal. The articles are usually intelligible and provide credible overviews, but the reliability of the article is a
function of the references that support it. The footnotes not only provide a
warrant for the claims but more importantly they serve as entrance to more
credible sources. Lack of footnotes is a giveaway that the claims are not properly supported. In addition, Wikipedia can hardly be expected to provide reliable information on politically controversial issues.

5. Pedagogical suggestions

A useful exercise is to divide the class into two groups to research the information pro and con on a topic such as vaccination, and have them apply the
criteria of assessment to the various sources. It is also useful to ask students
where they go to find out information and how they tell whether it is credible.

Also, a useful assignment is to have the students view the 20 minute
YouTube version of "The Secret"[7] and identify the variety of fallacious
appeals to authority.

References

Bailin, S. and Battersby, M. (2016). *Reason in the Balance: An Inquiry Approach
to Critical Thinking.* Hackett Publishing.

Battersby, M. (2016). *Is That a Fact?: A Field Guide to Statistical and Scientific
Information.* Broadview Press.

Boyd, R. and Silk, J.B. (2014). *How Humans Evolved.* WW Norton & Company.

Dancy, Jonathan (2013). "Moral Particularism", *The Stanford Encyclopedia of
Philosophy* (Fall 2013 Edition), Edward N. Zalta (Ed.), URL =
<https://plato.stanford.edu/archives/fall2013/entries/moral-particularism/>

EarthSky. (n.d.). "What is the Earth's age and how do we know?" Retrieved
August 26, 2017, from: http://earthsky.org/earth/how-old-is-the-earth

Freedman, D.H. (2010). *Wrong: Why Experts* Keep Failing Us–And How to
Know When Not to Trust Them* Scientists, Finance Wizards, Doctors, Relationship Gurus, Celebrity CEOs, High-powered Consultants, Health Officials
and More.* Little, Brown.

---

[7] https://www.youtube.com/watch?v=zdtqLNeK6Ww

Goldacre, B. (2014). *Bad Pharma: How Drug Companies Mislead Doctors and Harm Patients*. Macmillan.

Hardwig, J. (1985). Epistemic dependence. *The Journal of Philosophy*, 335–349.

Hooker, B. (1998). Moral expertise. In Craig Edward (Ed.), *Encyclopedia of Philosophy*. Routledge.

Locke, J. (1948). *An Essay Concerning Human Understanding*, 1690.

Murdock, S. (2017, March 11). A satire website posted fake news to Trump supporters. Many believed it. *Huffington Post*. Retrieved from: http://www.huffingtonpost.com/entry/a-million-trump-supporters-fell-for-this-absurd-fake-news-site_us_58c42653e4b0d1078ca7222e

Pinker, S. (1997). *How the Mind Works*. New York: Norton.

Surgeon General of the United States. (2006). The health consequences of involuntary exposure to tobacco smoke. *Atlanta, GA: US Department of Health and Human Services, Centers for Disease Control and Prevention, Coordinating Center for Health Promotion, National Center for Chronic Disease Prevention and Health Promotion, Office on Smoking and Health, 709.*

Tetlock, P.E. (2017). *Expert Political Judgment: How Good is It? How Can We Know?* Princeton University Press.

Walton, D. (2010). *Appeal to Expert Opinion: Arguments from Authority*. Pennsylvania State University Press.

Walton, D. (2014). On a razor's edge: evaluating arguments from expert opinion. *Argument & Computation, 5*(2–3), 139–159.

About the author:

Mark Battersby is Professor Emeritus at Capilano University, where he taught for over 40 years. He has also taught critical thinking at the University of British Columbia, Simon Fraser University and Stanford University, and has presented numerous workshops. He was founder of the British Columbia Association for Critical Thinking Research and Instruction and led a Ministry curriculum reform initiative based on learning outcomes. He has written numerous articles on critical thinking, and is the author of *Is That a Fact?* (Broadview, 2nd ed., 2016), and, along with Sharon Bailin, *Reason in the Balance: An Inquiry Approach to Critical Thinking* (2nd ed. Hackett, 2016). Translations of both of books have been published in China. *Inquiry: A New Paradigm for Critical Thinking* (Windsor Studies in Argumentation, 2019) is, a selection of his and Bailin's papers on their innovative approach to critical thinking. He and Bailin collaborated on CRITHINKEDU, a major European project to infuse critical thinking into higher education.

19

Logic and Critical Thinking

G.C. Goddu

Introduction

This chapter is a primer on basic logical concepts that often appear in various critical thinking textbooks—concepts such as entailment, contraries, contradictories, necessary and sufficient conditions, etc. The chapter will not provide a historical genealogy of these concepts—in some sense critical thinking, argumentation theory, and formal logic all trace their roots back to at least Aristotle over two thousand years ago. As a result, for many of these concepts, determining whether the concept was a logic concept co-opted by critical thinking, or a critical thinking concept co-opted and changed by logic and then co-opted back again, is extremely difficult. Regardless, a brief orientation of the relationship of critical thinking and logic is in order.

Critical thinking, at least as it is most often justified, is a practical, skill-building exercise with the goal of improving our reasoning. This motivation, of understanding and improving our reasoning, has also been the motivation behind the development of logic over the past several thousand years. While we could study and understand each piece of reasoning individually, it is much more efficient to look for reasoning *patterns* that recur over and over again, to distinguish those patterns that are good from those that are bad, and so to find principles underpinning our reasoning that help us distinguish good reasoning from bad reasoning across the board. This push to generalize and theorize with the patterns of reasoning generated numerous formal logical systems, including the syllogistic and modal logics of Aristotle.

However, logic, especially formal logic, has not been constrained solely by the goal of understanding and improving our reasoning. Like abstract mathematics, the formal structures underpinning logical systems, are rich and complex enough to generate study all their own, with no concern for the original motivation that may have pushed us to study patterns of human reasoning.

Regardless, many of logic's concepts are still useful in organizing any study of reasoning.

In what follows I begin with a fairly substantial discussion of the core concept needed to understand the traditional logical concepts such as entailment or contradictory or necessary condition—the concept of a possibility. Once we have this notion in play, the definitions of the standard logical concepts, which I provide in Section 2, are quite straightforward. In the final section, I discuss the potential for misapplication of various concepts or distinctions.

1. Possibilities

1.1 Possibility and reasoning

The core concept of logic is the concept of a possibility (a case, a scenario, an option, a way things could be). While logicians and philosophers continue to work on illuminating the nature of possibilities, we can, even without a precise definition, still intuitively grasp the notion. You could stop reading right now or you could keep going. England didn't win, but England could have won, if they had scored their penalty kick. That die, when rolled, will land on one of six possible sides. There are many things that might happen if the bill is passed into law. According to 18th century philosopher Gottfried Leibniz, God surveyed all the possible ways the universe might be and, being omnibenevolent, chose to create the best one (this one!?).

We appeal to possibilities all the time in our reasoning. Indeed, if there were but one way things could be and we knew completely what that way was like, then we would not need to reason at all—we would just know how things were going to unfold. But given that (i) we do not know completely how things are or how the future is going to unfold and (ii) we assume there are multiple possibilities for how the future might unfold, we need to reason about the ways things could be in order to learn how things are and how to best manage whatever the future brings. For example, the detective investigating a suspicious death gets a new piece of evidence—the deceased was killed by a rare poison. As a result, some scenarios are closed off as viable explanations of the death—e.g., the deceased was deliberately killed by someone who did not have access to the poison. Other scenarios, ones that may not have been in the detective's awareness before the new piece of evidence was acquired, become relevant—e.g., that someone who knew or at least had access to the poison was responsible for the death. As a result, a new line of inquiry opens for the detective: find out who had access to the poison. Similarly, a doctor runs a series of tests to try to eliminate certain possible explanations for a given patient's symptoms. Given certain results the possible explanations get narrowed down to one (and hopefully a treatment is available); given other results multiple possibilities remain and the doctor has to decide which tests may be required for progress to be made; unexpected results, while eliminating some possibilities may open up new possibilities that the doctor had not originally been considering. Finally, you are trying to decide when and in which order to run a list of errands. You take into account the likely lines at each location at different times of day, and the likely traffic at different times of day. After evaluating the possibilities, you choose the best option for you.

1.2 Types of possibilities

1.2.1 Physical and epistemic possibilities

Given the ubiquity of possibilities in our reasoning, theorists often classify the possibilities. For example, physicists are interested in distinguishing the physical possibilities (the possibilities consistent with the laws of physics) from the physical impossibilities (the possibilities inconsistent with the laws of physics). Other general types of possibilities include epistemic possibilities—scenarios consistent with what we know; moral possibilities—those consistent with a given moral code; legal possibilities—situations consistent with what is permitted by a given legal code. We can even combine these types—epistemic physical possibilities are those that are consistent with the laws of physics as we currently know them. If what we know about the world changes at a fundamental level, what once was epistemically physically possible (measuring time independently of motion or gravity) may become epistemically physically impossible. Like for the detective and the doctor above, new, unexpected evidence may require an adjustment by the scientist in what possibilities are under consideration as viable explanations.

1.2.2 Equally probable possibilities

Two other sorts of possibilities deserve mention. Probabilistic reasoning depends on possibilities of a very special sort—equally probable possibilities. To determine the probability that a fair coin will come up heads we assume that there are two equally likely possibilities, "heads" and "tails" (we usually ignore the extremely unlikely, though still physically possible situation in which the coin lands and stays on its edge). Failing to consider the relevant equally likely possibilities can make our probabilistic reasoning go awry. You will either win the lottery or you will not. There are two possibilities here, but treating them as equally likely is certainly an obvious mistake. Assuming the lottery is fair, the relevant equally likely possibilities are that each individual ticket (or set of numbers) will be the winner. If your ticket is one of many, then the probability you will win the lottery is much lower than the probability of your losing. Less obvious, but equally problematic is the following sort of case:

> Three drawers contain the following mixture of coins—one contains two gold coins, one contains two silver coins, and one contains one gold coin and one silver coin. Without looking you pick a drawer, open it, and pick out a coin. When you open your eyes, you see the coin is gold. What is the probability that the other coin in that drawer is gold?

Many will reason as follows. The coin came from either the gold/gold drawer or the gold/silver drawer. Each drawer is equally likely and if it came from the gold/gold drawer the other coin is gold. But if it came from the gold/silver drawer the other coin is silver. Hence, the probability the other coin is gold is ½ or 50%. Unfortunately, the two possible drawers are not the relevant equally likely possibilities (no more than your winning or losing were the relevant equally likely possibilities in the lottery case). The relevant possibilities are opening a drawer and picking out a coin without looking. There are six different equally likely ways that could happen, one for each coin. Once you gain the new evidence that the coin you picked is gold when you open your eyes, you can eliminate three of the six possibilities, i.e. the ones in which you pick a silver coin. Of the three possibilities left two are such that the other coin is gold, i.e., the two possibilities in which you pick one of the two coins from the gold/gold drawer. Only in the gold/silver case is the other coin silver. Hence, the probability of the other coin being gold is 2/3. The moral here is that accurate probabilistic reasoning requires identifying and using the relevant equally likely possibilities from amongst all the sorts of possibilities that may present themselves—not always an easy task.

1.2.3 Practical possibilities

Another significant type of possibility, especially in our everyday reasoning, is practical possibility—possibilities that are consistent with our means, desires, and will (or perhaps our epistemic practical possibilities—the possibilities that, given what we know or believe, are consistent with our means, desires, and will). When deciding how to get to an important meeting across town you are likely to not even consider the possibility that you flap your arms and fly, or the possibility that you use your personal matter/energy transport device, or even the possibility that you sprint all the way there. The first is physically impossible; the second, while perhaps physically possible, is beyond our current technological means; and the third, while certainly physically possible, is quite likely beyond your will and most certainly contrary to your strong desire to not arrive at the important meeting sweating profusely and gasping for breath. Instead you consider what your actual transportation options are (your own car, Uber, taxi, walk, subway, or some combination), how much time you have, how much money you are willing to spend, and then you try to find the optimal possibility (usually constrained by the desire to not spend too much time actually calculating the optimal possibility). Mundane decisions about which possibility to actualize like this happen all the time: what to eat this week, which movie to go see, what to do after dinner, when to get your hair cut, etc. Though mundane, they are still of interest to critical thinking or argumentation theorists since businesses and advertisers spend billions of dollars and devote millions of work-hours to trying to influence your desires and will in order to persuade you to choose their product.

Of more social significance are your individual choices that impact larger groups—in particular (if you live in a democracy) your voting choices, your decisions about how much effort you put into monitoring the outcome of your voting choices, and what the individuals or policies you voted for end up doing. In an optimal world, your political representatives would enact policies that benefit the most people in the most cost efficient, affordable, and just way. Of course, there may be little agreement about what is the most affordable, or just, or beneficial option, especially if what elected representatives take to be the best option is what will get them re-elected rather than what is actually good for their constituents. Regardless of the complexities and intricacies of public policy debate and decision-making, at the core is an attempt to find and agree upon a practical possibility, from amongst the myriad available, to actualize for our mutual benefit.

Given so many types of overlapping sets of possibilities, many of which differ for different individuals or groups of individuals—your set of practical possibilities does not likely match that of your neighbor even if the two sets overlap significantly; compare your set with someone of quite different socio-economic means and the sets overlap even less—and it is no surprise that numerous problems can arise when reasoning with and about possibilities. Individuals can consider too many possibilities, or more commonly, fail to consider all the relevant possibilities. For example, human beings are quite prone to confirmation bias—taking confirming instances as justifying an already-accepted theory or explanation rather than actively seeking out or testing for disconfirming instances. Detectives, or doctors, or researchers can become so fixated on the explanation they already believe to be correct that they are blind to the alternate explanations that are still consistent with the evidence available. In the case of probabilistic reasoning, we already saw cases of considering the wrong set of possibilities. Reasoners can also illegitimately shift the set of possibilities under consideration or shift the value assigned to various possibilities mid-reasoning. An egregious example can occur in public policy debates over the negative consequences of potential policies. When negative consequence X is a potential consequence of the opposition's preferred policy it is judged to be likely enough to count as a reason against the policy, but when negative consequence X is a potential consequence of one's own preferred policy, it is judged not to be likely enough to count as a reason against the policy. Identifying the correct set of possibilities and correct relative values of those possibilities is essential to reasoning correctly in numerous situations and yet identifying and ranking possibilities is often an extremely difficult task.

1.2.4 Logical possibilities

One way to try to sidestep some of these problems is to determine what reasoning holds no matter what the possibilities in question are—to determine the patterns of reasoning that work in *all* the possibilities. After all, if a piece of reasoning works no matter what possibility you are considering, then you do not need to worry whether you are considering the right set of possibilities or not. Hence, one goal of formal logic is to be able to identify the structure that defines *all* the ways things could be, i.e., the logical possibilities.

The rough and ready notion of a "logical possibility" is a possibility that has no contradiction in it. Whilst it is not logically possible for an individual to both exist at a particular time and place and not exist at that time and place, which is contradictory, it is logically possible that the person exist in Montana in one instant, and then exist on one of the moons of Jupiter, say Io, in the next. There is no contradiction in the possibility that you exist in Montana in one instant and on Io in the next. But this possibility, while logically possible, is not physically possible. Given the distance from Montana to Io, we would need to violate the physical restriction on moving matter or energy (currently travelling below the speed of light) faster than the speed of light to get from Montana to Io from one instant to the next, so such travel is physically impossible.

Earlier I said that philosophers are still investigating and debating the nature of possibilities. But, whatever they are, there is one actualized one and lots of unactualized ones. In Leibniz's argument that this world is the best of all possibilities, God examines all the possibilities and then actualizes the best one. Even if you doubt Leibniz's argument, of all the myriad ways this universe could be, it is in fact one way, namely, the possibility that is actualized. The detective has numerous possibilities in mind about who is responsible for the deceased's death; the detective hopes that by finding more evidence the possibilities can be reduced to one, the actual one. When you are deciding what to do tomorrow, you consider numerous possibilities and then engage in actions that make one (hopefully the one you wanted) actual.

But since there are lots of unactualized possibilities and only one actual possibility, how do we distinguish the unactualized possibilities from each other? Quite simply by what is true and false at each possibility. I flip a coin twice. There are four possible outcomes. Heads for the first flip and heads for the second; heads for the first and tails for the second; tails for the first, and heads for the second; and tails for both. Suppose the coin comes up tails on the first and heads on the second—that is the possibility that got actualized. How do we distinguish the three non-actualized possibilities? Well, in the first and second it is true that the coin first came up heads, but in fourth it is false that the coin first came up heads. But possibilities one and two differ in what is true and false of the second coin flip.

1.3 Declarative sentences and propositions

Given that we distinguish possibilities by what is true and false if they are actualized, one proposal for understanding possibilities is just as sets of declarative sentences. For example, the first coin flip possibility would be the set {"the first flip of the coin came up heads", "the second flip of the coin came up heads"}. While initially appealing, the problem with this proposal is that sentences are not as well behaved as is needed to demarcate possibilities. Why?

Sometimes different sentences describe the same possibility or state of affairs. For example, "George is a bachelor" and "George is an unmarried male of marriageable age" describe the same state of affairs, but are different sentences since they are composed of different words. But since they are different sentences, sets that differ only in regards to which of these two sentences they contain are still different sets, and so different possibilities. Yet, we agreed the sentences were just two different ways of talking about the same possibility.

Alternatively, sometimes the same sentence can be used in different ways to describe different possibilities. For example, the sentence "The movie was a bomb" used in the United States likely describes a state of affairs in which the movie was bad, but the same sentence used in the United Kingdom likely describes a state of affairs in which the movie was good. But if one sentence can be used in different ways to describe different possibilities, then, once again, we cannot identify possibilities merely with sets of sentences.

To avoid the vagaries of sentences, logicians usually resort to propositions—what it is that declarative sentences express. "George is a bachelor" and "George is an unmarried male of marriageable age" express the same proposition about George's marital status. "England won the World Cup in 1966" expresses a true proposition about the English national soccer team; "2 + 2 = 5" expresses a false proposition about the sum of 2 and 2. We use declarative sentences to express propositions directly, but other language use often involves them. For instance, when we ask, "did Hungary win the World Cup in 1938?" we wonder whether the proposition that Hungary won the 1938 World Cup is true or false. If we get the correct answer (they did not win—they lost to Italy 4-2 in the finals), then we stop wondering whether it is true or false and start believing it is false (and if the *belief* if strong enough and acquired in the correct way, we might even *know* that the proposition is false).

Instead of treating possibilities as sets of sentences, many logicians treat possibilities (or at least model possibilities) as sets of propositions. There are technical details that might require modifying even this proposal, but since the resolution of these details is unlikely to be relevant to the critical thinking project, we can take possibilities to be sets of propositions. The propositions that are members of a particular possibility are said to be true or obtain at that possibility. Propositions that are not members of a particular possibility are false at that possibility or do not obtain at that possibility. Armed with the concepts of (i) a possibility and (ii) propositions being true at or obtaining at possibilities, we can define many of the logical concepts that pervade logic and critical thinking textbooks. So even though some of the logical concepts that are forthcoming are, in some textbooks, defined in terms of sentences, the more common way is to define them in terms of propositions.

2. Logical concepts

2.1 Types of propositions

I begin by discussing some common types of propositions that arise in our reasoning. The most basic is a *simple* proposition, propositions expressed by such declarative sentences as "George is a bachelor" or "the sky is blue" or "Romeo loves Juliet." Simple propositions attribute something to some object(s) or thing(s). In the first case, of George, that he is a bachelor, and in the third case, of Romeo, that he loves another object, namely Juliet. *Negations* of simple propositions, propositions expressed by such declarative sentences as "George is not a bachelor" or "Hungary did not win the 1938 World Cup" say that the simple proposition does not obtain. Of course, we do not speak declaratively solely by affirming either simple propositions or the denial of simple propositions; we combine or modify our simple propositions such as in:

(1) "George is a bachelor, and so is Todd";
(2) "Mary loves Antonio, but he does not love her back";
(3) "George went to Sophie's house or he went to the movies";

(4) "If the butler did not do it, then the cook did";
(5) "If I take the subway, I will be on time for my meeting";
(6) "Every student in this class is eligible";
(7) "Someone deliberately killed the deceased";
(8) "In order to be on time for your meeting, you must take the subway";
(9) "England did not win the game, but they might have if they had scored their penalty kick in the last minute."

The first two sentences express *conjunctions*. For a conjunction to be true, both sub-parts of the conjunction have to be true. So for "George is a bachelor *and* so is Todd" to be true, both "George is a bachelor" and "Todd is a bachelor" must be true. [For ease of exposition I will often omit the phrase "the proposition expressed by" before mentioning sentences as I just did above.]

The sentence "George went to Sophie's house *or* he went to the movies" expresses a disjunction. There are two sorts of disjunctions—inclusive and exclusive. For an *inclusive disjunction* to be true, at least one of the sub-parts must be true. For an *exclusive disjunction* to be true, exactly one of the sub-parts must be true. If our sentence about George expresses an exclusive disjunction, then for it to be true George needs to be in exactly one of two places—at Sophie's house or at the movies. This is likely to be the usage of someone trying to tell us where George is at a particular moment. If, on the other hand, the sentence expresses an inclusive disjunction, then it will be true if George went to one of those locations and is still true if George went to both. This is likely to be the usage of someone just trying to lay out where George might have gone over a period of time. While some languages have different words for expressing inclusive and exclusive disjunctions. English relies on context or background knowledge, sometimes with limited success, to try to distinguish which type of disjunction is being expressed. Legal documents, in order to avoid the ambiguity of 'or' in English, often spell out exclusive disjunctions as "A or B and not both A and B" while representing inclusive disjunctions as "A and/or B".

Sentences such as: "*If* the butler did not do it, *then* the cook did" and "*If* I take the subway, [*then*] I will be on time for my meeting," express conditional propositions. Conditionals are frequently used in natural languages such as English, yet there is little agreement on how they are to be analyzed logically. (Some theorists even go so far as to deny that conditional sentences express propositions at all.) Usually the disagreement concerns determining exactly what it takes for conditionals to be true, but there is widespread agreement that declarative conditionals are false if the 'if'–part, the *antecedent*, is true, and the 'then'–part, the *consequent*, is false. If it is true that I take the subway, and false that I will be on time for my meeting, then the conditional "If I take the subway, I will be on time for my meeting," is false. As a consequence, logic has defined a minimal version of the conditional, called the *material conditional*. *Material conditionals* are false if the antecedent is true and the consequent is false, but true otherwise—in other words, material conditionals are the most permissive when considering what it takes for a conditional to be true. There has been much debate about whether *indicative conditionals* such as "If the butler did not do it, then the cook did" just express material conditionals or rather express something stronger. Despite the disagreement, the most common articulation of conditionals in introductory logic texts is in terms of material conditionals, and it is most often this sort of conditional that is co-opted into critical thinking texts. One merely needs to keep in mind that the work on understanding conditionals is far from finished.

"*Every* student in this class is eligible" expresses a *universal* proposition—a proposition that attributes something to every member of a specified group. For a universal proposition to be true there can be no instance of a member of the group not having the specified attribute. If "Every student in this class is eligible" is true, then there is no student in the class who is not eligible. Oftentimes the group is not fully identified in the sentence used to express the proposition. For example, saying "All the beer is in the fridge" or "All horses have heads" are unlikely to be taken as expressing that every single beer in the universe is in a particular fridge or that there is no single instance of a headless horse anywhere. Depending on the context of use, likely plausible interpretations of those sentences would be: "All the beer we brought home from the store (and which has not already been drunk) is in the fridge" and "Typical, normal live horses have heads." But once the group is fully specified, for a universal proposition to be true, every member of the group must have the attributed property or properties.

Instead of saying that everything in a given group has a stated attribute, we often merely want to convey that *at least one* thing or *some* things in the group have a particular property as in "Someone deliberately killed the deceased." Such propositions are *existential* propositions. They are true when at least one object in a specified group has a specified attribute. For example, "Some student is eligible" is true just so long as at least one student is indeed eligible.

So far, most of our examples of propositions can be true or false given a single possibility. Suppose we restrict ourselves to just the actual possibility—then it is either true that George is a bachelor at the actual possibility or it is not; if, at the actual possibility, there is no student in the class who is not eligible, then the universal "Every student in class is eligible" is true at the actual possibility and otherwise false. But some of our declarative sentences are not just about one possibility; rather, they depend on multiple possibilities. Sentences such as the last two on our list, which express *modal* propositions are examples. (They are called "modal" because expressions such as "must", "can", "might", "would", etc., were said to indicate the "mode" of the component proposition.)

Different modal expressions have different truth conditions. Consider, for example, the sentence—"In order to be on time for your meeting you must take the subway." For it to be true, all the possible ways (probably some set of practical possibilities constrained by the background in which the sentence is uttered) in which you make the meeting on time include your taking the subway. In the case of England losing, but winning if they'd scored their penalty, the first part is a negation that is true just so long as England won is false. So the first part tells us what the actual possibility is like. But the second part tells us what the relevantly similar possibilities except for England scoring their penalty, are like—namely, that England won in at least one of those possibilities. Compare that with the stronger claim that England would have won if they had scored their penalty—that claim will be true just so long as England wins in all the relevantly similar possibilities. (Part of the debate about conditionals is whether even conditionals without explicit modal terms, such as 'might' or 'would' or 'must', etc. are really expressing propositions concerning multiple possibilities, and not just the actual one—again, a debate I will not be able to resolve here.)

This list is not at all meant to be exhaustive of the type of propositions we express via our declarative sentences. Rather, it is meant to give a flavor for the sorts of propositions dealt with in first and second logic courses, the sorts of propositions that logicians attempt to model and define clearly and precisely in their basic systems. Why are logicians interested in these sorts of propositions? Because they show up in many of the reasoning patterns that we use over and over. For example, if I tell you George is either at Sophie's or at the movies, and you tell me he is not at movies, we both hopefully reason that we should check for George at Sophie's house. Another example: If the US Internal Revenue Service says that all US taxpayers satisfying their three specified conditions can claim a particular deduction, and you're a US taxpayer who determines that you satisfy those three conditions, you should reason that you can take that particular deduction. It is by recognizing these types of propositions, and the patterns that result in combining them, that formal logic, which focuses on the patterns, gets its impetus. But regardless of whether one is focusing on the goodness of patterns or more generally on the patterns and content of reasoning, both critical thinking theorists and logicians need to take special care in determining what proposition a given sentence in a particular context expresses, for without understanding the correct proposition we will not be considering and evaluating the correct possibilities.

Even though understanding and classifying what propositions various declarative sentences express is an ongoing project, there is another classification scheme that logicians often appeal to—necessary truths (also called tautologies), necessary falsehoods (also called contradictions), and contingent propositions. The definitions are as follows:

Necessary Truth: A proposition that is true in all possibilities.

Necessary Falsehood: A proposition that is false in all possibilities.

Contingent Proposition: A proposition that is true in some, but not all, possibilities.

Sentences such as: "Either Socrates corrupts the youth of Athens or he does not", or "If it is raining, then it is raining" express necessary truths. For every possibility there is, either Socrates corrupts the youth of Athens in that possibility or he does not. Some have wondered if there any non-trivial tautologies, since the standard examples, such as the ones I just gave, seem to be pretty trivial, uninformative sentences. Many theoreticians hold that the truths of mathematics are all necessary truths and many of those truths are certainly non-trivial—they often take a lot of work for us to know that they are true. Others point out that even if many necessary truths seem trivial or uninformative, they are still very useful. Plato, for example, uses the Socrates sentence in part of his dialogue concerning whether Socrates should have been found guilty of a particular offense. Plato starts with the obvious truth that either Socrates corrupts the youth or he does not, but proceeds to argue that in either case, Socrates should not be found guilty.

Sentences such as "At a particular moment in time, Socrates is over six-feet tall and Socrates is not over six-feet tall" express necessary falsehoods. For any possibility, and any moment of time in that possibility, Socrates cannot be both over six-feet tall and not over six-feet tall. Necessary falsehoods, or *contradictions* as they are more commonly called, are useful as sign-posts of something having gone drastically wrong in our reasoning. If we can show that someone's position contains or leads to a contradiction, then we show that they aren't even talking about a genuine possibility at all, but rather an impossibility. Good reasoners generally want to avoid being committed to impossibilities, so they try to avoid being committed to contradictions in their reasoning.

Most of the propositions we deal with in our everyday reasoning are contingent ones. "The coin landed heads on the first flip" is true in some possibilities, but false in others. "George will arrive on time" is true in some, but false in others. Even complex propositions, such as "If I take the subway, I will make it to the meeting on time" are likely to be true in some possibilities (smooth running reliable subway system) and false in others (an unreliable or scanty subway system). The challenge for good reasoners, of course, is to try to figure out, on the basis of what we already know, and the acquisition of new evidence, which propositions are in fact true at the actual possibility and which are not true. The detective, the doctor, the scientist, the everyday reasoner, are all reasoning using various possibilities in order to try to determine which propositions are true or false at the actual possibility.

2.2 Relations amongst propositions

Given that reasoning is the moving from given propositions to other propositions, and logicians are trying to understand correct reasoning, many of the important concepts of logic concern not just types of propositions, but the relations amongst propositions, I finish this section with definitions, examples, and discussion of eight such relations.

Necessary condition

One proposition, A, is a necessary condition for another proposition, B, if there is no possibility in which B obtains and A does not.

If A is a necessary condition for B, then you cannot have B without A. For example, if it is true that meeting the eligibility requirements is a necessary condition for legitimately holding office, then there is no possibility in which one legitimately holds office and does not meet the eligibility requirements. But if it is false that meeting the eligibility requirements is a necessary condition for legitimately holding office, then there is at least one possibility in which one legitimately holds office and does not meet the eligibility requirements.

Sufficient condition

One proposition, A, is a sufficient condition for another proposition B, if there is no possibility in which A obtains and B does not.

If A is a sufficient condition for B, then A guarantees B. For example, if it is true that getting a perfect score on every assessment is sufficient for passing the course, then there is no possibility in which one gets a perfect score on every assessment and one does not pass the course. If it is false, then there is at least one possibility in which one gets a perfect score on every assessment and still does not pass the course.

In many elementary logic or critical thinking textbooks, necessary and sufficient conditions are treated as material conditionals. For example, "George attending class is sufficient for George passing the course" is treated as "If George attends class, then George passes the course." But necessary and sufficient conditions cannot be material conditionals, since denying a sufficient or necessary condition is not the same as denying a material conditional. For example, saying "George attending class is not sufficient for George passing" is not the same as denying the material conditional "If George attends class, then George passes the course" is true. Denying the material conditional is just saying that it is actually the case that George attends class, but does not pass the course, i.e., that the antecedent is true and the consequent is false. But denying that George's attending is sufficient for George's passing is not saying that George attends and does not pass, but rather says that there is a possibility, not necessarily the actual one, in which George attends, but does not pass. In other words, necessary and sufficient conditions are describing what is true of a range of possibilities.

Equivalence

Two propositions are equivalent just so long as there is no possibility in which one is true and the other is false.

In other words, for each possibility, the two propositions are either both true or both false. For example, "All Euclidean triangles have three sides" and "All Euclidean triangles have three interior angles" are both true in all possibilities and false in none, so they are logically equivalent to each other. Similarly, "Either Peter failed to make the team or Abigail failed to make the team" is logically equivalent to "Abigail and Peter did not both make the team." If the first proposition is true, then, on an inclusive disjunction reading, at least one of the two did not make the team, so it is true that they did not both make the team. If on the other hand the first proposition is false, then it is false Pater failed to make the team (and so made it) and it is false Abigail failed to make the team (and so also made it), in which case both made the team and the second proposition is also false. Since the propositions are true in the same possibilities and false in the same possibilities they are logically equivalent.

Equivalence of proposition is not to be confused with the equivalence of sentences. Two sentences are equivalent, such as "George is a bachelor" and "George is a unmarried male of marriageable age" just in case they express the same proposition. Two distinct propositions, on the other hand, are equivalent just in case they are true or false in exactly the same possibilities. Of course, without a clear notion of the identity conditions of propositions, it is often hard to determine whether we have two sentences expressing one proposition, or two sentences expressing two distinct propositions that are equivalent to each other. [Like possibilities, theorists are still debating how to understand propositions. For example, here I have defined possibilities as sets of propositions, but some theorists reverse the order of dependence and define propositions as sets of possibilities, i.e., the possibilities at which they are true. Either way, having defined one concept in the terms of the other, the theorist still owes us an account of the undefined concept—a task theorists continue to pursue.]

Consistency

Two propositions are consistent with each other just in case there is at least one possibility in which both are true.

For example, "Sphere A is completely red" is consistent with "Cube B is completely blue" just so long as there is a possibility in which both are true. But "Sphere A is completely red" is inconsistent with "Sphere A is partly blue" since there is no possibility in which both are true.

Contrary

Two propositions are contrary to each other if there is no possibility in which both are true.

Contrariness is a kind of inconsistency. As we just saw, "Sphere A is completely red" is inconsistent with "Sphere A is partly blue" because there is no possibility in which both are true, i.e., because they are contrary to each other. But even though both propositions cannot be true together, they both could be false together, such as in possibilities in which "Sphere A is completely green" is true. But there is an even stronger kind of inconsistency, than mere contrariness.

Contradictory

Two propositions are contradictory to each other if there is no possibility in which both are true or both are false.

"Sphere A is completely red" is contradictory to "Sphere A is not completely red" since if one is true, the other is false and if one is false, the other is true. Similarly, if it is true that "Snow guarantees skiing" then it is false that "There is a possibility in which there is snow and no skiing" and vice versa.

One important reason to keep these two kinds of inconsistency separate is that reasoners sometimes treat inconsistency as if it were just the same as being contradictory—they reason that if two states of affairs are inconsistent, then if one is false, the other one must be true. But such reasoners miss or ignore the possibility that two inconsistent propositions might still both be false, and as we saw in the previous section, ignoring or missing relevant possibilities is prone to generate reasoning errors. Hence, knowing whether two propositions are consistent, or contrary, or contradictory gives us important information about which possibilities are still relevant to whatever inquiry or reasoning we are pursuing using those propositions.

Since logicians are motivated by the goal of distinguishing good reasoning from bad reasoning and at least one part of good reasoning is that what we reason from adequately supports what we reason to, logicians are very interested in relations of adequate support. One very special kind of adequate support is entailment.

Entailment

Proposition A entails proposition B just so long as there is no possibility in which A is true and B is false.

For example, "Sam's car weighs over 1000kg" entails "Sam's car weighs at least 500kg"—any possibility in which Sam's car is over 1000kg it is clearly at least 500kg. "Sam's car is a red hatchback" entails "Sam's car is red" and "Sam possesses a car" and "Sam's car is a hatchback". Instead of talking about what a single proposition entails, logicians are often interested in what a group or set of propositions entails. [A set of propositions entails another proposition just so long as there is no possibility in which all members of the set are true and the other proposition is false.] For example, "George went to Sophie's house or to the movies" and "George did not go to the movies" entail "George went to Sophie's house." On the other hand, "If Sally attends class, then she passes the course" and "Sally passes the course" does not entail "Sally attends class," since there are possibilities in which Sally can study well enough on her own and there is no attendance requirement, such that while it is true that "If Sally attends, then she passes the course" and true that "she passes the course", it is false that "she attends class".

Logic, especially formal logic, is primarily interested in entailment and other consequence relations. But at the elementary levels of logic at least the concept of entailment is applied to a concept that is also of interest to critical thinking and argumentation theorists—the concept of an argument. In logic, arguments are often modeled as a set of a set of propositions (the premises) and another proposition (the conclusion). [See Chapters 8 and 9 of this volume for a more detailed discussion of the concept of an argument.] Logicians define *validity*, a property of arguments, in terms of whether or not the entailment relation holds between the premises and the other proposition, the conclusion. If the premises entail the conclusion, then the argument is valid, i.e., there is no possibility in which the premises are true and the conclusion false, and otherwise the argument is invalid. [Validity here is not to be confused with the notion of 'valid' that is used in everyday speech to signify that something is "good" or "worthy of further consideration", as in: "She made a valid point, when she said ....". Nor is it to be confused with the notion of 'valid' that is used in survey research to signify the goodness or utility of a measuring instrument or the results of such an instrument—for that concept see Chapter 19 of this volume.]

In the previous section, I said that one of the motivations for studying logic was to try to find properties of good reasoning that would hold in all the possibilities. Entailment (and so validity) is one such property. If the arguments you make are valid, i.e. if your reasons entail your conclusion, then your reasoning, at least in terms of support, is good reasoning. Of course, other aspects of that reasoning might be problematic, but at least you know that your reasons, if true, guarantee your conclusion, no matter what set of possibilities is the relevant set.

But consider: Most of the coins on the table are heads-up and that quarter is a coin on the table, so it is heads up. "Most of the coins on the table are heads-up" and "That quarter is a coin on the table" do not entail that "That quarter is heads up" and yet in many situations we would likely say that the first two propositions give very strong reasons to believe the third. In other words while entailment is a sure sign of inferential goodness in reasoning, the lack of entailment does not necessarily mean there is a lack of inferential goodness. Sometimes we say our reasoning is good enough, even if our reasons do not entail what we infer from them. If, in the possibilities in which our reasons are true, enough of them also have what we infer to be true, then we can say that the inferential link is good because the reasons sufficiently support our conclusion. The general definition of sufficient support is as follows:

Sufficient Support

Propostion A (or a set of propositions) sufficiently supports a proposition B just so long as, in enough of the possibilities in which A (or the set of propositions) is true, B is also true.

What counts as "enough" often varies from context to context. For example, in civil litigation, the conclusion of wrongdoing has to be supported by a preponderance of the evidence, i.e., the possibilities in which the defendant did what they are accused of, should be the case in more than 50% of the possibilities in which the provided evidence is true. But in criminal cases, the conclusion of wrongdoing should be supported beyond a reasonable doubt (which, at least if we take the vast majority of judges' views on what that means, is above 80%). Statistical significance for supporting various hypotheses in the sciences is often set at 95% or higher. Determining what should count as "enough" in various contexts is often extremely challenging. At the very least, some of what counts as "enough" depends on the importance of the outcome. For example, since criminal sanctions are so much higher than civil sanctions, we demand more assurance that the evidence supports the conclusion of wrongdoing in the criminal case than in the civil case.

Logicians, I said, are primarily interested in consequence relations such as entailment. Different types of logic study these relations in different domains. For example, temporal or tense logics are interested in determining the consequence relations amongst uses of temporal phrases, such as, "in the future", "in the past" and "now". Modal logics study the consequence relations amongst propositions containing modal terms such as "must", "can", etc. But in addition to distinguishing types of logics by the types of propositions being modeled, logics are also categorized in terms of the type of consequence relation being studied. At the most general level, there are two types of logic—deductive and inductive. Deductive logic is concerned with entailment. Inductive logic is concerned with consequence relations weaker than entailment. Unsurprisingly, since there are many consequence relations weaker than entailment, inductive logic is a much less unified field of study than deductive logic. As we shall see in the next section, there are other uses of the terms 'deductive' and 'inductive', but these are generally misuses—the key difference between inductive and deductive logic is the type of consequence relation being studied.

I conclude this section with a final point about these eight definitions. They have all been given in terms of possibilities in general, i.e., logical possibilities. But for each definition, we could restrict the possibilities we are talking about and get restricted versions of these definitions. For example, physically necessary truths are those that hold in all the possibilities in which the physical laws hold. Morally necessary truths are those that are true in all the possibilities with the same moral code, etc. A set of propositions would physically entail another proposition if there is no physical possibility in which the propositions in the set are true and the other proposition is false. Two propositions are morally contradictory if there is no moral possibility in which both are true or both are false.

Even though explicit talk of these restricted kinds of logical concepts is rare, the theoretical apparatus is available and useful for trying to get clear on what various reasoners or arguers are in fact claiming. For example, in common discourse, when someone says that A entails B, I suspect they rarely mean that there is no possibility whatsoever in which A obtains and B does not; rather, for some contextually determined (though usually unspecified) group of possibilities there is no possibility in which A obtains and B does not. Similarly, for necessary and sufficient conditions; when someone says that snow is necessary for skiing, they probably do not mean that there is no possibility whatsoever in which there is skiing but no snow (there are in fact numerous possibilities—water skiing, roller skiing, sand skiing, skiing on artificial pellets, etc.), but rather that our typical conception of skiing requires snow. In the sciences, they are rarely concerned with logically necessary and sufficient conditions, but rather with causally necessary and sufficient conditions—conditions that require or guarantee something else in all the possibilities consistent with the causal laws. The moral for critical thinking is that even when one encounters terms such as 'entails' or 'contradictory' or 'necessary condition' they may not be being used in their strictly logical sense, but rather being used over a subset of relevant possibilities.

3. Logic and the activity of reasoning

3.1 Logic and reasoning

I conclude with some final comments about the application, and misapplication, of logical concepts in the study of reasoning. Logical systems are models. In particular, they are models of consequence relations between propositions. Some of the models are quite limited. For example, standard sentential or propositional logic systems ignore the internal structure of simple propositions and focus solely on connectives such as 'and', 'or' or 'if,…then'. Others add elements to model 'must' and 'can' while still ignoring everything else, and so on. The hope is to ultimately get a model, or group of models, that illuminates the standards of good reasoning, at least with regards to inferential support. Like most models, logical models can be very helpful when properly applied within the domain they model. Trying to use the model outside the proper domain, however, can have drastic consequences. For example, claiming that the standard sentential logic system is a good model for explaining instances of good reasoning utilizing modal claims is clearly a mistake. (This is true not just for logical models. For example, using the "model" of the north star as a fixed point is extremely useful for general terrestrial navigation, but using the same model for routing certain sorts of messages, which requires quite precise location determination, gets poor results.) Similarly, since logic focuses on support relations and good reasoning usually involves not just adequate support, but good reasons as well, it is a mistake to think logic is the whole story of good reasoning. Indeed, logic has little to nothing to say about what makes reasons good reasons, but rather focuses on what can legitimately be inferred from whatever good reasons we find.

3.2 Arguments and explanations

Clearly the target domain we are trying to understand and improve—the activities of reasoning, arguing, justifying, persuading, etc., are much more complicated than any of the various logical systems that logicians produce to model certain aspects of those activities. And yet many theorists still try to find distinctions in the models that are really only distinctions in the activities and not really the concern of logic at all. For example, logicians and argumentation theorists have spent a lot of time trying to distinguish arguments from explanations. But suppose I lay out several reasons (including some reasons about what I think will happen in the next six months) why you should believe a particular company will fail in the next six months. Six months go by and the company fails and someone else asks "Why?" and I trot out my reasons again. Nothing has changed about the propositions involved, so, from the perspective of logic, there is one object, one set of propositions, here. Yet, how that object has been used has changed. Initially the reasons are used to argue that the company will fail. After the fact, the reasons are used to explain the company's failure. We argue for propositions we are not sure of (or to convince others of propositions they are not sure of), but we explain propositions we are sure of, some of which may have been proved to us by argument, in order to understand *why* they are true. [Note that unlike my example, there are plenty of cases where the reasons one might give to argue for a proposition, which turns out to be true, need not be the reasons given when explaining why the proposition is true. For example, if something unexpected happens in the six months that contributes to the company's failure that is likely to be a part of the act of explaining even though it was not part of the act of arguing.] The fact that there is a difference between acts of arguing and acts of explaining does not mean that, in the domain of logic, we should find separate kinds of things—arguments on the one hand and explanations on the other.

3.3 Inferring and implying

Going in the other direction, no one doubts that, considered in terms of propositions and support relations the inference from A to B and the implication of B by A are the same thing. But it is a mistake to think that the act of inferring is the same as the act of implying. You assert a group of facts (with the intention that I draw conclusions from those facts). I, being a good reasoner, draw those conclusions. You *imply* those conclusions and I *infer* those conclusions. Put another way, if I ask someone what they are inferring, I am asking about reasoning going on in their head, but if I ask someone what they are implying, I am asking about reasoning they hope to be going on in other people's heads. Put yet another way, reasons do not infer conclusions, but rather imply them. People, when considering those reasons on their own, infer those conclusions, but do not imply them.

3.4 Deductive and inductive

Sometimes concepts are misapplied in both the model and the target domain. For example, some logic textbooks and critical thinking textbooks try to distinguish deductive arguments from inductive arguments, but from the perspective of logic there is nothing about the sets of propositions that compose arguments that make one kind of set deductive and another set inductive. For every group of reasons and a given conclusion we can ask whether the reasons entail the conclusion or not (the domain of deductive logic) or whether those very same reasons offer some support weaker than entailment or not (the domain of inductive logic.) Nor is it clear that we reason deductively or inductively—when we reason, we infer one or more propositions from others. Of that reasoning we did, we might wonder whether it is good or bad. The answer to that question will, in part, depend on what counts as good enough support in the situation in which I am using the reasoning. If the context requires entailment and the reasons do entail the conclusion, then the reasoning is adequate with regards to its support relation. If the reasons do not entail the conclusion, then it will fail to be adequate in such a situation. Similarly for a required support relation weaker than entailment—if reasons support the conclusion at or above the required level, then the support relation is adequate, whereas if it is below the required level the support relation is not adequate. The reasoning is one act of reasoning—whether the actual support relation of that reasoning is adequate or not depends on the situation. But none of this suddenly makes it the case that there are two distinct kinds of reasoning going on (even if there is a felt difference between realizing some reasons entail a conclusion versus realizing some premises only strongly support a conclusion.)

3.5 Linked vs. convergent arguments

One final example. The push for general principles often takes something that may track a real distinction or property in a certain specific set of cases and try to generalize it to all cases. For example, there is a strong intuition that reasons such as: "If you pass the test, then you will pass the course" and "You pass the test" work together to support the conclusion "you will pass the course" whereas reasons such as "You read all the supplemental material" and "You took good notes" and "You went to the tutor consistently" independently support the conclusion that "You are prepared for the test." This intuition is strong enough, that numerous textbooks, especially those that use argument diagramming as a tool, try to distinguish arguments with linked premise structures from arguments with convergent premise structures. The problem here is two-fold. On the one hand, attempts to actually provide a rule for determining when a set (or subset) of reasons are linked or not have, to date, all failed, at least if we trust the intuitions that generated the drive to generalize the phenomena in the first place. On the other hand, the underlying judgments of whether premises are working together or are independent seem to vary from person to person and context to context enough to suspect that the distinction may not be tracking a real phenomenon that deserves to be represented or captured in our logical models.

4. Last word

Despite these injunctions to take care with the proper application of various concepts that have made their way into various textbooks, the core logical concepts of Section 2, such as *sufficient support* or *consistency* or *necessary condition* are useful in any study of reasoning. Even if good reasoners need to be careful and work diligently to determine which propositions are being expressed, and which possibilities are relevant, and what the needed standard of sufficient support is in a given situation, once these tasks are accomplished, we can evaluate our reasoning for inconsistencies and determine whether our reasons entail or at least adequately support our conclusions.

About the author:
G.C. Goddu has published extensively on the foundations of argumentation theory for the past twenty years. He is on the editorial board of the journal *Informal Logic* and is a two-time winner (2007, 2010) of the Association for Informal Logic and Critical Thinking's annual essay prize. He is currently the James Thomas Professor of Philosophy at the University of Richmond.

20

Abduction and Inference to the Best Explanation

John Woods

... Peirce is a major star in the firmament of philosophy. By thrusting the notion of abduction to the forefront of philosophers' consciousness he created a problem which—I will argue—is the central one in contemporary epistemology.

❖ Jaakko Hintikka (2007)

1. Critical thinking

Arising from the Greek word *"kritikos"* for critic, critical thinking is said to be the intellectual capacity and wherewithal for judgment and discernment. According to the United States National Council for Excellence in Critical Thinking, critical thinking is the intellectually, analyzing, synthesizing, or evaluating information gathered from or generated by, observation, experience, reflection, reasoning, or communication, as a guide to belief and action.[1]

Some writers tend to view it not as a first-order mode of reasoning or family of such modes, but rather as more of a meta-reasoning mode of reflection, designed to maximize the rationality of human thinkers. In the opinion of Carmichael Kirby, the human thinker doesn't employ critical thinking to solve problems. Critical thinking is used to improve the process of thinking (Kirby 1997). From that point of view, a critical thinking textbook could be seen as a manual of self-help for the ratiocinatively challenged.

Strictly at odds with the meta-reasoning approach is the opinion of Kerry Walters, who proposes that rationality must be more than the ability to operate the "calculus of justification" and must include "cognitive acts such as imagination, conceptual creativity, intuition and insight" (Walters 1994, p. 63). These capacities focus more on discovery than on linear, rules-based procedures for problem solving. The linear and non-sequential mind in a recipro-

[1] "Critical Thinking Index Page" at http://www.criticalthinking.org//

cally nourishing partnership is what a human being's full rationality requires. Walters's point enjoys a fairly substantial empirical backing from various of the sciences of cognition. It raises a methodological question for philosophers: Is there an established approach to epistemology that gives this feature of "full rationality" the heed that's due it? For the most part by far, CT theories operate on background "command and control" epistemologies. These are epistemologies in which the executive centre of reasoning and decision is the human intellect, operating of its own volition to run the engines of inference and choice. Polar opposites of command and control epistemologies are "causal response" theories in which the cognitive devices that do most of the work of inference, belief-change and decision, operate subconsciously—out of sight of the mind's eye, beyond the reach of the heart's command, and unengageable by tongue or pen (or keystroke). Given that critical thinking is an indispensable facilitator of knowledge, CT theories have a stake in those epistemological issues.[2] If, as I myself believe, Hintikka is right about the centrality of the logic of abduction to contemporary epistemology, CT theorists would also have a stake in an appropriately epistemologized account of abduction.

My remit here is to reflect upon the present state of theories of abductive inference (A) and inference to the best explanation (IBE). Since this chapter is part of a volume on tools of critical thinking, it behooves me to say a little something of the connection, or want of it, between the two research literatures. The abduction and inference-to-the-best-explanation literatures are large and wide-ranging. The critical thinking literature(s) range even more widely. But, for all their respective robustness, there is little in the way of productive intersections of them. Not only don't these literatures talk to one another (much), they don't even talk all that much to themselves. However, on the whole the A&IBE literatures are the more interactive and unified of the two. One of the reasons that the CT literatures are less unified is that the disciplines in which they are sited, don't normally talk to each other. The three dominant disciplinary sectors of the present-day CT literature are those that cater capaciously for informal logic, argument, and speech communication.[3] In Chapter 1 in this volume you will find a summary of where the CT literatures are to be found. All that there is space for here is to make some mention

---

[2] For a fuller discussion see (Woods 2017).

[3] Two somewhat more recent developments should be noted, both offered as contributions to the theory of argument. One is the emergence of highly complex mathematical and computational models of attack-and-defend arguments. See here the contributions of Barringer *et al.* (2002). The other is an even more expansive move to legal reasoning. See, for example, Douglas Walton (2008) and John Woods (2015).

of where contributors to the CT literatures hook up with A&IBE agendas. In the section below, I'll list some of the leading A&IBE works, indicating those scant few by authors of some prominence in the CT sector.

On the other hand, those parts of the CT literature in which we might expect to find some mention of A&IBE have so far left few footprints on the A&IBE literature and none that is either weighty or enduring. So the point is made: These are literatures that have yet to talk to each other about these matters of common interest. This helps in framing a course of action for what lies ahead in this note. A good part of what I aim for here is help to open an A&IBE backchannel to CT.

2. Peirce on abduction

We owe the modern notion of abduction to C.S. Peirce (1839-1914), although there are undeveloped intimations of it in 4th century B.C. in Aristotle's concept of *apagogē*. These need not detain us here (see Aristotle 1985). Peirce famously sees abduction as inference in the form,

(1) The surprising fact C is observed.
(2) But if A were true, C would be a matter of course.
(3) Hence there is reason to suspect that A is true. (*CP* 5.189)[4]

Peirce's schema covers not all of what an abductive inference is, but only what I'll call the "inference stage". It is preceded by the "selection stage". At the inference stage a claim is inferred about a hypothesis, namely, that if premisses (1) and (2) are true, it follows that there is reason to suspect that a given hypothesis A is true. At the selection stage—not schematized here—Peirce reflects on how hypotheses are arrived at in the first place. The logistics of neither stage are all that easy to discern, but the selection stage poses the rougher challenge by far. Here is more of what Peirce had to say about them.

(i)   Abduction is triggered by surprise. (*CP* 5.189)
(ii) Abduction is a form of guessing, underwritten innately by instinct. (*Reasoning and the Logic of Things*, p. 128.[5] *CP* 5.171, *CP* 7.220)
(iii) Abduction provides no grounds for believing the abduced proposition to be true. (*RLT*, p. 178)

---

[4] C. S. Peirce, *Collected Works*, Cambridge, MA: Harvard University Press, 1931-1958. A series of volumes first appearing in 1931. "*CP* 5.189" denotes p. 189 of volume five. Line numbers are mine.

[5] C. S. Peirce, *Reasoning and the Logic of Things: The Cambridge Conference Lectures of 1898*, K. L. Kettner, editor, Cambridge, MA: Harvard University Press, 1992. Hereafter "*RLT*".

(iv)   Rather than believing them, the proper thing to do with abduced hypotheses is send them off to experimental trial. (*CP* 5.599, *CP* 6.469-6.473, *CP* 7.202-219)

(v)   The connection between the abduced hypothesis *A* and the observed fact *C* is subjunctive. (*CP* 5.189)

(vi)   The conclusion licensed by the abduction is not proposition *A*, but rather that *A*'s truth is something there is reason to suspect.

(vii) The "hence" of the schema's conclusion is not characterized at *CP* 5.189, but it is clear from context that it denotes a nonmonotonic relation.

The present-day literature reveals different streams of thought about bringing the Peircean paradigm into a more unified and systematic theory. There isn't space in this note to adjudicate these differences. Interested readers could consult to advantage the somewhat selective works noted in the Appendix, arranged there in chronological order.

Abductions of Peirce's sort are entirely commonplace, and the fact that human beings are fairly good at drawing them makes a large contribution to the success of *homo sapiens* in negotiating the shoals of life's dangerous waters. Imagine Fred, a middle aged man, married to Kate, an accountant, whose three grown children live away, two married and with busy careers, and a third who is a student in residence at an out-of-province university (the family lives in Canada). One December day Fred returns from his Court Clerk's job at his usual time of five, parks in the garage at the back. As he starts walking towards the rear of the house, he sees that the back door is wide-open. The downstairs lights are on, triggered to do so automatically around 5:00 p. m. This is the door from which Fred leaves the house every morning on the dot of 6:30 for a pre-work visit to the gym. He has never before failed to close it properly. Kate is driven to work by a neighbour, and always leaves through the front door. Her own unvarying after-work routine takes her from office to gym, and from there to the market where she does her daily shopping, finally arriving home by bus at 6:00. It is said that the philosopher Kant was so regular in his walks that the citizens of Königsberg could set their watches by when he started or ended. Fred and Kate were like that too.

In Peircean terms, the open door was the surprising fact *C*. What Peirce means by a "surprising" one is a fact that is somehow off-course, irregular, or aberrant. The open door was not how things were supposed to be at Fred and Kate's house. The open door also posed an *ignorance-problem* for Fred. He wanted to know why it was open, and yet nothing he presently knew answered his question. Fred's ignorance wasn't something to make light of. There were innumerable things Fred didn't know then and there, such as the size of Montenegro's population, for example. Of course, had he wanted to know it, he could have pulled out his iPhone and found out in a flash. The open door was different. It was a cognitive irritant, and was not something Fred could or should simply have put aside. And no answer awaited him on his iPhone.

Given this cognitive irritant (not necessarily something psychologically annoying), Fred wanted to find a hypothesis A with respect to which, were it true, the open door would have been a matter of course. Suppose that A were the hypothesis that Fred had simply forgotten to shut the door securely. If that had been what actually happened, then with no one left in the house to spot it open, it would be entirely a matter of course that Fred would be the first to discover it later on. In Fred's household, a closed door at 5:00 p.m. is a reliable but not strictly universal generalization, certainly not universal in the logician's sense. Colloquially speaking, it was "never" open at 5:00 p.m. But while a perfectly accurate one so far, the regularity is defeasible. It admits of possible exceptions. What Fred wanted to know in this case was what caused the exception to this regularity. Not knowing of any, it was time for him to use his head. Was there, he wondered, a *hypothetical* fact, which, were it actually true, would have provided the exception that induced the open-door surprise? In so asking, Fred was looking for a Peircean hypothesis A.

It is here that a second difficulty arises. There are more possibilities than one to consider. It is possible that Kate had come home early and was in process of hanging some laundry on the outdoor clothesline. But there were two things wrong with this. In that same sense of "never" in which the back door is never left open, it is never the case that Kate comes home before Fred, and, Kate might for the first time have come home sick, but wouldn't that pretty well rule out the late-laundry hypothesis?

Perhaps Pete had come home from university for an unannounced weekend visit. But Pete was in the middle of final exams in a tough computer engineering programme. Besides, he'd never done that before, and would always have called ahead were he have decided to do so. Kate and Fred are entirely self-sufficient by choice. They share all household duties, including spring cleaning and all the rest. They do all their own lawn mowing, gardening and snow removal. No one has a key to the house beyond the five members of the family. Nice Mr. Chapman across the street once had one for emergency purposes. Childless and long retired, Mr. Chapman had recently died, and Mrs. Chapman shortly after had returned to her native England to live with her sister in Cambridge. The key had never surfaced, presumably now an inadvertent resident of that pleasant but chilly university town.

Fred and Kate's house hadn't been equipped with a security alarm. All three external doors were of solid construction set in sturdy frames, and provided with superior locks. The house lies in a quiet neighbourhood, and had never been broken into before. Nor had there been any evidence of any earlier attempt to do so. As he made his way towards the house, four different versions of line (2) of Peirce's schema might have somehow or other entered Fred's mind.

(2^1) If it were true that Fred had forgotten to shut the door this morning, then its being open now would have been a matter of course.[6]

(2^2) If it were true that Kate had come home early, then its being open now would have been a matter of course.

(2^3) If it were true that Pete had paid a surprise visit, then its being open now would have been a matter of course. (Pete is notorious for not shutting doors.)

(2^4) If it were true that the house has been burgled, then its being open now would have been a matter of course. (Flight, not door-shutting, is the first priority for house-breakers.)

The known facts at the time countervailed against (2^1) (2^2) and (2^3) rather more than against (2^4). Fred "never" leaves the door open. Kate "never" comes home early. Pete "never" pays surprise visits. Even though the house had never been burgled before, houses rarely, if ever, are burgled in Fred and Kate's neighbourhood. Just as, in one good sense of the word, it is a *norm* that Fred closes the door properly, a norm that Kate gets home after Fred does, that Pete stays put on campus at weekends. Here too there is a norm about house burglary. It normally happens that when a house is burgled in a neighbourhood like theirs, it will have been for the first time. Note, however, that the first three norms carry more predictive weight than the fact that Fred and Kate's house had never before been burgled, which carries little, if any. Still, each of these four is an antecedent of a subjunctive conditional statement, which *if true* would trigger the Peircean conclusion,

(3*) Hence there is reason to suspect that the antecedent of (2^1) [2^2, 2^3, 2^4] is true.

It is important to emphasize that a reason to *suspect* that a hypothesis is true is certainly not evidence that it *is* true, and not reason to *believe* that it's true either. Peirce is insistent in saying that a successful abduction provides no grounds for believing the abduced hypothesis (Peirce, *RTL*, p. 178). From which we may derive two further observations about the situation Fred was in.

---

[6] "Had it been true that X " is more idiomatic English than "If it were true that X had ". But because the latter more closely fits the wording of Peirce's schema, I'll stick with it.

The productivity of ignorance-preserving inference: Even if at least one of these subjunctive conditionals were true, the hypothesis thereby induced would not have solved Fred's ignorance-problem. But it might have provided Fred with a reasoned but non-deterministic basis for action.

Here is the action that Fred actually took. He pulled out his phone and called 911. He called Kate on her cellphone, advising her that, upon arrival, she shouldn't enter the house until the police had checked things out. He followed that advice himself. As it turned out, the house had indeed been burgled. The thieves had used a glass cutter to remove a small basement window.

We now have at hand a nice characterization of the good that's in a good abductive inference. It also helps distinguishing successful abductive inference from valid deductive inference and strong inductive inference. While

- a valid deduction is *truth-preserving,* and
- a strong induction is *likelihood-enhancing,*
- a successful abduction is *ignorance-preserving yet action-motivating.*

Suppose, however, that after careful examination of the scene, the police had found no evidence of a break-in and Kate and Fred had found nothing missing or damaged. At that point, they both might reasonably have defaulted to the hypothesis of the antecedent of subjunctive conditional (2^1) and drawn the conclusion:

(3*) Hence there is reason to suspect that Fred forgot to shut door.

It is interesting that in the discussion surrounding the presentation of the Peircean schema the key terms "surprise", "matter of course" and "suspect" are neither defined nor explicated. Even so, the wording of the schema provides some contextual clues. As I've already suggested, a surprising event is something off-course or irregular, something that deviates from the normal workings of things. In *CP* 1.139, Peirce says "Now nothing justifies a retroductive [= abductive] inference except its affording an explanation of the facts." He doesn't say what he means by "explanation", but it is easy to see it working in the schema as an alternative wording of "would make them a matter of course." I'll come back to this later when we discuss *inference to the best explanation* in Section 4.

I think that it may now be said that Fred's reaction to the open door hits all the buttons of what Peirce has told us so far about abduction. Perhaps the most striking feature of the case of the open door is how long it's taken to recount it. In presenting this sort of everyday situation to a class on critical thinking, it wouldn't be at all unusual for students to leap to the punch-line well before the case has been properly laid out. This is bears on what Fred actually did. When he first spotted the open door, it was 5:04. When he started calling 911 it was 5:05. It took longer to answer the 911 operator's questions, hence longer to complete the call than to arrive at the point of making it. The situation that Fred was in is one of a kind that the students could easily see themselves being in. In each case, Fred's and their own, they moved like lightening. Yet every word laid out in Section 1 faithfully records most of what must have somehow or another been going through Fred's mind, and some likeness of what was going through the minds of the students to whom the Fred case is being recounted. Here are some highlights.

- There is a large presence of localized background information made up of numbers of defeasible household generalizations, supplemented by facts particular to those householders—e.g., that Fred knows what things are like in his city and in neighbourhoods like his.
- There is also the presence of a more global background information, having to do with Fred's largely implicit appreciation of the generalizations arising from his life-experiences to date and those of his ilk—e.g., open doors in December in northern Alberta, Canada make for cold houses.
- Also present were well-functioning filtration-mechanisms, keeping out of play myriad facts of Fred's explicit and/or implicit awareness that have no relevant bearing on the open-door problem—e.g., that Pete was born in August.
- There was also the fact that almost none of this relevant background information was processed consciously or formulated linguistically. From which we are invited to draw a further inference, perhaps the most important one so

The subconscious abduction thesis: Even though it is briefly and simply laid out, and Fred's actions comported with it, what he did not do was consciously instantiate the Peircean schema. There wouldn't have been time to call it to mind, and then give linguistic effect to the required substitutions for its schematic letters, in the interval between 5:04 and 5:05.[7]

Once again, this calls to mind the question of whether there is an epistemology that adequately takes this thesis into account.

This last point calls for a bit more consideration. Although what happened that day at Fred and Kate's place was a singular event, it was but one

---

[7] The contrast between consciousness and unconsciousness is certainly a graded one. It used to be thought (and still is in many circles) that unresponsiveness is a secure marker of unconsciousness. Recent work with a functional magnetic resonance imaging (*fMRI*) scanner casts doubt on this. See Adrian Owen (2017).

instance of a more commonly experienced type. The way in which Fred's mind worked on that occasion wasn't peculiar to reactions to Peircean surprises. It is typical of human responses to the information imparted by the varying elements of life's passing scene. Imagine a student in a critical thinking class, straining to take good notes at a lecture about Fred's case or anything else covered by the course. The student couldn't do it without a good aural understanding of the professor's language, a decent command of its syntactic structure and lexical orthography, as well as a timely appreciation of the necessity to get it all down while fresh. When we consider the magnitude of what the note-taking student must know, we should be struck by how little of it makes footfall in the student's conscious mind. For all its indispensability in getting the note-taking job done, by far its contribution was transacted in his cognitively productive subconscious. Nor is this peculiar to the cognitive mechanics of note-taking in a critical thinking class. It is, in Peirce's words, a matter of course for how human beings subconsciously process the information that conduces to their quotidian knowledge, calling to mind the importance of the non-sequential mind in Walters' approach to a well-nourished human rationality.[8] This, we may now think, has crucial implications for how theories of knowledge and logics of reasoning operate.

3. Big heavenly bodies

For all its commonplace appearance, the open-door abduction is a made-up example of one. One of the attractions of made-up examples is that they expose themselves to tendentious employment. You can make a made-up example do what you want, even to fit the provisions of an awaiting theory. Better, we might rightly think, to turn our minds to some real-life ones, beginning with the one that launched planet Neptune. We begin this story with Uranus, whose orbital irregularities were noticed in the 1840s to discomport with Newton's laws of motion and gravity. It was widely believed that these irregularities would be a matter of Newtonian course were there an as yet unknown planet whose gravitational force was disturbing Uranus orbit around the Sun. In 1845 Urbain Le Verrier (1811-1877) in Paris and John Couch Adams (1819-1892) in Cambridge, operating independently, made calculations to help account for the nature of this planet and to locate its position. Both Le Verrier and Adams drew the same abductive inference. The sought-for planet was Neptune. The postulation of Neptune spurred a flurry of follow-up testing, and seventeen days after the Royal Society had

---

[8] For a fuller discussion, see (Woods 2013 or Woods 2014). See also (Woods 2012 and 2017); this latter pair of papers update the account of (Gabbay and Woods 2005).

bestowed the Copley medal on Le Verrier, William Lassell (1799-1880) had tracked down Neptune's moon Triton. The Berlin Observatory made telescopic observations confirming Neptune's existence. It was a high point in 19th century astrophysics, and a stunning re-confirmation of Newton's laws.

We see in Neptune's discovery every box of the Peircean schema ticked off to rich astrophysical effect. The inference of Neptune was abductively impeccable, and its dispatch to the tribunal of observational determination yielded up a verdict that transformed a reason to suspect the abduced hypothesis to be true to a reason for asserting it to be so. Abductions so perfect are not, as Peirce makes clear, guaranteed such happy outcomes. We see this in the abduction of Vulcan.

It all began with the perihelion procession of Mercury's orbit whose classically predicted value differed from the observed one by 43 arcseconds per century. A small perturbation to be sure, but one that discomported with the Newtonian laws. In 1859, using the same techniques that had done so well in restoring Uranus to Newtonian fidelity, Le Verrier's team abduced the planet Vulcan, placing it between Mercury and close to the Sun. In the forty-five year aftermath of the abduction, there was no settled observational confirmation of Vulcan. In 1915, Einstein (1879-1995) published the general theory of relativity, which put Newton's laws into honourable retirement and, in so doing, revealed Mercury's orbital perturbations to be a relativity matter of course. To this day, there are astronomers who think that what was taken for a planet in 1859, might now be explained by other inter-Mercurial objects, either previously unknown comets or asteroids.

There are two points of importance to take note of here. One is that the abduction of Vulcan was as good as the abduction of Neptune. The other is that all abductions, Fred's or Le Verrier's or anyone else's, are transacted in contexts of background information, none of whose particulars functions as a voiced premiss. What happened between Neptune and Vulcan was a background shift from Newton to Einstein.

Another of our everyday defeasible generalizations is that everyone knows that water is H_2O. However, many fewer know what "hydrogen" and "oxygen" mean here and, still less, the structure denoted by the combined chemical notation. Vastly more people know that Einstein's general theory of relativity ended the reign of Newton's theory of gravity, than understand the new laws. It sounds paradoxical, of course. How could people know so much without knowing what they are talking about? An answer proposed in chapter 9 of *Errors of Reasoning* derives from the mediaeval philosopher-Saint Anselm (1033/4-1109), who famously avowed *credo ut intelligam*—"I accept in order that I might come to understand."[9] The opposite view is the reverse avowal, *"intelligo ut credam"*—"I understand so that belief might be made possible." A question for epistemology in general is which, if either, of these Latin tags to favour.

One way out of the apparent paradox is that when everyone knows that water is H_2O, what they actually know is that "Water is H_2O" is a sentence that expresses a true proposition. Ditto for the likes of "Everyone knows that $e = mc^2$", and so on. On this characterization, it is perfectly consistent for someone to say that he really does know that p even if he doesn't know what he's talking about. This is as true of the man who first asserted the action at distance theorem, while acknowledging that he didn't understand it as it is true of the man across the street who says that $e = mc^2$, while acknowledging that he doesn't understand it. What Newton was saying, in effect, was "I don't understand the action at a distance theorem and yet there is reason to suspect that it expresses a true proposition." This, I think, is a good enough idea to have a name. We could call it "the Anselmian suspicion precedes understanding thesis", or for short "the suspicion of truth thesis". It would appear that the suspicion of truth thesis might have been purpose-built for a child's learning of the mother tongue. How likely that a little tyke would ever understand the utterances of parents and family without some antecedent primitive confidence of their reliability, buttressed by an also primitive testing of the abduction that generated the suspicion of the truth in the first place?

4. Explanation

In what must be considered one of the foundational papers, Gilbert Harman (1965, see pp. 88-95) picks up on an idea that we also see in Peirce's *CP* 1.139 (with apologies for repetitiveness):

> Now nothing justifies a retroductive [= abductive] inference except its affording an explanation of the facts.

Late in Section 2, I advanced the suggestion that what Peirce means by "explains" is wholly contained in premiss (2) of the Peircean schema. If so, a hypothesis A which, if true, would explain the surprising fact that C, would be the very one that makes C a matter of course. Peirce was never drawn to the idea that the inference to the best explanation is the keystone of scientific method. The very suggestion of it would have been dismissed upon arrival. The doctrine that suspicion of truth can both precede and facilitate subsequent

---

[9] Anselm, St., *Proslogion*, 1. This echoes remarks of St. Augustine of Hippo (354-430) in his *Tractates on the Gospel of John* 29.6: *"Crede*ut intelligas"*. ,* intelligas". *ut*ntelligas". *intelligas*

understanding is amply and convincingly instantiated in history. Neverthe-less, Harman (1965) writes:

'The inference to the best explanation' corresponds approximately to what others have called 'abduction', 'the method of hypothesis', 'hypothetic inference', 'the method of elimination', 'eliminative induction' and 'theoretical inference'. (88-91)

Peter Lipton (1991) writes in like vein:

According to Inference to the Best Explanation, our inferential practices are gov-erned by explanatory considerations. Given our data and our background beliefs, we infer what would, if true, provide the best of the competing explanations we can generate of those data (so long as the best is good enough for us to make any inference at all).

He goes on to say, quite rightly it seems to me, that

Inference to the Best Explanation has become extremely popular in philosophi-cal circles, discussed by many and endorsed without discussion by many more . Yet it still remains much more of a slogan, than an articulated account of induc-tion. (*Ibid.*, p. 58)[10]

We are now at the point of distinguishing what at present are the two most discussed schematic updates of Peirce's original one. Like his, each of these schematizes stage two—the inference stage—only. Let E be a Peircean sur-prising event for some agent, K be his knowledge-base at the time, H be a hypothesis, K(H) be a hypothetical knowledge-base got by addition of H to K, and let ↝ be an undefined conditionality relation. Then, according to the *AKM schema*, abductive inference has the following structure:[11]

---

[10] The same view persists in the 2004 edition of the 1991 book, *Inference to the Best Explanation.*

[11] The label "AKM" was proposed by Gabbay and me in our *The Reach of Abduction* 2005 in honor of some of those whose work is shaped by it, to wit: Aliseda 1997 and later 2006, Robert Kowalski, *Logic for Problem Solving,* New York: Else-vier, 1979, A. Kakas, R. A. Kowalski and F. Toni, "Abduction and abductive logic programming", *Journal of Logic and Computation,* 2 (1995), 719-770, Theo A. F. Kuipers, "Abduction aiming at empirical progress of even truth approximation leading to a challenge for computational modelling", *Foundations of Science,* 4 (1999), 307-323, Magnani 2001 and later 2009, and Joke Meheus, Liza Verho-even, Maarten Van Dyck and Dagmar Profijn, "Ampliative adaptive logics and the foundation of logic-based approaches to abduction", in Lorenzo Magnani, Nancy J. Neressian and Claudio Pizzi, editors, *Logical and Computational Aspects of Model-Based Reasoning,* pages 39-71, Dordrecht: Kluwer, 2002. Mind you, the

1. E
2. ~(K ↬ E)
3. ~(H ↬ E)
4. K(H) is consistent
5. K(H) is minimal
6. K(H) ↬ E
7. Therefore, H.[12]

A sizable percentage of the AKM community leans towards an explanationist interpretation of "↬" and a truth-preserving interpretation of "therefore" although variations have also been proposed. In some accounts, "↬" sometimes means "possibly explains", and "therefore" denotes high inductive likelihood, as reckoned up in the probability calculus. Whether "↬" means "explains" or "could explain", and "therefore" denotes truth-preservation or the enhancement of likelihood, there remains a question, any answer to which could be a hard sell. The question is, "What is an explanation?"

Hintikka writes in *Socratic Epistemology* that the idea that abduction is inference to the best explanation, while it "has a great deal of initial plausibility is seriously simplified at best." (p. 40) He continues,

> Part of the difficulty can be seen by asking, first what explanation is or, perhaps more pertinently, what explaining is. Most people who speak of 'inferences to the best explanation' seem to know what explanation is. In reality, the nature of explanation is scarcely any clearer than the nature of abduction. (*Ibid.*, pp. 40-41.)

> In one sense—the hypothetico-deductive sense—"explaining an explanandum E is to derive it from [a] background theory T plus a number of contingent truths that are relative to E and that have to be found in order for an attempt to explain E to succeed" (*ibid.*, p. 41).

If we accept this, it is easy to see that abduction is intrinsically *non*-explanationist. Let Hintikka's background theory T play the role of the AKM-schema's knowledge-base K and let Hintikka's derivation be the AKM "↬". On Hintikka's approach, the equivalents of H are contingent truths. But in

choice of the letters, "A", "K", "M" represents a small sample of the going literature. In a larger sample, many more letters would have been displayed.

[12] A couple of technical points. First, if we insist that K(H) be consistent, we will exclude the Newton-Leibniz calculus from Newton's celestial mechanics, thus wrecking it. The second point is a closely related one. It is sometimes overlooked how greatly a revision of K by the inclusion of H can change the original K. Think here of the impact on the science of light and all its supporting theories caused by throwing the quantum hypothesis into the mix.

Peirce's schema and AKM's too, they are hypotheses. They would be *disqualified* as hypotheses were their abducer to advance them as true. So for this kind of explanation—a widely held one in the philosophy of science—abduction cannot be inference to the best explanation (Woods 2011).

Perhaps the larger problem posed by IBE is the unruly ambiguity of "explain" compounded by variations in their theoretical developments. Riding alongside, is the uncertainty that dogs the "therefore" operator.[13] The second post-Peircean schema, the Gabbay-Woods schema, attempts to bring some clarity to this murk. Here is how it goes, informally expressed. Anyone (Bill, say) for whom E is a Peircean surprise has an ignorance problem. Bill wants to know what he doesn't know. But for the present he will settle for this. He would like to know what, if true, would remove the sting of surprise and would render E's occurrence a matter of course. He would then have some reasoned basis for making something of this hypothetical answer. He could set out to determine whether it is true. He could send it to the lab for experimental test, or he could put it to provisional use as a premiss in reasoning about things of the same subject-matter in which the ignorance problem arose in the first place.

To put this in schematic terms, let E be the surprising event and ?E the question whose answer Bill wants to know but doesn't. Let K be his present knowledge-base, K* be his present knowledge-base supplemented by new information within Bill's timely and easy grasp, let H be an hypothesis and let $\leftadots$ be the subjunctive conditional relation. C(H) is the Peircean conclusion that there is reason to suspect that H is true, and H^C is the decision to put H to whatever kind of test as seems appropriate to its subject matter. R denotes a response relation to the question posed by E. These are put to schematic work as follows:

1. ?E   [the question posed by E]
2. ~R (K, ?E)   [fact]
3. ~R(K*, ?E)   [fact]
4. H $\notin$ K   [fact]
5. H $\notin$ K*   [fact]
6. ~R(H, ?E)   [fact]
7. ~R(K(H), ?E)   [fact]
8. H $\leftadots$ R(K(H))   [fact]

---

[13] Here is the Oxford-Cambridge online provision for "to explain", slightly paraphrased: to make something plain, clear or intelligible; to give a reason so as to justify or excuse something; to be the cause of something; to be the motivating factor of an action or decision; to minimize the significance of something embarrassing; or to defend oneself against verbal or oral attack.

9. H meets further conditions $S_1, ..., S_n$ [fact]
10. Hence, C(H)   [subconclusion, 1-9]
11. So, H^C [conclusion, 1-10]

It is worth repeating that the G-W schema applies only to the second stage of Peircean abduction. As it stands, it has nothing to say about stage one, the stage at which H was selected from among rival hypotheses to do the heavy lifting of stage two. We should also note that the G-W schema, unlike the AKM, stands mute on the conditions that fall upon H and K(H). The reason for it is partly its rejection of the AKM conditions, but mainly because those conditions will have been exposed in a principled way in the stage-one or selection-stage (tentatively and incompletely developed in Woods 2017).

Even so, our question here is whether the G-W schema offers IBE a welcome home. The answer is that it might and mightn't for particular readings of K(H), but not for all. If we agreed that when the K(H) of a successful G-W abduction is an explanatorily coherent statement of a future epistemic state, we could say that explanatory coherence is a welcome bonus. Of course, it depends on when the bonus would take effect. From this we might arrive at an explanatory hypothesis of our own.

Explanatory coherence as a collateral benefit: There are cases in which an abduction is entirely successful, and such explanatory coherence as might await it is achieved in the post-H^C stage of the G-W schema. That is, it is achieved by further testing of H. There are also less dramatic cases in which the attainment of explanatory coherence is concurrent but not intrinsic to abductive success.[14]

Another less actively discussed schema for abduction is the J-J schema of Josephson and Josephson 1994.

1. D is a collection of data.
2. H explains D.
3. No other hypotheses can explain D as well as H does.
4. Therefore H is probably true.

Each premiss of the schema must be *plausible* if the conclusion is to be made plausible. In *Character Evidence: An Abductive Theory*, Douglas Walton (2006) adopts the J-J schema and provides it with dialectical adaptation for legal contexts.

---

[14] Lorenzo Magnani's 2009 *eco-cognitive model* is an interesting and ambitious attempt to enlarge substantially the reach of the two schemata in view here, and in so doing remove the necessity to see them as rivals.

    i.   F is a finding or a given set of facts.

   ii.   E is a satisfactory explanation of F.

  iii.   No alternative explanation E given so far is as satisfactory as E is.

  iv.   Therefore, E is plausible, as a hypothesis. (p. 167)

We find in these approaches an emphasis on plausibility that is not to be found in the Peirce, AKM or G-W schemata. Especially striking is the difference between Walton's terminal line and the three prior termini. There is all the difference here between having reason to suspect the truth of even something you don't understand and concluding that what you do understand is plausible. It might well be that plausibility has a load-bearing role to play in sorting out different intelligible hypotheses for possible selection. Whether a stage one matter and a stage two one as well, whether a matter for abduction alone or loading-bearing in other contexts, plausibility awaits a satisfactory theoretical working up, notwithstanding its importance and the foundational work of Nicholas Rescher (1976).[15]

To conclude ...

In this note, I have attempted to make some headway with the following matters:

- What are today's predominant approaches to abductive inference, and is any of them consistent with any other? I have responded with the AKM, G-W and J-J models, and have explained that each conflicts with the others. Conclusion: The logic of abduction is not yet "settled science."

- What is the relation between these models of abduction to inference to the best explanation? I have suggested that on some interpretations of "explain" IBE is consistent with the G-W model but not inherently part of it. Since the ↝ relation of the AKM model varies contextually between deductive implication and inductive strength, its tie to IBE remains obscure. A closer connection can be found between Walton's plausibility-reading of the J-J model, in which the tie to IBE is tighter. However, the plausibility-reading is at variance with some of the most important cases in abductive science. If, as I think it does, Walton's plausibility reading of the J-J model ensues from Rescher's plausibility calculus, it is incompatible with the G-W model. Since the G-W model captures utterly implausible but scientifically break-out examples, that is a reason to abandon the plausibility factor.

---

[15] For reservations see Gabbay and Woods (2005, pp. 222-238) and Woods (2014, pp. 279-287).

- The AKM, G-W and J-J models certainly don't exhaust the going approaches to abduction, chiefly those in computational logics and approaches to logic programming. I have omitted them partly for want of space, but also because of the likelihood of their soon influencing expected iterations of CT theory.
- Why does this note bother with rival approaches to epistemology? Isn't critical thinking a matter for logic and argumentation theory? My answer is that since belief-revision is an essential component of inference and decision, it is subject inescapably to epistemological constraints. To the extent that this is so, a misstep in epistemology could risk wrecking a theory of critical thinking.
- My chief purpose in this chapter has been to establish a back-channel from current theories of abductive inference and inference to the best explanation to mainstream approaches to CT theory. I hope that I have made some headway with this but, needless to say, that is something for the reader to judge.[16]

Selected readings on Peirce and abduction

The present-day literature reveals different streams of thought in bringing the Peircean paradigm into a more unified and systematic, theory. There isn't space in this chapter to adjudicate these differences. Interested readers could consult to advantage the somewhat selective works noted below, arranged in chronological order.

Fann, K.T. (1970). *Peirce's Theory of Abduction.* The Hague: Martinus Nijhoff.

Josephson, J.R. and Josephson, S.G. (Eds.). (1994). *Abductive Inference: Computation, Philosophy, Technology.* Cambridge: Cambridge University Press.

Atocha Aliseda, Atocha (1997). *Seeking Explanations: Abduction in Logic, Philosophy of Science and Artificial Intelligence,* PhD thesis. Amsterdam: Institute for Logic, Language and Computation.

Kapitan, Tomis (1997). Peirce and the structure of abductive inference. In Nathan Housser, Don Roberts and James van Evra (Eds.), *Studies in the Logic of Charles Sanders Peirce,* pp. 477-496. Bloomington: Indiana University Press.

Flack, P. and Kakas, A. (Eds.). (2000). *Abductive and Inductive Reasoning,* Dordrecht: Kluwer.

Magnani, Lorenzo (2001). *Abduction, Reason and Science,* New York: Plenum.

Lipton, Peter (2004). *Inference to the Best Explanation,* new revised edition. London: Routledge. First published in 1991.

[16] Warm thanks to J. Anthony Blair for skillful editing of an earlier draft of this chapter.

Thagard, Paul (2000). *Coherence in Thought and Action,* Cambridge, MA: MIT Press.

Gabbay, Dov and Woods, John (2005). *The Reach of Abduction: Insight and Trial,* Volume 2 of their *A Practical Logic of Cognitive Systems.* Amsterdam: North-Holland.

Walton, Douglas (2005). *Abductive Reasoning.* Tuscaloosa: University of Alabama Press.

Aliseda, Atocha (2006). *Abductive Reasoning: Logical Investigations into Discovery and Explanation.* Berlin: Springer.

Pietarinen, Ahti-Veikko (2006). *Signs of Logic,* a volume in the *Synthese* Library. Dordrecht: Springer.

Thagard, Paul (2007). Abductive inference: From philosophical analysis to neural mechanisms. In A. Feeney and E. Heit (Eds.), *Inductive Reasoning: Experimental, Developmental and Computational Approaches,* pp. 226-247. Cambridge: Cambridge University Press.

Hintikka, Jaakko (2007). *Socratic Epistemology,* 2007

Schurz, Gerhard (2008). Patterns of abduction, *Synthese,* 164, 201-234.

Magnani, Lorenzo (2009). *Abductive Cognition: The Epistemological and and Eco-Cognitive Dimensions of Hypothetical Reasoning,* a Cognitive Systems Monograph, Berlin: Springer.

Park, Woosuk (2017). *Abduction in Context: The Conjectural Dynamics of Scientific Reasoning,* a volume of Studies in Applied Philosophy, Epistemology and Rational Ethics, Berlin: Springer.

References[17]

Anselm (2009). *Proslogion.* In Ian Logan (Ed.), *Reading Anselm's Proslogion: The History of Anselm's Arguments and its Significance Today,* Burlington VT: Ashgate Publishing.

Aristotle (1985). *Categories.* In Jonathan Barnes (Ed.), *The Complete Works of Aristotle.* Princeton: Princeton University Press.

Augustine of Hippo (1888). *Tractates on the Gospel of John* 29.6. John Gibb, translator, *From Nicene and Post-Nicene Fathers,* First Series Volume 7, Philip Schaff (Ed.). Buffalo, NY: Christian Publishing Co.

Bacon, Francis (1905). *Novum Organum.* In R.L. Ellis and J. Spedding (Eds.), *The Philosophical Works of Francis Bacon,* pp. 202-387. London: Routledge, p. 292. *Novum Organum* first published in 1620.

Barringer, Howard, Gabbay, Dov and Woods, John (2012). In *Argument and Computation* 3, 143-202.

---

[17] Works prefixed with the asterisk "*" denote those that may have made some footfall in mainstream CT theories.

Flandern, Tom van (1999). Status of the NEAR challenge. *Meta Research Bulletin*, 8.

Gabbay, Dov and Woods, John. (2005). *The Reach of Abduction: Insight and Trial*, Volume 2 of their *A Practical Logic of Cognitive Systems*. Amsterdam: North-Holland.

*Harman, Gilbert (1965). The inference to the best explanation. *Philosophical Review*, 74, 88-95.

*Hintikka, Jaakko (2007). Abduction—Inference, conjecture, or answer. In Jaakko Hintikka, *Socratic Epistemology: Explorations of Knowledge-Seeking by Questioning*, pp. 38-60. New York: Cambridge University Press. First published as What is abduction? The fundamental problem of contemporary epistemology. *Transactions of the Charles Peirce Society*, 34 (1998), 503-533.

Josephson, J.R. and Josephson, S.G. (Eds.). (1994). *Abductive Inference: Computation, Philosophy, Technology.* Cambridge: Cambridge University Press.

Kakas, A., Kowalski, R.A. and Toni, F. (1995). Abduction and abductive logic programming. *Journal of Logic and Computation*, 2, 719-770.

*Kapitan, Tomis (1997). Peirce and the structure of abductive inference. In Nathan Housser, Don Roberts and James van Evra (Eds.), *Studies in the Logic of Charles Sanders Peirce*, pp. 477-496. Bloomington: Indiana University Press.

Kirby, Carmichael (1997). Letter to Olivetti. Laguna Salada Union School District, May.

Kowalski, Robert (1979). *Logic for Problem Solving: Empirical Progress of Even Truth Approximation Leading to a Challenge for Computational. New York: Elsevier.

Kuipers, Theo A. F. (1999). Abduction aiming at modelling, *Foundations of Science*, 4, 307-323.

*Lipton, Peter (2004). *Inference to the Best Explanation,* new revised edition. London: Routledge. First published in 1991.

Magnani, Lorenzo (2001). *Abduction, Reason and Science.* New York: Plenum.

Magnani, Lorenzo (2009). *Abductive Cognition: The Epistemological and Eco-Cognitive Dimensions of Hypothetical Reasoning,* a Cognitive Systems Monograph. Berlin: Springer.

Meheus, Joke, Verhoeven, Liza, Van Dyck, Maarten and Dagmar Profijn (2002). Ampliative adaptive logics and the foundation of logic-based approaches to abduction. In Lorenzo Magnani, Nancy J. Neressian and Claudio Pizzi (Eds.), *Logical and Computational Aspects of Model-Based Reasoning*, pp. 39-71. Dordrecht: Kluwer.

Owen, Adrian (2017). *Into the Gray Zone: A Neuroscientist Explores the Border Between Life and Death.* New York: Scribner.

Park, Woosuk (2017). *Abduction in Context: The Conjectural Dynamics of Scientific Reasoning,* a volume of Studies in Applied Philosophy, Epistemology and Rational Ethics. Berlin: Springer.

*Peirce, C.S. (1931-1958). *Collected Works.* Cambridge, MA: Harvard University Press. A series of volumes first appearing in 1931.

Peirce, C.S. (1992). *Reasoning and the Logic of Things: The Cambridge Conference Lectures of 1898,* K. L. Kettner (Ed.). Cambridge, MA: Harvard University Press.

Pietarinen, Ahti-Veikko. (2006). *Signs of Logic,* a volume in the *Synthese* Library. Dordrecht: Springer.

*Pinto, Robrt C. (2001). *Argument, Inference and Dialectic: Collected Papers.* Dordrecht: Kluwer.

Quine, W.V. (1966). *Selected Logical Papers,* New York: Random House; enlarged edition. Cambridge, MA: Harvard University Press, 1995.

*Rescher, Nicholas (1976). *Plausible Reasoning: An Introduction to the Theory and Practice of Plausible Inference.* Assen: Van Gorcum.

Rescher, Nicholas (1996). *Priceless Knowledge? Natural Science in Economic Perspective.* Lanham, MD: Rowman and Littlefield .

Russell, Bertrand (1937). *The Principles of Mathematics,* second edition. London: Allen and Unwin. First published in 1903.

Soames, Scott (2014). *The Analytic Tradition in Philosophy,* volume I *The Founding Giants.* Princeton: Princeton University Press.

Walters, Kerry S. (1994). *Re-Thinking Reason.* Albany: SUNY Press.

*Walton, Douglas (2005). *Abductive Reasoning.* Tuscaloosa: Alabama University Press.

*Walton, Douglas (2008). *Witness Testimony Evidence.* New York: Cambridge University Press.

*Walton, Douglas (2013). *Methods of Argumentation.* New York: Cambridge University Press.

*Woods, John (2004). *The Death of Argument: Fallacies in Agent-Based Reasoning,* Volume 32 of the Applied Logic series. Dordrecht: Kluwer.

Woods, John (2011). Recent developments in abductive logic. *Studies in History and Philosophy of Science,* 42, 240-244.

Woods, John (2012). Cognitive economics and the logic of abduction. *Review of Symbolic Logic,* 5, 148-166.

*Woods, John (2013). *Errors of Reasoning: Naturalizing the Logic of Inference,* Volume 45 of Studies in Logic. London: College Publications. Reprinted with corrections in 2014.

*Woods, John (2015). *Is Legal Reasoning Irrational? An Introduction to the Epistemology of Law,* Volume 2 of Law and Society. London: College Publications.

Woods, John (2017). Reorienting the logic of abduction, in Lorenzo Magnani and Tommaso Bertolotti (Eds.), *Springer Handbook of Model-Based Science*, pp. 137-150. Heidelberg: Springer.

About the author:

John Woods has done foundational work in several branches of philosophy. He is co-founder of the Woods–Walton Approach to fallacies theory, an early pioneer of the formal semantics of literary discourse and of conflict-resolution methods for the non-empirical sciences. His historical investigations have prompted the reconsideration of the structural importance for dialogue logic of Aristotle's "immature" writings in *The Organon*. In collaboration with Dov Gabbay, the logic of relevance went causal, and abduction was framed as ignorance-preserving reasoning. More recently, Woods has generalized the causal aspects of relevance to a naturalized logic of inference and legal reasoning. A new book on fiction abandons formal semantics in favour of a naturalized logic of reference and truth. Woods is the recipient of national and international awards and honorary degrees. Elected Fellow of the Royal Society of Canada in 1990, he is currently Director of the Abductive Systems Group at UBC.

21

The Unruly Logic of Evaluation

Michael Scriven

1. Overview

The interest of this topic from the critical thinking/informal logic point of view is that it refers to the huge and important range of common and professional discourse aimed at supporting or contesting evaluative conclusions, and it raises the possibility of greatly improving the quality of such discussions by means of a largely informal logic approach, an especially interesting challenge given the failure of deontic logic to achieve that end.[1] As a practical goal for work in this field, though this particular presentation is not long enough to justify its attainment, one might propose as an aim for work on this topic that it should try to ensure that every respectable text in critical thinking/informal logic (and why not every text in the philosophy of the social sciences and ethics) will include a section on the logic of evaluation.[2]

Evaluation is the process of determining merit, worth, or significance (m/w/s); an evaluation is a product of that process.[3] Professional evaluation is evaluation done in a systematic and objective way with a degree of expertise that requires extensive specific training or learning. The logic of evaluation is concerned with (i) how, if at all, professional evaluation is possible; (ii) its

---

[1] See the valuable survey in the *Stanford Encyclopedia of Philosophy* (online) under this heading.

[2] With that goal in mind, the author would greatly appreciate receiving comments, critical or amplificatory; they can be sent to mjscriv1@gmail.com.

[3] This definition is a synthesis of the definitions in most dictionaries and the professional literature, with the unfortunate exception of the mother of them all, the *Oxford English Dictionary*, which seems unable to grasp the move beyond estate appraisal and mathematical formula calculation, despite many decades of prompting. (Recent editions of the single-volume Oxford dictionaries are somewhat less perverse.)

nature and its location in the organization of knowledge, and (iii) the logical structure of its inferences.

Four groups of issues in this branch of logic will be addressed here, even more briefly than they deserve, the first two of them philosophical, the third conceptual, and the last procedural. The philosophical issues concern the barriers that have been supposed to render the entire enterprise impossible—variants on (a) the so-called "naturalistic fallacy", and on (b) the alleged impossibility of objectivity. The conceptual issues concern various attempts to capture the essence of professional evaluation—either its nature or its operation—usually via a key metaphor. These issues, and the procedural issues, which concern how the practical logic of evaluation does and does not operate, are naturally of interest only if it is not founded on a fallacy. We'll stay with that sequence, except for beginning with one of the easier conceptual issues—the geography of evaluation.

2. The territory of evaluation

Evaluation has an extremely extensive territory, since it includes the substantial portion of everyday discourse devoted to proposing, attacking, and defending evaluative claims about food products, football teams, human behavior, global warming, and almost everything else. The domain of professional evaluation is still very extensive: we here distinguish seven standard sub-divisions of it, and four other specialized domains which are less commonly categorized or recognized as part of evaluation's domain, although substantially devoted to it.

The standard sub-divisions, which we'll call the satellite subjects, are: performance evaluation, product evaluation, personnel evaluation, proposal evaluation, program evaluation (which includes practice, procedural, and process evaluation), policy analysis, and portfolio evaluation (there is a small amount of overlap between some of these). The specialized or core domains include two for which I coined names now quite widely used—meta-evaluation (the evaluation of evaluations), and intradisciplinary evaluation (the evaluation of data, experimental designs, hypotheses, etc., which is part of normal professional practice within every discipline). The other two specialized domains are standard disciplines not commonly classified as divisions of evaluation but substantially concerned with that activity as a main subject matter, not merely for procedural (i.e., intradisciplinary) use: ethics (normative ethics in particular) and logic (because it includes the evaluation of arguments).

The logic of evaluation has general features and processes that are the same in all of these areas, and in the everyday business of evaluation, but it also includes some features that are specific to sub-sets or to individual members of the group. Many of the standard sub-divisions have had specialists working in them for a lifetime and have of course evolved sophisticated technical vocabularies and models of their own. Of course, some of this specialized knowledge will usually have to be mastered in order to make a contribution to the sub-area, although the amount varies considerably by area.

Perhaps the limit case of specialization is in the category of intradisciplinary evaluation, where it is generally thought that to be good at evaluating theories in particle physics, for example, or explanations in medieval history, or programs in international aid, you need to be a fully qualified specialist in the relevant area. However, this turns out not to be entirely correct; the study of the logic of evaluation does yield some results that include refutations of, or substantial improvements upon, the practice of intradisciplinary explanation; and studies of the logic of causal explanation in educational research have uncovered flaws and finer points missed by the mainstream professionals. Two good examples of this can be found in areas of current high activity—the general evaluation of research,[4] and the evaluation of causation in international aid.[5] So the logic of evaluation is sometimes not only of interest in itself, but can be of some value to the general scholarly enterprise and to all the social efforts that depend on results from that enterprise, e.g., the social enterprise of poverty reduction.

From the comments already made about the geography of evaluation, it should be clear that evaluation has a rather unusual dual role in the country of the mind. It is of course a discipline, or family of disciplines, in itself—in fact, even within one subdivision such as program or personnel evaluation scores of entirely specific books, journal issues, and conferences mark every year. But it is also a "service discipline" in the same way as logic or—to a more limited extent—statistics, because every discipline is heavily involved in evaluation. This goes somewhat beyond the way in which each discipline uses intradisciplinary evaluation, which mainly involves the evaluation of methodological entities, since every discipline evaluates its own students as well as practitioners (personnel evaluation), research proposals submitted for funding (proposal evaluation), its journals, websites, doctoral programs, and associations (product and program evaluation), etc. For this reason, evaluation is sometimes referred to as a transdiscipline—one that operates across

---

[4] Documented in the Summer 2008 issue of *New Directions in Evaluation* (Vol. 2008, Issue 118, pp. 1-105) eds. C. Coryn and M. Scriven; the entire issue is devoted to the evaluation of research.)

[5] Will be supported in the discussions with the Ministry of Foreign Affairs at Tokyo (July, 2007), and in an article in #8 of the online *Journal of MultiDisciplinary Evaluation*. Earlier issues of this journal contain earlier discussions of this topic.

many other disciplines as well as autonomously.[6] Logic is the only other transdiscipline that operates across all academic disciplines, but evaluation also operates across all physical disciplines, e.g., tai chi, marathon running.[7] But is it based on a logical error?

3. The possibility of evaluation

The Humean argument that is a precursor to the naturalistic fallacy was appealing enough to rationalize the ban on evaluative research (the "value-free doctrine") that largely prevented the social sciences from directly addressing most issues of social concern for the greater part of the 20th century. Following the conventional interpretation of Hume, it was argued that since one cannot validly infer evaluative conclusions from "factual" (here used, incorrectly, to mean naturalistic, a.k.a. empirical) premises, it followed that science cannot support them. This is an invalid argument with a false premise into the bargain. The premise is false, following Searle, since from the observable fact that Jones promised to repay his debt to Smith, it follows that he should do so—an evaluative conclusion— using the tautological (definitionally true) inference warrant that promises incur obligations. The argument is invalid, since science includes far more than factual (i.e., non-evaluative) claims: it is, by practical necessity and of its very nature as a discipline, suffused with evaluative claims, without which it would not be either functional or distinguishable from charlatanry. These claims range from evaluation of the quality of observational data and instruments, and the merits of experimental designs, hypotheses and theories, to evaluations of the worth of research proposals and scientific papers submitted to journals for publication, and to evaluations of the merit of scientific works and scientists. The difference between astrology and astronomy is essentially a difference in the quality of their data and the inferences from it. In fact, the nature of any discipline, including not just the sciences but also history and jurisprudence—the very reason they deserve the name at all—lies in the extent to which they meet the standards of quality that learning to practice requires every practitioner to master. Since science itself contains, at the heart of its practice and conclusions, many evaluative claims, the assumption that it is only concerned with

---

[6] Note the difference from 'interdisciplinary' meaning "relating to more than one discipline", and from 'multidisciplinary,' implying relevance to more than two disciplines.

[7] However, if one thinks that all 'logic of....' subjects are part of logic, logic would include the logic of evaluation, and hence, in this extended sense, the rules governing evaluation in the physical disciplines.

claims that can be established as (non-evaluative) facts directly, or by inference from other facts, is wrong.

Against this commonsensical refutation of the value-free doctrine, two
defenses are often produced. It is sometimes argued that the doctrine was only
meant to exclude the intrusion of *political and ethical* values into science, not
these workaday values. However, political and ethical values are excludable
simply on the grounds of irrelevance—when they are indeed irrelevant—so
there was no need for a new doctrine to keep them out. And a glance at the
arguments provided for the doctrine shows that they are arguments that are
entirely general about value claims, not restricted to a sub-species.

Again, it is sometimes argued that the kind of evaluative claim that is
commonplace in science is acceptable "because it can be translated (loosely
speaking) into factual claims": but, of course, it is plausibly arguable that
this is also true, loosely speaking, about most evaluative claims—and equally,
of course, it was exactly this claim about translatability that G. E. Moore
rejected, and labeled the naturalistic fallacy.

Here we come to a number of further variations in the general case against
evaluative claims as scientifically (or logically) respectable. To a substantial
extent the case was based on three confluent mistakes—one error of misclas-
sification, one of overgeneralization, and one about definability and translatability—and each of these comes into one or another of several defenses of the
value-free position or its grounds. The first error was the supposition that the
typical value claim was a statement of personal taste or preference, which of
course lacks the quality of universality that was thought to be requisite for
objectivity—here taken to mean universality in the sense of intersubjectiv-
ity—and hence scientific status. The error here was to over-generalize: while
personal preferences are indeed one kind of value, they are not the only kind.
For example, "Murder is wrong," "The reliability of cars is a prima facie-
valid criterion of their merit," and "The average vehicle on a United States
highway still contributes more than twice as much in emissions as the average Chinese vehicle" are all clearly evaluative but strongly general, two true
by definition and one a matter of evaluative fact (albeit timebound and with
particular names as descriptors).

The second error, closely related, was the supposition that objectivity
requires anything approaching universal generalization, clearly an error since
large parts of science (as well as history and jurisprudence, where objectivity
is equally important) are both objective and highly particular, obvious scientific examples being geology, forensic science, and planetary astronomy.

The third error, Moore's error, was the assumption that definability/trans-
latability is a matter of logically necessary connections. In fact, most common
concepts—especially the most important and general ones—in science as

well as in common experience, are "cluster concepts" that are learnt, explained, and defined in terms of a cluster of properties, few if any of which are *necessarily* connected to the concept. These properties are more commonly just criteria for the concepts, correctly said to be part of their meaning, but not necessarily connected to it. In some scientific cases, temperature being a well-known example, the concept at one point may have been "defined" in a certain way and thus briefly appear to be fully specified in terms of a set of necessary and sufficient conditions, but subsequent events clearly demonstrate that its full meaning extended far beyond the supposed definition, which consequently had to be revised— several times. Thus, coming to understand the significance of Wittgenstein's language games overpowered Moore's attempted proof of fallacy. Hence, 'good' might be naturalistically definable even though not logically equivalent to any determinate (finite[8]) set of naturalistic properties.

And there is a more complex point involved. The main reason that there is no naturalistic equivalent of 'good' is not because of the fallacy of thinking that Moore's hypothetical equation was the condition for meaning equivalence, but because the term is learnt only in context: we learn what makes X good, for a thousand Xs, not by learning what good is and combining that with our understanding of what X is. Good, by itself, is a function word, not an abbreviation for a set of properties; it simply reminds us of that second set of properties for each X, the set that we have learnt increases its merit or quality or value or worth, A good apple, for example, is one that lacks worms and bruises—but worms and bruises are not part of the definition of apple. (However, it's true that we tend to learn at least a little about what makes a good X along with learning what makes an X, so the notions are often genetically connected, at a simple level).

This logical point is of great importance in the practice of evaluation, since the first step in many evaluation projects is to unpack the meritorious variant of the concept of which the subject of the evaluation[9] is an instance—a health clinic, a curriculum innovation, a drunk-driving policy—into its constituent criteria, which can then be tied to empirical indicators for field investigation. And in doing this, we often need highly specialized knowledge, because knowing what makes a good clinic, for example, requires knowing what equipment it needs, and you don't learn much about that when you learn what a clinic is. That's partly because the needed equipment changes as medicine changes, and part of the utility of 'good' is that it's a pointer term that points us towards getting these updates.

[8] A finite list seems to be the relevant consideration, since Moore's argument loses plausibility if the list is not finite.

[9] The term for whatever is being evaluated is 'evaluand.'

Hence, it's perfectly possible for 'good' to refer only to naturalistic properties even though no finite list of them is possible in the abstract because it's a different list for each evaluand and the list of evaluands is indefinitely extensible, hence not determinate.

However, since many criteria of merit are not themselves naturalistic—for example, the criteria of merit for arguments—the project is impossible for other reasons. The bottom line is that 'good' is a concept that is analyzable into everyday functional concepts, not a referent to some transcendental property.[10] So the naturalistic fallacy provides, for more than one reason, no argument against the possibility of rational evaluation. Note that many people were and are influenced into abandoning or even ridiculing the value-free doctrine for a completely different reason, based on a total misunderstanding of the doctrine. It was argued, notably by political radicals of the 1960s and 1970s, who were rightly incensed by the discovery that social scientists had been providing technical help to dictatorships in South America, that the idea of value-free science was absurd because scientists were obviously affected by their own values in their choice of careers, and their choice of applications of their work. But of course no one arguing for the value-free doctrine had ever suggested the contrary; the doctrine is about keeping the inner workings of science—its inferences, its data, etc.—free from value judgments. Having motives for doing or applying science is obviously universal, and would not be denied by anyone with a college degree; the idea that science could not justify evaluative conclusions was entirely different and supported by arguments that looked good to good scientists.

The argument against objectivity is even less formidable. It is normally based on the claim that no one is without bias, often supported by the previous argument that scientists often have evident political biases. However, that premise does not imply that no group, e.g., a group of scientists or historians in a particular field of expertise, including those with a wide range of political and ethical preferences, is incapable of generating claims that we can have good reason to believe to be objective. The counterargument, which is an induction from the historically common discovery of bias even in such bodies of claims, does no more to support skepticism than the analogous argument supports it about the truth of similarly supported claims such as the claim that vaccination against smallpox works very well. Of course, the skeptic's argument does support constant vigilance and avoidance of overconfidence, but these are already ensconced as primary imperatives in the scientific attitude. We are often wrong, even when we had been certain, but 'often', although it

---

[10] Or, if you like this phrasing better, it refers to a non-naturalistic concept that is epistemologically on a par with the concept of a dimension, i.e., a property that is mildly abstracted from a set of naturalistic properties (length, width, etc.).

refers to a numerically large number of cases, refers only to a minute fraction of the cases where due diligence supports a firm conclusion. So this argument is simply an illicit exaggeration of a bad statistical inference; or, if you prefer, a misunderstanding of the meaning of claims of truth or objectivity.

Which brings us to the topic-specific logic of evaluation, that is, to the logic underlying practical reasoning in the field. It involves two levels of generality, corresponding roughly to the levels distinguished in ethics as normative ethics and metaethics. We'll begin with the more abstract level, which is the effort to convey the general nature of (professional) evaluation. Historically, this has mostly meant program evaluation, since that is the sub-area in which most of the theorizing has been done, but we'll look at the answers (a few of them) in terms of their accuracy for all areas.

4. Conceptions and misconceptions of evaluation

In the development of the various branches of evaluation, most of them intensely practical in their aims, very little crosspollination has occurred. This is partly due to the bizarre episode in the history of thought we have already discussed, where evaluation was tabooed by the mistaken ideal of "value-free social science". This ban on the legitimacy of any kind of evaluation of course deterred any efforts to develop a general theory if taken seriously in areas like medicine and engineering, where many of the workaday tasks were largely evaluative—no-one supposed that the doctor should not make recommendations about your diet or medications, even though they were of course evaluative. And it was not taken seriously in, for example, personnel and performance evaluation, where the name of the game was to a large extent to provide better ways to select the best applicants or candidates for promotion or discharge. But it was taken seriously enough in mainstream sociology, where it originated with Max Weber, in political science, in much of social psychology, as well as in many departments of psychology, to scare almost everyone away from serious treatment of serious social problems, which of course is heavily dependent on the evaluation of the proposed solutions. This made them largely useless where needed most; but since the practical demand was great, the opponents of evaluation did propose what amounted to a behaviorist surrogate for serious evaluation, one that could be found in almost every text for many decades in mid-twentieth century social science. The grip of this surrogate was so strong that even today one frequently hears or sees it proposed online as the right way to go about (social) program evaluation. The suggestion was simple enough, and goes like this: (i) identify the goals of the program; (ii) convert them to behavioral objectives (or as near as you can get to that); (iii) find or create tests for measuring the behaviors specified in those objectives; (iv) test the program participants to see if they have achieved these objectives; (v) analyze the results to see if they have, in which case the program is successful; if not, it has failed.

The absurdity of this suggestion would have been obvious if anyone had been thinking about the general logic of evaluation, because everyone does product evaluation all the time and everyone knows that you don't evaluate products against the intents of their makers but against the needs of their users or prospective users (see any issue of *Consumer Reports*). But the surviving evaluators were hiding out in their own silos, so the absurdity was not apparent for a long time. There are half a dozen flaws in the "goalachievement model" of evaluation. Getting to the goals may only show they were set too low, not that the program was worthwhile. Not getting to them may only show they were set too high, not that the program wasn't marvelous. The goals may be immoral, or they may be irrelevant to the needs of those served. Getting to goals that are perfectly matched to needs may still represent a trivial achievement; or it may be important, but overshadowed by side-effects, whose existence is not mentioned in this model for doing evaluation. Doing wonderful things is boring from the practical point of view if it costs far too much; or if the costs were moderate, if it could have been done another way for less. Doing even a little good may be worthwhile if it cost very little. And so on, and on.[11]

Goals are for guiding action; for planning and managing. They are not the key issue for evaluators—as ethicists have long noted in their territory, "the road to hell is paved with good intentions"—although they are something that must be commented on at some point in an evaluation. The key issue for program evaluators is the effects the program actually has, measured in terms of what they mean to those you affected (and those you did not reach), whether or not you meant to have those effects; plus how much it costs to do what you did do; and what alternatives there were; and how you got to where you got (since the end does not justify all means); and other things, e.g., the potential uses of the program by contrast with the uses under examination.

The introduction of "goal-free evaluation" and the demonstration that it was feasible and in significant ways superior to "goal-attainment evaluation" finally established—but only in the community of professional evaluators who keep up with the subject's development—that the goal-based approach was just a reflection of the fact that program evaluation mainly began as an effort funded by program managers and planners, whose interest was of

---

[11] See "Hard-Won Lessons in Program Evaluation" by the present author in *New Directions in Program Evaluation*, Summer 1993, (Jossey-Bass), whole issue.

course mainly in whether their goals had been met.[12] Ethically, and to an increasing extent politically, the consumer's point of view must be taken as primary.

However, the main threat to establishing evaluation as a respectable subject, or profession, or discipline, was much more fundamental: it was the claim that for basic logical reasons, there could never be a scientific or indeed a rational basis for evaluative conclusions, and we've already looked at those arguments.

Once program evaluation got past the barrier of the value-free doctrine, following personnel and performance evaluation (the latter being the category into which all student testing falls), and the cartoonlike effort of the goal-achievement model, it began to generate many justificatory accounts of the real nature of evaluation. These began with the relatively simple checklist models like the CIPP (Context, Input, Process, Product) model and went on in three directions. One of them led to more sophisticated checklists, e.g., the still-primitive DAC model used widely in international aid evaluation, and the Key Evaluation Checklist from me (on line). Another led to the formulation of national standards for program evaluation—a formidable and impressive project. The third was less structured, and led to a long and still-expanding list of original and interesting "models" ranging from the goal-free approach, through the "advocate-adversary" model based on the legal metaphor, to the more recent participatory, collaborative, and empowerment models (involving increasing amounts of involvement of the evaluees as partners or authors in evaluating themselves or their programs), and the "appreciative inquiry" approach (which strives to emphasize a more constructive approach than the common critical one seen as leading to much of the negative reaction to the use of evaluation in many organizations). Many articles and several books have been devoted to taxonomies and critiques of these models, so I will omit almost all of them, but recommend those discussions for those interested in how a new discipline seeks to rationalize and reform its own processes.[13]

---

[12] See *"Prose and Cons About Goal-Free Evaluation", in *Evaluation Comment*, December, 1972, Center for the Study of Evaluation, University of California in Los Angeles. Reprinted in *Evaluation Studies Review Annual*, Vol. 1, Gene Glass, ed., Sage Publications, August, 1976; reprinted in Hamilton, D., Jenkins, D., King, C., MacDonald, B., and Parlett, Michael., eds., *Beyond the Numbers Game: A Reader in Educational Evaluation*, Macmillan, 1977, pp. 130–171.

[13] A recent and one of the best of these is: *Evaluation Theory, Models, and Applications* by Daniel L. Stufflebeam and Anthony J. Shinkfield, Jossey-Bass, April, 2007, and Dan's 2018 update of the CIPP model.

We have already covered two such models (three if one counts the transdisciplinary account as a model) and it is worth looking at what is probably the most popular common model today, since it is based on a misconception that may be as serious as the goal-based error. According to this model, referred to in the United States as the logic model approach, and in the United Kingdom often called the realist or realistic approach, evaluations should begin with and to some extent (or a large extent, or completely, depending on the author) be based on an account of how the program works (or is supposed to work, according to other authors). To cut to the bottom line of a refutation, this looks as if it's based on a simple confusion of the aim of evaluation with the aim of explanation. The strong counter-examples are from the evaluation of medicine, where we were evaluating aspirin for fifty years without the slightest idea of how it worked; or from the evaluation of claimed faith-healing, where the supposed explanation is supernatural intervention, but the evaluation can proceed entirely without commitment for or against that view. However, these counter-examples have not proved persuasive so far, and it is possible that this is because there are more subtle benefits to be reaped from the logic model approach. It goes without saying that it would be a notable benefit if the evaluator could in fact provide explanations of whatever it is that s/he finds—success or failure.

But that's absurdly ambitious since in many cases where an evaluation is called for, e.g., in investigating a new approach to reducing melanoma or juvenile delinquency, the best experts in the field have been unable to determine an acceptable explanation. And explanation is at best a side-effect of the main goal that, in this case, should dominate the investigation, which is to determine whether success or failure occurred (more accurately, to determine the kind and extent of the benefits or damage wrought). Moreover, it is not true that having an explanation of X's effects makes a substantial contribution to the evaluation of X in a particular context, since we may know how X works but not know whether its effects were net positive or negative, or even how large they are, in this context or even in general. So the explanation is not only not necessary for evaluation, but not sufficient for—not even substantially contributory to—evaluation.

The potential costs of this approach are considerable. They run from simply wasting some resources on explanation-hunting to spending so much time and/or other resources on this hunt that one fails to do the evaluation task at all. It's hard to avoid the conclusion that the evaluators favoring this approach are driven by the urge to make a significant contribution to explanatory science, perhaps because many of them were originally trained in a scientific field, and a lack of understanding of the difference between the two enterprises.

There are other interesting efforts at conceptualizing evaluation, of which perhaps the most interesting ones now popular refer to the spectrum encouraging some degree of participation of the staff of the program or design team responsible for a program or product. The benefits of this approach are access to data and insights not always made available to the external evaluator, increased "buy-in" and hence better implementation of findings, and reduced anxiety/opposition to the evaluative effort. Costs of this approach depend on the degree of shared responsibility and co-vary with that, along the dimensions of credibility, utility, validity, and ethicality (the latter comes in since the targeted consumers, and other impacted groups, are still not involved in the usual versions of these models).

But now it's time to move on to the more specific level of evaluation: procedural logic.

5. The basic logic of evaluation

5.1 Types of value claim

It is important to distinguish half a dozen of these types since each of them requires somewhat different data to support it, and each legitimates somewhat different conclusions. We begin with: *(i) Personal preferences (wants).* Often offered as the paradigm of value claims, in order to denigrate them, these are in fact the least important from the point of view of professional evaluation. Nevertheless, it should be absolutely clear that, although paradigmatically subjective in the purely descriptive sense, these claims are entirely objective in the evaluative sense that they make an intersubjectively testable and hence scientifically respectable claim. The evidence we all use to verify or falsify them is of two main kinds: evidence bearing on the veracity of the claimant, and behavioral evidence of the obvious kind. If, for example, someone claims to prefer classic literature to contemporary fiction, we expect to see their library and their movie-going reflect that taste, of course as a norm from which not only exceptions but general deviations can be justified without refuting their claim—and we know the difference between a justification and a cover-up for a lie. This type of claim is extremely important in the logic of evaluation because it can provide the main value premise required for support of evaluative conclusions with exactly the same circle of applicability as the premise, namely the person or people said to have the preferences. In order to give people advice about, for example, the best car for them to buy, or the best investments for them to make, expert advisers need input about their preferences. Now, when groups of people share certain preferences, we can often move to an even more objective form of value premise, namely...

(ii) Market value. This kind of value has a specific legal status and definition[14] that references the verification procedure, so it is not only objective but quantitative.

But the market value is not the most important value; in many cases, an expert adviser will say, "Well, there's no doubt that the market value of this property is X, but it's seriously overpriced—we can find you a much better value, in fact a better property for less money." That is, there's something that we refer to as the "real" value that is sometimes, not always, different from market value. This has other names, e.g., ...

(iii) Real, true, essential value. This is a theoretical construct based on abstracting from the properly established criteria of merit for an evaluand. When we talk of a change as "really significant" or a doctoral thesis as "truly excellent," we are stressing that a truly careful evaluation will reveal the result we are claiming. This sense of value is the one that professional evaluation seeks to uncover, and it is the one that evaluation as a discipline is all about, just as the "real truth" is what the professional journalist or scientist seeks. To reach it, we usually have to assemble a number of values and a number of facts, and integrate (synthesize) them in a way that calls on a couple more types of value. The first of these is:

(iv) Public value. Public values are the kind to which we appeal when we are trying to establish the m/w/s of some evaluand (a program, product, or person) in a way that will be intersubjectively acceptable, as for example when it is to be paid for with public money, or is intended to receive public acknowledgment for its m/w/s.

There are many species of these, including legal, ethical, cultural, logical, scientific, educational, historical, professional, and expert values, and the context determines which one(s) it will be relevant to consider. (The name for these is intended to suggest the contrast with private or misleading values, e.g., personal preferences.) However, public values are general in nature, and in order to pin down an evaluative conclusion of the required specificity, we often—although not always—need a refinement of them, as follows:

(v) Standards and requirements. Standards are specific levels or amounts of public values that are set for certain evaluative or practical purposes. Some public values are so essentially tied to action that they are themselves referred to and formulated as standards—a good example is safety standards, which are normally expressed in exact terms, e.g., "A fire extinguisher of type X must be located and visible in standard working conditions within five feet of

---

[14] In the real estate market, one definition is: The most probable price (in terms of money) which a property should bring in a competitive and open market under all conditions requisite to a fair sale, the buyer and seller each acting prudently and knowledgeably, and assuming the price is not affected by undue stimulus.

each machine operator's normal location." But in many cases, the standards will be context dependent, and stated for specific evaluative tasks or contexts, for example: "An A on this test will require a mark of 85%." (The formulation of a set of standards like this one, covering all grades, is called a rubric.)

The preceding five categories are the main types of value, but there are a couple more that should be mentioned to avoid confusion.

(vi) Contextual values. There are many contexts in which a statement of bare empirical fact has evaluative significance. (This is one reason why the facts vs. values dichotomy is misleading.) It is a "mere" statement of fact that someone has just broken the world record for the hundred-meter dash, but of course it's also a statement about the m/w/s of the event and the sprinter. Hence, in an argument, it may be entirely appropriate to address the evaluative component of the statement rather than the factual one, e.g., by pointing out that the track was an exceptionally favorable one and the new record was only a hundredth of a second better than the previous one, set on an ancient track.

(vii) Illustrative and exemplary value. When someone talks of the "perfect crime" or the "perfect storm" they are not suggesting that the crime or the storm are ideal events in themselves, but only that they are ideal examples of their kind; Aristotle discussed the case of the "good thief" in the same way.

Now we need to look at the basic evaluative operations, and distinguish them.

We are all loosely familiar with them, but the exact definitions of the terms when used precisely are rarely quoted correctly, and once again, they need to be carefully distinguished because the data and analysis required to answer an evaluative request for any one of them is essentially different from that required for any other. (Note that the same names as below are used for analogous non-evaluative operations, and sometimes it's not clear which is intended.)

5.2 Types of evaluative operation

The following material may seem to duplicate what is found in educational measurement texts, but a careful reading will reveal that the focus here on evaluation leads to significant differences. Educational measurement is still taught as closely analogous to measurement in the physical sciences, but it is crucially different in that educational measurement is usually supposed to be measuring something of value, and that task requires specific and more complex consideration. We distinguish four basic operations, and add two refinements.

(i) Ranking or ordering (the term 'ordering' is more commonly used for non-evaluative tasks such as placing in order of height). Placing evaluands in order of m/w/s: strict ranking allows no ties (evaluands with the same rank), while weak ranking allows some ties, sometimes allowing only a small number of them (this number should be specified), and more commonly allowing only a small number of evaluands at the same rank (this number should also be specified). An evaluand's rank has no meaning except for its relative ordering against the other ranked evaluands. Ranking is the key operation for evaluative tasks like choosing which alternative to adopt in decision-making, which product to buy, who it to get prizes or scholarships or assistance. Note that the top-ranked evaluand in a set may have negligible merit, and the lowest-ranked may be superb (not in the same set, however). Note also that a ranking may be partial, i.e., the best or worst sub-set may be ranked and the others simply listed as "of lower/higher rank"; they are not of course tied. (This is not the same as an incomplete grading, where the remainder is of unknown rank, and therefore the ranks of those ranked so far are only tentative; contrast this with incomplete grading (below). Note also that ranking is automatically exhaustive, cf. grading.

Gap-ranking. This is a useful variant of ranking where an indication of the size of the interval between evaluands is given in addition to their rank order. This is common in horse-racing ("X is the winner by three lengths, Y next by a head from Z, who is third by a nose", etc.). Gap estimates can often be provided with considerable practical benefit in other cases, telling the buyer for example, that taking the runner-up at a much lower price would be a good buy, or that in an election where our candidate loses, that it was "very close". When scores are involved, we can often give precise quantitative measures of the intervals.

(ii) Grading. This is the operation of placing evaluands in one of a set of categories (the grades) which are defined in three ways: (a) each evaluand in a particular grade is superior in terms of X (the evaluative property within the large group of properties indicating m/s/w that is being used as the basis for grading) to all in a lower grade, and inferior to all in higher grades; (b) each grade is named with a term that has some degree of independent meaning in the vocabulary of m/s/w, a meaning that must of course be consistent with condition (a); (c) the set of grades is exhaustive, i.e., all evaluands are included in one or another. Of course, there can be unlimited ties in a graded group, by contrast with (all strict and most weak) rankings. The most familiar example of a set of grades is perhaps the set A through F (in the U.S.) A though E (in the U.K.), or the roughly equivalent sets such as Excellent / Very good / Good / Marginally acceptable / Unacceptable). Note that condition (b) is violated by the so-called "grading on the curve" procedure, which is log-

ically self-contradictory and ethically abhorrent (since those "failed" by the curve's definition may in fact have done acceptable work)[15]. Note also that a set of grades must be exhaustive, i.e., so defined as to cover all probable cases.

Note also that a partial and incomplete grading should not require any reconsideration when it is completed, since grades are determinate predicates, all of whose relevant conditions are considered when the grade is awarded, unlike ranking.

The essential difference between ranking and grading is that neither can do the job of the other. Each adds something to the story the other tells: the grade adds the "absolute reference" to a set of external standards; the rank adds the inter-evaluand comparison element absent in grading (if the ranking is not too weak). Each provides answers to questions the other cannot answer: ranking answers the quest for the best and the better; grading answers the quest for true quality, good enough quality, etc.

Profiling. A variant of grading, with great evaluative utility. A profile can be constructed of either an evaluand, in which case it shows strengths and weaknesses, a good way to express the results of an evaluation in a graphically direct way (or a simple table); or it may be the profile of a consumer or market or community, where it will show the relative importance of their wants or needs. The graphical version is a vertical bar graph of an evaluand, one on which each bar represents one of the criteria of merit. (More details in the following section.)

Part of the importance of a profile is that it avoids the need, when evaluating something, to convert the result into a single overall scale, in order to give a single grade to the evaluand. To do that, one must determine the rela-

---

[15] Grading on the curve was and is an example of the extremes to which the value-free adherents (or quantitative enthusiasts) were prepared to go in order to avoid actually making a judgment of quality. It is often defended as an acceptable way of avoiding the errors of "subjective" judgments of quality in large classes, but of course its validity depends on three weak assumptions—that classes do not vary significantly from time to time, and that the test is of unvarying difficulty, and impregnable security. Granted there are substantial interinstructor variations in the definitions of grade quality amongst random samples of faculty, it has long been known how to reduce them to minor dimensions, so continuing to use grading on the curve is a confession of inadequate training of faculty. And ultimately it was a futile gesture, since it depended on scoring, which depends on the fundamental judgment of quality in the allocation of every single point on the scale, e.g., in the judgment that a correct answer to the nth question on the test is worth m points. When the test is multiple-choice and each question is allocated one point, it's obvious that this judgment is false for almost every test, so this is hardly a valid foundation on which to build a test grade.

tive importance of the dimensions of merit, a requirement that is sometimes extremely difficult to justify. While a profile thus provides a multi-dimensional portrayal of a multi-dimensional reality, it isn't good enough if what the evaluative question requires is a ranking, a single winner for the best car to buy or the best proposal to fund or the valedictorian. Then the evaluator must do the reduction to a single scale, usually by appeal to the profile of the relevant consumers/users/voters.

(iii) Scoring. The application of a m/w/s measurement scale to the evaluand(s).

This is the quantitative approach to evaluation, sometimes the best approach, often impossible, quite often absurd. The best case is exemplified in the evaluation of athletic performances where the stopwatch is the measuring instrument, and can be used, in conjunction with suitable rubrics and databases,[16] to yield both ranking and grading. The absurdity shows up in the faculty handbooks used in some major universities where the faculty are instructed to award grades based on scores in some specific way, e.g., "The grade of A is to be given if and only if the student's mark on a course is between 85% and 100%." But as every faculty member in the humanities knows very well, this is an absurd suggestion since essay tests are the norm there, and it is much more appropriate— and is the standard practice, regardless of what the handbook says—to give the answers a grade rather than a score and calculate or estimate a weighted average of the grades in order to get the test grade (which are in turn cumulated to get the course grade). It is also invalid where it is normally used, in science and math courses, since it rests on the assumption that all items (and other scored assignments) are of equal difficulty, a highly unrealistic assumption. Getting 86% on a test may be a sign of a middle B, even a C, or an A , depending on the test's difficulty and the response's originality, presentation, etc. as everyone knows. But some administrator with a quantitative obsession wrote the handbook, so—if the faculty (or students, or alums) knew anything about the logic of evaluation—this regulation would make the institution look absurd. But, since it's often been there for half a century, one should probably conclude that the conditional does not apply.

(iv) Apportioning. This is the fourth and last of the basic evaluative operation we'll distinguish. It involves the distribution or allocation of valuable resources to a set of evaluands in a way that reflects their relative m/w/s. A good example is the distribution by a department head between the members

---

[16] And, in serious athletic competition, a recently calibrated altimeter, since the international athletic associations have determined the extent to which altitude must be used to discount athletic performance that is to be considered for world or country record status.

of the department of a sum of money, S, allocated to the department for merit raises. If one can find a valid measure of their relative merit on a scale of, say, 1 to 10, possibly the most plausible way to do this would be to add up the total of all their scores on this scale—let's call the result M—and allocate the nth member of the department, whose own score is N, N/M x S. This is a simple case of the general problem of portfolio construction. In the more difficult case of constructing a solution when your investment is to be into a number of stocks or bonds or other investments, each of which has different profiles of probable performance in different respects (safety, short-term income, long-term growth, etc.) and given your own profile of values for each of these aspects of performance, there is no publicly known algorithm of any real plausibility, although investment managers at large funds undoubtedly have their own strategies based on massive trials of computer models. So the portfolio evaluator has no ideal against which to compare actual cases.

However, there are a number of ways not to do it, and one can at least learn to avoid them. A simple example of these, on a related problem, is this: if the total organization budget is cut from S to 90% of S in a later year, a common error is to think that an across the board cut of 10% in the submitted department budgets would be an appropriate, perhaps even the most "fair" response. It is a bad response because it simply rewards those who have padded their budgets the most, and will encourage that response in future years from smart department heads. The correct first step in a response to the budget cut problem is to trim all budgets to the same standards of economical use of resources, albeit imprecisely.

6. Refining the evaluative tools

The vertical scales of a profile can just show units of measurement for each dimension (criterion) but more usefully, after conversion using the standards (rubrics) for each dimension (these are available since it's usually a value), it shows their grades on a single common scale, the vertical axis. We may take these to be A through F, for discussion purposes; here can add two or three useful refinements to this representation.

First, we can mark what are called "bars" on these scales, whether in their raw or evaluative form. The most important bar is a horizontal line showing any absolute minimum value (on the raw scale) or grade (on the converted scale) that must be attained.

For example, if we are profiling the qualifications of a candidate for a staff position where fluency in Spanish is absolutely necessary, we put a bar under B, or A (for fluency equivalent to a native speaker) across the scale referring to Spanish competency. Of course only some scales have bars, and in a particular case all or none might be barred.

Bars must be very carefully applied, since failing to clear the bar on any scale eliminates the candidate from any further consideration, no matter how well they score on other dimensions. (For this reason, dimensions without bars are sometimes called "compensatory".) Because of the power of bars, when evaluating a new candidate it is usually good practice to start by checking the barred dimensions (called "autonomous"), since it will save time (and favors) to find failings there first.

In addition to bars on particular scales, there may be a holistic bar. For example, in admitting a candidate to graduate school in a doctoral program, one may require certain minimum scores on the GRE math scale, a masters degree from a certified college, and a 3.5 grade point average across their courses in that degree program; but one may also be unwilling to admit a candidate who just scrapes over all the bars. This bar might translate as requiring a B average on all dimensions considered, and can be shown on the evaluative profile as a dotted horizontal line at that grade level across the whole chart, meaning that average is required.

For some (rare) purposes, it may be useful to also use a "high bar" on some scale meaning one that if cleared, implies that the evaluand is to be admitted, appointed, or purchased, regardless of their score on all other scales. This has been called the "Einstein bar" meaning that if Einstein applied for a position at your university in any year after 1905 (the "anna mirabilis" when he published several papers each of which is often said to have been deserving of a Nobel prize in itself) he would be judged as clearing the high bar on the scale of research competency and thereby bypass any consideration of his performance on the other two bars on which faculty candidates are assessed (teaching and service).

Second, one can also show differential weights on a profile, representing the differential importance of various dimensions if this is something that needs to be represented. For example, an undergraduate college might consider teaching to be twice as important as research or service, and show this by doubling the width of the teaching column. Using this device, the best candidate then shows up as the one with the largest area under their profile (the line through the points representing their achievement on each dimension) rather than the one with the highest average score (as long as the profile does not dip below the minimum bar on any scale). It should be noted however, that validating differential weights is extremely difficult (it requires deciding whether teaching should be twice as important as research, 50% more important, three times as important, etc.).

In evaluating programs, the five key bars—analogous to the three used in evaluating faculty—used in the Key Evaluation Checklist approach are process, outcomes, cost, comparisons, and generalizability, and the first four have minimum bars on them. Of course, the details turn out to be where the professional skills come in, and a minimalist expansion of these runs 12,000 words at the Checklists in Evaluation website, i.e., 50% more than this paper (under Tools and Resources at evaluation.wmich.edu).[17]

By giving details on the profiling refinements, we have in fact done a good deal of work on one of the great methodological problems unique to evaluation, the synthesis problem—how to combine the "factual premises" with the value premises.

7. Conclusion

It is perhaps best to conclude by mentioning something interesting still on the table, so here is one example of material not approached here but falling under the article's title.

There is currently a major war going on in evaluation circles over the single question of how outcomes are to be determined in program evaluation, that is, it concerns only one sub-topic of one of the five main criteria for one subdivision of evaluation. This dispute has brought in the entire literature on causation, and the outcome of it will determine the use of at least five billion dollars a year of direct expenditure.[18] So this article is only an introduction to its subject, but it may be enough to suggest to people seriously interested in the domains of critical thinking/informal logic, and the philosophy of the social sciences, the serious possibility that evaluation now constitutes an area in which some mapping has been done, some value has resulted, and important work remains unfinished.

The title of this essay refers to the "unruly" logic of evaluation. Why not just call it "mixed methods"? Because none of the methods in the mix is tidy; and because there is something else involved that's quite different from what's involved in the mixed methods as currently conceived. That "something more" is the method of linguistic microanalysis that is buried in the Wittgensteinian approach, as refined by the Oxbridge efforts of the 1950s and thereafter. To formulate and validate an account of this approach and its link to the process of reasoning to evaluative conclusions, I believe one

---

[17] There are a dozen texts on the market that expand on evaluation at greater length, of which the one by E. Jane Davidson (*Evaluation Methodology Basics: The Nuts and Bolts of Sound Evaluation*) sticks closest to a serious logic of evaluation approach and is not exclusively focused on program evaluation.

[18] Some further discussion of this topic will be found in the reference in note 5 above.

has to reanalyze the concepts of definition and translation and thence reconsider abductive and probative inference—tasks for another day. Or two. The results, if successful, might be called the "paralogic" of evaluation. Till then, "unruly".

About the author:

Michael Scriven was born in the United Kingdom, went to Australia from age 12 through a BA & MA at Melbourne in honors math. Returning to Oxford, he received a D.Phil. in philosophy (thesis on explanation theory). He then held appointments (about four years each) at Minnesota, Swarthmore and Indiana; did summer teaching at Wesleyan and Harvard; did research in primatology in Austria; and two Institutions for Advance Study (on democracy and on the behavioral sciences). Next he spent 12 years at Berkeley, with eventually a split appointment between philosophy and education. He left UCB to start an institution for evaluation research at the University of San Francisco; ran an evaluation consulting business; was a Professor of Psychology at Claremont Graduate University; served was co-head of the School of Education at the University of Western Australia for twelve years; now back at Claremont as co-director of the Claremont Evaluation Center.

Index

A

abduction Ch. 20 *passim* ...
  big heavenly bodies 337
  subconscious 330
  successful 335
  abductive inference 331, 335, 337
  abductive inference schema 331, 340f.
abstraction, principle of 138
acceptability 19, 186, 200f. 203, 261f., 272-274, 287
Acceptability, Relevance & Sufficiency 200
actions performed by definitions 260f
Adams, John Couch 337
advice to teachers 32
advocating a meaning, definition 263f.
Agora 244
algorithmic search 229
algorithmic studies 232, 241
Allen, Derek [Ch. 3], 38, 49
ambiguity 16, 130, 214, 264, 315, 342
American Philosophical Association 15n2
Amsterdam school 173
Anselm 104
antonym definition 257
argument, arguments ...
  argument₁ 88, 91
  argument₂ 88ff.
  construction, teaching 51-55
  concept of [Ch. 9]
  context of 77f.
  convergent vs. linked 144, 146f., 272, 327
  deductive, deductively 142, 176, 196, 198f., 202f., 215, 272, 286, 327
  inductive inference 33ff., 259f., 335

  interpreting 17, 86, 93f., 149, 191
  judging [Ch 13] 21, 94, 153, 192, 246
  linked 142-145
  making 181f., 185-187
  mapping [Ch. 10] 34, 115-118, 124, 135, 191, 193 ...
    computer-aided 117f., 120
    history of 146f.
    software 122, 131
  mining [Ch.11] 104, 171, 173 ...
    multi-layered 135, 138
  multiple 194
  theory of [Ch. 9] 330
  uses of argument 102
  senses of the word 38, 87f., 92, 101f.
  as rational persuasion 102
  pro and con 75-77
  reason-claim complexes 91-92
  recursive 107, 166-168, 177, 250
  restatement of 197
  simple 102, 105
  strength of 78
  types of 154-156, 172, 175, 199
  weighing & balancing 79-80
argumentation 92-93
artificial intelligence 153, 171f.,176
Aristotle 187, 209, 215, 217, 219, 307
ARSD standards 274, 283, 286f.
assumption 9-11, 18-20, 23. 53, 128, 141, 143, 148, 174, 186, 196, 227, 244, 366n15
associated conditional 195f.
Assisted Dying example 72ff
audience 19, 21, 52, 89, 140f., 181-188, 209f., 215, 220, 275 ...
  adapting to 185

B

Bailin, Sharon [Ch. 7], 30, 81
Barnett, Ashley [Ch. 10], 85
Battersby, Mark [Chs. 7, 18], 30, 81, 305
Bayesian network model 149
bCisive^{TM} 148
Beardsley, Monroe 146
belief-worthiness of scientific claims 296
behavioral targeting 235
bias 8, 15, 22, 155, 170, 232, 237, 240-242,244,
     253-256, 282f., 286, 295, 200, 303, 311, 357f
Black, Max 255
Blair, J. Anthony [Chs. 2, 8, 13], 31, 35, 87, 104,
     177, 191, 200, 203, 272, 288, 345
Blair, June xii
Blue Feed/Red Feed 234f.
Bowell, Tracy [Ch. 5], 29, 57f., 59
burden of proof 55, 77, 79, 159, 178, 182-184,
     187, 193, 212, 218

C

Checklists 370
cluster random sampling 279
Carneades 149, 244
cognitive environment 201, 241f.
compromise 61ff.
computer-aided argument mapping [Ch. 10] 35
conditional 38, 47, 109n8, 130-132, 159, 196f.,
     315-317, 367 ...
     material conditional 316., 319f.
     subjunctive conditional 334
confidence level (polling) 277f.
conjunction(s) 123, 172, 195, 315
consensus 14f., 62, 78, 291-295, 297f., 301
consistency 138f., 155, 159, 265f., 297n4, 321,
     328
Consumer Reports 359
content dimension of definition 264-267
contextual values 364

contingent proposition, truth 318, 341
contradiction 47, 312, 318,
contradictory 313, 321,
contrary(ies) 321
controversy(ies) 89
Comey, James 96-98
co-premises 118, 127, 133, 141-145, 149
counterexample(s) 52, 207, 273, 361
credible claims, information 78, 238f., 289-292
credible experts 158
credible sources 290f., 297, 301, 303f.
credibility 291, 297
critical 34
critical spirit 12
critical thinker 12, 21, 23f., 32, 91, 94, 194, 227,
     231, 237f., 240 ...
     active vs. passive 7f.
     character trait 8
     dispositions 21f., 61
     moved by reasons 12
critical thinking abilities 8f.
critical thinking and ...
     argument 16, 93f.
     communications 16, 20-24, 95-96, 227f., 231,
          243, 329
     creative thinking 19, 22-24
     criteria 13, 15, 18f., 22, 74, 78, 94, 98
     evaluation [Ch. 21], 191, 206, 217, 237, 242,
          244, 272, 289, 303
     good thinking 15, 21, 24
     information 9, 16f., 21, 96f., 118, 120, 213,
          228, 230, 232, 249, 262, 289, 299, 303, 336
     logic [Ch. 19], 307ff., 312, 322f.
     observation 16, 20, 355
     persistence, care 22, 57, 80
     rationality 12, 183, 243, 329f., 327
critical thinking as ...
     active thinking 7, 16, 18, 20, 32, 80, 95
     cognitive skill 15
     a disposition 3, 8-10, 17, 21ff., 61, 237f., 254
     fair-mindedness 9, 10, 11n1,

metacognition 16, 237
sensitivity to context 13
self-regulation 20, 57-59
a skill Ch. 1 *passim*, 8, 10-13, 15-24
critical thinking attitudes 12, 15, 32, 61
critico-creative thinking 22f.
definitions of critical thinking ...
Delphi definition 15
Dewey's 7
Ennis's 9
Fisher and Scriven's 16
Lipman's 13
Paul's 11
strong sense 10ff., 13
weak sense 10f., 12
Woods's 329f.
tests of critical thinking 8

D

Dai, Yiwen [Ch. 17], 288
Davies, Martin [Ch. 10], 85
debate 88-89
definition actions 249
definition content 249
definition forms 250
Dewey, John 7f., 14 ...
definition of critical thinking 7
deliberation 61
Delphi Method 15f., 21 ...
Delphi definition of critical thinking 15
dialectical tier 272-274
dimensions of a definition 249
dispute 88
Duckman, Ellen xii

E

Eemeren, Frans H. van 154, 173, 182, 196, 199n3

Ennis, Robert H. [Ch 16], 6, 9f., 14, 17, 22, 196, 270 ...
definition of critical thinking 9
entailment 38, 308, 322-324, 327
epistemic authority 289f.
equivalence 267, 320 ...
meaning equivalence 356
equivalent expression definition 253-255
essential value (see also real, true value) 363
evaluation [Ch. 21] ...
checklists 360, 370
criteria of merit 357, 366, 370
defined 351
goal achievement model 359
goal free 359
intra-disciplinary 352
logic model approach 361
meta-evaluation 352
paralogic of 371
performance evaluation 253
personal preference 355
personnel evaluation 352
policy analysis 352
portfolio evaluation 352
program evaluation 352
proposal evaluation352
transdiscipline 352f.
evaluation operations ...
apportioning 367
gap-ranking 365
grading 365
ordering 365
profiling 236, 366, 368, 370
ranking 365
evidence-based approach to teaching 31-33
expert teachers 32
experiments 280 ...
vs. polls & surveys 280
experience 300 ...
maturation experience 282
expertise 282, 297-301, 351 ...

and argument 325

explanatory coherence 343

extended synonym definition 256

external validity 281, 283

F

Facebook *Demetrictor* 242

Facione, Peter 9, 14f., 17, 18, 19, 20, 21

fakespot.com 239, 241

fallaciousness [Ch. 14]…

accent 214

ad verecundiam 216

Aristotle's conception of 213-216

Aristotle's lists of 213f.

begging the question 215

many questions 214

FeedViz 242

Flynn, Michael 96

Fisher, Alec [Ch. 1], 26 …

definition of critical thinking 16

Fisher & Scriven 9, 16, 17, 96-98

footnotes 302f., 304

formal logic 38, 118, 307, 317, 322

Freeman, James 104

G

Gabbay, Dove 340ff.

Gelder, Tim van [Ch. 10], 85

generalization …

generalization-establishing arguments
271-273, 285

generalization-using arguments 272f., 286f.

genus-differentia definition 250

Glaser, Edward 8f., 14, 17 …

critical thinking abiliti es 9

definition of critical thinking 8

God's existence example 54

Goddu, G.C. [Ch. 19], 105, 106, 328

gold standard for medical research design

Golden Rule, The 143

'good', meaning of 356

Google Scholar 238, 302

grading 365

Groarke, Leo xi

Grosser, Ben 242

group exercise 52, 80, Ch. 6 *passim*

guilt by association 211, 217

Guarini, Marcello 110, 177

H

Hample, Dale [Ch. 17], 288

Hansen, Hans V. 177

Hardwig, John 290

Harman, Gilbert 339f.

Hattie, John 29, 31-33

Hintikka, Jaakko 329, 341

Hitchcock, David [Ch. 9], 85, 87, 113

"Holding Hands" rule 141f.

Horn, Robert 148

Hume's fact/value argument 354f.

Hundleby, Catherine 177

I

illustrative value 364

infer and imply 326

inference to best explanation 335, 339ff.

Innocence Project 91

Innocenti, Beth [Ch. 12], 85

inquiry Ch. 7

internal validity 281f.

interpreting 17, 281

invalid 39

J

Jackson, Sally [Ch. 15], 181, 227, 244f., 248

Johnson, Gregory Lee 167

Johnson, Ralph H. xi, 4, 177, 200, 216n6, 272

Johnson & Blair 200n4
Johnston, Dave xii
Josephson J.R. & Josephson, S.G. 343

K

Kahane, Howard 14
Kahneman, Daniel 102
Kingsbury, Justine [Chs. 4, 5], 29, 51ff., 55, 57ff.
Kirby, Carmichael 329

L

Laar, Jan Albert van [Ch. 6], 30, 69
language strategies 186
level-consistency, principle of 138f.
Lipman, Matthew 13f. ...
    definition of critical thinking 13
linked arguments/reasoning/premises 106, 117,
    142-147
    vs. convergent arguments 327f.
Lipton, Peter 340
Locke, John 289
logic [Ch. 19] ...
    and possibility 308, 310-313, 316-322
    logical possibility 39, 312f.
    logical impossibility 39
    of evaluation [Ch. 21]

M

mapping software packages 131
margin of error 276
market value 363
Mebane, Waleed xii
Middle Ground [Ch. 6]
missing premise(s) 140f., 159, 177, 196 ...
    "Holding Hands" rule 141
    "Rabbit" rule 141
modal auxiliaries 172
modal logic 307

modal propositions/claims/expressions/terms
    317, 324f.
modal qualifiers 38, 147, 203
modality 38, 46, 118
Moore, G.E. 355
Mulvaney, Tamilyn xi
multi-modal 92

N

naturalistic fallacy 352, 354
necessary and sufficient conditions 18, 38, 42,
    174, 251f., 254, 256, 266f., 307, 356
necessary falsehood 318
necessary truth 31, 324
Neptune, discovery of & abduction 337ff.
Norris & Ennis 9, 17
Nosich, Gerald M. 11

O

objectivity 352, 355, 357
O'Keefe, Daniel J. 87, 91
operational definition 257f.

P

Palgrave Handbook of Critical Thinking 3f., 151
para logic 371
partial definition forms 258-260
patterns of ...
    arguments 217
    beliefs 9
    consistency 265
    inference 3
    reasoning 19, 34, 113, 307, 312
    studies 285
Paul, Richard 10f., 17 ...
    definition of critical thinking 11
peer evaluation 294
peer critique and feedback 34, 58

378

peer review of scientific claims 291, 296f., 300, 302, 304

Peirce, Charles Sanders and abduction 101, 331-337 ...

   selected readings on 345ff.

personal preference or taste 362

Philosophy for Children 13

physical possibility 324

Pinker, Steven 290

Postman, Neil 227, 243, 246

practical ...

   inference 160-162

   possibilities 310f., 317

   reasoning 154, 160, 163f., 168f.,171-173, 358 ...

      value-based 162f.

premise vs. premiss 101n2

presumption 182-184, 187, 218

principle of abstraction 138

principle of level-consistency 138f.

propositions 207, 313f. ...

   types of propositions 314 ...

      complex 318

      conditional 315

      existential 316

      simple 314

public value 363

Q

quarrels 87-90

R

Rabbit Rule 141

radical reform in CT instruction 34ff.

random sample 169, 201, 276, 279, 281, 366n15

ranking 365

range definition 255

Rationale™ 131

reactive effects of experimental circumstances 283

real value (see also true, essential value) 363

reasoning 314-319 ...

   abductive reasoning schemes 169, 171

   causal reasoning schemes 109

   deductive and inductive 327

   deductive reasoning schemes 109

   embedded suppositional reasoning 108

   errors of 321

   good vs. bad 322f., 325

   inductive reasoning schemes 109

   linked 143f.

   logic and reasoning 325

Red Feed / Blue Feed 234f.

reflective thinking 7, 9, 23

relevance 182, 184, 187, 200f.

Relevance, Acceptability & Sufficiency 200

reporting a meaning, definitions 261f.

Rescher, Nicholas 344f.

Rhetoric (of Aristotle) 187, 213f.

rubric 364, 367, 369

Russell, Bertrand 2

S

Salmon, Wesley 216

sample size 281

scoring 367

Scriven, Michael xi, [Chs. 2, 21], 9, 16, 18, 20, 24, 30, 34f., 371

Scriven's radical thesis 34

Searle, John 354

self-assessment 32

Siegel, Harvey 9, 11f. ...

   definition of critical thinking 12

slippery-slope arguments 71, 76, 155, 166-170, 177, 212n2

Socratic ideal 7, 11, 213

Sophistical Refutations (by Aristotle) 213f., 219

sophists 231, 213n4

sound 34, 205

soundness 20, 198, 207

standards 10f., 16, 19f., 23, 29, 98, 182, 204, 206, 210, 243, 246, 273f., 282, 286f., 325,354, 360, 363f., 366, 368

stem cell example 165f.

stipulating a meaning, definitions 262f.

stratified random sampling 201, 278

stereotypes 22, 281, 273, 286

stock issues 182, 184, 186

straw man/straw person 206, 216f.

structure of arguments 108, 118 ...

   critical algorithm studies 232, 241

style 182, 186f., 230, 233

sufficiency 182, 186, 198, 200f., 205, 273-274, 287

Sufficiency, Relevance & Acceptability 200

sufficient condition 38, 252, 272, 319f.

sufficient support 296, 323, 328

sunk costs argument 155, 163f., 164, 166, 169f., 176

surveys 275, 280, 284

synonym definition 255f.

T

tautologies 318

textbook publishers 4, 205

Thomas, Stephen 147f.

tiers of reasons 135

Tindale, Christopher W. [Ch. 14], xi, 85, 177, 206, 221

Toulmin, Stephen E. 103n3, 113, 147, 203

Triton (Neptune's moon) 338

true value (see also essential, real value) 363

U

universal generalization 109n8, 333, 355

universal proposition 316

universality 355

uses of arguments 102

using arguments to inquire [Ch. 7] 74

V

validity in logic 37, 322 ...

   deductive [Ch. 3], 38-39, 203, 210, 215, 253

   inductive 215

validity in survey research 265, 366 ...

   external 281, 283

   internal 281-283

value-based practical reasoning 162f.

value claims, types of 355, 362

value-free doctrine 355, 358ff.

visible teaching and learning 31-33

W

Walters, Kerry 329

Walton, Douglas N. [Ch. 11], 85, 179, 200

Walton, Reed, Macagno 155

Watson-Glaser Critical Thinking Appraisal 8

Weber, Max 358

Whately, Richard 146

Wigmore, John Henry 146

Wikipedia 230, 304

Wittgenstein, Ludwig 370

Wohlrapp, Harald 104f.

Woods, John [Ch. 20], 349

Y

Yelp 240